Is the Chu... Biblical?

An Anglican Ecclesio....

Colin Buchanan

DARTON·LONGMAN+TODD

First published in 1998 by
Darton, Longman and Todd Ltd
1 Spencer Court
140–142 Wandsworth High Street
London SW18 4JJ

ISBN 0–232–52134–4

A catalogue record for this book is available from the British Library.

Phototypeset by Intype London Ltd
Printed and bound in Great Britain by
Page Bros, Norwich, Norfolk

Contents

Preface   v

Introduction   1

Part I Biblical Data

1 Scriptural Authority   29

2 The Old Testament   38

3 The New Testament and Christology   43

4 The New Testament and Derived Ecclesiology   56

5 An Assessment of the Biblical Data   142

Part II The Early Church

6 The Authority of the Early Church   147

7 Apostles and Apostolicity   151

8 The Universality of the Church   164

9 The Early Development of Sacraments   169

10 The Unity of the Church   180

Part III The Church of England Then and Now

11 The Reformation   189

12 Scripture and Tradition   195

13 The New Testament Church and the Church of
England   213
14 A Sacramental Church   238
15 The Ordained Ministry   254
16 The Character of English Anglicanism   266
17 Whither, then, the Church of England?   291

Part IV Appendices and Notes

1 Notes to Chapters   295
2 The Worldwide Anglican Communion   344
3 The Establishment of the Church of England
  – A Shameful Captivity   349
4 Making Epsicopacy Credible   352

Notes and references   357
Index   368
  Scripture references   368
  Index of biblical names   372
  Index of names   372
  Index of subjects   374

Preface

This book was conceived around 30 years ago, but, gestating in a life filled with a great range of both theological and practical concerns, it still would probably not have come to birth had it not been for the provision by the parish of St Mark's, Gillingham, in combination with Gordon Oliver, the training officer of Rochester diocese, for me to have a sabbatical in autumn 1996. This meshed well with an invitation from Oak Hill Theological College to be a guest 'fellow' for a term, and to live without charge in a college flat, contributing a little teaching, but basically getting time for study myself; and I owe a debt of thanks to Gordon Bridger, the principal who first invited me, and to his successor, David Peterson, who was in post when I came, and who, with all his staff, made me wonderfully welcome, and enabled this book to be shaped and in large part drafted.

The sabbatical was drastically affected by my recall to episcopal office in my old age, and the sabbatical ended abruptly with the book still unfinished when I took up my new post as bishop of Woolwich in the Southwark diocese in December 1996. Since then, life has been a whirl of practical activity. The upshot is a book written and presented not as I would, but simply as I could. It does not provide an exhaustive set of definitive answers to a linked battery of enormously difficult questions; measured against such a standard, it is more like a preliminary sketch. Its shortcomings are well known to its author.

I add a couple of words about the text of the New Testament. I have presented the canonical books at their face value, in line with my conviction that they are in principle the inheritance of the whole Church, and that most people will have to take them as they find them. So I have not dealt with issues like whether Paul wrote the Pastorals, or Peter wrote 2 Peter, or whether the gospel stories emerge from a later 'creative community' rather than being near to eye-witness accounts (admittedly selective and edited ones) of Jesus in his incarnation. I am not unaware of such questions, and I endeavour not to be blinkered in relation to them; but, for the purposes of winkling out what the apostolic Church believed, I do not think that such questions can here help us much, and I am certain that treating them at serious length would distort my object and distract from my theme.

At virtually every point where the New Testament is rendered in English, I take responsibility for the particular translation myself, usually without drawing attention to it. If sometimes that brings it near to a published version, well, that published translation may or may not have been running in my mind – but I have almost always worked from the Greek. If my version is different from some well-known version, I have probably had good reason for varying from it, even if I do not discuss it. As, for obvious reasons, I would not want to acknowledge copyright claims in the field of New Testament translations, similarly I do not attempt to make any such claims – Bible translations traceable to me are open to any to employ without attribution.

While at all kinds of places I reproduce, consciously or unconsciously, material I have tried out elsewhere, there is one point where I have deliberately drawn upon the text of an essay I was commissioned to produce under another aegis. I wrote a paper, 'The Anglican Ordinal', for the theological conference held between the Church of England and the EKD (Evangelische Kirke Deutschland) at Emmaus House, Hayes, Kent, in March 1996, and I have incorporated part of it almost verbatim into Chapter 15 below. It is published in an edited version of its original form in *Visible Unity and the Ministry of Oversight: The Second Theological Conference held under the Meissen Agreement between the Church of England and the Evangelical Church in Germany* (Church House Publishing, 1997).

Finally, I should note that, having been, as they say, 'around' for 40 years – and 40 years of astonishing change – I have not hesitated to write in first-person terms at various points. As I had to say of my book on disestablishment, so I repeat here: whatever first-person bits and pieces inevitably enter the story, this book is not an autobiography, and is at no point organised, covertly or openly, in the interests of being such. It does have an element of personal credo about it, but its theme is the Church of Christ, with some resultant attention to the Church of England.

Colin Buchanan
January 1998

Introduction

The Church of England purview

The Church of England is an institution both wonderful and improbable, with good claims to be part of the true Church of God, and yet an astonishing ability to combine effortless superiority with an inability to state its claims aright. The nearer one gets to the actual organisation and running of the institution, the more astonishing it seems that it functions at all. It preaches unity, but obstructs it for secondary reasons; it preaches economy, but only practises it three days a week; it preaches that ministers are servants, but succumbs to a rampant clericalism; it believes itself to have good news, but few of its members can articulate it; it cheerfully requires its ministers to accept its doctrine and discipline, but makes little attempt to define the one or enforce the other; it runs an electoral roll for its members in each parish, but it does not have any clear idea who its members are; it has a mythical but much-trumpeted notion that it supplies a ministry for every square inch of England, but would still claim this if the whole land were but one parish with one incumbent to hold 'the cure of souls' for the whole 40 million. To have Christian beliefs and to live in England is certainly to be faced with the sheer fact of the 'C/E', and most adult Christians have to adopt some kind of a stance (for or against or whatever) in relation to the Church of England. And a major difficulty is that the Church of England loves fantasy and unreality, invents rationales no one can actually believe, conceives that fudge is better than principle on many major issues, expands minor issues into major principles, and hates having to grapple with reality. I confess that I abhor these characteristics and yet am regularly sucked into them. But I do think that much of our trouble derives from half-baked ecclesiological assumptions in one half of the Church of England and from well-baked ecclesiological error in the other half.

At this point I have to stop and clarify. I use the adjective 'Anglican' fairly freely below; I had hoped to write as for the whole Anglican Communion, but have been defeated by lack of time and space. I am still hopeful that a book which attempts to grapple with basic theological principles, for all that it is most obviously rooted in specifically English Church history, will be of service to the whole Communion which has sprung from the Church of England.* I do need that adjective 'Anglican', even though the book is just for the English scene, and, unless otherwise emphasised, the Church of England alone is the limit of the scope of my discussion of things Anglican.

I permit myself here just one point about the whole Anglican Communion. My own ecclesiological thinking leads me to prefer a worldwide approach to Anglicanism to the rather insular, and occasionally even exclusive, 'Church of England only' mentality – a hybrid bred by the natural English superiority complex out of a combination of establishment, historic assets, episcopacy, and the old Adam. This mentality is showing signs of breaking down on the English front, as the old stiff English are affected by the new multi-ethnic and multicultural English, and as establishment becomes incredible, historic funds run down and episcopacy is reduced to size (though the ecclesial old Adam proves to be still in place). What is clear is that an effective apologia must have the potential for universal application; and the slow fading of an English Anglican apartness from world Christianity offers hope that the point will be recognised even in England. The provisionality to which I refer below is all the greater because I could not here handle the growth of the world Communion and the ecclesiological issues integral to that.

Anglican Evangelicals

I write in the first instance, if not primarily, for Evangelicals in the Church of England. It is they who have lacked a well-founded and informed mind on ecclesiology, and have

---

*Appendix 2 reflects on the growth of the worldwide Communion, and on the extent to which my earlier reasoning is applicable universally.

inadvertently found themselves with what I have called above 'half-baked assumptions'. Those assumptions have in turn governed their understanding of Scripture, and this in turn has lain behind their relations with both non-Anglican Evangelicals and non-Evangelical Anglicans. So I write as an Evangelical Anglican for Evangelical Anglicans, but in the hope and expectation that others on both flanks will look over our shoulders and engage with my attempt at rethinking.

Evangelical Anglicans who engage with others represent a relatively recent rebirth in the life of the Church of England. Their predecessors were squeezed in the nineteenth century by Anglo-Catholicism on the one hand and by theological liberalism on the other. They lost intellectual confidence in the early years of this century, and, while rallying to the infallibility and authority of the Scriptures, became simply shrill in their protestations, and were thus unable to contend intellectually with those whose positions threatened them. As far as can be told, virtually all serious Evangelical Anglican literature ceased early in the century – probably dying with Nathaniel Dimock just before the first world war.

The last 40 years have seen an astonishing revival, which has not only brought Evangelicals (of all denominational loyalties) above ground to contend for the Bible, but has also seen them gain enough space intellectually to engage in pedagogy and controversy on a thousand-and-one secondary points relating to the application of biblical truth to the life of the Church and of the world today. However, where Evangelicals can unite across denominational frontiers for a vast amount of this kind of exercise, and can agree, for instance, on the doctrine of the Trinity, or even the atonement, it is a different matter when it comes to the doctrine of the Church. At that point denominationalism is bound to raise its head somewhat adversarily. Individual histories, family loyalties, love of forms of worship, and deep personal emotional and spiritual investment in a particular denomination, tradition or even local assembly, are bound then to colour the handling of Scripture and of history and to stir a defensiveness which makes true dialogue difficult. I am in no way proof against such pressures myself. Ecclesiology will inevitably have more marks of subjectivism than most other theological studies, and equally inevitably it will sweep into itself a great range of stances on other issues – from patristics to hermeneutics, and from missiology to ordination. Evangelicals are vaguely aware of the depth of study properly required; and thus, when joining with each other across denominational barriers for any particular purpose, have usually solved their ecclesiological problems by ducking them. But realistically, to hold to most other points of evangelical theological accord, while ducking what ought to be a major factor in that total theological position, is to create a danger of getting the proportions of other doctrines wrong and thus distorting the total picture.*

Personal involvement

I therefore declare my hand. Brought up in vague attachment to non-conformity, and coming to faith during my last year at school and my first in the army doing national service, I not only found myself at an early stage a 'Bible-believing Evangelical', but also found myself drawn to the Church of England; and thus I was confirmed more than 40 years ago in my first year as an undergraduate, and was confirmed, no doubt with many less than worthy motives, but behind it and under it because I believed in what I would now call the unity of the visible Church. Ordination followed, and was indeed already in view at the time of my confirmation.

I was ordained at a time when Anglican Evangelicalism was on the one hand growing numerically (partly in the wake of Billy Graham), but on the other hand was still very conscious of being an *ecclesiola* within the very comprehensive frame-

---

*For example, Billy Graham, in his great days in England in 1954 and 1955, proved to be an evangelist who could draw support from across the denominations, and with that support he preached the Gospel powerfully. But by definition his call to respond to the Gospel could not include any mention of the need for baptism, and the enquirers' cards – which in St Paul's day would have been bound to have started by asking 'Are you a baptised believer?' – were similarly without mention of baptism. I make no criticism of the need to get together – I merely point out that inevitably everyone's doctrine of baptism (and of the relationship between baptism, conversion and membership of Christ and his Church) was being distorted by the suppression of that feature of the New Testament Gospel.

work of the established Church's legal parochial structure.* There was a 'backs to the wall' persecution complex – no Evangelical ever became a bishop; the Evangelical colleges and their whole theological stance were dubbed 'Stone Age' by the rest of the Church; the Evangelical clergy were placed in benefices almost entirely through the agency of Evangelical patrons, with bishop's patronage very rarely exercised on their behalf; and few voices of this persuasion were to be heard in the Church Assembly or in broadcasting, and very few books by contemporary authors of this persuasion were in the bookshops. The Church of England was still led by the liberal Catholic hegemony which had dominated it in the first half of this century, and the atmosphere of that hegemony was not only breathed by all, but had become regarded as the normal and proper atmosphere, the natural genius even, of the Church of England.

Opening positions in evangelical ecclesiology

Latimer House, Oxford, was founded in 1960 to provide on a Church of England front something comparable to the work of the Inter-Varsity Fellowship on an interdenominational front – and particularly to grapple with issues that were coming up for review on the Church of England's agenda, such as liturgical revision and relations with other Churches. Jim Packer left Tyndale Hall, Bristol, where I was a student, in spring 1961 and became warden of Latimer House.[1] He formed a Doctrine Study Group round Latimer House, and it was a meeting of that group at Oxford in early 1963 which has always struck me in retrospect as a vital watershed in Evangelical ecclesiology. The occasion of our meeting was the Report of the Conversations on Anglican–Methodist Unity, published in February that year.[2]

The Conversationalists had included (typically) no Evangelical Anglicans; and the dismay of our group at the Report was perhaps predictable. We found ourselves gazing with some

---

*I revisited my school some time around the point of my confirmation. The headmaster enquired about my life, and, on learning I was being confirmed, asked a question to which I boldly replied, 'I am an evangelical'. His response (this would be in 1956) was, 'I prefer something more intellectual myself'.

horror on statements on Scripture and tradition, on episcopacy and ordination, on priesthood and sacraments, and on the 'reconciliation' of ministries – statements which we could not but oppose – and we had a dread sense that 'they' would steamroller us whatever we said or did. As we gazed, however, we were sufficiently delivered from paranoia to be led to the positive question on the wider horizon: 'Suppose, *mirabile dictu*, these questions were answered right, would we *then* favour a union of Anglicans and Methodists?' The initial answer from the most eminent theologian there was, 'No, for it would be no better and would promise no more life than taking two corpses to a wedding!' The response of others was, 'Is not the visible unity of the Church part of its holiness? If it is, you pursue it, along with other features of holiness, *all at once*, and you do not allow yourself to say, "Let us first pursue holiness; and then, when we have made progress there, then will be the time to address reunion".' The watershed was crossed with this response; and in the group's first publication, the 'two corpses in one coffin' had ceased to be a serious ground for opposing the quest for visible unity, but instead was actually cited as an Aunt Sally to be quickly demolished, while the essays in the symposium addressed biblical ways in which a genuine quest for visible and organic unity could be pursued.[3] At an academic-cum-policy level, a corner had been turned. From then on, serious Anglican Evangelicalism viewed the nature of the visible Church and its unity as a doctrinal concern not only worthy of sustained study, but actually demanding it urgently for the sake of the contemporary scene. Ecclesiology was on the agenda, even if there were few to address it in any depth.

My own reading now of the 1960s would attribute great importance to the twin thrust of a restored neo-Puritan theology and a rise in numbers of ordinands.* Until that

---

*I have traced what I have called successive 'phases' of theological fashion among Evangelicals in an article I wrote years later for the first issue of *Anvil* ('Evangelicalism: the state of the party', in *Anvil* Vol. 1 no. 1 (1984) pp. 9–12). The neo-Puritan era, short-lived in one sense but highly formative in another, is closely associated with the name of Jim Packer; and it involved a strong reaction against the simple pietism of the previously dominant public school Evangelicals (being public school, these were usually Anglicans long before

decade a high proportion of Evangelical Anglicans justified their belonging to the Church of England on opportunistic grounds, namely 'It is the best boat to fish from'. This kind of rationale, depending as it does on alleged results rather than a true scrutiny of ecclesiology, not only failed to convince non-Anglicans but also, with the advent of the neo-Puritans, came under grave question from within the constituency which was propounding it. For the Puritan theological approach meant in principle that theology had to provide the measure of the whole of creation and of the whole of life, and thus the end could not justify the means, and evaluation of a church structure could not be kept down to the narrow limits of evangelistic results. And this in turn meant that, however immaturely their doctrine was enunciated, Anglicans of this formation had to justify their churchmanship in terms that were doctrinal – and not merely opportunistic, let alone dynastic or facile.

Alongside the opportunistic defence there existed a kind of dogmatic rationale of the Church of England to appeal to Evangelicals, and it needs to be noted. This was a strictly constitutionalist position. Its characteristic exposition was to say: 'The Church of England is bound by its foundation documents in the Thirty-Nine Articles of Religion, the Book of Common Prayer, and the Ordinal – and possibly the Homilies. The Thirty-Nine Articles have pride of place in these documents. We Evangelicals are those who are loyal to those formularies. All others seem to have strayed into a liberalism about Scripture and faith or into an ecclesiasticism of Anglo-Catholic teaching – or both – and, to the extent that they deviate from the formularies, they are *not* the Church of England. We Evangelicals hold the title deeds, and must make it clear that other pretenders to the title are imposters.' This exposition was of course good for morale; it promoted a tiny handful of Evangelicals, a remnant, from being on the fringes into being the norm, the yardstick, for loyal Anglicanism. It provided a clear rallying-point. It furnished an apologia to offer non-Anglican Evangelicals (who were often sceptical of

_____

they were vital believers), who did their best to function with an A–B–C gospel (and a tendency to Arminianism) and a 'best-boat-to-fish-from' apologia for their Anglicanism. At intervals this Introduction draws upon the analysis I provided in that article.

their Anglican friends' Anglicanism). It was principled and
easy to understand. It kept hopes alive during a very difficult
period. But of course it would not actually do. For it created
several problems at once:

1 It quickly lost touch with reality. If only 10 per cent, say,
of the Church of England *was* the Church of England, then
communication became difficult, as enormous qualifiers had
to be put into every proposition.

2 It was difficult to sustain. If an ordinand found a kindly
disposed bishop who prayed with him and for him, and duly
gave him his charge and ordained him, then (with Letters
of Orders in his hands) it was not easy for the man to say,
'That bishop, my bishop, is not really part of the Church of
England'. There might be qualifications to put against one's
bishop, but a denial of his being truly 'C/E' demanded a
rigorously blinkered approach to reality which only the most
ideologically ruthless could sustain.

3 It raised an intriguing question (which has been in my
mind throughout this book): is a Church, any Church,
formed or defined simply through an outworking of its doctrinal position? Or does any element of what it is come not
from the doctrinal trust deeds but rather from the living
company who have arisen in the present generation? (This
is discussed more fully in Chapter 12.)

4 It froze Evangelicals into a backward-looking stance (not
unlike what we have seen on a large politico-religious canvas
among Unionists in Northern Ireland). Such a stance is
sometimes necessary, and particularly when under supposed
outside threats – but it is neither native to biblical Christianity (of which *'ecclesia reformata semper reformanda'** is
the proper rallying-cry) nor health-giving to those who hold
to it.

5 Consequently, this position was highly separatist and thus
created an over-strong us-and-them polarisation. Quite
apart from the tendency of such a stance to create harsh
pharisaism, it also meant the rest of the Church of England
was always then viewed as embattled to persecute the godly,

---

*'A Church which has been reformed is up for reform permanently
thereafter' (a sixteenth-century Reformation maxim). See also p. 31
below.

or at least to disdain them – and that again, whether the perception was accurate or not (which in practice actually varied), made any joining with 'them' for any serious purpose inadvisable or even impossible. I can well recall pointing out to fellow-Evangelicals in the early 1960s that they knew how to be less than 10 per cent of the Church of England (namely, to bare their teeth and attack anything that moved, and to embrace their persecution complex and go down fighting if they had to – while all the time insisting that they were the 'true' Church of England); and also they knew how they would conduct themselves if ever they became more than 50 per cent of the Church of England (namely, they would use their majority power to enforce discipline and thus run out the ungodly and erroneous); but they really had no idea of how to go from being less than 10 per cent to being more than 50 per cent, and unless they had it would never happen. Very soon after this I found myself as the sole Evangelical on the Liturgical Commission, asking myself exactly that question: not, 'how can I go down heroically with the ship?' but 'how can I so judge what is primary and non-negotiable and what is secondary and admitting of varied solutions in such a way as to enable positive new steps to be proposed which I can then commend to my Evangelical peers?' I think I may have been the first to undergo this painful mind-concentrating experience.

6 The sheer separatism inevitably made the individual parish the test of orthodoxy, the locus of policy-making, the natural autonomous unit of church government. The inheritance of the Church of England and the constitutional position of parishes and patrons (let alone the parochial individualism of the Catholic movement in the Church of England) bolstered this defensive separatism; but the separatism itself undoubtedly blunted the ability and willingness of Evangelicals to think both positively and supra-parochially about ecclesiology.

My own analysis would suggest that, in the early 1960s, Evangelicals were realising their isolation, which followed from this rigid position; and, as numbers grew and they found themselves in actual positions of helping the Church of England look to the future, they were conscious both of the need for a realism in their doctrinal position and of a need within themselves for a reappraisal of what made them Anglicans at all.

Developing trends over three decades since Keele

Keele and its aftermath
All that was in the background and build-up to the Keele Congress of April 1967.* While the 1960s, from the point of

---

*The actual history of the months leading up to Keele encapsulated the swirling dynamics of this transition extremely well. Originally, the Congress had been planned to reproclaim Evangelical fundamentals, and various big guns had been placed in position to fire their salvoes from the platform. The then younger clergy started to show signs of restiveness, which came to head in November 1966 at the Eclectics Conference at Swanwick. The cry for a participatory congress reached the organising committee and late that month (i.e. less than five months before the congress of a thousand people took place), they virtually threw in their hand and decided:

a The big guns would fire, but not at the congress itself, but in a book available in advance – this became J. I. Packer (ed.) *Guidelines: Anglican Evangelicals Face the Future* (Falcon/CPAS, 1967);

b The congress itself would instead write a Statement of Contemporary Policy for Evangelicals;

c A drafting committee would be appointed immediately and would prepare drafts to be fed into the various groups engaged at the Congress in drafting.

The drafting committee was theoretically chaired by Jim Packer, but he was in the USA most of spring 1967 and the three-man drafting committee was in effect Gavin Reid, Philip Crowe and me (with some correspondence with Michael Green). I found myself drafting initial statements on 'The Church and its worship' and 'The Church and its unity' – both areas where Evangelicals suffering from a persecution complex tended to turn reactionary, and Evangelicals with the Scriptures in their hand and a sense of space in which to move tended towards brinkmanship. Each group appeared to the other group (and still does appear – for some of the division is still around) as though embracing totally wrong-headed, inapplicable and subversive policies – the reactionaries appear to the progressives as though they are digging last ditches and occupying them under inner compulsion when they are not actually being attacked; whereas the progressives, as they get near the brink, simply appear to the reactionaries like a bunch of lemmings. What Keele discovered was that, with some caution, the Evangelical constituency at large was ready to move, ready to move forward out of the last ditch, ready even to move without being absolutely sure what the point of arrival would be, but

view of most historians of the Church of England, were the decade of John Robinson and of the 'death of God', Evangelicals in the Church of England were (almost unnoticed) growing in numbers, confidence and venturesomeness. And Keele, with its participatory style and its clear statement at the end, caught that point of growth at just the moment in history when it needed articulation. Wonderfully the thousand participants were a widespread cross-section of old and young, ordained and lay, men and women – and the youngish and the lay were more than half the total. In the process of the writing of the Keele statement in that first week of April 1967, there was an unconscious shift of ecclesiology – and that has been the key to a rising tide of Evangelicalism in the Church of England ever since.

For Keele proclaimed that Evangelical Anglicans really belonged to the existent contemporary Church of England, warts and all. It proclaimed our readiness to treat people on their own profession as in Christ with us, even if we thought them deficient in their understanding or adherence to the Gospel. It stated that we were ready to learn truths from others which we had missed partly through our purblindness, partly through our separateness. It made it clear that we were not all teetering on the edge, about to secede if things did not go our way. This pronouncement led to a serious breach of relationships with Free Church Evangelicals. It took a positive approach to reunion questions, not excluding dialogue with Rome. And it revealed a principled high sacramentalism, including a desire to work towards the celebration of the Eucharist as the main service of each Sunday.[4]

Keele provided a turning-point, one to which Evangelicals and others alike have ever since looked back on as very significant. Since then, Evangelical Anglicans have been found fully engaged in the life of the Church of England, its synods, commissions, boards and at every level. From the swelling ranks there have appeared bishops (and an archbishop), authors, and pioneers of every sort. Even the tinpot publishing empire of

---

with a deep sense that, under God and with due regard for his word and for the realities of the Church and the nation, there were certain moves which were right in themselves to take, irrespective of narrow issues of advantage and disadvantage.

Grove Books in which I have involved myself is, in the strictest sense, a post-Keele phenomenon – not only because its origins were chronologically post-Keele (the numbered series began in December 1971), but also because the ethos of the publications has been frontier-work – not definitive statements of positions set in concrete, but kite-flying and venturesome proposals; the authors have been Evangelicals not now making predictable statements to reassure their own gallery, but instead writing exploratory material for the whole Church of England and for many far beyond it. Thirty years on from Keele, Evangelicals are in a place of astonishing influence in the Church of England, one that could hardly have been foreseen at that hastily but imaginatively re-formed congress in April 1967.

Yet the very success of this grouping in the Church of England has also had its fissiparous tendency. Indeed it is arguable that difficulties have arisen not only because of the shedding of the last-ditch mentality, but also because the underlying shift in ecclesiology which Keele represented has never been properly charted. That is part of the reason for this book, which has been in the making all these years. But some mapwork of the different directions taken by Evangelicalism may be relevant here.

The ecclesiologists
First of all, there were the very people who had steered Keele and given content to it. Broadly the younger clergy of the 1960s were to be found in this stream, and so were the staffs of the Evangelical theological colleges, and many on the staffs of missionary societies. A great range of Evangelicals had begun to sense, whether their convictions were opportunistic or more severely ecclesiological, that they were a growing force in the Church of England, and that, if they got properly aboard, they might well give direction to its future. In the 1960s and 1970s they began to take an ever-increasing place within their deaneries and dioceses. Evangelical clergy appeared in some strength at the first elections to General Synod in 1970, beginning to match a vigorous voice of younger Evangelicals in the House of Laity, who had appeared through the 1959 and 1965 elections. However late in the day, Evangelicals had to be taken seriously in relation to that

Anglican–Methodist Scheme.[5] They made a significant impact in the late 1960s on the work of the new Doctrinal Commission.[6] They were even found in dialogue with Roman Catholics.[7] They were deeply involved in liturgical renewal, including whole new patterns of family services, creativity in hymnody and music, visual communication, and textual proposals.[8] They were pioneering in fields of theological education. Their marginalisation, which had been so evident, had by 1970 or so become a positive, deeply committed involvement in the corporate life of the Church of England. The theological shift at Keele, combined with the rising numbers and relative optimism under God about the future, had brought about a major reorientation. They were, if we may characterise them by a label I have adopted with the benefit of hindsight, the new wave of Evangelical 'ecclesiologists'.[9] The only snag was that, for all one might retrospectively title them as 'ecclesiologists', there was a grave lack of a developed ecclesiology to which to relate – for, while a half-underground doctrine was evident at Keele and was motivating this wide swathe of people, there was little laid out in serious theological works.*

The charismatic movement
Secondly, there has been the burgeoning rise of the Charismatic Movement (which I shall accord capitals just this once). I have written elsewhere about the likely causes in human terms.[10] Suffice to note that in the 1950s Pentecostalism was assumed by most Anglicans to be a gut-level or emotional form of Christianity which a cool head with adequate grey matter would soon cure; and it was a matter of some surprise when Lesslie Newbigin, in *The Household of God* (SCM, 1952), treated the Pentecostalist Churches as somehow adult among the world Churches, and as carrying a respectable strand of church life which should be added as a third force to existing

---

*It is often noted that the memorable part of Archbishop Runcie's word to the National Evangelical Anglican Celebration at Caister holiday camp in April 1988 was a challenge to formulate a coherent ecclesiology. It struck a chord (and, I suspect, had been suggested to him by one or more Evangelicals); and it too had its part in pushing the present work into execution. That was 21 years on from Keele.

Catholicism and Protestantism.* At the same time David Du Plessis, a world-leader in Pentecostalism, was urging ecumenism upon his own denomination, and was looking for Pentecostalism to emerge in the 'main line' world Churches. And so it happened: in Anglicanism it began on the West coast of the USA at the end of the 1950s, and broke out in England in many persons and parishes, not least (and probably first) in 1962 in St Mark's, Gillingham, Kent – the parish of which I have myself recently been incumbent. In England (unlike other parts of the Anglican Communion) the outbreak came largely within the existing Evangelical constituency, and therefore affected people who already had a great love of the Bible. I detect that one of the main distinguishing features of the first decade of this outbreak was that, along with Keele and all that, existing Evangelicalism appeared to charismatics as spiritually dry and ever more cerebral, whereas they themselves were being irrigated with living waters, renewed inwardly by the Holy Spirit. Apart from actual theological arguments, the difference in ethos was enormous, and the two groups tended to polarise until some fairly representative leaders were brought together through the statement of a joint theological group, *Gospel and Spirit* (1977),[11] and by an honest conjunction at the second National Evangelical Anglican Congress at Nottingham in 1977.

At this point I write as a sympathetic fellow-traveller with a large amount of experience of the movement. I have had reason recently to observe that the phenomena which have appeared to be most highly valued within the movement have altered over the years. In broad terms, in the 1960s it was 'baptism in the Spirit', 'prophecy', 'tongues' and 'interpretation'. In the 1970s there was a shift in favour of healings, exorcisms and 'spiritual warfare'. In the 1980s there appeared John Wimber and 'words of knowledge'. In the 1990s the whole world has gone after 'Toronto', and that which was quite widely

---

*Since getting to know Lesslie Newbigin in his old age, I think I have heard him say that, at the time he wrote in these terms about Pentecostalism, he had never actually met a Pentecostalist. He characterised his 'three forces' in world Christianity as the Church of the body (Catholicism), of the word (Protestantism), and of the Spirit (Pentecostalism).

known before (and was characterised as 'being slain the Spirit') has latterly become *the* great test of the presence of the Spirit. Alongside charismatics in the historic denominations, there has also been an enormous growth of the 'new churches' (in the early stages often called the 'house churches'), and these have both drawn members from the Church of England and also provided the Church of England with ordinands. It has to be said that the volatile growth of the new churches does not appear to have included a commensurate pattern of theologising, and, if the doctrine of the Church is neglected among Evangelical Anglicans, and is not particularly prioritised among charismatics of any denomination, the new churches, for all their growth, are at this point weaker still. They are virtually without interest in ecumenism and have been no part of the recognised Churches in the various ecumenical structures in England.*

What I have done in this book is to try to attend to those features of the charismatic movement which refer themselves to Scripture, and to attempt to work closely at the exegesis of those passages. But clearly there are all kinds of further distinguishing marks of charismatics which are part of the culture, the spirituality and the linguistic currency of the movement, and have become 'recognition symbols', and actually have no particular need to justify themselves from Scripture, *unless* they are to be taught as 'generally necessary for salvation' or as uniquely indicative of the presence of the Holy Spirit. This may open up a gap between us. It is my judgement, for instance, that there is less in Scripture about 'gifts' than charismatics have assumed. I also offer (from academic conviction) reasons to hesitate about the received charismatic understanding of both 'baptism in the Spirit' and 'tongues'. As long as the features of the culture are not contrary

---

*To be fair, this is the general experience of new movements. The history of the Quakers, the Methodists, the Irvingites, the Brethren movement, the Salvation Army and a host of others is of people taking up positions and forming a movement without any thinking through in advance the principles on which it is to function for hundreds of years ahead. Theology then gets formed in arrears, as reflection upon, and defence of, the existing institution start to require some justification.

to Scripture, and as long as they are not overstated, they may
well be valuable. But they may also open a gulf which exists
just beneath the surface – for there is a real issue as to whether
charismatics wish to be led by Scripture (and would identify
that with being led by the Spirit) or whether they are so drawn
by lived experience as to be proof against the true testing by
Scripture. With the former, we may well explore the kinds of
experience of the Spirit promised and described in Scripture;
but with the latter the dialogue has to be conducted from two
sets of differing premises and is extraordinarily difficult.

The greatest contribution charismatics have made to Christianity in this country may well prove to be not so much the
bubbling experientialism in itself, but the awakening of the
notion of every-member ministry (a fair outworking of a strong
attachment to the 'body' imagery). The sense that all believers
have a vital contribution to make to the work of Christ on earth
today is one that has been grasped and propagated wonderfully
among our latter-day pneumatics. The goal of making all
members articulate in the things of Christ in the assembly is
an extension of this, and it is a wonderfully refreshing corrective to the traditional Anglican liturgical programme, which a
believer could attend for 50 years or more and *never* be asked
to say anything personal about his or her faith in Jesus Christ
and consequential discipleship. When in recent years the
Church of England has finally stirred itself and provided new
emphases on evangelism, believers may have found themselves
being urged by the clergy or other leaders to 'speak for Jesus'
in their world of work, when they had never, over all their
previous years, heard themselves say anything to God or about
God in the presence of others, even in the sympathetic sur-
roundings of 'church'. Refreshingly, charismatics have shown
few inhibitions on that front.

Women's ordination
But, thirdly, Evangelicalism has seen a very different development alongside the charismatic one. In the 1980s and 1990s
there has been a reaction against Keele, and a revival of the
strictly 'constitutionalist' way of thinking. While there have
always been some such reactionaries around, many of them
taking the view that Keele was a mistake and a wrong turning,

the matter has come to a head since the voting in the Church of England General Synod on the ordination of women as presbyters in November 1992. While Anglican Catholics provided the main opposition to this move, much of the grounds they alleged against the change was not directly scriptural. Among Evangelicals, however, it was inevitable that the debate should focus on Scripture; and, while the majority of them reached a conclusion that was in favour of women's ordination, they found they could only do so by interpreting some passages of Scripture about the role of women in the Church as 'historically conditioned'.* This led to a strong reaction by the minority – Evangelical opponents even forecast that such an invoking of 'historical conditioning could and would set a precedent for similar treatment of the denouncing of homosexual practices in the New Testament'. As the Church of England has in fact been sorely riven by exactly that controversy in the five years since the vote on the ordination of women, the prediction of the 'domino' impact of an evasive principle of exegesis may well have looked plausible, and thus perhaps increased the hard-line reactionary responses among Evangelicals. It would be my contention that a firm set of core beliefs is entirely scriptural and should be as deeply entrenched as possible – but that the Church should also have an awareness of a distinction between primary and secondary issues, and should be ready to live (as 1 Corinthians would have us live) with a degree of anomaly in secondary matters. It is part of the intention of this book to help such Evangelicals do the requisite map-work, and to find not only themselves, but also those with whom they disagree, on the ecclesiological map.

'Post-evangelicals'

There is yet another division of post-Keele Evangelicals which has to be noted, those who are starting to call themselves 'post-Evangelicals'. The man who has invented the name and given it currency by the title of his book does not appear himself

---

*Everyone acknowledges *some* historical conditioning, as, for instance, in relation to women's hats. But its unrestricted application obviously could remove the sharp edge from all New Testament injunctions and ethics. (The issue of women's ordination is discussed in Appendix 1, pp. 333–6.)

to be, or to have been, an Anglican.[12] But he has written at length – and stirred the correspondence columns – in a church weekly, and there is reason to think that he has an Anglican constituency. His stance would appear to have little theological basis – indeed its motivation seems to be anti-theological or, to put it another way, the thrust is a reaction against the Evangelical culture, the 'dos' and 'don'ts' which tend to develop in tight Evangelical circles. But we should be very clear that a reforming or radical Evangelical does not have to be bound by any feature whatsoever of the existent culture, and, true to the dynamic of being subject to Scripture, is seeking to reform, refine and even perfect that which has been inherited as Evangelicalism. To walk away from it, and to define yourself by what you now are not, is a short-lived and unhelpful programme – whereas to be the people of the revealed word of God is a very distinct position, and should provide a place of great rallying and far-sighted vision.

The start of serious ecclesiology

Having said that there has been a dearth of Evangelical books on ecclesiology – and for most of the time since Keele there have been none at all – I now find myself needing to note two recent and very significant and useful ones. I mention them in the opposite order from that in which they were published for reasons which will be clear from their contents.

The first of these is Kevin Giles, *What on Earth is the Church? A Biblical and Theological Enquiry* (SPCK, 1995). It is almost entirely a biblical enquiry, and is both thorough and illuminating in its handling of Scripture – and is warmly to be commended for that. I do not view my own enquiry (which in various ways does not have the same depth of scriptural treatment) as dependent upon his; and I have found myself asking slightly different questions which have perhaps produced slightly different answers – but I am fascinated by it, and keep going back to it.[13] The major problem I would have with Kevin Giles is his conclusion that the believers in, say, Corinth were not one congregation, but a fluid agglomeration of persons to be found sometimes together, sometimes 'in the house of [a named person]', and that therefore a multiplicity of congregations of different denominations on an urban scene is a perfectly scriptural fulfilment of that Corinthian pattern.

The other book is Tim Bradshaw, *The Olive Branch: An Evangelical Anglican Doctrine of the Church* (Paternoster, 1992). This is a most demanding but very rewarding book for the specialist. Bradshaw is the clean opposite of Giles: thus he does not begin at the beginning historically – but instead plunges in with an opening chapter dominated by Newman and Barth. He follows it with 'An Anglo-Catholic synthesis'; and that in turn is followed by 'The ARCIC synthesis'.

My discernment of these two books – a discernment which has become my motivating impulse to write this present book – is that Kevin Giles lives in the New Testament, and hardly ventures beyond it, while Tim Bradshaw engages with the highly complex ecclesiastical position of today without catering sufficiently for those who would like to know why they are here in the first place. It has thus seemed sensible to me to give large space to discovering biblical principles, but then also to see how these principles apply to the Church of England today.

My methodology

In my treatment of the scriptural evidence I have tried to discover what the books of the Bible are saying to us, without the intervention of issues, questions or interpretations of a later date. Yet the handling of the New Testament down two millennia cannot be avoided entirely. Obviously, I am aware of historical interpretations of the New Testament and at intervals need to take them into account. Obviously, they are likely to tinge any enquiry any modern Christian makes of the biblical text. Obviously, there is a need of such questions if biblical answers are to arise which can serve the Church of today and answer its questions. And I suppose that the kind of ecclesiological questions I have faced for over 30 years have particularly driven my enquiry, so that I cannot pretend to a wholly detached, 'purist' look at the New Testament as if in a vacuum – which all the hermeneutical disciplines tell us is impossible anyway. But I have nevertheless initially striven to live in Part I of this book solely within the New Testament itself, and I have then indicated that I am aware I have varied my approach whenever I have had to invoke sources or questions from more modern times. These usually take the form of 'Notes to Chapters' in Part IV, where I have engaged with the New Testament specifically to seek an answer to a disputed or pressing latter-day question.

My handling of the New Testament has attempted to fulfil the criteria I myself have set out within the section – that is, that diligent study will discover reasonably clear teaching; and careful awareness of ordinary hermeneutical procedures may enable that teaching to be applied to today's Church.

Part II is entitled 'The Early Church'. It is not, and does not pretend to be, the whole of the first five centuries – indeed, it is almost entirely pre-Constantinian. It is confined to the questions: Was there development (legitimate or illegitimate) going on in the doctrine and institutions of the Church? And did the pre-Constantinian Church expect or want to create such developments or innovations? While I have always had a suspicion that the patristic era tended to be presented in our times in ways which established a developing tradition as autonomous, my rereading of the authors of the earliest centuries actually points in the opposite direction, and I have endeavoured to demonstrate this.

Part III addresses the Church of England of Henry VIII's times and since. The treatment is, inevitably, excerptive as well as provisional. While I have generally pursued my self-appointed task of seeking a biblical ecclesiology, I have also found myself responding to the discussion by Stephen Sykes, Bishop of Ely, of the pros and cons of what he calls 'NSD' – 'No Special Doctrines'.[14] His target is those Anglicans (emanating, I judge, from the Tractarian movement of 1833) who claim to be simply historic Christians, adhering to the 'original' faith of the early Fathers, distinguished from others merely by the fact that the accretions or subtractions of Papist and Protestant alike have not affected us – such writers claim that we are a kind of unadorned, perhaps slightly quaint, norm of historic Christianity. It will be obvious at once that, even if the 'simple unadorned original Christianity' claim could be sustained, it would not really amount to 'NSD'. As well might the modern driver of a horse-drawn hansom cab claim he had 'no special vehicle', when that had once been true, perhaps a century before, but mere inspection might well reveal the cab now to be unique. Sykes tackles 'NSD' head-on, but more academically than this illustration would suggest. He insists that it is exactly in distinguishing the place one's Church occupies on the world ecclesiological map that one comes to the 'special doctrine'. If others can be thought to be in error, then defining ourselves over against them is both requisite and distinguishing. Sykes, however, is only asserting the propriety of such defining; he is not actually doing it.

It has been inevitable for an Introduction to this particular book to speak specifically to Evangelicals. But it is also written for the whole Church of England, and would be useless to Evangelicals if it had not a 'whole Church' purview. To non-Evangelicals I address a summary few words as follows: I find myself ever more 'Catholic' in respect of the worldwide organic unity of the visible Church (both as given and as to be sought) and in a cognate high sacramentalism. But I believe that to accord a kind of autonomy to 'Catholic tradition', when in fact that has to mean that all Anglicans have to pick and choose for themselves what they are going to treat as authoritative tradition, is self-defeating as well as at odds with the supremacy of Scripture; and the particular instance of this which most confronts us is the treating of episcopal succession and the threefold orders of ministry as non-negotiable, despite their totally inadequate warrant from the Bible or even, as I try to show below, from the whole of the first two centuries.*
There is a cartoon Anglican genius around, one which I all too frequently encounter; it is totally unbothered about the standing of biblical doctrines in a local congregation, but is

---

*My quarrel is with making a non-scriptural doctrine to be of the *esse* of the visible Church. A Catholicism which is merely bound up in exotic ceremonial, or luscious music, or simply a love of ritual for its own sake, while it may emerge in what are known as 'Catholic' contexts, may nevertheless prove on inspection to be not Catholicism at all but a subjective aestheticism. If so, the difference from Catholic belief needs grasping. Perhaps all too many lay people (and clergy too?) are where they are along the spectrum of Anglican worship-styles not because they have worked through the doctrinal stance of a particular parish, and adhered to it themselves, but rather because they rather like the particular culture – or have been loved by the particular local folk.

up-in-arms if a hymn-tune is changed or a pew moved. We seem to be getting near this when a partisan theory of orders which has no basis where it needs it – i.e. in Scripture – becomes somehow foundational to ecclesiology and church life.

This latter point becomes a puzzle to somone trying to write a biblical ecclesiology, for so many Anglican writers have concentrated on issues of 'orders' as both to appear to make this central to Anglican thinking and correspondingly to require refuting at similar length. Those who were once pursing a serene journey of enquiry into the doctrine of the Church, but have been hijacked *en route* into a captivity to the necessity of certain doctrines of orders, may well have to fight at length, in a conflict not of their own choosing, to free themselves from this captivity in order to resume their original journey. So I have inevitably had an eye on the issue, but I hope I have not been over-tempted into disproportionate refutation by the sheer outsize proportions of the advocacy lavished upon 'orders' by others.

To attempt a work of this compass is to tread in the fields of biblical studies, church history, historical theology, dogmatics, liturgy and even phenomenology. There are some such areas into which my studies have frequently taken me over the years, but there are others where they have not. So, as lack of time in each day and abundance of time already lived suggest foreclosure and publication, I can visualise readers from different disciplines saying: 'But hasn't he read [this or that groundbreaking author]?' The answer in many cases may well be, 'No, he has not'. In others it may be, 'Well, he has, but he doesn't show much knowledge of it'. In either case my endproduct can hardly be magisterial. Instead this book will be best understood as modelling my own doctrine of imperfection and provisionality, put out in the hope that it will at least prove seminal, a starting-point for more exact investigation and fuller exposition. Time and again I have had to content myself with a mere outline, sometimes little more than a hint, of how I think a particular theme should be developed. Its very provisionality betrays the eschatological tension within which Christians ought to function – morally, doctrinally and academically doing the best they can in the present, but knowing that doing better in the future is the divine imperative.

There is also a case, alongside admitted imperfection, for what I have come to conceive as 'intermediate scholarship'. There is need for a new start in ecclesiology across a wide constituency, including a great variety of grass-roots persons. The most useful debate will therefore be reasonably general in order to afford maximum accessibility for those to whom the shape of the questions is new. The size of the subject-matter is limitless; yet the amount of space between two covers is severely limited. The inevitable issue as to what to include and what to omit has therefore been determined not only by my scholarly limitations, but also by the estimated threshold of appetite of the targeted consumer.

A friend of mine composed a slogan for Grove Books when it first became a limited company, a slogan still seen in the blurbs and advertising of the company. It went like this: 'Not the last word on a subject, but very often the first'. That is how I have viewed my own task in putting together this rather larger enterprise. It is an overtly tentative, unpolished and clearly undefinitive exploration of a theme almost entirely neglected by Evangelical writers of the last half-century. After 30 years of gestation it had to be brought to birth quickly, and those marks are on it. It cries out for confrontation, debate, adjustment or even refutation. Even those who write a 'first word' may covet for others the dialogue which might lead to a 'last word'. I can only repeat that I am conscious that the 'last word' is yet at a long distance from the 'first'.

Addressing existent Evangelical ecclesiology

I have judged a 'first word' to be needed primarily because, in the absence of sustained thinking, Evangelicals fall quickly into an individualistic Gospel, in which the Lord Jesus is one's personal Saviour, and 'Church' is wherever and whenever like-minded people happen to get together. It is convenient for finances, buildings etc., if some medium-term permanence can be established, but no attender has any real duty to belong other than friendship, and individuals may move around con-gregations or stay put as suits them best. If people are not like-minded they would do better to split. Church is in any case a kind of hobby – admittedly often an all-consuming one – which is additional to the basic life of discipleship, and may be varied at will without relating to that personal salvation. It corresponds very closely to a general atmosphere in church-going in England today, and is thus constantly reinforced in ordinary conversation, in exercises like group Bible study, and in the actual behaviour of believers, and thus it subliminally affects the reading of the Bible and the individual's church membership. I have been long convinced that evangelicals have been so hermeneutically blinded by these presuppositions that it is only with much human difficulty, or much iconoclasm by the Holy Spirit, that the New Testament Church and its application to the English scene today can be clearly discerned.

Addressing non-Evangelicals

I should nevertheless be very happy if those who do not call themselves evangelicals will read this. I hope that liberals (about whom I have said little so far) will merely content themselves with saying, 'Yes, I think Scripture does teach that, even though I do not reckon myself as compelled to believe Scripture as he does'. That could be the basis of a profound probing of Scripture. The difficulties liberalism raises are of two most obvious sorts: one is the sheer bypassing of the text of Scripture, as having demonstrated itself difficult, unauthoritative and irrelevant, and it is that which I hope probing would prevent. The other liberal Anglican syndrome is the love of fudge. I recall Jim Packer saying in my student days, 'Anyone else who gets hold of a convincing theological principle adheres to it and lives by it; Anglicans, however, look for ways they can compromise or fudge it.' Now I do believe that not all conclusions have to be immediately sharp-edged; I do reckon that much theological tension can only be worked through eschatologically; I do judge that much in the ecclesiological field requires degrees of preference or adherence rather than straight 'yea' or 'nay'; and I do conclude that in many secondary matters, a principle of faith or practice can be established without all variants from it being ruled out. But the *quest* for accuracy of formulation and for truthfulness in communication is surely right in itself, and to call off the hunt is surely to settle prematurely for the provisional or tentative as though they were definitive? To that extent the Anglican instinct for fudging (it can hardly itself be called a principle) is to be avoided, and sloppiness of thought (even if dignified as non-linear, or post-modern) must surely not be hailed as a theological virtue?

However, my long-term view is that theological liberalism is parasitical – it needs a conservative host-body on which to live and feed, and cannot really arise in any generation unless the conservative host-body is present. It has no power of self-propagation or self-sustaining. It is, of course, to be distinguished from the social radicalism which a true conservativism should generate; but its role in God's economy may well be that of keeping hard questions, not least that of social radicalism, before conservative eyes.

But it is Catholic Anglicans who are likely to find much of my treatment of the data of Scripture and history provocative. This is partly because, over a century and a half, so much of their position, having begun as sectional and even disloyal, has in turn slowly been tolerated and has then progressed to become a norm in a conventional understanding of Anglicanism, arriving sometimes triumphantly, sometimes subliminally. I do not know where the joint authorship about the nature of the Church (mentioned on p. 359: ch. 3, n. 2) would have got if it could have continued; certainly I owe a great spiritual debt to Anglicans Catholics of all kinds of hue, and want to put on record my conviction – well expressed at Keele, and well supported from experience – that there is much to learn from those with whom one disagrees; but, when the chips are down, I fear that not only are the premises of current Anglican Catholicism suspect, but that a divided and declining constituency is hard-put to make a convincing contemporary restatement of its distinctive principles.

I can hardly conclude this Introduction, however, without saying that the important issue is the God in whom we believe, and the Jesus Christ whom we confess as Saviour, Lord and God. Nor would I omit the Holy Spirit. Of course I want to hold out hands and sit down to eat with all believers. Ecclesiology is the sort of issue to be debated after eating, over the coffee. But then it is a serious debate.

Part I

Biblical Data

1 Scriptural Authority

Separation from Rome – asserting scriptural authority
Anyone who would with good conscience (and a modicum of inquisitiveness) belong to a church of the Anglican family must inevitably be driven to examining the point of the historical origins of a Church of England separate from Rome, and separate too from its bonds of nearly a thousand years previously with Rome. There, then, we start.

The Church of England gained its independence from Rome in the sixteenth century (actually in 1533–4) through a flurry of political activities, not least the declaration that Henry VIII was the supreme head on earth of the Church of England – just as he was (and by the same token as he was) supreme head of the nation of England. Despite all constitutional verbiage, let alone the arbitrary despotic overtones, of this legislation, some assertion of the supremacy of Scripture as a matter of principle was to be found under it all, and that principle was to expand in coming reigns, becoming vital to the rationale and life of Anglicanism.

We trace the principle in this way. The monarch had earlier appealed to the pope to grant him a dispensation to marry his deceased brother's widow, Catherine, and the pope had granted it. Then, in circumstances well known to all, Henry went back to the pope to ask him to cancel the dispensation, declare the marriage null and void, and release Henry to contract marriage as a fancy-free bachelor. A pope in other generations might well have agreed – but this pope, held captive by Catherine's nephew, was not well-placed to accede to the request. Henry then appealed, via Cranmer's mission, to the universities of Europe with this question: 'If Scripture has forbidden a certain step, can the pope dispense from that prohibition?' The answer, though apparently slightly uncertain and less than unanimous, was 'No, he cannot'. This then became the charter for the break from Rome – there was to be no appeal from Scripture to the pope, but instead the appeal was from the pope to Scripture, and therein lay the key to the future.

The principle was duly developed in Edward's VI's reign, and was clearly spelled out in the Reformation formularies. In the Thirty-Nine Articles (1571), Article VIII states: 'The Three Creeds ... ought thoroughly to be received and believed: for they may be proved by most certain warrants of holy Scripture.'* This a crucial test-case, for the creeds have often come near to claiming an independent, indeed autonomous, life of their own (two of them, for instance, form a side of the 'Lambeth Quadrilateral', i.e. as a second side quite apart from the side represented by Scripture; but here in the Articles all other distinctive claims of theirs are set aside – the Church of England does *not* receive the creeds simply as coming from General Councils; she does *not* receive them according to the 'Vincentian Canon' as having been believed everywhere, always and by all people;** she does *not* receive them as a valuable ingredient in the inherited riches of the traditions of the Western Church. These attributes and buttressings of the creeds are no doubt of great interest, but the Church of England cuts through all those possible qualifications – the authority for receiving the creeds is to us that they encapsulate the teaching of holy Scripture.

The Reformation formularies spell out this supremacy of Scripture in dozens of ways, but the ordination services are a key example. From 1550 onwards the intending deacons were asked: 'Do you unfeignedly believe all the Canonical Scriptures of the Old and New Testament?' And the intending presbyters and bishops were asked: 'Are you persuaded that the holy Scriptures contain sufficiently all doctrine required of necessity for eternal salvation through faith in Jesus Christ?'[1]

---

*This form of words must mean 'proved to the satisfaction of a listening and enquiring mind'. See below.

**Quod ubique, quod semper, quod ab omnibus* – 'that which has been believed everywhere and always and by all' – a principle of faith enunciated by Vincent of Lerins (in his *Commonitorium*, AD 434.)

Instances could be multiplied, but these are sufficient for the moment to indicate that the secondary formularies of faith of the independent reformed Church of England in the sixteenth century pointed to a primary formulary in the text of Scripture and entrenched the actual life of the Church within the teaching of that Scripture. It also thereby implicitly entrenched a principle enshrined in a famous Reformation tag – *'Ecclesia reformata semper reformanda'* ('The church which has been reformed is always to go on being reformed', or, 'A reformed church is always up for further reform') – and established that principle as operable thereafter under the authority of the primary formulary, Scripture. As Scripture exposes shortcomings in the life of the people of God, so those people are to be subject to Scripture's teaching, and obey God's word to them.

If this principle is taken seriously, then Anglicans need to be able to root their doctrine of the Church in Scripture and to be ready to adjust their self-understanding, their universal ecclesiology, and their ways of life and practice in accordance with Scripture. That is what this book is about.

However, Scripture is not a series of tightly written theological statements like the Westminster Confession of Faith. It does not provide a series of blueprint answers which can be read off from it as soon as the questions are framed. And this means that some procedural warnings have to be given, before we venture any inferences from it about a possible modern Anglican ecclesiology.

Deploying scriptural authority

Firstly, there is a real question as to whether Scripture is clear – or 'perspicuous', as the pundits have it. This is not only a question as to whether the thought of the writer of each book is clear in itself; it is also a question as to how that thought applies to the life of the individual or Church or society today. And the dilemma is this: if the original thought of the author and manner of contemporary application are deemed transparent, easily visible and accessible to any individual with the ability to read, then it is astonishing that Christians differ from each other so much; but if the access to that original thought is only available to persons trained in certain academic disciplines, then we have removed Scripture from the 'common person' and made it the stamping ground of the elite: and, as we enunciate the programme, by that very process we inhibit interest in reading or studying the text of Scripture among 'ordinary Christians'. If we have eliminated an interpretative hierarchy of the Church of Rome only to replace it with a hermeneutical priesthood of the academic elite, we might well wish ourselves safely back within the walls of the Vatican.*

Whatever the temptation to declare Scripture perspicuous at sight – for that would cut so many corners and deliver a simple and credible doctrine to us ready-made – it cannot quite be done. So we have to affirm some simple qualifiers or provisos, preferably ones with some transparency or self-authenticating validity. The simplest form I can conceive for these now follows:

1 Scripture yields its meaning to persistent study;

2 All Scripture has more yet to teach as generations pore over it;

3 No Scripture will yield its truth in the face of a simple evasion of the need to discover its original meaning (ideally in its original language) in its original setting for its original addressees;

4 No Scripture will be truly comprehensible if we overlook its literary genre;

5 No Scripture will help us if we are blind to the limitations of our own generation and to the blinkers with which we are likely to read the text;

6 No Scripture will help us if we do not attempt to relate it to other Scripture so that a consistent whole may be found;

7 No Scripture will help us if we insist on grappling with it as an individualistic task without reference to what others

---

*To illustrate this I cite David Jenkins, former bishop of Durham. It is not only that his doctrine of a non-bodily resurrection of Christ is wrong, but also that, even if it had been right, no reader of the Scripture – ignorant or learned – could ever have lit upon that doctrine. The Bible then becomes a closed book to the vast majority – it allegedly does not mean what it clearly says, and of itself not only gives us no clues as to what it does mean, but delivers us into either total confusion or the passing esoteric intellectual fancies of the priesthood of academe!

have done with the text in the past and are doing around
us at the moment;

8 No Scripture will help us if we are determined not to act
on its teaching once discovered;

9 No Scripture will help us if we do not hold to some
provisionality in our understanding of it, pending such
further light as may affect our understanding.*

These are admittedly fearsome warnings with which to hedge
the revelation of God: but one can see them at work in the
doctrinal debates of the fourth and fifth centuries about
the nature of the Trinity, and they led then to a virtual consensus which was not so much imposed by hierarchical
authority but rather was expressive of a growingly common
mind about the teaching of Scripture. It is safer and truer
(and a hundred times more helpful) to affirm the principle of
transparency in Scripture, however qualified by the procedural
warnings set out above, than it is for one moment to concede
that the Bible is a privileged book in a special code to which
only certain categories of people have access.

The warnings are needed – but they are qualifiers to the
general principle: that Scripture was written to be read and
understood within the life of the people of God. Thus we can
still at root even assert the controverted principle of 'private
judgement' – *if* we mean that Scripture is to make its own
impact upon its readers, without that meaning being pre-
cluded, coloured or warped in advance by imposed hierarchical
interpretations or by equally tyrannical rationalistic presuppositions.** Interestingly, there are strong hints of that actual

---

*The stating of such general principles is not to say that occasional
guidance or other help from God may not be available through a text
quoted out of context and without regard to its original meaning –
but we do distinguish a happy result from a revealed purpose, and
the former cannot be transmuted into the latter.

**The fineness of these qualifications is illustrated by 2 Peter 1,
where Peter says that 'no prophecy of Scripture is of private interpretation' (2 Pet. 1:20). If the banned 'private interpretation' is judged
to be that which might be brought by the latter-day reader, then
Peter is asserting that there is in Scripture a 'mind of the Spirit' (cf.
1:21), and that people are not to twist, wrest or evade that mind by
individual perversity – and on this view he is not attempting to say
that the Scripture should not be allowed its proper impact on the

force of Scripture (i.e. in providing the unmediated truth of God) in the latter part of the question to candidates for the episcopate and presbyterate quoted on p. 30 above: 'And are you determined . . . to teach nothing, as required of necessity to eternal salvation, but that which you shall be persuaded may be concluded and proved by the Scripture?'

The overt sixteenth-century Anglican presuppositions here are threefold:

1 Scripture has a discoverable and trustworthy meaning;
2 the individual minister at least has to let that meaning impose itself upon him;
3 that meaning has to be taught to the lay people.

It has to be confessed that the Reformers held to a very strong distinction between the ministers who were to teach the faith, and the laity who were to receive their teaching. Nevertheless there exist under the overt presuppositions three less overt ones:

1 lay people have open Bibles;
2 they too have to be 'persuaded' that any particular teaching is scriptural;
3 they may therefore in principle challenge the exegesis of any teacher (though they were usually liable to be in trouble if they tried this in some Tudor or Stuart reigns).

In this interactive dynamic we are approaching an understanding of the way in which the supreme authority of Scripture is to be understood and exercised within the Church.

---

individual (and is certainly not saying that there is somewhere in the offing a protected authoritative interpretation of the Church, and personal understanding must be brought to conform with it). It is instructive to read his later remarks about Paul (2 Pet. 3:15–16) – where he says (a) that Paul writes 'Scriptures' (the only place where the New Testament term for the Old Testament writings is itself applied to newly existent Christian literature which we now call 'New Testament'); (b) that he expects his readers to have been reading Paul, and reading him to their own benefit; (c) that nevertheless Paul's writings are in parts 'hard to understand'; (d) that some people 'distort' them to their own destruction; (e) that, although such distortion is occasioned by difficult bits of Scripture, the real cause of it lies in the 'unlearned and unstable' character of the particular readers. So both chapters of 2 Peter which refer to Scripture apppear to witness to a broad perspicuity of it, to be accompanied by care and humility in reading and expecting to understand it.

The Bible is to be in the hands and hearts of all, and all other expressions of the faith – creeds, Articles, liturgy, sermons, lectures, commentaries, synodical resolutions or whatever – are in principle all provisional and negotiable, subject to reformulation in the light of what the Church of any generation may be 'persuaded' is the teaching of the Bible.

Approaching ecclesiology

The issue then looks simple: we identify the doctrine of the Church by which any particular church lives today; we put it under ruthless analysis in the light of biblical teaching on the Church; and we then come up either with a strong programme for reform, or with a despairing, 'If I were going to Dublin, I wouldn't start from here'. In practice, however, it is not so easy, and it may help at the outset to look at the difficulties.

1   The Bible itself may not prove too easy, and it may well be a matter of debate as to what biblical material even bears upon the question.

2   There are literally *hundreds* of autonomous Churches in the world, with a vast variety of self-understandings. Some of these self-understandings are dogmatically entrenched, but others are not explicit in prose, but are simply to be discerned as a function of the kind of association they have come to be. People act under pressure of events in history, form groupings almost by instinct (and/or by conversions) and only later attempt rationalising ecclesiogies. The problem then, in drawing an ecclesiological map of today, is not only to provide the self-justification naturally sought by any grouping, but also to give some account of the place on the map which any grouping would accord to all the others. It is little use a large or small denomination saying, 'We are formed on New Testament principles', if they have achieved that supposed accord with the New Testament by cutting off all other Christians from their account.* The effect in life, of course, is to produce a more or less separatist stance, in which there is little sense of duties towards those who are

---

*Bishop Thomas Deacon of the later Non-Jurors wrote: 'If then the Church of Rome has erred, and the Churches of the East have erred, and the Church of England that now is has erred, where then is the true Church to be found? I will tell you – in Manchester.'

'not on the map' – and surely some solipsist unrealism when seen from where the angels sit?

3   For a study of the doctrine of the Church to be useful, we have to ask the New Testament (and, indeed, the early Church and the Church throughout history) a series of questions, not all of which were uppermost in the minds and writings of the biblical authors – and some of which might even lead the authors of Scripture to protest that the priority we give to our current questions itself shows we have departed a long way from their presentation of the Gospel.[2] And, although I have attempted here to set out some biblical data first so as to express the supreme authority of Scripture over the life of the Church, I am also aware that the very issues I wish to tackle may well have so determined the selection and presentation of the data that I have subconsciously built my conclusions into my premises. If this is so, by definition only others can judge.

4   We have a much less tidy historical situation to chart than a similar study of, say, the doctrine of the Trinity would have. The doctrine of the Trinity was the subject of enormous and virulent debate all over the Mediterranean for over a hundred years in the fourth and fifth centuries. It was then resolved for most practical purposes; and it was resolved with an exactness of language which in general enables orthodoxy on the points at issue to be ruled off from heterodoxy almost at sight. No one could urge that ecclesiology poses *harder* questions than does the nature of the Trinity; but the ecclesiology questions are highly complex, and more variegated than the trinitarian ones – and the answers so far available differ among themselves and are consequently to be reckoned far more provisional. So a doctrine of the Church not only necessitates a large book rather than a Chalcedonian formula, but it also poses complex questions and exhibits, through history, different and often mutually exclusive answers to those questions surviving and thriving alongside each other. To leave aside for the moment all Reformation issues, one has only to cite the issues separating the Eastern Orthodox from the Church of Rome – along with the anathemas issued in the interests of their respective positions – to recognise the warring and unresolved

character of many ecclesiological issues. Add back in the Reformation issues, and the position becomes complicated. Add on again the new manifestations of the seventeenth, eighteenth, nineteenth and twentieth centuries, and the task is harder still.

Nevertheless, however hard the charting may be, every separate development of Church life, every coming to birth of a new denomination, and every consequent question of relationships between denominations, has given birth to an ecclesiology. It has often not been an overt ecclesiology; it has indeed often remained at gut level. Thus there has arisen a great range of ecclesiologies. They have had most imprecise formulation among Evangelicals; but they have so often been derived indirectly from an individualistic Gospel – and sometimes from a schismatic tendency – that they are in great need of open evaluation in the direct light of Scripture.

2 The Old Testament

The story starts in the Garden of Eden. The perfection of creation 'in the image of God' is marred by the Fall. From the Fall there is to be a redemption. God creates for himself from the seed of Abraham a people who will be his instrument for bringing salvation to the world. He is their God and they are his people by covenant. They are to be a nation, but they are also to be his nation. He gives circumcision to Abraham both as a pledge or sign of that promise, and also to bind him and his seed in obedient response. They live by the promise of land and seed, and for the two generations from Abraham to Jacob (or Israel) the promise of the land is contained within the chosen one out of two children – the promise passes each time to the younger son, Isaac in the first generation (the one born of promise to a woman past child-bearing) and Jacob in the second generation (the election of God being worked out as Esau trades in his birthright for a 'mess of pottage'). Then the settling in Egypt of the twelve 'children of Israel' does turn the promise of seed into the provision of a nation, though it is a nation at that point with seed but no land. The nation retains its identity even in captivity in Egypt, and still retains in that captivity in Egypt the hope of the Promised Land also.*

The deliverance comes. It comes through the sheer faithfulness of God to his covenant with Abraham. God raises up his deliverer, Moses; he brings his people out of slavery 'under the blood of the lamb'; he orders them an annual feasting celebration of this passover as part of their covenant relationship with him; they flee; then they are, as a people, 'baptised into

---

*As borne out by the burials of Jacob and Joseph (Gen. 49:29–50:14; Gen. 50:24–6; Exod. 13:19; Josh. 24:31).

Moses in the cloud and in the sea' (1 Cor. 10:1); cut off by the Red Sea (and its point-of-no-return character) from going back to Egypt, willingly or reluctantly, they go together to Sinai under Moses' leadership; at Sinai, God affirms that, subject to the conditions of obedience, he will make of them his 'treasured possession . . . a kingdom of priests and a holy nation' (Exod. 19:5–6); and at Sinai God invokes his covenant relationship, and then starts to impose his directive moral will and ceremonial guidance upon them. This Sinaitic covenant is predicated entirely upon his prior covenantal grace – 'I am the Lord your God who brought you out of the land of Egypt, out of the house of bondage: therefore you shall . . .' The 40 years in the desert become years of attempting rebellion, disobedience and lack of trust towards God, and years of being rebuked, corrected and rebuffed by him back into loyalty, obedience and trustful dependence. The people retain their identity, and are taken by Moses to the very brink of the Promised Land.

They duly enter, conquer and occupy under Joshua. They now have in full the redemption story which sustains their corporate identity and reinforces their separateness from the nations around. They look back to the promise to Abraham, the deliverance from Egypt and the bringing into their own land as the peculiar favour and love of God towards them; and this is an assurance with enormous contemporary implications in each generation as he is still their God, the same God, and they are still his people, the undeserving apple of his eye, called by him to be the obedient servants of his will. To our Christian eyes, God has a long-term view as to his own purposes in creating such a people. To the generations which follow the occupation of the land, the great first duty is to be grateful to God and worship him, and in grateful response hold fast to his law and find from it the prescribed pattern of corporate living. The book of the Judges records that they in fact ignore his law, doing marginally better under the right leadership, but always returning to corrupt ways after the death of a judge (Judg. 2:18–19).

There comes the day when they seek a king. Kingship is duly established, rather as a concession to their earth-bound nature than as a true expression of God's best purpose for them. Nevertheless, both in the history of a dynastic kingship on the one hand, and in the poetry and worship which accompanies royal festivals and regal honour on the other, God affirms his own kingship, and makes the house of David a kind of sacrament of his own rule over his people, and, in the promise to David of an heir always to sit on his throne, gives shadowy outline to 'great David's greater Son'. In the second generation of the Davidic kingship, that is, in the reign of Solomon, he also establishes the temple as the permanent abode of the 'tabernacle of testimony'. This becomes in turn the symbolic dwelling-place of God on earth, and thus the headquarters of the priesthood, the centre of worship, the place of pilgrimage, and the reassurance that God is 'in the midst of his people'. The promises to the house of David are linked with the significance of the continuity of the temple.

All this is blasted apart in the division of the kingdom after Solomon's death. Whether the blame be attributed to Jeroboam's rebellious spirit or Rehoboam's tyrannical programme, in the tenth century BC the kingdom comes apart. Ten tribes become the northern kingdom, called Israel, Samaria or Ephraim, under the rule of the upstart rebel and with a centre of worship at Bethel; and two tribes, Judah and Benjamin, form the southern kingdom, usually called Judah, remaining loyal to the house of David, and retaining the city of Jerusalem and thus the temple and the instituted worship. The books of the Kings tell the story of the schismatic Israel until its destruction by the Assyrians in 721 BC (see 2 Kings 17), after which the second book switches to Judah. The books of the Chronicles tell the story of Judah from the original division, concentrating on the saga of the house of David and on the temple – that is, on the two supposed authentic 'notes' that God is with them.* Yet both lines of accounts date themselves by political and other changes (usually the death of a king) in the other kingdom, and both therefore march together in telling the story of a people of God that is in origin one, that

---

*The last stages of this equivocal concept is to be found in Jeremiah's denunciation of those who think that if the fabric of the institution is intact, then God is with them and will protect their identity and inheritance *irrespective of what they do* (cf. Jer. 7:4–11 – and note v.12, 'Go and look at Shiloh').

at its best worships the same one God and acknowledges each other as brothers and sisters, but is to be found ruled over by two different sets of monarchs, diverging often from each other in their ways of life, and occasionally even forced by events or turbulent people into confrontation and warfare with each other. Interestingly there is a more forceful and flourishing sequence of prophets raised up by God in Israel than there is in Judah, during those two centuries or more in which the two kingdoms lived alongside each other in bonded tension. Perhaps the northern kingdom was more corrupt; perhaps because of what they lacked they were more needy; or possibly their prophets were recorded in greater detail; but God gave them Elijah, Elisha, Hosea and Amos. In the southern kingdom only Micah is recorded from that period, with Isaiah coming above the horizon as the northern kingdom disappears.

After the sack of Samaria, the northern tribes were forcibly dispersed and resettled, and intermarried with people of their locality and are lost to ethnic history.* They also seem to be virtually lost to religious history by the same token. Thereafter their fate haunts the southern kingdom, where the people at times reassure themselves that, having the kingship and the temple, they have talismen which will secure them against disaster; but at times are told that no such security is available to them. The sack of Jerusalem duly comes in 586; the people are carried into exile in Babylon; but they remain a people, as they had in Egypt, and they have prophecies of a return, of a rebuilding of the temple, and of a restoration of Judah and Israel into one nation again.

Cyrus sends them home from 535 onwards. A new temple is built. The people are back in the land. But it is not what it

---

*This seems undoubted (cf. 2 Kings 17:24–41). The Samaritans of Jesus' time (and a tiny community of Samaritans which has apparently remained to this day) would appear from the Old Testament account to be the nearest claimants to being demonstrably ethnic descendants. The claim of the 'British Israelites' between the wars was based, it would appear, upon the superstitious self-regarding persuasion that God *must* have chosen the British race for some uniquely favoured place in his economy, rather than upon either Scripture or respectable anthropology. History – and more enlightened views of ethnicity – now make the claim seem not only wrong, but also both wrong-headed and (metaphorically!) antediluvian.

was before. Clearly the promises of a glorious restoration, while prefigured in the return, are nothing like fulfilled. Something more is awaited. The people are still a people, still in their own eyes the people of God. They sin, they backslide, they rebel – and they suffer. Yet through the years of occupation by Alexander, Antiochus, and Rome, they dream of autonomy, of freedom, and even of a Messiah, a deliverer, God's anointed one. And God's years go ticking on till the days of Herod the Great.

(See Appendix 1, pp. 295–6, for a Note on the Greek word *ecclesia*.)

3 The New Testament and Christology

Jesus is the centre of the New Testament. Christians are Christ-ians – or they are nothing. The person of the incarnate Son of God cannot be evaded, sidetracked or short-circuited. The issue for this book is both his person and the purpose he came to serve. To put it another way: if he came to save the world, we need to know not only *from* what he came to save us, but also *for* what. In the process of investigation, I shall try not to linger too long on known events or history. Furthermore, I need to take almost for granted the way in which an individual is converted to Christ by coming to put his faith in him. This book is not directly a treatment of the conversion of the individual, and no argument bears directly on the point. But the ecclesial (including the sacramental) implications for such conversion are attempted here, and should in passing put that individual experience into a rich biblical context.

The New Testament writers are in no doubt about the role Jesus fulfilled in relationship to his followers. He came to 'save his people from their sins' (Matt.1:21). The people of God are to be *his* people. Paradoxically and amazingly he came to find and call 'his people' from within the existing people of God. He drew followers to himself, and, as they followed him, so they related to each other. They belonged to him within this company, and modelled in their persons a bonding with each other which was nevertheless centred on him. Anyone joining Jesus as a disciple inevitably joined the band of disciples and was thereby committed to common living, physical proximity, and actual loving. Their relationships were being monitored and enriched by Jesus from the start, and at root these relationships had two dimensions to them: firstly that they were to exhibit a loving company before the world, and sec-

ondly that they were there for the world's sake and it was only
as they loved each other that they had any prospect of loving
the unbelieving world around. Their love on both fronts was
to be unlike that of unbelievers, for they were to love those
whom by nature they would not have loved, and to exhibit a
supernatural bonding which has few parallels in the class,
gender, wealth and intellect divisions of society around us. If
we may so put it, oddballs entering the company of Christ's
church were to know they would be loved and would be
included informally as well as formally.

The word 'ecclesia', drawn (as we see in Appendix 1,
pp. 295–6) from the Septuagint but translated in the New Testament as 'church', was in regular use in the Pauline letters
(almost certainly written between AD 47 and 65). It is, however,
not regularly used by Jesus in the gospel narratives; the exception to this is that he does make reference to 'the church' in two
places in Matthew's gospel: he will found his Church on Peter –
or possibly on Peter's confession (Matt. 16:18); and if anyone
has a reason to complain against another, after various earlier
stages he or she is to make the complaint 'before the church'
(Matt. 18:17). The question whether Jesus 'intended to found a
Church' is virtually answered in these two citations – there was,
on the basis of the former citation, to be a worldwide timelong
institution, cosmic in its dimensions, and transcending death in
its vigour; at the same time there was, on the basis of the latter
citation, to be a locally gathered community, existent in defined
time and space, before which any two persons might appear on
a particular day to air a particular grievance. It appears from
the verses immediately following the second of these citations
that there is a strongly corporate character to both the proclamation of the gospel of forgiveness (18:18) and the worship of
the Father through Christ (18:19–20). And both these manifestations – the timelong cosmic and the local limited – are 'the
Church'. It would seem tightly logical, therefore, to see the disciples as being, in embryo, the Church – but most of the
references by Jesus are prospective, and relate to what 'you' (the
disciples) will be doing *after Jesus' death and resurrection* –
prophecies which are of great value when the gospels are being
later compiled and edited. We may illustrate this from an infer-
ential feature of the gospels: clearly, during Jesus' earthly

ministry, there were people still living in their own homes who were disciples, and there were occasional persons who, being 'not against us', were deemed to be 'for us' (Mark 9:38–41). Certainly there is no tidy picture. It seems fair to say that the people are being prepared to be the Church; but it would be hard to say they are already it.

Indeed, it is an arguable and very satisfying approach to view the 'true Israel' as not only contained within 'Israel after the flesh', but, in the person of Jesus, coming down to one representative person – as Paul says, the 'seed, being one person, the Christ, not seeds, being many' (Gal. 3:16). The one who dies on the cross dies both alone, and yet for all, and very distinctively contains within himself all who would ever be delivered by him and through him – for they are reckoned in the economy of God to have died with him and in him (cf. 2 Cor. 5:14). The sheer plurality of the people of God is built into the one who dies on the cross, and their actual cleaving to Christ, stemming from the resurrection and enlivened and empowered by the coming of the Spirit on the day of Pentecost, starts thereafter to expand the membership within Judaism until the day, quite soon to arrive, when it bursts the confines of Judaism altogether.

The resurrection not only vindicates the Lord, and 'powerfully declares him to be the Son of God' (Rom. 1:4), but it sets him alive for evermore among the world's people, offering them immediate access to him, ever-present and ever-living among them. Faith starts there, for, while it must always recognise the demonstration in the gospels of who Jesus is, it can never consist simply of careful attention to the historical incarnation, but must include actual faith-cleaving to this same Jesus, alive from the dead. Once that livingness of Jesus is known, then we are ready for yet another dimension in his living on earth today: it is not only that he lives 'in' or 'among' us; it is also that we are members of him.

There are two New Testament images which enforce this most strongly: the body and the temple. The first of these is so strongly in line with Jesus' bodily resurrection as to warn us to be wary of the very word 'image'. We are stating reality – a reality becoming more detailed as we use sentences like 'we

are members of him'.* Of course heavenly realities are seen
through earthly imagery; but here the imagery is not just a
human simile, but a drawing upon Christ's historical bodily
risen reality. Paul wrote, 'we who are many are one body in
Christ' (Rom. 12:5, cf. 1 Cor. 12:27), and John Robinson
expounds it thus:

> He is not saying anything so weak as that the Church is
> a society with a common life and governor, but that its
> unity is that of a single physical entity: disunion is dis-
> memberment... It is to be noted how uncompromisingly
> physical is the language in which Paul depicts Christians as
> going to compose the resurrection body of Christ.[1]

The use of 'body' language grew in Paul's own understanding
as his own years went by. The Ephesians–Colossians use of it
includes a very cosmic and glorified picture, in which at first
sight we are 'in Christ' because he is the 'head of the body'
(Eph. 4:15), unlike the apparent Corinthians–Romans use,
where the mutual interdependence of the members appears to
make the 'body' both local (so that the members are accessible
to each other), and in its totality coterminous with Christ.

I say 'apparent Corinthians–Romans use', as the disjunction
should not be made too great. Thus in Romans 12 Paul says
'*we* ... are one body in Christ', when he was a thousand miles
from the Romans, had never yet met them, and did not even
know what reception awaited him. Correspondingly, in Ephesians 4, although Christ is the 'head' (verse 15), and the source
and point of origination of all growth and nourishment in the
body (verse 16), yet he is also the measure of the complete
growth and maturity of the body (verse 13) – almost as though
the members were both currently 'in Christ' and yet by growth
in both numbers and discipleship were to fill out the true
measure of Christ's body. In Colossians 3:12–17, the 'body'
imagery is being orientated towards the local relationships at
Colossae, although the general thrust of the 'body' terminology
in Colossians is, as in Ephesians, strongly cosmic.

The other evocative imagery is that of the temple. The

---

*We are so used to 'membership' of clubs and teams that we easily
forget that '*membra*' are the limbs or organs of a body.

temple also is part of earthly reality, a living parable rather than a mere verbal metaphor. And Jesus himself mixes together the language of rebuilding a temple and his own bodily resurrection (John 2:19–22). Paul also links body and temple imagery in a series of varying allusions:

1   In 1 Corinthians 3 we are (bodily) the temple of God (in verse 16, 'you' is plural, but 'the temple' is singular: cf. 2 Cor. 6:16); the Spirit of God indwells us (as the *shekinah*-glory dwelt in the sanctuary of old), and, although our bodies are not mentioned, bodily indwelling is implied.

2   In 1 Corinthians 6, Paul emphasises that the importance of our bodies stems from what God has done in raising Jesus from the dead (verse 14). Our present bodies are under two overwhelming constraints: firstly, that they are to be raised from the dead and should not be compromised or tainted in this life; and secondly, that they are here and now 'members of Christ' (verse 15) (and cannot therefore be 'joined to a prostitute' and become 'one body with her' – verse 16). No: 'your' (plural) 'body' (singular) is the temple of the Holy Spirit (verse 19), and you are to glorify God (a temple activity!) in your body (verse 20). There is a subordination to Christ as well as an incorporation into him, as 'you are not your own, for you have been bought with a price' (verse 19).

3   In Ephesians 2 the reconciliation of Jews and Gentiles in Christ is spelled out with both sets of imagery: the Gentiles who were debarred 'far off' from the physical Jewish temple are now 'brought near' by the blood of Christ (verse 13); the wall of partition (a feature of the inner exclusive courts) has been broken down (verse 14); and the result is 'one new man' (or 'human being'), for the 'two' have been reconciled by Christ 'in one body' (verse 16). And then comes the fullest picture of a temple (verses 20–22): a foundation of God's truth ('apostles and prophets') leads to the rising building, with the Gentiles built into the fabric, and the resultant whole providing (as any authentic temple should) a dwelling-place for God by his Spirit. This latter part of the chapter leaves behind the 'body' imagery, but instead provides a kind of vivid pictorial model to which the purple passage about the body in 4:11–16 later conforms.

Some of these thoughts are complex. But the two imageries conspire together to show that, for Jesus' disciples – those who are 'in Christ' – there is both an intimate connection with a Christ who has purchased our salvation with his blood, and an irrefragable bonding with, or binding to, each other to become an organic unity.

The Petrine temple imagery (1 Pet. 2:4–9) has almost exactly the same force. The temple of God is not made of mute inanimate materials, but of 'living stones'; the stones are so built together as to form a single unity, bonded primarily by belonging to the 'chief cornerstone' or 'capstone', Jesus himself, the true 'living stone'; and as the imagery grows, the living 'spiritual house' of verse 5 transmutes into a holy 'priesthood' offering 'spiritual sacrifices' as true worship.

Pauline Christology certainly bears out this 'being members of' (the body) and 'being built into' (the temple). There are two archetypal men – Adam and Christ. The opposition and polarisation between them is set out in complexity and profundity in Romans 5:12–21 and in 1 Corinthians 15:21–2 and 45–9. Each of the passages sees the whole human race as compassed within the persons of Adam and Christ, and each sees the destiny of the people concerned as corporately bound up in the destiny of their respective heads, Adam or Christ. In the Romans passage the emphasis is upon the disobedience of Adam, which has constituted us all as sinners in God's eyes* – reckoned as belonging collectively to the race which opposes God, under the headship of Adam. This is reversed by the obedience of Christ, not simply by his constantly doing the Father's will, but specifically in his being 'obedient to death, even death on the cross'. There, by the death of Jesus, the guilt of all is put away, we are counted as 'in him', and as we were 'constituted sinners' by Adam, so we are 'constituted righteous' by Christ. It is wonderfully summarised in a Pauline sentence, the corporateness of which is often overlooked: 'There

---

*In Romans 5:19, 'constituted' is the correct translation, and *not* 'made'. It is the *position* of the human race before God which is being discussed, not its *disposition*. If this is grasped, then the parallelism in the second half of the verse, where justification is understood as being 'constituted righteous', will also deliver the correct sense.

is therefore now no condemnation to those who are in Christ Jesus' (Rom. 8:1).

In 1 Corinthians 15 the emphasis is subtly altered, the major concern being about death and resurrection. Adam is the figure of death, and those 'in Adam' die. Jesus defeated death, and rose as the first-fruits of a harvest which will be fulfilled at his second coming. In him all shall be made alive. And we who 'have borne the likeness of the earthly man' will, by a kind of mirror-image reversal, 'bear the likeness of the heavenly man' (1 Cor. 15:49). The opposition is of death and resurrection – the likeness of the former is of the dust of the earth; the likeness of the latter is of the heaven to which we are resurrected. Again there are two alternative 'heads' – the second overtaking the first, and transferring those in Adam to himself. Each passes his own destiny into the lives of those who are his; and in the process we find the category of thought that believers are 'in Christ'. This is a key category in the epistles, even in the many other passages where the contrast with being 'in Adam' has dropped out of sight. As earlier writers put it, we belong to one of two 'federal heads', and, in scriptural terms, our destiny is that of our head. Thus those who are 'in Christ' belong, by that very 'incorporation', to each other.

In the Acts of the Apostles this visible pattern is easy to discern. Before the day of Pentecost the 'brothers', numbering 120, 'joined together constantly in prayer' (Acts 1:14–15). On the day of Pentecost, they were 'all together in one place' (2:1). The Spirit came; Peter preached; and with the first baptisms 'about 3000 were added to them that day' (2:41). Thereafter they 'devoted themselves to . . . the fellowship, to the breaking of bread, and to the prayers' (2:42). They circulated round each other's homes; they shared their goods, they loved each other and supported each other practically – all as part of their discipleship. In a word, they *belonged* to each other as believers; and thus, as their message – a message of their corporate way of life, as well as of the Jesus who indwelt them – took root in others' lives, so 'the Lord added to their number daily those who were being saved' (2:47). If the word 'church' has not yet appeared, yet the concept that the Lord is 'adding to them' (2:41, 47 – the word 'number' does not come in the Greek) suggests a single entity of the believers, an entity

which is expanding as others are 'added' to it, and is of a more
stable and enduring character than simply those in attendance
at any one meeting.

What we have here are the outlines of future church life.
New believers are baptised as they profess faith (and their
children are probably baptised with them – a theme pursued
on p. 75ff. below); they move into a strongly corporate 'fellowship' (which is an objective description of a given bond between
them, not a subjective description of how wonderful it feels);
the fellowship is characterised by a common set of beliefs
('doctrine'), a common cultus ('the prayers'), and a common
way of life ('breaking bread' and 'sharing goods'). These determinative features or 'notes' of the Church are set out not only
in Acts 2:42–6, but are largely repeated in Acts 4:32–5. The
word 'church' does not appear at first in the early chapters,
but that may well be without significance, as Luke calls them,
apparently artlessly, 'the brothers' (1:15, cf. 6:3), 'the believers'
(2:44; 4:33; 5:12), 'their own people' (i.e. from the standpoint
of Peter and John, 4:23), 'the disciples' (6:1, 2, 7; 9:1, 10, 19),
most notably, 'those of the Way' (9:2), and, seminally, 'the saints
[*or* holy people]' (9:32).* And the title 'the Church' begins after
a while to appear among these words – as in 5:11 and 8:1 and
3. It may be initially a local term, describing a particular
assembly – and yet it is not simply *as assembled* that the
believers are so described, for the Church is an entity which
is in existence even when dispersed in homes, and would, one
senses, still be *'the* Church' if it existed in more than one city.
For, within a short time, that entity is not found only locally
in Jerusalem: there is a passing yet pregnant line in Acts 5:16:
'Crowds gathered also from the towns around Jerusalem'. (Is
this stage two in the fulfilling of 'You shall be witnesses to me

---

*What they are *not* called in these early stages is 'Christians'. That
comes first in Acts 11:26, and apparently stems from unbelievers –
and may mark the transition to being a Jew-and-Gentile-together
church. The disciples were being gently mocked as 'Christ-ians' – i.e.
people who went on about the Christ, the Messiah. The word would
have been very confusing in Jewish-only days, and actually only
recurs twice more in the New Testament (Acts 26:28 and 1 Pet. 4:16),
in both of which cases it looks like a nickname used by opponents
rather than the term believers chose for themselves. I try to be
somewhat sparing about the use of it also.

in Jerusalem, in all Judaea, in Samaria, and to the ends of the earth?' – Acts 1:8.) Thus 'the church in Jerusalem' (8:1) is not a tautology, but an identification of one (leading and highly significant) outcropping of the believers among what may have been many. And the use of the term in the next chapter then expands the concept further; for in 9:31 Luke refers to 'the church which was throughout Judaea, Galilee and Samaria' – a singular collective noun which embraces not only the individual believers, but also, presumably, a series of separate congregations who are identified as in some sense one unit by this use of the singular term 'Church'.

A further characteristic feature of the early chapters of the Acts is the disciples' unshakeable conviction that the Lord Jesus is with them, or among them, or in them. It is he who chooses Matthias (1:24); it is he who pours out the Spirit (2:33); it is he who adds new believers to them (2:47); it is he who effects healing (3:16); it is he who will return to reign (3:20–21); it is he who turns people from their wicked ways (3:26); it is he whose name is powerful in both healing and salvation (4:11–12); and the list could be extended without effort. While all kinds of dealings with individuals are scattered through this list, there is a strongly ecclesial context throughout. The story of the Acts is self-evidently the continuation – the second volume – in direct sequence to 'the previous account of all that Jesus began to do and teach until the day when . . . he was taken up' (Acts. 1:1–2); and this is a very strong hint that the Acts tells the story of all that Jesus *continued* to do and teach through his presence among his disciples and his power working through them by the Holy Spirit. The infant Church is not just the agent of an absent landlord, but is corporately the working presence of Christ on earth in respect of his communicating with the unbelieving world, and of his purifying his people to serve his purposes the better. They are the em-bodi-ment of Jesus – it is hardly surprising that the concept of the people of Jesus as being his body is woven through the New Testament.

This is sometimes seen as the 'extension of the incarnation'. The point is not simply that of the godhead living 'bodily' on earth (Col. 2:9), but of the 'bodiliness' being adapted to a particular people, place, time and customs. It is the ideological

backdrop to Jesus saying to his disciples, 'As the Father has
sent me, so I send you' (John 20:21); they in turn are sent
into the world with God's mission – indeed, like Jesus and in
sequence to his incarnate ministry, they *are* God's mission,
both embodying the godhead, and yet belonging to their own
times, and conveying the good news of the kingdom in their
words and deeds. In an earlier book a team of authors of whom
I was one preferred to see this concept as the 'extension of the
resurrection', partly because the Jesus Christ whom we
embody is the crucified and risen Christ, and to speak of
extending the incarnation is half to suggest that his death,
and its reversal in resurrection, were slightly complicating
distractions from the primary function of incarnation; but also
partly because it is in his resurrection that Jesus finally lodges
the full responsibility for witnessing and evangelising to his
people, and promises to be with them always (Matt. 28:16–20;
John 20:21–3; Acts 1:6–8).[2] His resurrection is, of course, a
bodily resurrection – for there is no other. It is only as he
appears in the body that Jesus appears or is known in any
way at all to his disciples. So the initial criteria of the incarnation are still fulfilled, but the transition to the age of the
Spirit has begun; the purpose of his incarnation is now fulfilled
as far as it concerns his own bodily ministry on earth, but it
is, according to this account, 'extended' by his 'sending' of his
Church into the world – and that sending, that 'mission', is
the sending by the risen Christ of those who are to live the
risen life of his risen body within the world. He is physically
to depart, and, pouring his Spirit upon them, he will equip
them now to continue his work, to extend his risen presence,
into all the earth down to all generations.

What is clear is that to be Church is to be God's mission.
The full character of the mission may need further exploration,
but the principle involved is inescapable – becoming Church
was 'being sent'. There was no idea of Church as a comfortable
club of happy associations but no responsibilities. When those
who received the good news submitted to the love of God, they
became his active servants in the Church which is his mission
on earth

So, as the mission begins, we have to ask: 'What is *forming*

the Church? What is causing its beginnings and growth?' And
to this there is a threefold answer.

Firstly, there was the Old Testament. This is most strongly
brought out in the exposition of Jesus himself speaking to the
two disciples on the road to Emmaus. ' "Ought not the Messiah
to have suffered these things and to have entered into his
glory?" And, beginning from Moses and all the prophets, he
expounded to them in all the scriptures the things concerning
himself' (Luke 24:26–8). And exactly the same pattern is found
on the day of Pentecost, for Peter first cites Psalm 16 ('You
will not abandon me to the grave, nor allow your Holy One to
see corruption' – Acts 2:27); then shows how it could not apply
to the author of the psalm, King David ('His tomb is with us to
this day' – Acts 2:29); and then concludes that it does apply
to the Christ who has overcome death (Acts 2:31). In the
economy of God, the Gospel first takes root among Jews; it is
indeed 'to the Jew first'; and it takes root precisely because
the Jews know the Scriptures and it is those Scriptures, held
in common between speakers and listeners, which provide the
starting-point in building a community of believers. The
authority of the Old Testament is unquestioned – the only
question is the character and scope of its messianic teaching,
and whether or not that has been fulfilled in Jesus.

Secondly, there is the fulfilment of the Old Testament Scriptures in Jesus himself. This element is also strong in the
account of the conversation on the road to Emmaus. The disciples told a story of Jesus ('We thought he would restore the
kingdom to Israel'), and in Luke this leads into the story Jesus
himself told – about himself. And again it is matched in Acts
2 – Peter's preaching is about 'Jesus of Nazareth, a man
marked out by God for you by miracles and wonders and
signs' (Acts 2:22). And in Peter's preaching the truth of the
resurrection is not simply told deductively from Psalm 16 –
quite the reverse: it is testified by the actual witnesses to the
resurrection (Acts 2:32 – with a hint, through the lack of a
parallel with David, that of Jesus it would properly be stated
'his tomb is *not* with us to this day'). The citing of the Old
Testament is one strand of evidence; the eye-witness account
of Jesus is the other. Telling them about Jesus is what brings
them to ask, 'What are we to do?' (2:37). The accounts of

Jesus, including his teaching, healing and other features of his
earthly ministry, as well as his death and resurrection, were
clearly carefully conserved by oral repetition in the first
instance, and by slow compilation into edited 'gospels' in the
second.

Thirdly, the New Testament company of believers is formed
on the basis of a message of the Gospel which includes both
the Old Testament and the stories of Jesus (including his
death, resurrection and ascension), but has a further word or
words within it. The telling of the story begins to include
detailed exposition of the meaning of the death and resurrection of Jesus, the telling of the coming of the Holy Spirit, the
missionary and ethical implications of being followers of Jesus,
the inclusion of the Gentiles within the fold, the ways in which
Christian communities are to run their communal life, the
assurance of the Lord's return, and a host of other features,
some apparently integral to the message, some perhaps secondary. The Acts, the epistles, and even the book of Revelation,
contain more stories of the communities, and a plethora of
case-histories, fine judgements, revolutionary injunctions and
apostolic *obiter dicta*. They were coming to birth alongside
both the expositions of the Old Testament* and the telling of
the stories of Jesus. Paul is prepared to claim that there is a
revelation of God's truth – particularly in respect of the
'mystery' of the inclusion of the Gentiles in the Church – in
'the apostles and prophets'. In this reference, in Ephesians
3:2–6, he virtually says that what has been revealed to the
apostles and prophets can be read *here in his own writing*,
and he is in fact both expounding the mystery in detail (see
pp. 99–100 below), and stating that the Church is built upon
the foundation of the apostles and prophets (Eph. 2:20). These
Pauline writings were clearly received as of great authority,
and we must assume that, when a particular company had
original letters from Paul, they not only guarded them, but
allowed Christian visitors from other towns to copy them, so
that within a generation from Paul's death around AD 65, a

---

*It is arguable that 'to the Jew first' in the economy of God was
specifically designed and intended to ensure that the books of the Old
Testament were well entrenched in the Christian consciousness
before the Gentiles came into the company.

known collection of Pauline writings was starting to appear –
and was viewed as 'word of God' in a way comparable to the
standing of Old Testament books and gospel narratives
(whether or not these were yet written down). There was, of
course, a direct witnessing to Jesus going on by those who had
known him in his earthly ministry and had been witnesses to
the resurrection (Acts 1:21–2); and there was Paul, who
claimed by divine exception to be of that same number (1 Cor.
9:1; 15:8). But, as the first-generation persons and their first-
hand oral message faded from the first-century scene, the
definitive form of their message in the three sets of writings
(*graphai,* script-ures) became the controlling norm. Scripture
mediated the knowledge of Jesus, and Jesus ruled among his
people by the Scriptures.* These alone could not be queried;
they were the non-negotiable core of Christian revelation.

None of this is to deny that faith is the gift of God, and the
Church the creation of his Holy Spirit . . .

---

*That is not to say that all 'lay' members of their company possessed
written Scriptures or could read them.

4 New Testament and Derived Ecclesiology

How then did this New Testament community live its earth-bound life as the body of Christ, the temple of the Holy Spirit? For the purposes of answering this question, I shall now largely take for granted that the first disciples were above all to be followers of Jesus, confessing 'Jesus is Lord', and living with the Lord Christ dwelling in them by his Spirit. That primary and all-enveloping loyalty and orientation is presupposed in what follows, and is not restated solely for the purposes of presentation.

The disciples as a loving company

First of all Jesus called them to join him as a *company*. He told the greater to serve the less. He told them that they were to be known by their love for each other. He left them at his ascension waiting together for the coming of the Spirit, and it was in that togetherness that they sought a successor to Judas. They were duly together at the dawning of the day of Pentecost; and when, by that same evening, the infant Church had grown from 120 to 3000, togetherness was the most characteristic mark of their activities recorded in Acts 2:42–7. Certainly in Acts 2:42, 'the teaching' derived from the apostles, but 'the fellowship', 'the breaking of the bread' and 'the prayers' were presumably experienced in groups without apostles always physically present; and the pattern of moving daily from house to house for joyful meetings and generous sharing implies every possible form of networking and loving relationships. 'Togetherness' was basic to being Christian in the first generation in Jerusalem, and we must infer that, as Jewish–Christian groups from Pontus, Phrygia, Egypt and Rome returned home from that life-changing Pentecost in

Jerusalem, so they too met in groups and sustained a pattern of common life. The implication from the 'continued stead-fastly' (or 'devoted themselves') of Acts 2:42 is that they viewed themselves as under a binding obligation to meet, and that this was not simply a joyful overflowing of fair-weather Christianity (such as could be asserted about Acts 2:42–7, when they were still 'enjoying the favour of all the people'), but was also found in bad weather, adverse employment conditions, poverty and hardship, and actual opposition and persecution. The succeeding chapters of Acts make this abundantly clear. And the togetherness was sealed not only in the feast the Lord had commanded (see pp. 106–13 below), but also in the 'holy kiss' to which Paul (and Peter) refer at the end of their letters.[1]

Fellowship

By being a company, the disciples continued in the apostles' 'fellowship'. 'Fellowship' is the regular translation of the Greek *koinonia*, though it is sometimes rendered 'communion' (as, for example, in 1 Cor. 10:16 in some versions), or 'participation' (as in other versions of the same verse – or, with the adjective *koinonoi*, as in 2 Pet. 1:4). It is a word of considerable significance for the nature of the Church, as our earlier inspection of Acts 2:42 has suggested. But, as the English word 'fellowship' has drifted away from its biblical meaning, it is all the more important to establish that meaning clearly.

We begin with 1 John 1:3–7. John is proclaiming the incarnate Christ. He says of himself (with a hint of a royal 'we', though that is alleviated by the implication that he is typical of believers and thus the use of 'we' is justified), that he has 'fellowship' with the Father and the Son (1:3). His readers are to believe what he writes of Jesus, 'so that you may have fellowship with us' (1:3). But the converse may sadly be the case – that those who claim to have 'fellowship' with God, when their lives are actually in darkness, are simply liars (1:6). Those who walk in the light have 'fellowship' with one another (1:7).

This brief example is beginning to clarify the meaning. The strong thrust of this passage is that believers have some deep objective bonding with God and with each other. 'Fellowship' is a totally objective concept. It does not describe likes or

dislikes; it does not describe situations we may enjoy or may
not enjoy; it does not describe our feelings; and it does not bear
upon issues of cosiness, spiritual warmth, or even heightened
awareness. It is a 'given' from God, given in common to all his
people.

We return from this interim assessment to look at other New
Testament examples (including not only the abstract noun,
koinonia, but also the adjective and verb from the *koinon-*
stem, and from its compound *sunkoinon-*):

- Acts 2:42: 'remaining in the company of the apostles', or
  'in the company originating from the apostles', or
  (possibly) in the light of the following verses, 'in the practice of sharing with each other characterised or modelled
  by the apostles'.
- Romans 11:17: 'you are sharers in the nourishing sap of
  the olive tree'.
- Romans 12:13: 'sharing in the needs of the holy people'.
- Romans 15:26–7: 'The Macedonians and Greeks have been
  pleased to share a contribution [i.e. by giving it] with
  the poor among the holy people in Jerusalem . . . for if the
  Gentiles have shared a contribution of their [the Jews']
  spiritual things [i.e. by receiving it], then they also ought
  to minister to them in material things'.
- 1 Corinthians 1:9: 'into the fellowship of his Son Jesus
  Christ our Lord'.
- 1 Corinthians 9:23: 'I do all things for the sake of the
  gospel, that I may share [in its benefits]'.
- 1 Corinthians 10:16: 'a sharing of the blood [body] of
  Christ'.
- 1 Corinthians 10:18: 'those who eat the sacrifices are
  sharers with the altar'.
- 1 Corinthians 10:20: 'I want you not to be sharers with
  demons'.
- 2 Corinthians 1:17: 'sharers of our sufferings'.
- 2 Corinthians 6:14: 'What fellowship is there for light
  with darkness?'
- 2 Corinthians 8:4: 'a sharing in this service to the saints'.
- 2 Corinthians 9:13: 'the liberality of your sharing [money]
  with them and with all'.
- Galatians 2:9: 'the right hand of fellowship'.

- Galatians 4:6: 'Let him who is being taught the word share in all good [material?] things with him who is teaching'.
- Ephesians 5:11: 'take no part in the fruitless works of darkness'.
- Philippians 1:5, 7: 'your partnership in the gospel . . . sharers in God's grace'.
- Philippians 2:1: 'If . . . there is any fellowship of the Spirit'.
- Philippians 3:10: 'I want to know the fellowship of his [Jesus'] sufferings'.
- Philippians 4:14–15: 'shared well in my troubles . . . no church but you shared in giving and receiving'.
- 1 Timothy 5:22: 'and do not share in the sins of others'.
- 1 Timothy 6:18: 'ready to share'.
- Philemon 6: 'active in sharing about your faith'.
- Philemon 17: 'If you consider me a partner'.
- Hebrews 10:23: 'you shared with those who were so treated'.
- 1 Peter 4:13: 'as you have been sharers in the sufferings of Christ'.
- 1 Peter 5:1: 'one who will share in the glory to be revealed'.
- 2 Peter 1:4: 'sharers in the divine nature'.
- 2 John 11: 'whoever welcomes [this sort of man] shares in his wicked work'.
- Revelation 1:9: 'I am a sharer of your suffering'.
- Revelation 18:4: 'take no part in their sins'.

In English the general sense conveyed by these instances is that of a commonality, partnership, or mutual participation of an objective sort. Clearly the word itself is morally neutral – it may in its different uses describe participation in the divine nature (2 Pet. 1:4) or sharing with demons (1 Cor. 10:20). Many of its uses describe giving and receiving monetary gifts. Most would imply that we do not live to ourselves (cf. Rom. 14:7). But we do not discover either a club-like group called 'a fellowship' or a subjective experience of *enjoyed* sharing, such as could be, and today might well be, called (in a selective sense) 'having fellowship' with others. The Church of God is in partnership with God himself (though not necessarily on the crest of a wave of subjective joy); the members participate (in 'communion') in the body and blood of Christ; they are in fellowship with each other (which means loving each other and supporting each other materially); so there is a deep, but surely unselective, mutual belongingness established by being in Christ together, which in biblical terms is defined and asserted far prior to any of the more subjective questions of cosiness or mutual confidentiality

The Church living by the word

We have already seen how the Church was to live by the 'word', and the Acts 2:42 words 'continued steadfastly' applied to the new disciples' hold on the apostles' teaching, as well as to the hold on each other's company. The apostles themselves, finding life overcrowded and organisational tasks getting out of control, delegated all these in the interests of 'devoting ourselves' to 'prayer and the ministry of the word' (Acts 6:1–6).* We have also seen how the 'word' was a three-legged stool consisting of the Old Testament, the direct rendering of Jesus' earthly ministry, and apostolic judgements on new situations as they arose (see p. 55). Indeed, the very provision of 'deacons' in Acts 6 appears to be an instance of 'the ministry of the word'; for 'the twelve' had clearly reached a decision of their own before they summoned the 'full number of the disciples' to put it before them. The word then starts to take on a dual characteristic – it often involves a response to new situations where the word, however based on precedent, comes as instant judgement for instant action; but it also involves handing on a deposit of faith in verbal form.

A good instance of the two elements of the word is to be found in 1 Corinthians 15. Here the central deposit of faith is 'that Christ died for our sins in accordance with the [Old Testament] Scriptures, that he was buried, that he was raised on the third day in accordance with the Scriptures' (15:3–4). It is this which Paul had both 'received' and 'passed on' (15:3). These truths were vital for *all* practice of Christianity, and *all* converts had to take them aboard. They included the Old Testament and the account of the passion and resurrection of Jesus, and an element of assigning significance to Jesus'

---

*The Greek verb ('*proskartereo*') is the same as in Acts 2:42, suggesting a stripped-down single-mindedness of life and life-patterns in both cases.

deeds – for he died 'for our sins', a significance derivable both
from the Old Testament and from the words of Jesus himself.

But Paul is writing this chapter to 'remind' (15:1) the particular Corinthians of the central truths because they had got
themselves into error. They were denying the resurrection of
the dead; and so Paul launches into not just an assertion of a
well-witnessed event (though he has plenty of evidence for
such an assertion), but also into an exploration of the implications of their denial ('[on your assumptions] we are of all
people most pitiable') and a confrontation of their rhetorical
polemic, 'How are the dead raised?' ('As we have borne the
likeness of the earthly man, so we shall bear the likeness of
the man from heaven'). In the process the apostolic 'word' is
being expanded in conformity with the Old Testament and the
Gospel narratives, and the Church at Corinth is being corrected and matured through the application of the word. The
difference between this and the organisational need in Acts 6
is that now the word, needed at a distance from the apostle, is
mediated by being written, and thus receives a definitive form,
whereas in the early apostolic Church the new word was *at
the time* oral, and was perhaps repeated, discussed or amended
as spoken words may be. The developing of the written word –
as the apostolic letters were written and the epistle collections
were gradually standardised and the gospel pericopae were
edited – meant that by the time the apostles were dying out
(about AD 70) the 'word' of their personal witness was
being slowly replaced by their written word in definitive and
non-negotiable shape. The word itself was, of course, continuous and ran on in the day-to-day life of the Church without
a break – but its continuity and normative character for the
Church was assured by the coming of the written form,
matching the non-negotiable 'given-ness' of the Old Testament
Scriptures.

In the process we are beginning to winkle out a principle of
church life in relation to the word. It has sometimes been said
(on behalf of an exaggerated view of churchly authority) that:

1   the Church produced the New Testament writings and
    therefore has not only a guardianship role in relation to
    them but also a God-given protected authority to interpret
    them;[2]

2   the Church in the second century decided which books should be Scripture thus reinforcing these roles.

But a truer view of the dynamics of church life in apostolic times and of the actual content of the Scriptures would be that the Scriptures did not so much represent and reproduce church life (as a church-based journal by, say, a bishop might do), but rather *confronted* existent church life. The word is God speaking to his people *to put them straight*. They are out of kilter doctrinally, ethically, mentally and emotionally, and the word – white-hot from God himself – not only exposes their need, but meets it. The ministry of the word is accompanied by the work of the Spirit, an entirely understandable activity by the one who gave the word in the first place. The Church's role is to be open to God's word, that by the word his Spirit may work the reconstruction and remaking that is God's purpose for his people. And to this day, for all that the epistles, for example, may be handling cases of Gnosticism in Colossae or idol-meats and sexual misdemeanours in Corinth, yet that same word confronts the present-day Church and calls, from God himself, for correction and redress. If the word is turned into a kind of household pet of the Church – to be seen in small selected ways in the liturgy, but not to be disruptive or out of control – then it is also rendered toothless and liable to be ineffective. We possess little evidence of how individual churches responded when they received one of Paul's letters (though at the very least the evidence is that the letters we possess never reached the waste-paper bin, but were kept and copied as valuable). But the evidence is strong that, within a generation, the letter that overtly addressed a particular situation in a particular local congregation at a particular point in history, had become part of the total word of God to all his people down all time.

Kingdom

To follow Jesus, to be a company, to have sharing or participation with each other, to experience the gift of the Spirit – all these made the young Church an eschatological community. They were a community of the kingdom of God (in Matthew's gospel always called 'the kingdom of heaven', but otherwise undistinguishable from 'the kingdom of God' in the rest of the New Testament); and that kingdom, the New Testament teaches, had already come and was already established in the person of Jesus and was to be found present 'among' the people of his time.* But Jesus also taught them of a kingdom of which they were a kind of advance guard. And he also taught them of an eschatological kingdom to be ushered in – quite possibly apocalyptically rather than by gradual growth – at the end of time. While in no sense are there three kingdoms, these different aspects of the one kingdom do invite separate consideration.

The Greek word, *basileia*, itself has some nuances of meaning. In its contemporary Gentile usage it meant a nation which had a king, and its territorial implications would have been much the same as in our use of 'kingdom'. Thus Jesus can say, 'Nation will rise against nation, and kingdom against kingdom' (Luke 21:10). The spatial or territorial understanding of the word can appear in a metaphorical use, as when Jesus says to one of the scribes, 'You are not far from the kingdom of God' (Mark 12:34). But more usually in the New Testament, the concept of the 'kingdom of God' is not territorial or spatial, and might be better translated as 'the reign of God'. That translation also avoids any suggestion that 'kingdom' is a collective noun, and brings us instead to actual relationships of a king to his subjects. To think of a sphere (or realm!) in which God is king over his people may bring us back near to the spatial or to the collective noun – nevertheless the distinction remains important. The kingdom of God has an overt inauguration on earth in the person of Jesus, and spreads into other lives as his disciples increase.** 'Kingdom of God' is used in this way, as in effect identifiable with the Church of Christ, in various places in Acts and the epistles,

---

*Note Jesus' words in Matthew 12:29, where not only is the person of Jesus, in his exercising power over demons, evidence that the kingdom of God has come 'upon' his disciples, but also there is a hint in the verb for 'come' (*ephthasen*) that the kingdom has come unexpectedly, or ahead of schedule. Jesus being present 'among' his people is a quotation from Luke 17:21, where, in answer to a question from Pharisees about when the kingdom would come, Jesus insists on its present reality, being incarnated among them in his own person.
**Thus John the Baptist, who had announced the kingdom, is treated by Jesus as not belonging to it (Matt. 11:11, etc.).

though the term's occurrence there is relatively rare compared with the frequency with which it appears in the teachings of Jesus (see, for example, Acts 14:22; 20:25; 28:23, 31; Rom. 14:17; 1 Cor. 4:20; 6:9; 15:24, 50; Eph. 5:5; Col. 1:12–13; 4:11; 2 Tim. 4:1, 18; Heb. 12:28; 2 Pet. 1:11).

Some of these references, however, like many of the parables, have an eschatological perspective. The kingdom will be fulfilled or come to fruition at the end of the age. This is in line with the Lord's own prayer: 'Your kingdom come; your will be done on earth as in heaven.' There is a strong 'not yet' about the coming of the kingdom, and an equally persistent 'and that will be the end of the world' attached to it also. The upshot will be that the king will *be* king, so that in the last of the eschatological parables in Matthew's gospel ('the sheep and the goats'), while the 'kingdom' is not mentioned, yet the Lord is presented as 'the king'. The kingdom comes in, not as a spatial or measurable physical or populous entity, but as the beginning of the reign of the king, and it is centred in the role he plays in relation to his creation, and particularly his creatures.

The question remains as to the way the kingdom grows from its mustard-seed beginning on the day of Pentecost to the reaching of its full measure at the end of time. Is this simply another way of saying that the Church of God is his people on earth, his chosen vessels to promote his kingdom and form the channels of his blessing to the rest of the world? Is it, alternatively, a way of saying that the Spirit of God is found within the lives of the people of God, and it is he who is working for the consummation of the age? Certainly the Spirit belongs with the Church – whether exclusively or not! Certainly the Spirit is the herald of the end.* But is the *current* sphere of the kingdom of God wider and more inclusive than the Spirit-led people of God, the Church?

The answer has to be frankly speculative, or, to be more exact with an analogy, extrapolatory. The Church has an embryonic character in relation to the ultimate kingdom of

---

*See, for instance, the concept of the Spirit as 'first-fruits', leading to a 'groaning' for the final harvest (Rom. 8:23); or the Spirit as the present 'deposit' or down-payment, as a pledge of final redemption (Eph. 1:14).

God. Properly speaking, it is a 'sign' of that kingdom – that is to say, it should be exhibiting within itself the values and styles of the kingdom. The issue is whether it can and should promote or undergird the values of the kingdom in society so that, independently of individuals turning to Christ, the purposes of the kingdom, the actual instances of the reign of Christ, are to be found – partially and proleptically – in the life of that society. Such features of the kingdom need not spring from conscious obedience to God's law among this world's rulers, but may still reflect it; and an understanding that there are purposes of the kingdom to be pursued which embody God's justice and love, even without direct evangelism and church-building, may unlock for the Church the character of its overall mission. And if the structures of this world's societies – as, for example, in monogamous marriage or fair wages or accountable government – retain any hint of the God who made them, then perhaps that is also a hint of his coming kingdom. Even if the principalities and powers have a strong foothold in today's world order, they surely do not have an exclusive monopoly of power there? God is not without his witness, and the coming kingdom may be provisionally discerned on a much wider canvas than his Church.

But there remains a coming kingdom. It is long delayed. The first believers probably knew it might be long delayed, and they ought not to be represented as having expected it, for example, in AD 48, 'tomorrow', and as then having to rewrite their plans when it did not occur. The Thessalonians may not have properly grasped that those who died in Christ were safe, and may have needed reassuring (1 Thess. 4:13–18); but Paul himself, whose own conversion stemmed from the death of the first martyr Stephen, can hardly have fathered the error or needed to change his teaching when he heard of their uncertainty or distress. Similarly, there is no real evidence of the disciples generally, or of Paul in particular, either declining to look forward or aborting plans already laid, on the grounds that the second coming would supervene. In Acts, first Peter and then Paul appear to be acting on the basis of Jesus' parting words, 'You shall be witnesses to me ... to the ends of the earth'. Thus, when the first Gentiles were converted in about AD 40 (or even earlier), the horizons for the Gospel must have seemed limitless. Paul himself must have been told by Ananias (Acts 9:15–16) that he had a worldwide mission, with suffering built into it. On his first missionary journey, he revisited on returning the churches he had founded on his outward journey, and took steps to provide elders everywhere (Acts 14:23), and encouraged them by telling them the road was hard. It all reads as though churches were being planted to endure where they were, rather than to be suddenly delivered into new heavens and new earth. The preaching in Acts 13 and 14 shows little or no sign of an immediate expectation of the end – quite the reverse: the turning from Jews to Gentiles looks to be the laying a new foundation for a Church to last for generations. When Paul, in Acts 13:47, quotes from Isaiah 49:7 to give a warrant for this turning, he thereby invokes 'the ends of the earth' as the Gospel's purview.

On the second journey, Paul works a fairly complex plan with Silas and Timothy to give the best coverage of churches he is founding in Greece, and when, on the way back to Jerusalem, he stops briefly at Ephesus, he says, 'I will come back, if it is God's will' (Acts 18:21). He returns on his third journey, and spends three years in Ephesus, before going round Greece again, and now saying, 'After I have been there [to Jerusalem], I must visit Rome also' (Acts 19:21). When he writes to the Romans from Corinth on this journey, he is planning to go to Jerusalem with the money he has been collecting for the church there (Rom. 15:25–8); but he not only hopes, after that, to get to Rome (Rom. 1:10), but also, after staying for a while with them, to go on to Spain (Rom. 15:24, 28).

All this middle-term planning is hardly characteristic of someone expecting an imminent parousia, and the sense that it was thought to be immediate would seem to depend upon the wording of 1 Thessalonians 4:15: 'We who are alive, who are left to the coming of the Lord, will not precede those who sleep'. But surely Paul is simply here speaking out of the situation then current, that some Thessalonian believers have died and he himself and his readers are still alive, and the two groups, divided in just that way, are then used to explain the two different ways in which all believers will share in the general resurrection. It does not have to involve any judgement about whether or not he will himself in fact be alive at the

parousia. In 1 Corinthians 15, he expresses it more indiffer-
ently – 'We will not all sleep, but we will all be changed' (1
Cor. 15:51) – and writes as though a generation has died, and
has not missed out, or somehow broken the rules, by doing
so.* If it be objected that, by the time 1 Corinthians was
written, Paul had already revised his eschatology (because the
end had not come), then the reply must be that the literary
basis for his supposed earlier view is extremely narrow (being
at most the last six verses of 1 Thessalonians 4). In the Thessalonian correspondence Paul is certainly eschatologically aware,
as his essentials of conversion are described in 1 Thessalonians
1:9–10: 'You turned to God from idols to serve the living and
true God and to await his Son from heaven, that is the one
whom he raised from the dead, Jesus who delivers us from the
wrath to come.' It is similar in 2 Thessalonians 1:10: 'when he
comes to be glorified in his saints and to be wondered at among
all who those who believe, because our testimony was believed
by you.' This puts the Thessalonian readers among those who
are alive at Christ's coming, the event which they have been
awaiting. But, despite Paul's eschatological vividness, it must
be remembered that his argument in 1 Thessalonians 4 is
about the fact that it does not matter in relation to believers
dying that the end is *not* yet; and he goes on to say the event
will be a surprise – but a surprise which comes when people
have got used to it *not* happening (1 Thess. 5:1–2). His next
verses use the prospect of the parousia as an incentive to
sobriety (as in Rom. 13:11–14), but even then, lest he be heard
as too univocally asserting its imminence, he slips in that the
purpose of Christ's death was that, *whether we wake or sleep*,
we should live together with him. If he dare not offer them
generations of believers before the end come, he equally will
not back off from ordinary instructions about work (1 Thess.
5:12–15; 2 Thess. 3:6–13), prayer, love and perseverance.

So we return to Acts 1. Jesus is physically departing. One
day he will physically return. Meantime his followers are to
take the Gospel to the ends of the earth. Then indeed the end
may come (though there are no precise measures). So, for the

---

*Many have 'fallen asleep' (1 Cor. 15:6, 18, 20), and the question is
not, 'How can they be saved, or safe?', but, 'With what body will they
come?' (1 Cor. 15:35).

purpose of our present study, the Church is set on earth to exercise a stewardship over its own life and mission for which it will one day answer to God. To plan ahead (even if with the blessed proviso 'DV') is reponsible discipleship from the start, and to shape an institutional and abiding structure is not faithlessness but obedience.

But the end will come. And the Church will reach the fullness of the measure of the stature of Christ in the twinkling of an eye. And people of God and kingdom of God will be one.

Boundaries of the Church

Clearly the basic division between being Christian and not being Christian was faith in Jesus and overt confession of Jesus as Lord.* However, from the start the Church proclaimed the Gospel by word (for it was 'good news' – *evangelion* – and 'news' is for proclamation and communication), but also called upon those who believed it to be incorporated into Jesus and into the company that is his body by a symbol – that is, by baptism.

This is interestingly expressed in the words of Jesus. His 'great commission' (Matt. 28:16–20) takes this form:

There is given to me all authority in heaven and on the earth;

[you] therefore,
having got moving,
make disciples of all the nations,
by baptising them into the name of the Father and the Son and the Holy Spirit
and by teaching them to observe all that I have commanded you:
and, lo, I am with you always, even to the end of the age.

---

*There is no need to stay on this, but it would appear, both from the New Testament and from the sheer logic of ministering Jesus Christ today, that the actual dividing line runs very close to an acknowledgment that *this Jesus rose bodily from the dead*. I say 'very close' as (amazingly) a Jew, Pinchas Lapide, has written a book defending the historical resurrection but denying that Jesus was the Son of God – and, equally amazingly, we have in recent times had to cope with a bishop denying the bodily resurrection of Jesus.

I have set it out like this, as translations frequently obscure the fact that there is only one imperative in the commission ('make disciples'), and that the three Greek participles, one before and two after the 'make disciples' imperative, have different functions: the first ('having got moving') is in effect a temporal clause, defining an order of events ('you won't be able to evangelise the nations if you are not prepared first to *go*'); but the second and third are *causal*, indicating *how* the disciples are to 'make disciples'. The translations often suggest there are two other additional tasks to be fulfilled after making disciples (i.e. to baptise and to teach), making three separable tasks in all.* But it is highly unlikely that the Greek means that (or that Jesus meant that), and both the assurance of Jesus' authority (in the first line) and the promise of his continual presence with that authority (in the last line) are meant to attach to his single command to the eleven, so that there is no mistake as to their all-pervasive application.

Baptism, then, is an integral and vital part of making people disciples. It is exactly how, only ten days later, it was presented on the day of Pentecost at the end of Peter's preaching the good news: 'Repent and be baptised every one of you for the forgiveness of sins, and you will receive the gift of the Holy Spirit' (Acts 2:38). And Acts goes on to say, 'Those who received his word were baptised . . . that day, about 3000 of them' (2:41). We must conclude that baptism was an essential element of what was preached (the *kerygma*) in the initial expansion of the Church.

It is perhaps hard for twentieth-century Christians – particularly those living in post-Christendom – to visualise this practice. Throughout Acts, baptism was administered *as the Gospel was being received*, both as reinforcing God's promise of love and faithfulness in Christ to the recipient, and as a means of marking that person as the Lord's possession from

---

*The distinction can be recognised in English if we say, 'He cycled on his bike, wearing a coat and whistling as he went' and 'He cycled on his bike, pressing hard on the pedals and using all the gears'. The former of these has second and third activities which are merely incidental and perhaps coincidental with the first; the latter has a mention in second and third place of two actions which are together contributory and integral to success at the real activity.

then on. The recorded instances of baptism wholly validate this conclusion:

- Acts 2:38 (Pentecost): 'that day';
- Acts 8:12–13 (Samaria): 'believed . . . and were baptised' (even before the evidence of the coming of the Spirit)*;
- Acts 8:36, 38 (Gaza desert): 'See, here is water; what prevents . . .?'
- Acts 9:18 (Paul in Damascus): 'And immediately . . . he got up and was baptised';
- Acts 10:47–8 (first Gentiles): 'Can anyone forbid water that these people should not be baptised?' (*or* 'Quick! Get the water – the Spirit has beaten us to them');
- Acts 16:14–15 (Philippi): 'When she and her household were baptised';
- Acts 16:33 (jail in Philippi): 'In that same hour of the night . . . immediately he and all his household were baptised' (a Gentile with no Jewish background);
- Acts 18:8 (Corinth): 'and many Corinthians, hearing him, were believing and being baptised';
- Acts 19:5 (Ephesus): 'When they heard this, they were baptised into the name of the Lord Jesus';**
- Acts 22:16 (Paul repeating his own Damascus story): 'What are you waiting for?'

This picture is amply confirmed by the passing references in the epistles. Baptism is assumed to have been received by all the recipients of the letter, and it is never suggested that any unbaptised persons, such as enquirers or 'hearers' or catechumens, are present. So clear is it that all in the New Testament assemblies have been baptised that discipleship can be traced equally and interchangeably to the coming of faith or to the receiving of baptism. Thus Paul writes in Galatians 3:26–7:

---

*There are many puzzles about the Samaritan episode (see pp. 88–90): but if there is one certainty above all contradiction it is that Philip was prepared and even eager to give baptism immediately upon profession of faith without waiting for evidence of the coming (the 'illapse') of the Spirit.

**The Ephesian disciples, who 'knew only the baptism of John', are another puzzle (see pp. 88–90). But we need only here note that, as soon as Paul had determined that they should be baptised, they *were* baptised.

- 3:26: 'For you are all sons of God through faith in Jesus
  Christ';
- 3:27: 'For all of you who have been baptised into Christ
  have put on Christ'.

For the purposes of his argument, it would have been entirely
appropriate to have followed through his first line with a
(perfectly consistent) second line: 'For all of you who have
believed in Christ have put on Christ.' It is not very difficult
to recognise that a latter-day Evangelical would here have
instinctively stuck to references to faith. But with Paul, faith
and baptism spring equally easily to his lips or his pen as the
pinpointed starting-place in the life of discipleship.

From this kind of evidence we may draw other conclusions:
1   The New Testament authors are totally unembarrassed
about 'categorical' language in baptism. They quite naturally
state that it effects what it signifies, and, once that principle
is grasped in the explicit references to baptism, then it will
become obvious that passages which are not quite as explicit
also include a reference to baptism. Instances would be:
John 3:5 ('born of water and the Spirit'); 1 Corinthians 6:11
('but you are washed'); Ephesians 5:26 ('cleansed her by the
washing of water with the word'); Titus 3:5 ('the bath of
regeneration'); 1 Peter 1:22–3 (where some have thought
that the whole letter is a baptismal homily – cf. 1 Peter 3:21
and its 'now'); and some other even more allusive texts. If
the 'performative' language is warp and woof of the New
Testament anyway, then we can be serene about these passages and not mind the varying possibilities that baptism is
fully or partly in view. The Galatians 3:26–7 citation above
is a good instance of this. Not only so, but we shall then not
find ourselves unwilling to believe that water-baptism is in
view in the places in Acts and the epistles where the word
'baptise' and its cognates *are* in use, and shall not need to
argue against that obvious prime point of reference.*

---

*I suspect that the obviously metaphorical references to baptism in
Jesus' own teaching (Mark 10:38–9; Luke 12:50) are the only points
in the New Testament where we are justified in treating the term as
solely metaphorical, though the 'baptism in the Holy Spirit' (for

2   We must not let baptism get theologically marginalised by those with a fear of anything too 'performative' being affirmed in our own use of baptism. The defence against overstatement is all too often a rationale making baptism a mere outward demonstration of something that has already happened separately and interiorly, and a form of 'witness' which is valuable to the individual, and indeed encouraging to the Church; but that its value is essentially that of a dramatic form of testifying, and its occasion is the moment that seems right to the individual disciple when he or she is moved to ask for baptism. None of that splitting of God's taking possession of a life by the Gospel from the ritual of baptism would be doctrinally possible if we insisted that, whatever our practice may be, our doctrinal thinking should be formed from the New Testament. There, the practice of 'immediately' ensures that we see baptism as integral to the event of conversion, not as a loosely drifting rite to be explained in some less-than-biblical terms so as to make it clear that it is *not* conversion! We may have three separate steps visible in the lives of adult converts – namely, conversion, baptism, and joining a church; but in the New Testament such a separation was unthinkable: the Church grew as newcomers were 'added' to it, as people were converted to Christ in baptism into his Church. However such issues may present themselves today, in the New Testament the Church is formed as a visible corporate organism through converts being added in and by baptism. Indeed, we would be wise to be hesitant about calling them 'converts' prior to their baptism – arguably they were 'enquirers' or 'applicants' until they went through the waters of baptism, and can only be reckoned to have become converts as they confessed Jesus as Lord in the waters.

3   Despite all the above, it is clear that baptism was *not* an automatic or invariable (let alone magical) means to actual new birth by the Spirit or to other features of discipleship. The New Testament would not countenance such corner-cutting, despite its 'performative' language. Not only is it

---

references, see pp. 296–9) might be viewed as a metaphor drawn from water-baptism.

logical that a person can be a believer and a disciple without baptism – and whole denominations, such as the Salvation Army, today exist to testify to that logic, even though their refusal of baptism appears unbiblical; but the contrary is also true – that people may go through the ritual of baptism and emerge still unregenerate. And arguably the risk of that result is all the greater if, in observance of the New Testament practice, you baptise within minutes of people's first profession of faith. And that self-evident logic must have been known to the apostles, for it is reinforced by a warning passage of Paul:

I would not have you ignorant, brothers, that our fathers were all under the cloud, and all passed through the sea, and were all baptised into Moses in the cloud and in the sea, and all ate the same spiritual food and all drank the same spiritual drink (for they drank of the spiritual rock that followed them, and that rock was Christ); BUT with many of them God was not well pleased . . .

AND these things occurred as types of us, that we should not be . . . [as they were]. (1 Cor. 10:1–6)

Paul could hardly spell out more clearly that what he means by the last line here is: 'You Corinthians have all been baptised into Jesus as your Lord and have all shared in the food and drink of the Lord's Supper but it may well be that with many of you God is not well pleased.' The 'all . . . all' is in stark contrast to the 'many' – the passage makes very clear that there is no automatic salvation through the mere external conforming to a ritual. If lives are not changed, baptism has not inaugurated a discipleship.

4 Baptism once given is given for life. In the 1 Corinthians 10 passage above Paul does *not* say: 'All crossed the Red Sea, but only some were baptised' – but rather 'all were baptised, though not all were pleasing to God'. This again is a clear pattern in the New Testament: however ungodly in their lives particular Christians or congregations may be, the letters still say, in effect, 'you have all been baptised'. This has a triple set of implications: firstly, that the definition or demarcation as to whether or not a particular event is to count as a baptism cannot be suspended upon the

answers to questions about the inward state of the recipient, but instead, however paradoxical it may appear, the definition must be couched in terms of the outward administration;[3] secondly, the appeal to the meaning of baptism (as, for example, in Romans 6:3–4) must be viewed as functioning with a category of people *who are entitled to be treated as Christian* (this is a surprisingly obvious category, but ignored in much theoretical debate by many an Evangelical pastor in local congregations) – and it means that baptism may in fact (even if undesirably) come first and its significance only dawn later, or conversion may come first and baptism be added quickly; thirdly, the appeal to baptism is an appeal to what it means *here and now* to be a baptised person or baptised group, and *not* what recollection the readers or hearers may have of the actual event of their baptism years before, let alone of their state of heart when they were going through the event.

In short, we shall understand the individual significance of baptism in the New Testament if we conceive of it like a branding of cattle (however invisible it is), for it lasts like a branding even if the recipient is not apparently in the possession of the one whose brand-mark has been given.

But it is the ecclesial significance which concerns us. Baptism is the boundary which the individual crosses into the life of the Church – and crosses once for all, for life. Paul writes 'By one Spirit (in common) we were all baptised into one body' (1 Cor. 12:13). Thus, whatever of inward gifts is conveyed (or not conveyed), a formal or visible membership of the Church is conferred for life in baptism, and the bonds which bind believers together include 'one Lord, one faith, one baptism' (Eph. 4:4). All the practice of baptism in Acts adds newcomers *to the Church*; and there is no precedent for any notion that it is an individual step of faith, taken as it seems fit in the individual's maturation in Christ. Baptism changes the context of the person, and he or she then belongs closely to the local believing community – and to the worldwide one. In theory, then, the Church ought to be in a position where baptism genuinely divides between believers and unbelievers and between the Church and the world. Baptism itself, in its actual daily practice as well as in academic theory, should set up the notion of an alternative kingdom, a new community of love, an anticipation of heaven. Baptism is the badge of discipleship, a discipleship which is to be exercised by the people of God in a corporate or societal way.

A clutch of residual baptismal questions

The assertion that baptism goes with faith, and that the unbaptised faithful should be baptised quickly and that the baptised unfaithful should be led into faith, leaves many loose ends in biblical terms and in present-day church life.

1 Should infants be baptised?

The question of baptising infants is in the Church before us today. There is a very strong tradition of infant baptism, and the tradition has accumulated its own rationale – notably in Augustine's treatment of baptism in relation to original sin. But the issue is: does Scripture warrant this practice?

I have dealt with this at some length elsewhere.[4] There are convergent lines of evidence which pick up some of the points made above about baptism in general, and which, if we are allowed to cumulate them and, so to speak, keep them in play, go very far in making the baptising the infants of believers a better choice, biblically and pastorally, than not baptising them. Here in summary are the lines of evidence.

Firstly, there is Old Testament circumcision. It is clearly initiatory, and is a sign of God's covenant of love. Paul says that Abraham 'received the sign of circumcision, a seal of the righteousness that came to him through faith when he was still uncircumcised' (Rom. 4:11). That meaning is identical, in the reasoning in the letter to the Romans, to the meaning of baptism in Romans 6:3–4. Yet that same sign, with that New Testament meaning related to it by Paul, was in fact given to newborn sons. And while it is conventional to say that circumcision witnessed to an automatic inheritance (i.e. by fleshly descent), in fact in the two generations from Abraham to Jacob there was nothing automatic, only one of the two sons was the 'heir of the promise', and yet both sons were treated alike and both were circumcised (see p. 38). That appears extraordinarily like a precedent for giving an initiatory sign to newborn children today, where believing parents may properly lack absolute certainty about how the children will grow up, but nevertheless run a Christian home *treating their children as believers without distinction* and with good and well-founded hopes that in the long run they will prove to be believers. If the significance of the Old Testament sign is truly the conveying by God of 'the righteousness which comes through faith', then at first blush any Christian initiatory sign which replaces circumcision is properly given to infants.*

Clearly baptism did replace circumcision for Christians. We are left to wonder why; and the New Testament itself, while juxtaposing the terms in Colossians 2:11–12, never quite argues through the transition. Two lines of thought appear fruitful:

1   John the Baptist came with a new prophetic sign to be administered *to those already in Israel*. The transition is effected by his confronting with a need for a new initiation those who were *already* members of 'Israel after the flesh'. The transition is effected by introducing the one sign before overtly abolishing the need for the other. Christianity accordingly starts within Judaism, and only bursts its confines as the Gentile mission begins a few years later.

2   Circumcision, by definition, was for men only. Women belonged to the covenant in the Old Testament basically by belonging to a man, and were thus only mediately within the people of God. The replacing of circumcision with baptism makes the sign the same for both sexes, and not

---

*An interesting New Testament test-case would be among proselytes. Proselytes are only mentioned four times in the New Testament (and in modern translations they are not always rendered *as* 'proselytes') – Matthew 23:15; Acts 2:11; 6:5; 13:43. Of these, Acts 2 is the significant passage for our purposes. If there were proselytes present on the day of Pentecost, and they had come into Judaism by the fathers being circumcised and their sons with them; and if those fathers were now being told that the heart of Judaism was Christ, and that they were to be baptised in his name (Acts 2:38), would not their own expectation have been that they should take their own children into baptism with them? And, of course, they were being told 'the promise is to you *and your children* and to those far off' (Acts 2:39, my italics). If there ever was infant baptism in apostolic times, then it is very appropriate that we discover it first employed on the day of Pentecost! Were there indeed infants and children of all ages within the count of 3000 'added to them' that day?

only exhibits men and women alike as one in Christ (Gal. 3:28), but also reinforces the contrast between a 'physical' or 'fleshly' approach in the Old Testament with a more 'spiritual' (though still sacramental) style in the Gospel era.

So much for the speculative side. Circumcision remains the first line of thought in the cumulative case.

Secondly, there is a further line of argument of a similar sort from proselyte baptism. This practice was known in the Judaism of the late first century AD, and may well have arisen because, in the Roman empire, women were taking independent autonomous action and seeking to become Jews in their own right, and not simply as a consequence of their husbands being proselytised (including being circumcised). Such women, the argument runs, needed some liminal ceremony, some rite of passage, to assure themselves and others that they truly had become Jews. While we cannot prove that such a practice existed as early as the time of Jesus' ministry on earth, Jeremias has argued strongly for this practice to be understood as the part of the background to the New Testament. If so, then the later evidence about the practice may bear upon the New Testament, for it looks as though, irrespective of its original *raison d'être*, it was in fact given to whole families together, infants included.*

Thirdly, there are the instances of household baptism. These come in Acts 16:15; 16:33; and 1 Corinthians 1:16 – and the same practice is strongly implied at Acts 18:8 and might even be part of the picture in Acts 10:44–48. However, the first three instances alone state clearly that a whole household was baptised, and the case need not be argued by reference beyond

---

*If there existed a Jewish baptism of proselytes prior to John the Baptist's appearing, then there is reason to think that the *concept* of baptism was not a novelty with his ministry. If the fact of baptism was already known when the Baptist opened his ministry, then the searing scandal of his practice lay not in the use of baptism in principle, but in his requiring the 'chosen people', the circumcised and clean, to undergo it. The prophetic feature of the sign is the judgement it involved on those who thought themselves safely within the fold – the entirely proper challenge to the outsider was being astonishingly redirected to those who were surely, on all previous Jewish accounts, the righteous.

those three. In each instance the collective noun *oikos* ('house' or 'household') is used. The argument is threefold:

1   The noun is wholly *inclusive*, and could not have been used by Luke and Paul if they had wished to restrict the reference to those who had reached certain known levels of ability to articulate, or to reflect, or to understand, or to be independent, or to take decisions. That is not to assert that there actually were infants in each of the stated households, but it is to insist that the language fully allows that possibility; and, as part of a cumulative argument, the existence of household baptisms in the New Testament give us grounds for baptising (and thus including in the Church) the children born of Christian parents.

2   The household pattern suggests a parental, or head of the household, decision. The households include that of Lydia (Acts 16:15), who must, presumably, have been the head of a household. Whether she was a widow with children, or simply a single woman who owned slaves, or whatever, on any account she had a household, and they followed her into baptism.

3   The argument continues that the baptised are thereafter treated as believers (a category of thought discussed above on p. 74), and that became the position in respect of the children within a believing *oikos*.

Fourthly, there is the universal expectation that all the recipients of Paul's letters are baptised, and children were among them. This is simply a matter of inspection. The references to baptism in Romans 6:3–4 is cited to enforce a point about not living in sin – it is not a point about baptism itself, and it would have only partial usefulness for its purpose if any of the recipients of the letter had not been baptised. In 1 Corinthians 1:13 they have obviously all been baptised or the question would be absurd; in 10:1–4 the text actually says 'all' (see discussion on p. 74): in 12:13 again the text says 'all'; in Galatians 3:27 the 'all' of verse 26 must carry through to verse 27 (see discussion on p. 71); in Ephesians 4:4 baptism has to be exactly as wide in its application as 'one Lord' and 'one faith' are in theirs. And so we could go on.

The question is not, therefore, 'Can we identify specific cases of events at which infants were being baptised?' but, 'Are children from the start addressed *as* baptised?' And the answer to this latter question is 'Yes' – for, once we have seen that baptism is taken for granted as the common initiatory sign of all the believers to whom the letters went, we simply need to recognise that children of all ages were in the congregation. No doubt we could wish for more overt mention of them – and even for more about the correct nurture and maturing of them in faith. But their presence cannot be doubted (see Ephesians 6:1–4; Colossians 3:20–21, 1 John 2:12). This line of argument also is not conclusive of itself, for it is open to opponents to say that all implicit references to children as baptised presuppose that they were of age or understanding to have articulated the faith. It appears more natural to assume that households or families with children of any age appeared in the assembly *together*, had Paul's letters read to them *together* (presumably with that range of ability to understand which goes with variation in years – but, for the purpose of this argument, listening to letters addressed to them all equally), and were all reckoned to be in Christ *together*, not least in and through being members of the body of Christ together through baptism. It is worth reinforcing this with a closer look at Ephesians 6:4: the fathers are to 'nourish' or 'nurture' their children 'in the training and instruction of the Lord'. One could hardly have a more explicit statement that children are one with their parents in the Lord. They are members of the body of Christ, sharing in full in the privileges and responsibilities of the Church. So we ask: are these children all the children there are, of all ages, belonging to the particular church (in this case Ephesus – though the letter may be a circular to many churches)? Or is there a concealed (and unmentioned) group of children who are under a certain age, and/or not allowed into the assembly, and/or unbaptised, and/or to be regarded as unbelieving and needing the Gospel proclaimed to them until they come to faith and are baptised? It sounds extraordinary – but unless the references to the children in the letters are permitted to refer to *all* the children of believers, then this excluded, unmentioned, theologically banished class must be posited. And we never hear of any of them at any point qualifying for baptism through getting converted – they stay as silent and unseen throughout as they have been in their infancy.

Fifthly, there is the argument from the scriptural pattern of baptising as early as possible rather than delay enquirers with a probationary period (see pp. 69–70). If the Church does not test them over a period of time before baptism, then it must be willing to treat people as Christians on the basis of a simple warrant – presumably the confession of faith in Jesus, or an instantly changed life. The earlier argument has demonstrated this for the normal (that is, in Scripture, largely adult) run of new believers. The question is: is it appropriate to treat our own children thus? And, if it is appropriate, at what point do we administer baptism to them?

The alternatives are obviously that we should administer baptism very soon after birth, or that we should delay it until some particular watershed is reached in the child's life. If we pursue the latter alternative, then the parallel with the agreed patterns of adult conversion in the New Testament would lead us to look for that first moment of actual belief. The infant is, presumably, through lack of articulate faith, classified as an unbeliever. Baptism, rightly understood, comes at the beginning of the Christian life – but the Church has to recognise when that watershed moment is happening. If the Church has an arbitrary threshhold (e.g. a youngest age-limit – say, five years old), then it risks withholding baptism from a believing child; and that risk includes both leaving the child officially in a non-Christian limbo and also, when in due course the child is admitted to baptism, making baptism appear not as initiation but as a kind of prize for certain progress or maturing within the Christian life. The Church, if it is truly bounded by baptism, simply does not include young children; and the true believers straddle the baptismal boundary – some within, some without. It is a curious way of invoking the New Testament to correct the alleged error of infant baptism.

If we go back to the alternatives, and believing parents are able and willing to bring their offspring for baptism straight after birth, then it is true that such parents cannot know the future beyond all question and cannot therefore guarantee that the children will persist in the faith. But, if we return to the New Testament, then we have to acknowledge that the same lack of absolute guarantee obtains if adults are baptised within minutes of being converted, or, more strictly, as part of the process of being converted. The New Testament Church contained a 'mixed multitude' (even though they lived in a 'normal' atmosphere of being persecuted), and, although in due course concern for the witness of such a Church led to delay in administering baptism, within the New Testament there was no such delay – and there were many who, after being baptised, backslid or apostasised. No baptism, at whatever age or stage, contains that unobtainable absolute guarantee that the baptised will *never* depart from the faith. But baptism incorporates the candidate into the Church and *treats* him or her as Christian. So infant baptism is the Church *treating the newcomer as Christian*. Yes, the child may later lapse from the faith – but that is only in line with how adult converts behaved in the scriptural accounts. The issue will then be: what rule of thumb will warrant the Church treating a relatively unloquacious, recently born infant as qualifying for baptism in exact parallel with the way a profession of faith in Jesus Christ would be qualifying a more articulate adult?

Sixthly, there is the straight question: how will you bring up your children? This question rests upon what we have seen in Scripture, but presses believing parents harder as to their intentions about their newborn child. The biblical boundary of baptism appears to offer parents a straight choice: you bring up your child as a baptised believer from the start, treated as Christian, included in the life of the Church and expected to live as a disciple; *or* you acknowledge that the child is an unbeliever, cannot be treated as a believer until he or she shows credible signs of conversion, cannot be expected to live as a disciple, and is actually therefore on the other side of a serious boundary from his or her parents. It is from the two discernments of the way to view a newborn child that the two alternatives logically polarise from each other, though in fact opponents of infant baptism will frequently be found teaching their children to pray (including the Lord's Prayer with its 'Our Father'), training them to live as disciples, helping them to understand that Jesus Christ is with them always, and in many other ways including them within a Christian circle. But the argument then presses: why do you refuse to mark them as Christian in baptism, and leave them formally outside the life of the Church, while informally you treat them as within? And, if the answer to this question is something like, 'Because I cannot know and be persuaded without spoken testimony', then we return to this category of having sufficient warrant to treat people as believers (including giving baptism) even when we do not know their hearts exactly. Further reflection indicates that we rarely get beyond 'warrant to treat people as believers', even with adults. That is what most pastors are doing most of the time with people who come new into their congregations and sing the hymns and articulate their faith.

Against these arguments the great cry has always been that baptism follows belief, and that the pretended baptism of infants has no standing, warrant or precedent in the New Testament.* There is little guidance in the New Testament about the standing of infants in the eyes of God or in the life of the Church. But the areas of silence affect both sides of the argument, and it has been noted above that there is an equal silence about the later baptism of the children of believers (as, for example, might have been happening at a revisit by the apostle to a home or church where children were now growing into an age or maturity of Christian experience to qualify for baptism). There is, of course, no such event recorded in the New Testament. There is silence.

There are two further implications for the Church in relation to the baptism of infants:

---

*This sometimes takes the naïve form of saying that the New Testament tells us that repentance and faith should precede baptism, and this is demonstrated by the kind of proclamation we find in 'Repent and be baptised' (Acts 2:38), or the kind of history we find in 'Many of the Corinthians . . . believed and were baptised' (Acts 18:8). To this the reply which is on the same level as the assertion will go to Matthew 28:19 where disciples are made 'by baptising and teaching' which (by parity of handling texts) would suggest that baptism should come before teaching the faith! At a deeper level we should be ready to argue that ideally repentance and faith come *with* baptism, and that the infants of believers, being treated as believers from the start are to be reckoned as repenting and believing. If this sounds difficult, it is not half as difficult as treating your own children as impenitent and unbelieving.

1   Infant baptism must be the 'one baptism' of the New Testament and must fulfil the role that baptism fulfils in the New Testament, including giving distinct boundaries to the Church and placing doctrinal and ethical leverage on the recipient. An infant baptism which has a rationale which splits it from adult (or other post-infancy) baptism cannot be defended from the New Testament.

2   A careful rereading of the lines of evidence upon which a biblical case for infant baptism is based reveals that every single feature of the argument is a line about how believers qualify their children for baptism – and thus how they should treat their children thereafter. There are no grounds here for baptising infants or children from unbelieving homes.

2   The mode of baptism

A kind of secondary contest has continued alongside arguments for and against infant baptism – a contest relating to the mode of baptism. The two sets of issues do not necessarily march in step with each other, but in general those who affirm infant baptism are ready to baptise by one of several modes, while those who are opposed to infant baptism tend to want to insist on submersion. It is worth opening up some of the relevant considerations.

Firstly, it is clear that, in the New Testament, water was needed for baptism. Without water there may be some other rite, but it cannot be called 'baptism'.

Secondly, those who insist on submersion are virtually bound to depend upon four lines of argument:

1   that the verb '*baptizo*' in the New Testament itself means 'to dip below water';

2   that the New Testament practice of baptism universally conformed to this;

3   that the determining motif in the administration of baptism is union with Christ in his death and resurrection (as in Romans 6:3–4);

4   that the act of baptism, to be baptism, has necessarily built into it a dramatisation of that its richest meaning.

Those who would resist this insistence may still value submersion very highly, use it as they have opportunity and see fit, yet still wish to emphasise that other forms of ministering baptism may still be perfectly valid.* They meet the above lines of argument as follows:

1 Etymology cannot prove meaning (see pp. 295–6); and, even if it could, it is not clear that the background of *baptizo* necessarily refers primarily to a *mode* (i.e. dipping), but may equally be focused in the *result* (i.e. cleansing).

2 It is impossible to demonstrate a universal practice in the New Testament; admittedly we learn that John the Baptist baptised at Aenon 'because there were many waters there' (John 3:24),** but the onus of proof is on those who would insist that the 3000 on the day of Pentecost, the Ethiopian in the desert, Cornelius and his company in his own home, and the Philippian jailer in the middle of the night (when the earthquake must surely have broken any large containers?), were all baptised by submersion using a sufficient depth of water for all necessarily to go 'right under'. It is difficult to believe. We might add that if there were any emphasis upon the actual submersion as crucial to the event, it is very surprising that Paul (in 1 Corinthians 10:1–4) should invoke the crossing of the Red Sea as a 'type' of baptism – for in that instance those who stayed dry were saved and those who were submerged drowned. It must rather be that crossing the water separated the Israelites' new life in the desert pilgrimage from their old life in Egypt, and the sense of being separated by water from the old and committed to the new ('baptised into Moses') prevails over all considerations as to who went under the water – or how far under.

---

*As this is the first time the concept of 'validity' has arisen, it is worth a moment's inspection. Any rite which is to be conferred once-for-all-for-life must inevitably raise questions as to whether, in any particular instance, it has actually happened. That is why baptisms (like marriage) must be carefully witnessed and certified. Ordination raises the same questions, and the question of validity is plain common sense (though not all answers to the question are). The issue of the 'validity' of a particular Church's eucharistic celebrations, on the other hand, is a rather different, though still important, matter. **'*Polla hudata*' might presumably mean 'water with much depth', but one wonders rather whether it does not mean 'a good supply' of water (cf. NIV 'plenty of water'), i.e. a supply that would not dry up at particular seasons, without reference to its depth.

3   While the 'death and resurrection' motif of baptism is important, it is highly arbitrary to erect this into a sole determining principle to control the invariable practice of baptism. Other motifs abound – 'repentance and cleansing' (John the Baptist, cf. Acts 2:38; 22:16), 'the descent of the Holy Spirit' (Acts 2:38; 10:44–8), 'coming under saving headship' (1 Cor. 1:13; 10:1–4), 'being grafted as a limb by a transplant into a new body' (1 Cor. 12:13), 'putting on Christ as a garment' (Gal. 3:27), 'rebirth' (John 3:5, Tit. 3:5), 'the pledge of the resurrection of the body' (1 Cor. 15:29) etc. *All* that is involved in being Christian is, it would seem, implied or symbolised somewhere within the use of baptism; and thus one important, perhaps even the most important, theme (namely, death and resurrection) ought not to be made the sole controlling one in the absence of any differentiating discussion in the New Testament.

4   Even if the motif question were conceded, a further jump in the argument is needed if we are to accept that, for a sacrament to *be* its own sacrament, it must be expressed by a dramatic representation of that which it signifies, and that this representation must be so close to the thing signified as to draw a theological distinguishing line, on one side of which the dramatisation is close enough for the sacrament to be valid, and on the other side of which it is not. This appears doubtful, firstly because sacraments do not obviously gain their status from our power of dramatisation, but from the command of Jesus attached to an action to which the Holy Spirit, in and through Scripture, attaches both meaning and power; and secondly because, if it were the case, we would never actually know how to draw that theological distinguishing line. Of course, eating bread and drinking wine (if we may start the case with the other dominical sacrament) have some message about inner feeding and nourishing (and it is odd that, down history, the Church has been tempted to use the elements for almost anything except eating and drinking); but to believe that we are somehow conveying a *dramatisation* of Calvary, or that the power of the sacrament stems from our ability to dramatise the death of Jesus on the cross by manipulation of bread and wine – those rationales both show that we have neutral-

ised the horrors of crucifixion and suggest that we have failed to grasp the foundational principles of a sacrament in use. If we now apply this to baptism, then, although there is a totality of being swamped in the act of submersion, there is so much that is non-negotiably unlike a death, burial and resurrection that one is left saying that the closeness of imitation is being asserted verbally in the rite rather than actually being visible without explanation. (Anglicans, when they submerge – and they do – tend to submerge three times, which makes it very clear that they are not particularly enacting an attempted dramatic resemblance to Jesus' death, burial and resurrection!)

If any one of these four necessary assertions is weak, then the alleged necessity of submersion starts to disappear. It is, of course, further weakened by a practical consideration which has theological issues attached. Could God be commanding us to perform an action which, in some parts of the world (or at some seasons of the year), cannot be performed? Or, to put it in more specific terms, are all baptisms to be suspended in times or places of drought? Or why were the Anglicans far ahead of the Baptists in evangelising in the Arctic, and submersion only came when central heating came?

It may then be helpful to get our terminology clear as well as our practice. The following verbal usage is strongly recommended (in descending order of quantities of water):

- Submersion: going right under (i.e. 'sub');
- Immersion: everything short of submersion – as, for example, the candidate standing, sitting or kneeling in water and having further water poured or showered over him or her;*
- Pouring: from a receptacle or even cupped hands, a visible stream or strickle of water alights on the candidate;
- Sprinkling: spots of water (rather than a stream) alight on the candidate;
- Smearing: water is directly applied by the finger.

---

*There is a Free Church tradition of speaking of 'total immersion' for that which is here called 'submersion'. This usage has tended to fall off into the unqualified simple term 'immersion'. The usage of 'immersion' actually to mean 'submersion' has done nothing but complicate discussion.

In dramatic terms each of these is visibly less impressive than the one which precedes it. The last is probably only appropriate to the baptism of a baby in intensive care. It is certainly sad when the liturgy is not used to the full with visual drama. But, however we enrich the movement, colour and visual effect in the administration of the sacrament, we should neither believe we are dramatising the death and resurrection of Jesus, nor believe that the central force of a sacrament derives from our power to dramatise.

3   The formula of baptism

Most Western Churches are used to a liturgical formula being uttered at a baptism, drawn from Matthew 28:19: '[Name], I baptise you in the name of the Father and of the Son and of the Holy Spirit'.* This has a very long (though not unbroken) tradition behind it. But at intervals individual Christians – or groupings among the 'new' Churches – pick up the Acts references to baptism 'into the name of Jesus Christ' (Acts 2:38; 8:16; 10:48; 19:5), and swing away from the trinitarian formula, even in extreme cases undergoing baptism a second time, on the grounds the first was invalid through an improper formula. What are we to say to these things?

Perhaps we could think round these formulas for a minute or two. In the early third century in Rome, so Hippolytus records, candidates for baptism stood in the water, and were asked three questions in turn: 'Do you believe in God the Father?' 'Do you believe in his Son Jesus Christ?' and 'Do you believe in the Holy Spirit in the holy Church?' To each of these the candidate replied 'I believe', and was then in each case (as Hippolytus says) 'baptised' (i.e. presumably received a single submersion or immersion). Here the interrogation (with the right answers) *is* the 'formula' of baptism. No one would dream of saying it was not a valid baptism – and it was, presumably, baptism 'into' the holy Trinity. Was it or was it not a faithful fulfilling by the Church of the Lord's command in the great commission?

Then let us ask ourselves what happened at apostolic baptisms. It looks as though the candidate had to say 'Jesus is

---

*The Eastern Orthodox Churches use it in the passive: '*N* is baptised in the name of the Father, the Son and the Holy Spirit'.

Lord', or something very like it (as well as the actual baptismal occasions in Acts recorded above, many of the juxtapositions and equations which put 'Jesus' and 'Lord' together very probably reflect that practice – cf. Romans 10:9 and 1 Corinthians 12:3). So what did the baptiser then say? It is an open question as to whether it was, 'I baptise you in the name of Jesus as Lord', or something more like the interrogation, 'What do you say of Jesus, the Son of God?' 'Jesus is Lord.' 'Then in the power of his name, be baptised into him as Lord'. The point is that it cannot be traced, may well have varied, and, we dare opine, actually does not matter.

It does not matter, because clearly in both the great commission and the accounts in Acts we are handling not a formula but a theology. The precise wording might vary between the two sources, but the meaning of Christian baptism was the same. And those who said 'Jesus is Lord' (and may also have experienced the Spirit in power, though that is less evident in some cases than in others), might truly be said to be 'baptised in the name of the Father and the Son and the Holy Spirit'. The right relationship to a rightly confessed Jesus is actually (at a more profound level) a right relationship to the holy Trinity. We must determine whether an event is a baptism by the theological context, the application of water, and the general thrust of the word attached to the element. The trinitarian formula has in practice been deemed least open to misunderstanding or pre-trinitarian heresy, but that only makes it safe, not binding.

4 Confirmation

Michael Ramsey wrote in 1936, 'Baptism therefore (with the laying-on-of-hands as its normal completion) is the first significant fact about a Christian.'[5] In a simple passing bracketed phrase he thereby epitomised the Anglican problem about 'confirmation' (though, to be accurate, he does not actually use the word 'confirmation'). Between 1890 and 1970 there was a great weighting of a post-baptismal laying on of hands among Anglicans – and the persuasion took the form that:

- this was the normative second part of sacramental initiation (note Ramsey's 'completion'), based on Acts 8:14–17;

- that the laying on of hands imparted the Holy Spirit;
- that the 'early Church' had always had water-baptism and the laying on of hands administered together as an 'integrated' rite;
- full initiation, full membership and participation in the Eucharist came through confirmation.

It is frequently characterised as the 'Mason-Dix' line, being associated particularly with two theologians, A. J. Mason and Gregory Dix – the former opening the period, the latter (a contemporary of Michael Ramsey) bringing it to its zenith.[6] Since 1970 it has been easier than it had previously been to respond that this persuasion is unbiblical, unhistorical, and theologically unsustainable.

The simplest statement of the biblical material is that, in the nine separate instances of water-baptism recorded in Acts, there are only two where the laying on of hands followed the baptism (Acts 8:14–17; 19:1–6). In other cases – as, for example, that of the Ethiopian in the desert (Acts 8:26–40) – it looks as if it could not have happened.* And it appears perverse and rash to posit that it was happening in all the instances where it is not mentioned. The same is true of all the references to baptism in Paul's letters. Baptism itself, we have seen above, is assumed to have been universally given to all who name the name of Christ; but a post-baptismal laying on of hands is an exceptional event, not a normal or normative one, and the sacrament of entry into the Church is water-baptism, so that the boundary to the membership and life of the Church is set by water-baptism alone.

At the risk of anticipating later material on the post-apostolic Church, I point out that the earliest Christian literature subsequent to the New Testament also has baptism alone, without mention of any completion by another ceremony. This is true in the West of Clement, Hermas and Justin (that is, through until the second half of the second century), and in

---

*Certainly Philip, the same evangelist who had sent for the apostles in Samaria, was presumably not qualified to administer the laying on of hands after baptism; there is no mention that he did (rather the strong implication that he and the eunuch parted quickly); and he did not send the man back to Jerusalem to be 'confirmed' by the apostles, but rather let him go on his way 'rejoicing'.

the East of Didache, Ignatius and even Chrysostom (that is, until the fourth century). It is incorrect to refer to an original 'integrated' rite, which in later centuries 'disintegrated' – incorrect as historically not the case, and incorrect as subtly importing indefensible value-judgements, for 'integrated' sounds healthy, and 'disintegrated' unhealthy! It looks biblically, historically, and theologically, as though the norm is 'sacramental initiation complete in baptism'.[7]

(See Appendix 1, pp. 296–9, for a Note on baptism in the Holy Spirit.)

Life within the Church

The early believers knew themselves to belong to a worldwide company. Wherever they were on earth, they received good news of Jesus which, in terms of the evangelists who brought it, came ultimately from Jerusalem. They inherited the words of Jesus in the great commission, and presumably also the words of Jesus as recorded for us in Acts 1:8: 'You shall be witnesses to me in Jerusalem, in all Judaea, in Samaria and to the farthest parts of the earth'. They found themselves spreading the word – as, for instance, the Thessalonians did (1 Thess. 1:7–8), or finding it elsewhere and bringing it to their own people – as seems to have been the role of Epaphras (Col. 1:7 and 4:13). Whole provinces were being evangelised by people travelling out from capital cities (as, for example, opponents testify, perhaps with some exaggeration). They were accustomed to travellers coming and going, and the Mediterranean basin, with assured sea-routes and Roman roads on land, seems to have been alive with movement.* After an

---

*Lest we think this was distinctive of Paul, we can note that the 'scattering' of the Jerusalem church (Acts 8:1) led not only to the mission in Samaria (8:4–25), but to Philip going South (8:26) and to others, unknown to us, founding churches in Damascus (9:2, 10–25), Galilee (9:31), Lydda (9:32), Sharon (9:35), Joppa (9:36–43), and other 'foreign cities' which Paul later says he had visited in order to persecute the Church in them before he set off for Damascus (26:11).

internal struggle they found that 'in Christ' they were both Jew and Greek. They sent letters of commendation as people moved on (Acts 18:27, cf. 2 Cor. 3:3). The Gentile believers found themselves sending aid to the Jerusalem church – indeed, Paul anticipated their sending the aid through couriers of their own, men who would be travelling the Mediterranean as Christ's people doing his work (1 Cor. 16:3). Letters would arrive from apostles from a great distance.* The believers enjoyed in common across the face of the known world not only 'one Lord, one faith, one baptism', but also in consequence a common 'citizenship in heaven' (Phil. 3:20) and a common engagement on earth with 'principalities and powers and the rulers of darkness'. They did speak of Jesus as king, and of his reign or kingship as both due and already present.

In the light of this perspective it is fair to conclude that those who were divided from each other in the society of their times were united in Christ. It did not matter whether that division was geographical, or was ethnic, intellectual, social, sexist, political or financial – in Christ they were made one. This was true catholicity. It was exemplified from the start in Jerusalem where they all shared common meals, took care of

---

There are many examples of travelling Christians throughout Acts and the epistles (some named, some anonymous) – not to mention the legendary stories of the missionary apostles (Thomas, James, Mark). It appears that any Christian congregation in a city, at a crossroads, or in a port, in the first century AD, may well have had more visitors and strangers appearing than virtually all English parishes would have had at least until the middle of the nineteenth century.

*Specific letters were addressed to specific churches, though they might often be intended to be copied or taken on to others (as, for example, the Colossians and Laodiceans were to interchange letters (Col. 4:16)). But in addition there were 'general epistles', a category we know from the collection of 'catholic epistles' by James, Peter, John and Jude. And it is arguable that Hebrews is not far from being of the same order, and there is some reason (both internal and external) to think that 'Ephesians' was actually being taken to every city on Tychicus' route from Rome to Colossae (cf. Col. 4:7–8; Eph. 6:21), but that the copy which fathered most of the later manuscripts was the one which went to Ephesus and therefore had 'Ephesus' in the blank spot in 1:1 – the only reason we know it as 'Ephesians'. Romans too has much of a general character, and large parts may well have recurred in other missives of Paul.

each other's needs, and built each other up in faith. They were simply fulfilling the command of the Lord, emphasised at the footwashing before the Last Supper, that they should love one another and do so by washing each other's feet. To belong to Jesus was to have a deep, indeed unbreakable, sense of belonging in Jesus to all his people. The fact that you could physically be with some who were local, but not with those at a distance, was not viewed as a dividing point of principle. The bonds were still the same – as Paul emphasises to people he has not yet met in Romans 15:21–9 and Colossians 1:9.

This in turn means that the basic meaning of 'Church' must surely be 'the believers throughout the world'? Obviously the first Matthean use (Matt. 16:18) must refer to all believers all down time (see p. 44). Certainly the second use (Matt. 18:17) looks like a physically gathered 'local' church, but closer inspection suggests it could conceivably have a wider meaning – though nothing hangs on that possibility. In Acts we have seen that, as early as Chapter 9, it was natural for Luke to write of 'the church throughout Judaea, Galilee and Samaria' (9:31).* This matched the other non-geographical terminology, 'those of the Way' (9:2; 22:4; 24:14). When, for reasons of distinguishing a locality, a place is mentioned, the word 'church' may still bear its universal connotation. The first such use is in Acts 8:1 – and it reads quite strongly as though Luke means, 'The church, i.e. that part which was in Jerusalem'.** This is similar to the charming phrase 'the church

---

*Admittedly there is a variant reading giving the plural 'churches' (which actually involves six word-changes of article, noun, verbs and participles to give full grammatical consistency); but the manuscript evidence for this is very poor, and the principle of *difficilior lectio* would certainly point to the authenticity of the singular.

**Our own use of territorial language may illustrate what I suggest the New Testament is telling us. If I land at Calais I may say, 'Ah, so this is France; and these are the French'. In so saying I am being perfectly truthful, but I do not thereby imply either that France is anything less than a massive nation of which I am merely encountering one corner, or that the structure of France has to be understood by our first identifying the 25,000 local entities in which one may accurately say, 'Ah, so this is France' – and then mentally cumulating them till the measure of the country has been built up. So it is that we should approach the concept of 'the church, i.e. that being in Antioch' (Acts 13:1).

which is in their/her/your house' (Rom. 16:5; 1 Cor. 16:19;
Col. 4:15; Philem. 2) – which is not of itself proclaiming an
irreducible basic localised unit of the (universal) Church to be
a more-or-less autonomous 'church' in the particular home. It
is more like a pastorally useful manifestation of *the* Church in
a particular place, without doctrinal or organisational implications. If these local uses enable 'church' to have a plural
('each church' – Acts 14:23; 'churches' – Rom. 16:3; 16:16; 1 Cor.
7:17; 10:16; 16:1; 2 Cor. 8:9; 8:18; 11:8; 11:28; Gal. 1:2; Rev. 1:4;
1:20), yet it appears a derivative from the single worldwide
entity which (at the level of ideas) has priority in Acts. The
plural 'churches' astonishingly hardly occurs in Acts at all
(16:5 appears to be a lone use); and a wonderful uniting of local
and universal senses of 'church' is to be found in Paul's address
to the Ephesian elders in Acts 20, where (in 20:28) the Church
(universal) has been purchased by the blood of God's own one,
and it is also the church (surely local?) in which the Holy Spirit
has made them 'overseers' (or 'bishops'), as a consequence of
which it is their task to 'take heed to all the flock' and 'feed the
church' – which must primarily refer to the church in Ephesus.
They were, after all, 'the presbyters of the church at Ephesus'
(20:17). In Revelation the seven churches of the seven cities of
Asia are put in the plural (Rev. 1–3; 22:16), but for the rest
of the book the people of God, in their eschatological manifestation, appear under different metaphors (bride, city, etc.) and
the word 'church' does not appear, rather as though the term
belonged to our contemporary earthly period, but was superseded by the ultimate redemption.

At first sight we can set this over against the use of the
imagery of 'body'. It is temptingly easy to say that 'body' in 1
Corinthians 12 or Romans 12 so clearly relates to the interaction of the members in a local gathering, that the local
church is being viewed as a single body – with the 'belongingness' all local, and the body entire and self-sufficient as a
unit.[8] This is then contrasted with the use in Ephesians and
Colossians (see p. 46). However, as with Paul's address to the
Ephesian elders, we may well discover that this provides an
over-sharp contrast.

In 1 Corinthians Paul is obviously dealing with local errors
and their redress. He wants the Corinthians to be in harmony

with each other. And it is true that he says to them 'you are
the body of Christ' (1 Cor. 12:27). But his use of 'body' is not
as confined as that. Earlier he writes, 'Because there is one
bread, we who are many are one body, for we all share the
one bread' (10:17); and 'The body is one and has many parts . . .
So it is with Christ, for by one Spirit we were all baptised
into one body' (12:13). Both these instances (with their own
sacramental references) unite Paul (who is writing from
Ephesus, and is no sense local to them) with his Corinthian
recipients – experiencing a common baptism by the one Holy
Spirit into the one universal body of Christ, they continue one
in that body as they share the common bread. That is the fuller
doctrinal background in chapter 12 to his more particularised
appeal – now from the one place, Ephesus, to the believers of
another place, Corinth – that they should live in actual
harmony with each other. And thus when he says, 'you are the
body of Christ' (12:27), again it is unlikely that he is saying
that you are a complete body or a self-contained body. 'You are
body' has a similar scope to 'you are family' – a term which
would demonstrate that they belonged to each other but did
not deny that they also belonged to others elsewhere. 'Body'
here has no article in Greek, so the translation 'you are body'
is perfectly in order. Furthermore, though it is not often well
remarked, in 1 Corinthians 12:28 Paul says, 'God has placed
in the church some as apostles' (italics mine). Surely here he
cannot be referring solely to Corinth? He is making a
generalised point about the Church of God, the worldwide
Church – and, far from the chapter having a purely local
reference, it is stating for the Corinthians points of principle
which are drawn from Paul's understanding of the Church as
a single worldwide body, the body of Christ. This in turn would
mean we must not be surprised if local congregations do not
always exhibit a complete range of talents, or have everything
necessary for total self-sufficiency.

A similar reasoning applies to Romans 12. Paul has, in
Chapter 11, been viewing the universal Church as a single
entity (particularly as uniting Jew and Gentile) using the
imagery of an olive tree (with branches grafted in and others
cut out) which has as a whole a continuity from the old covenant into the new. For all that Paul is concerned about right

attitudes and right behaviour in the local church, in Romans of all letters he puts these local considerations against the fullest possible background. And, sure enough, when he introduces the 'body' imagery, he includes himself with them – despite his writing from Corinth, not only from a great distance but also to people he has never met. But as he wrote to the Corinthians, so he now writes, 'Just as we have many members in one body and the members do not all have the same function, so we who are many are one body in Christ and individually members of each other' (Rom. 12:5–6). Of course there are individual functions; of course there is need for local harmony in Rome. But the practice is to be based upon a larger foundation than, 'You at Rome form one body in Christ'. He is one with them in Christ himself, and this is symptomatic of the fact that it is the worldwide Church which comes first in his thinking.

The universal Church gets the higher profile in the later prison epistles. In them, quite apart from some allusive references, there is clear mention of 'the body of Christ' in a churchly sense in Ephesians 1:22–3; 2:16; 4:4; 4:13; 4:16; 4:25; 5:23; 5:30; and in Colossians 1:18; 1:24; 2:19; 3:15. These vary from the visionary and apocalyptic ultimate perfection in Ephesians 4:13–16 to the uniting of Jew and Gentile in Christ through the reconciliation effected in the cross (Eph. 2:16); and from the test of schism deriving from heresy (Col. 2:19) to the simplest basis for loving each other with straightness and integrity (Eph. 4:25, Col. 3:15). Although some of these passages differ from the earlier picture in making Christ the 'head of the body', others are fully compatible with Christ being the body – and it may be that other (non-corporal) references to Christ's headship, which is certainly a regular theme, have spilled over into the 'body' references. Thus Christ's headship over all creation, particularly in its final fulfilment, is being asserted without reference to 'the body' in Ephesians 1:10 (and probably in Colossians 2:10); and it looks as though, in the places where 'head' and 'body' are connected, the connection arose when Paul found himself naturally referring in the course of his argument to Christ as the 'head' and then, almost as though by a semiconscious reflex, he tacked in a side-reference to the body as though he had been organically led there. This is certainly the appearance of Ephesians 1:22–3; 4:15–16; 5:22–3 and would also be quite plausible in relation to Colossians 1:18; 2:19. If those references are set aside, the remaining ones look less grand, more everyday, and entirely appropriate as a basis for calling believers to more immediate ethical conduct. They are not only compatible with saying that ' "the body of Christ" means "the body which is Christ" ', but they almost demand such a meaning in Ephesians 2:16; 4:4; 4:13; 4:25 and Colossians 1:24; 3:15 (and compare with this 3:9–11).

It has been conventional in Protestant circles to see the more cosmic references to the Church as the body of Christ in these two letters as primarily eschatological in so far as they relate to the unity of the body. There are of course strong eschatological thrusts in the two letters, and particularly in connection with the church (in Ephesians 1:10; 2:7; 4:13 and in Colossians 1:17–19). But it does less than justice to the text to see the unity of the body as merely 'invisible' now and only to be realised in heaven. This rationalisation appears to derive from two facts of later church history: firstly, a desire to say, ever since the Reformation, that belonging to the Church does not of itself save, that church members are not necessarily of the elect, and that therefore the 'true' Church idealised in these two letters must be currently an 'invisible' Church ('the Lord knows those who are his') and it is not to be confused with the visible institutional Church; and, secondly, that among the various denominations we already have the 'invisible' unity to which the imagery of the body here refers, and therefore have no great duty (above that of mere convenience or efficiency) for seeking to unite visibly with anyone else. Paul himself would reply that we belong to each other both worldwide and locally already, and that in Christ we are to seek each other, love each other and bond with each other here and now – and, if one can extrapolate but a short way from what he writes, he would be very impatient of rationalisations that enable Christians to stand apart from each other in the way the Protestant and Evangelical Churches have always tended to do.

Indeed, the actual bonding here on earth is a large part of Paul's battle over the inclusion of the Gentiles. There is no doubt in his mind that the Gospel of Jesus is 'to the Jew first', and that the Church of God is in some continuity with the Jewish community though it has now burst the bounds of that community (compare the imagery of the olive tree in Romans 11, which is discussed above). The promise to Abraham of a seed and a land did have an interim or provisional (but necessary) fulfilment in the birth of Isaac and of Jacob and then of a nation as numerous as the stars of heaven, and also in the entry of that people into the land through Moses and Joshua. But that physical mode of fulfilment was only provisional, and the promise has now been completely fulfilled in a non-physical way – 'If you are Christ's then you are Abraham's seed and heirs according to the promise' (Gal. 3:29). This is the conclusion of the argument that 'there is neither Jew nor Greek, slave nor free, male nor female; for you are all one in Christ Jesus' (Gal. 3:28). Galatians gives us the crucial illustration of how practical this oneness is to be:

> When Peter came to Antioch, I confronted him face to face; for he was to be blamed, and this was why. Before some people came from James, he used to eat with Gentiles; but when these people arrived, he became fearful of the circumcisers, and withdrew from the Gentiles and kept himself separate. The other Jewish believers also joined him in this hypocrisy. (Gal. 2:11–13)

Paul does not say that Peter excommunicated the Gentile believers and told them they had neither part nor lot in Jesus until they were circumcised. No, his actions were much milder, much more subtle, than that: he simply withdrew from eating with them. Now, it may not have been necessary or even possible for him to say, 'No slight intended; the groups have got a bit large, and I find I get on better with the group that goes to synagogue on the sabbath – that's how friendships are made'. But Paul could see in the physical separation of two groups the rebuilding of the 'middle wall of partition', of a spiritual and ethnic–cultural apartheid which was fatal to the Gospel of free grace. If our 'oneness in Christ' is solely 'invisible' or eschatological, then, whatever innocent-sounding rationale we put up, we are in breach of the Gospel; for 'neither circumcision is of any account nor uncircumcision, but a new creation – so peace and mercy to all who walk by this principle, even to the Israel of God' (Gal. 6:16). So the nation of old has become the new nation – Jew and Gentile are together 'the Israel of God'. And therein lies a further worldwide imagery of the Church – one nation, which had once been within national borders but is at the turn of the Christian age scattered through the known world with a separate ethnic–religious identity, is to become a single multi-ethnic multicultural people of God throughout the world, sitting somewhat loosely by their earthly nationhood, for their citizenship is in heaven and is shared by people of every tribe and tongue and skin-pigmentation. That is the Church already dawning in this earliest of Paul's letters. It stands as a corrective to any forming of a 'church' which is monocultural or monochrome, tribal or ethnic, national or denominational.

This is very close to Jesus' prayer for his disciples in the Garden of Gethsemane:

> 'I am not asking for them [the present disciples] alone, but also for those who come to faith in me through their word, that all may be one, even as you, Father, are in me and I in you, that they may also be in us, in order that the world may believe that you have sent me. And the glory which you have given me, I have given to them, that they may be one even as we are one – I in them and you in me, in order that they may be perfected into one, that the world may know that you have sent me.' (John 17:20–23)

Here is a goal of oneness set out by Jesus himself, which mirrors the oneness of Father and Son within the godhead of the Holy Trinity. For Father and Son are not simply a good team or a useful alliance – they are literally numerically 'one', even while Jesus is using the first person plural 'we/us' in his prayer to the Father. There is a mysterious mutual indwelling which characterises relationships within the godhead, and that same mysterious mutual indwelling of one within another is equally, and equally profoundly, to characterise the relationships within the Church. The means to this end include receiving the glory of God through Jesus, and that may betoken the supernatural character of the unity for which Jesus prays. From our point of view, it is a bonding of a highly inclusive sort, for there are no exceptions: all believers down all time are, without differentiation, to be united in Christ. Nor can the union be left as an ethereal 'spiritual' uniting, for it is intended to have a visible impact 'that the world may know you have sent me'.

If we revert to Paul, and move to one of the latest of his writings (perhaps up to 15 years later than Galatians), we find the letter to the Ephesians delineating exactly the same problem. Paul writes as a Jewish Christian, and initially identifies with a group of Jewish background, calling his group 'we'. And he writes as to Gentile Christians, characterising them as 'you'. So the argument goes:

- **Pair (a) in separation**
  [We Jews] 'that we who were the first to hope in Christ might be for the praise of his glory . . .' (1:12).
  [You Gentiles] 'And you also were in him, when you heard the word of truth' (1:13).
- **Pair (b) in separation**
  [You Gentiles] 'And you, when you were dead in transgressions and sins' (2:1).
  [We Jews] 'In those transgressions all of us also all had our way of life' (2:3).
- **'We and 'you' united** (now 'we' is inclusive, as both groups are 'together')
  'But God, who is rich in mercy, made us alive together with Christ, and raised us up together, and seated us together in the heavenly places in Christ' (2:4–6).
- **Further back-reference to what 'you' Gentiles have been**
  'Therefore remember that you who are Gentiles as far as the flesh is concerned . . . were at that time separate from Christ, excluded from citizenship of Israel . . . But now in Christ Jesus you, who were once far off, are made near through the blood of Christ' (2:11–13).
- **The final breaking down of barriers**
  'He himself is our peace' (2:14)
  'he has made the two one' (2:14)
  'and has broken down the middle wall of partition' (2:14)
  'in order to create in himself out of the two one new man' (2:15)
  'so making peace' (2:15)

'and to reconcile both to God in one body by the cross' (2:16)
'and he came and preached good news to those who were near and to those far off' (2:17)
'through him we both have access through one Spirit to the Father' (2.18).

- **Final summary for the Gentiles in Christ**
'So you are no longer strangers... but fellow-citizens' (2:19).

- **Final theological summary, revealing the 'mystery'**
'In Christ Jesus the Gentiles are to be joint-heirs, fellow-members of the body, sharers in the promise' (3:6).

The imagery in Ephesians 2:19–22 then continues from the converted Gentiles as 'fellow-citizens with the saints' (i.e. all in one city or citizenry), to their being 'of the household of God' (i.e. part of the one family), and 'built together' (i.e. walls of a single common building) into a single temple. The uniting of Jew and Gentile is the model demonstration for Paul that all who are in Christ are one with each other in the most practical ways possible – bound in effect to 'eat with each other' on the local scene (i.e. in Antioch), but bound to each other in a single body throughout the world.

So the Church of Pauline teaching is in essence one throughout the world, enjoying one body and one Spirit, one Lord, one faith, one baptism, one God and Father of all, and, *for this doctrinal reason*, bearing with one another in love and striving to keep the unity of the Spirit in the bond of peace. That must surely mean full visibility and no shirking of actual tasks of mutual belongingness?

This strong sense of a single visible worldwide Church, conveyed in Acts and by Paul, is borne out by Hebrews and 1 Peter. In Hebrews there are few local references, and, although there are injunctions which have to be obeyed locally (such as, 'Let us not give up gathering with each other', Heb. 10:25) – yet the letter could be applicable in almost any believing community round the Mediterranean. It does not deal with the word 'church' (save in the tempting phrase of 12:22), but it does deal with those whom it calls 'the people of God' (a phrase which spans old and new covenants) as a single entity. There is a recurrent 'we/us' terminology which unites the writer with the readers. There is a strong sense that, by his once-for-all sacrifice for himself, Jesus has won (or 'sanctified' or 'perfected') a whole people for himself right down history (9:27–8; 10:10; 10:14), and he now 'appears in the presence of God on their behalf' (7:24–25; 9:24). The people of God form a 'house' or 'household' over which Jesus presides (3:6; 10:21). They inherit a city with foundations (11:10; 11:16; 12:22; 13:14). They are, it is suggested, 'aliens and strangers on earth' (11:14). They are already participants in the amazing list of unifying features of God's grace – 'Mount Zion, heavenly Jerusalem, the city of the living God, an array of thousands of angels, the church of the firstborn whose names are written in heaven, God the judge of all, spirits of righteous people made perfect, and Jesus' (12:22–4). They are receiving an unshakeable kingdom (12:28). They are the sheep of Jesus the great shepherd (13:30). Are they not one in Christ, with the mutual belongingness and duties of those in Christ, already?

1 Peter is not dissimilar. His readers are scattered through the provinces of what we call Asia Minor; they are probably Jewish and Gentile believers united into single communities, and they are, in terms that echo Hebrews, 'strangers on earth' (1:1; 2:11). The letter is going to them all and, although they are physically separated from each other, they are, by coming to Jesus (2:4), being built into a single 'spiritual house' and constituted a 'holy priesthood' (2:5); they are 'an elect people, a kingly priesthood, a holy nation, a people for God's possession' (2:9) – a marvellous crescendo of collective nouns. The terminology is from Exodus 19:5–6, where the Israelites, coming out of Egypt, just before reaching Mount Sinai are told how they are God's 'treasured possession, a kingdom of priests, a holy nation', specially chosen within God's rule of the world; and it is these words, specifically identifying the people of Israel as God's chosen people, which Peter then applies unblushingly (and probably not for the first time in his life!) to the church of Jew-and-Gentile-together-in-Christ. If the new people of God are not, in this passage, directly called 'the Israel of God', yet they are very nearly so. Indeed they are strikingly ruled off from 'the Gentiles' (2:12) – a term which must surely here mean not the physically uncircumcised but those separate from Jesus Christ – which confirms that they are 'the Israel

of God'? Thus 'Israel' has its new meaning, drawn in part from the corresponding new meaning of 'Gentile'!

In the terms used there are various rich implications – in 2:5 the temple, or 'spiritual house', is the place where the 'priesthood' is 'offering spiritual sacrifices to God'; and in 2:9 the people who are God's possession tell out praise to God for all the great works that he has done.* But the point worth noting for future reference is that the whole Church (like the nation of Israel in the desert) is a 'kingly priesthood'. This 'priestly' terminology, unknown in the gospels, Acts and Paul, is used rather differently in the letter to the Hebrews, but does recur in the heavenly vision of the book of Revelation, where in heaven the redeemed are said to be a kingdom of priests (Rev. 5:10, cf. 20:6). It is, of course, in each case a 'priesthood' belonging to the whole Church as a corporate entity – there is little ground in these rare uses either for making ordained ministers of the church 'priests' (see pp. 311–16), or for describing each individual member as being 'a priest'.

That is not to deny the strong local manifestation of the body, and the prime duty of working out belongingness, love and mutual support locally. What then does the New Testament give us of local church life?

The local church

Most of Paul's letters are written to correct and encourage local church life between the late 40s and the early 60s AD, and, with one or two exceptions, fairly precise dating is possible for them. Other New Testament letters may also be from the 60s though, because of their general character, dating them is more difficult. From the Pauline letters we receive a series of tantalising glimpses of the strengths and weaknesses of the church in various named towns of the Roman empire; and we

---

*There are two tricky features in translation here, and English versions tend to miss one or other or both. The 'tell out' or 'declare' (*exangeilete*) is likely to be a proclamation *in worship* (rather than in witness), an apt task for a 'royal priesthood' – and what is declared is the 'mighty works' or 'praiseworthy deeds' of the redeemer (*aretas*), a more concrete concept than simply 'praises'.

inherit from them those letters by which the apostle addressed the weaknesses on behalf of God.

That which makes a church 'local' is its rhythm of *meeting*. Actual bodily proximity gives to a set of disciples the ability to 'come together', and it is 'coming together' which constitutes the localness of the local church. There are various phrases used (for example, to 'be in the same place' – as on the day of Pentecost – Acts 2:1 – or at Solomon's Colonnade – Acts 5:12; or in 1 Corinthians 14:23), and clearly the new disciples on the day of Pentecost broke into a pattern of daily meeting including eating together and sharing goods, while on other occasions the apostles themselves summoned the disciples (e.g. Acts 4:23; 6:2). The verb 'to come together' (*sunerchesthai*) is characteristic of Paul's writings (e.g. in 1 Cor. 11:17, 20, 33; 14:26) and 'to be brought together' is found in Acts 11:26; 20:7 and 1 Corinthians 5:4. They were not to omit the 'meeting together' (*episunagoge* – Heb. 10:25). While it is very clear that the New Testament *ecclesia* remained the Church of God, even when it was not meeting, there also remained a spill-over from the 'assembly' meaning in classical Greek and Septuagint usage, so that 'church' is used frequently, if not primarily, to mean 'the assembled group'. Thus this is the more probable (though by no means certain) meaning in Matthew 18:18; it is the necessary meaning in 1 Corinthians 14:19, 28 and 35; and it has a surprising but understandable plural in 1 Corinthians 14:33–4. 'Church' is however also used of the whole membership of Christ locally, irrespective of whether it is actually meeting at that moment, and thus in this meaning it can be regularly used in the plural. It remains very clear, as we have observed earlier, that in the New Testament the 'catholic' or worldwide Church is logically prior to the local church, and that the local church is the worldwide 'body' outcropping locally. Thus we might say 'no [local] church is an island entire of itself'.

Characteristics of the local church

There seems little doubt that, despite all the qualifications set out above, the local church had to take large corporate responsibility before God for its own life-patterns, and for the credibility of the discipleship of each member. Some of this responsibility might be exercised by specific church officers, though the degree of authority and influence they might hold seems to have varied from place to place.* We look at the ingredients of their life-patterns, and then at the character- istics of their meetings or assemblies.

Doctrine

The first point of adherence in Acts 2:42 was 'the apostles' doctrine' (or 'teaching'). In each church the teaching of the faith was supposed to be going on. The teaching included 'as of first importance' that 'Christ died for our sins in accordance with the Scripture, that he was buried, and he rose again the third day' (1 Cor. 15:3–4). It included the ethical teaching that, when new disciples 'learned Christ (for you heard him and were taught in him as the truth is in Jesus)' (Eph. 4:21–2), then they were 'to put off the old self which is corrupt . . . and to put on the new self created in the likeness of God' (Eph. 4:22–4). They were taught in the gospel narratives.** And there are all sorts of signs in Paul's writings of catechetical or credal material, along with songs and other succinct phrases to remember.† There are also signs that they could go wrong in their teaching, and Romans, Galatians and Colossians in particular are precipitated by reports of wrong or inadequate teaching reaching Paul. The expectation that a letter from Paul would be read aloud in the assembly is strong guarantee

---

*The churches in Corinth and in Rome have no mention of such officers in either the opening greetings of Paul's letters or (and this is particularly noteworthy in Corinth) in the roles such officers might perform in redressing ills and exercising discipline in church life – or in simply passing on the truth of the Gospel. The respective churches are simply addressed as single corporate entities, able corporately to organise their own church life.

**There are overt hints of this in the evangelists (Mark 14:9; Luke 1:1–4; John 20:30–31), though the whole concept of collecting, editing and issuing gospels must surely have been based on the general tacit expectation that they would be read and taught!

†The quasi-credal include the baptismal confession 'Jesus is Lord' (Rom. 10:9), the summary of Christ's death and resurrection quoted in the main paragraph (1 Cor. 15:3–4), the fuller confession in Phil. 2:6–11, the various expanded phrases arising from the Old Testament confession that 'the Lord our God is one Lord' – e.g. in 1 Corinthians 8:6 or Ephesians 4:4–5, and, quite possibly and certainly very interestingly, in the assertion in Colossians 1:15–19.

that truth learned and sustained by word was fundamental to the stability and growth of the church. They were 'no longer infants, tossed about in the sea and blown all over the place by every wind of teaching . . . but instead, giving utterance to the truth in love, to grow up into him who is the head, Christ' (Eph. 4:14–15).

It looks as though some of the 'giving utterance' is mutual – the members are to teach each other, interact with each other, refine the formulation of the truth by conversing or even arguing with each other (which is why the warning corrective about doing it in love is included). No doubt much of the teaching would be supplied or reinforced by words or formulas used in a routine and repeated way (as we would say 'liturgically') in the assembly. The double thrust is found in Colossians 3:16: 'Let the word of Christ dwell in you richly, as you teach one another with all wisdom and instruct one another in psalms and hymns and spiritual songs, singing in your hearts to the Lord'. The whole context here is of mutual relationships 'as members of one body' (3:15). So the way 'the word of Christ' is to 'dwell in you [plural] richly' as they 'teach one another with all wisdom' would be at its richest as the 'word' is shared, developed, applied and moved around within the assembly. On the other hand, they are also to use the given words of 'psalms and hymns and spiritual songs'. We have considerable evidence of what songs they had in their repertoire – there were the Old Testament psalms, which were very much stock-in-trade of the New Testament Church; there were New Testament songs (such as those in the birth stories in Luke and those embedded in the worship of heaven in the book of Revelation – some of each with Old Testament backgrounds); and there was further creativity in song, such as is witnessed by Ephesians 5:14. While the form of songs might be more guaranteed by their musical setting, there were also said items of which we have some glimpses – not only the early creeds which we have noted, but also the Lord's Prayer (and other patterns of prayer),* and possibly features of the

---

*Note the words at the end of Acts 2:42 – 'and to *the* prayers' (emphasis mine). Most translations evade the 'the' and simply say 'to prayer', but the original suggests a regular rhythm of actual prayers, whether or not they were of set form and order. It would be interesting

Lord's Supper, including the account (the 'narrative') of the institution. All would be assisting the 'word of Christ' to 'dwell in you richly'. There was no substitute for word.

The cycle of meeting

It looks as though from the day of Pentecost onwards some at least of the disciples met together daily (Acts 2:46), but the developed pattern seems to have brought them together (perhaps as a minimum) on the first day of the week. They were of course Jews, and they observed the sabbath, the seventh day, as Jews. So they may have been motivated by mere convenience, along with a desire not to appear to break too thoroughly with sabbath patterns. At any rate the first day developed – as we find in Act 20:7 and 1 Corinthians 16:1, and possibly even (as 'the Lord's day') in Revelation 1:10. And as it developed it acquired echoes of the Lord's resurrection, for not only do all four gospels emphasise that the resurrection occurred on that day, but they also record in effect the first meetings of the infant church on that day's evening. John's gospel goes further, showing how Thomas missed out by not being 'in church' on the first Sunday evening, and how a week ('eight days' – counting inclusively) later he was there and did meet Jesus – it is easy to visualise the turn-of-the-century sermon based on this passage, exhorting the believers never to miss out by being absent on any particular Sunday.

The meal

The disciples shared the Last Supper with their Lord. At that meal, when Jesus at two separate points, passed round first bread and then wine with the words, 'This is my body' and 'This is my blood', they were also instructed by him, 'Do this in remembrance of me' (1 Cor. 11:24, 25). They did so, but they did so (as they had at the Last Supper) in the context of a larger meal. The major description we have is in 1 Corinthians 11:17–31, which not only sets the event more clearly in the life of the local church, but also probably antedates any of the three gospel accounts we have (John's gospel, while it has a detailed account of the Last Supper in chapter 13, does not

---

to know whether the Lord's Prayer (which the disciples received when they asked 'Lord, teach us to pray' – Luke 11:1) figured in the apostles' programme.

include the bread and wine components). Because the event
came in the context of the larger meal it did not have, and by
definition probably could not have, the reverent disciplined
atmosphere of celebrations of the Lord's Supper outside a meal
context which have characterised the practice of the Church
since the second century. We would expect such an *agape* to
include ordinary conversation as well as readings of Scripture,
exhortation, songs, prayers and the kiss of peace flanking the
sacred distribution at the two high 'sacramental' moments of
the meal. But we are left with largely guesswork – though
obviously there were discourses by Jesus at and after the
original Last Supper, and we know from two gospels that
the disciples sang a hymn at the end of it (Matt. 26:30; Mark
14:26). What is clear is that, whatever such components there
may have been, there was not the kind of event we would call
a 'church service'. Meals involve far more informality than
that – and in Corinth, far from becoming too formal, the meal
had deteriorated into an indulgence of greed.

There are a thousand other books to discuss the ways in
which Christ is present with his Church at the Lord's Supper,
to examine the chances that the Last Supper was or was not
a passover, or to speculate on the nuances of 'remembrance';
and there are as many again to set out full liturgical texts for
the celebration. The present purpose is to see how far the
celebration bears upon the character of the Church. But it is
worth picking up in passing the term 'Eucharist', not least
because it (and it alone) offers a satisfactory adjective –
namely, 'eucharistic'!

Jesus himself 'gave thanks' over the bread and cup in turn,
and the Greek verb used is *eucharisteo*. In the immediately
post-apostolic literature the term 'Eucharist' is already being
used for the Lord's Supper, by the idiom which permits the
part to be used for the whole (and is a further proof of
the irrelevance of etymology for ascertaining meaning). Alongside this, the New Testament itself provides the term
'communion', the word used in 1 Corinthians 10:16, though
this too (translating *koinonia*) is ambiguous, as *koinonia* itself
may be rendered 'sharing' or 'fellowship' and in Acts 2:42 is
actually distinguished from 'breaking bread'.

The inner meaning of the meal is the sharing in 'the body

and blood of Christ', the signification which Jesus gave to the respective elements at his institution of the Eucharist. Paul enjoys sliding from 'body of Christ' as the significance of the bread to 'the body of Christ' as the Church. This occurs in his two main citations of the Eucharist. In 1 Corinthians 10:16 he says, 'The bread which we break, is it not a communion in the body of Christ?' – the predictable sacramental sense. But then in 1 Corinthians 10:17 he says, 'Because there is one bread, we who are many are one body, for we all partake of the one bread'.* Here it is absolutely clear that he has shifted the meaning of 'body' from verse 16 to verse 17.

The passage is matched by the warning passage in 1 Corinthians 11 – as in 11:29, where the careless, selfish or scandalous participant is said to eat and drink without 'discerning the Lord's body'. I suggest that, as a formal matter, it is best to see the 'inner part of the sacrament' in the text only when both 'body' and 'blood' are mentioned, and that references to 'body' alone are, at least initially, to be taken as referring to the Church, the body of Christ. This is, in fact, wholly in line with the misdemeanours of the Corinthian participants – they were eating food under the noses of the hungry, without, it seems, having any conscience or care for those who were supposed to be 'one in Christ, one in his body' with them. The conclusion to which a reader of 1 Corinthians would naturally come is that such persons, whatever their own view of their direct relationship with God, did not really believe they had come into loving relationships with the members of Christ's body – in other words, they failed to 'discern the body'.

As these two occurrences are part of the run-in to Paul's use of 'body' in relation to the Church in 1 Corinthians, it is worth stopping to point out that the reference is by no means solely local. In 10:17 the 'we who are many' embraces both Paul in Ephesus and his readers in Corinth, and the 'one bread' is (like the 'one Lord, one faith, one baptism' of Ephesians 4:4) not so much the lowest number in a numerical count, as an insistence on one 'shared in common' perspective or attribute.

---

*Is it possible that he oddly reverses the normal order of bread and cup in verse 16 in order to get this juxtaposition which enables him to make his point? The reversed order is otherwise incomprehensible – or so casual as to have no significance at all.

Here, to translate one bread in common as 'one loaf' is not only to miss the point, but to make Paul say something which, at his distance from Corinth, was physically impossible. The bonding in Christ with them . . . indeed, the sharing in the Eucharist with them – at that distance is not only indication that the Church as 'the body of Christ' is a worldwide concept, even here in 1 Corinthians, but is also a pointer to the unseen 'communion' with each other at however great a distance that participation in the Eucharist entails. (It also, in passing, suggests strongly to us that all in the Church did share in the Eucharist – it was impossible to conceive of a non-participating believer.)

The body which is the Church in 1 Corinthians 11:29 is more visibly local – indeed, it is in view in the verse simply because it is local and tangible and present under the noses of our self-indulgent wealthy participants. Its message is obviously ethical – they ought to learn to share with the needy. It also perhaps includes a pastoral note for those struggling with the ethical demands of being the Lord's disciples in and through the Eucharist – you might do better to stay away from communion until you have sorted yourselves out! This is always risky, and in most congregations we would prefer the transparent hypocrisy of people coming in a less-than-perfect state of heart and spirit to the honest absenteeism (typical of the British) which says, 'I would be a hypocrite if I went to worship now'! Here in Corinth, Paul's point is more a debating one made in rhetorical style than serious pastoral advice – but, if he were taken seriously, he would be saying: 'These people are so bonded with Jesus, so built into this fellowship, that urging them not to partake for the moment is exactly what is calculated to bring them to a better mind and a better practice – and, for the moment, the church will be delivered from unedifying models of participation in our shared sacramental meal.'

What is very clear – a point to which we shall return – is that, if the people are excommunicated or do withdraw, they have nowhere else to go. This is the Church of God as it is found in Corinth, and there is no other 'fellowship' to which they may resort if they do not like it. The existence of but one eucharistic assembly in one city entails a belongingness which is total. And, for that very reason, the rich and poor may both sit at the same table – just as may the Jew and the Greek, the bond and the free, and the male and the female – and the joining them together in Christ is part of the glory of the body, part of what is being exhibited at the meal.

In the process we are perhaps gleaning a slightly wider set of eucharistic motifs than have usually been realised by Evangelicals:

1 There is no doubt that the death of Jesus is central. The Last Supper (simply by being 'Last') was eaten in an atmosphere of impending death. The passover references suggested that this was the 'Lamb of God' about to be slain. The values given to the bread and wine were of 'body given for' and 'blood shed for' you, and possibly (though this is speculative) the provision of the two elements separately – and originally separated to different parts of the meal – may have been a reinforcing of the separation of body and blood in violent death. Furthermore Paul adds a word of Jesus and a word of his own which reinforce this further:

- Jesus said, 'Do this in remembrance of me'* – and, while the 'remembrance' may not be taken up exhaustively by Jesus' death, it would be perverse to try to minimise or exclude that reference. There is a remembrance of Jesus' death which calls for outward corporate expression (by word or action or both) within the supper.
- Paul himself adds, 'As often as you eat this bread and drink this cup, you tell out the death of the Lord until he comes' (1 Cor. 11:26). This would appear to be a simple report back to the Corinthians of what they say when they are sharing the bread and wine – a practice of which Paul clearly approves and cites as virtually canonical, which would make it more or less binding on us. The Greek verb for 'tell out' is *katangellete*, a verb from the *angello* (and 'angel'/messenger) stem. The stem

---

*I say 'Paul adds a word of Jesus', as this command is not explicit in the gospel narratives (the Lukan citation is textually suspect, and probably inserted from Paul – or from liturgical usage – at a later date). But that is not to call in question its historical authenticity or theological value, and, in strict chronology, Paul's account and the liturgical tradition on which Paul draws antedate the gospel narratives.

is a speaking stem, and the reference is undoubtedly to articulating or reciting the death of the Lord, not to enacting or dramatizing it.* That said, the Pauline report nevertheless gives us important information about what was said at the celebration of the supper. It must have included something close to 'Christ died for our sins in accordance with the Scriptures'.

2   There is a question as to whether references to the death of Jesus should stand unqualified by proclamation of his resurrection. If the community is itself in continuity with the resurrection body of Jesus, then we might look for some mention of that – quite apart from any seasonal references at Easter time. There are two good pointers to this.

Firstly, there is the haunting phrase in Luke 24:35 – the two who had walked to Emmaus reported to the others that Jesus had been made known to them 'in the breaking of the bread'. At first sight, this might well simply mean that Jesus' manner of breaking bread was so distinctive, and so well known to them, that seeing their friendly stranger performing the action in their home opened their eyes and told them he was Jesus. But we have to recall that Luke was writing for the Church of the second half of the first century AD. What would be the significance to them of the phrase, 'He had been made known to them in the breaking of the bread'? Would there not be great overtones in their consciousness declaring to them in their turn that in the breaking of the bread the risen Jesus would be made known to them *as* risen?

Secondly, there are the secondary implications of, 'Do this

---

*If I labour this point slightly, it is because I constantly encounter people – often learned and sophisticated people – who expound and even create liturgy on the basis that the act of eating and drinking itself, dramatically, 'tells out' the death of Christ. No one dealing in the first instance with *katangello* could ever think that, but the situation has been queered for centuries by the AV translation, 'ye do shew forth the death of the Lord', which has so coincided with laudable Protestant prejudice in favour of a tight theological link between the supper and the crucifixion as to persuade readers of the AV not to ask what Greek verb lay behind the translation, but instead go straight for an exposition ('dramatically exhibit the death of the Lord') which the Greek will not sustain.

in remembrance of me'. 'Of me' cannot be exhaustively rendered by 'remember my death'. We do not and dare not simply give what an opponent once called 'peculiar mental attention to a particular past event'. We are engaged with the living Jesus, praying that 'We may live in him and he in us'. We remember one who is alive but unseen – of which we get a faint hint when we 'remember' relatives in Canada, or prisoners of conscience behind bars, but alive, today.

3   I think it is not unfair to suggest that the inner meaning of the supper – 'feeding on Christ' – is not exhausted by the exposition that we rely on his death and draw strength from his forgiveness mediated by his death. In the long passage in John 6 which appears to expound the inner meaning of the supper, Jesus says, 'I am the bread of life . . . If anyone eats this bread, he will live forever' (John 6:48, 51), as well as saying, 'Unless you eat the flesh of the Son of Man and drink his blood you have no life in you' (John 6:53). There is a clear thread running through the chapter which takes the form of, 'Whoever comes to me will never hunger, and whoever believes in me will never thirst' (John 6:35). The eating and drinking motifs are there, but they point to relating the recipients to the person of Jesus himself, as alive and ready to receive them. Again, as with Luke's gospel, all the more so with John's – we have to ask ourselves how John 6 would first have read to those who opened the Fourth Gospel new around AD 100. It is Jesus, as alive yet as saving through the effects of his death ('my flesh which I will give for the life of the world' – John 6:51), who is central to the chapter.

4   There is the strong churchly reference in the bonding of sharing a meal, in the slightly punning invoking of the meaning of 'body', and in the very practical injunctions to share with each other – in bonds of love that bring together rich and poor. While the word *agape* is not used in 1 Corinthians to mean a 'love-feast' (indeed it is used in the famous chapter 13 to mean the quality and practice of love, without reference to feasting), the actual character of the meal in which the bread and wine of the Lord's body and blood were shared led naturally on to its being designated a 'love-feast' – i.e. *agape* – a title found in the New Testament in

Jude 12. There could be no greater testimony as to the purpose of the eucharistic meal than love-feast – for all that that purpose was apparently being frustrated in practice in Corinth.

5   It is only a short leap from the above to see that there is an ongoing ethical outcome from the supper – that the disciples of Jesus, practising love among themselves, are thereby re-equipped for mission, witness and sheer love in the world. The 'rocks' in Jude's love-feasts (Jude 12) are people who feed with God's people 'without a qualm' – when, because of the people they are, they ought to have qualms, because the supper ought to conscientise them about the rest of their lives.

6   The Church is also reminded at the supper of its eschatology. Because we 'tell out the death of the Lord until he comes', we cannot help but know when we meet that he is coming – and the Church's cry, 'Maranatha' ('Lord, come' – cf. Revelation 22:20), while it is not demonstrably linked to the supper in the New Testament, fitted very naturally into it in the next century. The very use of the created order in bread and wine indicates a limited time-period for the sacrament – that is, the period of this world's time – and when the Lord returns, a different order of feasting will break out. So there is a strong forward-looking reminder in the celebration: we are like watchmen that wait for the dawning (cf. Rom. 13:11–12). And there is another close link made in that John 6 passage: Jesus says of those who feed on him that he will raise them up at the last day (John 6:39–40, 54), and that they will live for ever (John 6:51, 58).*

The unity of the local church

The emphasis on love and bonding at the Lord's Supper in 1 Corinthians 11 (with its poetic reinforcement in chapter) is only part of a larger picture in 1 Corinthians (and, up to a point, in Romans). The mutual belongingness of the local

---

*The promise 'I will raise him up at the last day' is the more remarkable because John's gospel has been so often viewed as the epitome of 'realised eschatology' (i.e. that believers have *already* passed from death to life, have *already* eternal life, are *already* enjoying the 'final' resurrection). But in these verses (as possibly also in 5:28–9) the eschatology is flagrantly unrealised.

community who are in Christ is brought out in a series of ways, etched all the more boldly because the Pauline exhortations are prompted by the errors – impending or actual – marring the life of the Corinthian church. Not all are direct sins, but rather they are matters where secondary issues are being magnified in importance among the Corinthians, thus causing people to take an unbending stance where it is inappropriate, and consequently threatening the unity of the believing community. If the community is to be disrupted or broken up, then that *is* a primary issue – there is no question, when we reach chapter 13, but that love is 'the most excellent way' (13:1), that love 'does not seek its own advantage . . . [and] keeps no record of wrong' (13:5), and that, among all spiritual qualities, 'the greatest of these is love' (13:13). After that, we find in chapter 15 that Paul is presenting the death and resurrection of Jesus as that which he had 'handed on' to them as 'among the primary [teachings]' (15:3–4); and thereby is probably indicating that, in many of the previous chapters about church life, he has been handling secondary issues. He handles them with great seriousness because of the very problem that people who take up a stance on secondary issues and on matters of preference often erect them into a primary and non-negotiable principle, as though they were comparable with the affirmation or denial of the death and resurrection of Jesus.

Firstly, the Corinthians were at risk of breaking into parties, possibly even into what we would call denominations:

> I call upon you . . . that you all agree with one another, lest there be schisms among you, and that you be equipped with a common mind and common judgement. For it has been revealed to me about you . . . that there are strifes among you. I am saying this: that one of you says, 'I am of Paul'; another, 'I am of Apollos'; another, 'I am of Peter'; and another, 'I am of Christ'. Is Christ divided? Was Paul crucified for you? Or were you baptised 'into the name of Paul'? (1 Cor. 1:10–13)

The rallying into opposed parties is contrary to the Pauline Gospel. It testifies either to a divided Christ or to a series of merely human saviours – Paul, Apollos, Peter. Both horns of that dilemma are unthinkable. The life of the local church has to testify to one Saviour, one Christ, one loving community. Hence Paul goes about cutting the profile of himself, of Apollos and of Peter down to size – as of no value over against Jesus, and, within the minor roles they have, as complementary to each other and in no sense rivals (1 Cor. 3–4). What he cannot contemplate is the founding of two or more groupings in the same city – two or more denominations, in our terms – an outcropping of the universal Church which he deems both illicit and unacceptable.

Secondly, Paul has to deal with litigiousness in Corinth (6:1–11). Amazingly (to latter-day eyes) he still does not name a leader or pastor who might reconcile the litigating parties – but he does make it clear he expects there to be *somebody* (6:5), and disagreements within the body are to be handled by reconciliation; and, if the matter is pushed to the limit, peace and harmony are to be sustained if necessary by one party being ready to lose out unfairly (6:7–8) – which is a real Gospel demand. No doubt, litigation before pagan courts in Corinth, irrespective of the result in the particular case, could only lead to division.

Thirdly, he has to deal with differing practices within the church arising from 'weak' and 'strong' consciences, tending to provoke the 'weak' to judge the 'strong' and the 'strong' to despise the 'weak' (see 10:29, etc., and cf. Romans 14:3). The argument begins at 6:12, where he appears to be quoting the slogan of the 'strong' – that is, the disciples who tend toward antinomianism and cite the freedom they have in Christ. Their slogan is, 'All things are lawful [*or* permissible *or* possible] for me'. At this point Paul simply raises the forthcoming issue – that adjustment to each other may be needed (that is, the question of what one may eat), and goes on to sexual licence where, it seems, the same slogan is being used as an umbrella for any licentious behaviour, and needs straight refutation rather than adjustment. In so doing, he is firing a shot across the bows of any who want to make 'All things are lawful for me' the basic principle of living.

He returns to the eating theme at the beginning of Chapter 8, and the significance of the issue emerges: the meat sold in the market may well have been offered to idols in the pagan temples of Corinth; and are all things then permissible to believers? There is a fundamental theological principle for believers that 'an idol is nothing at all in the world and there is no God but one' (8:4), and therefore, all other things being equal, there is complete liberty to eat anything sold in the market-place – for, as he says, quoting Psalm 24, when he returns to the subject yet again in Chapter 10, 'The earth is the Lord's and all that is in it' (10:26). So the strong – those who have got their theological starting-points right – are in principle free to eat.

However, it is not so simple. Other converts still have a conscience about the idol and the meat sacrificed to it; they have psychologically needed a complete break from the past, and have effected it. And that is possible for them. They are the 'weak' who are scrupulous, and who retain a conscience where God has said that in the light of his truth there is no need for scruple or conscience. They can indeed stop short of exploiting all the liberty God has given them, and they obviously cannot and should not be forced to eat just to prove they have liberty. But – and this is the rub – their weak consciences are then troubled if they see the strong eating cheerfully in the temple restaurant (8:10).

And the strong are correspondingly told that, despite the theoretical legitimacy of 'all things are lawful' (which recurs as Paul has his third go at the issue in 10:23), yet that principle may be overtaken or at least restricted by the greater principle, 'not all things are helpful' – and 'no one should be considering his own advantage, but that of the other person' (10:24–5). So the issue now is not how one person's approach can be deemed determinative and be imposed by authority or *force majeure* on another, but whether there are secondary issues in the life of the local believing community where one group, even if by most canons of judgement they have the truth with them, can nevertheless not only live with a group that sees the matter differently, but can also make concessions to the other group so as not to offend their consciences. This is going far beyond tolerance and is right into the field of love – and is Paul's remedy for splits in the local church, his recipe for visible tangible unity.

Fourthly, he gives similar advice in Chapter 7 across a series of different states of life. Here it is not that one position is right and another wrong; he expresses a mere preference, itself affected by the perspective that this world is passing away (7:31). This approach is all the more one in which no one set of mores is to overrule or extinguish another. This advice – all in the field of tolerance-moving-into-love – covers the following 'states of life':

1 There is a range of marital situations, in which Paul says 'it is good' (7:1, 8, 26) to take what often appears today as the more demanding path – though 'it is good' would seem to be bare permission ('it is OK, not reprehensible, if you go this way rather than that'):

- it is OK for the single to marry – or not to marry (7:1–9) – (cf. 7:25–38);
- it is OK for a wife (presumably under provocation) to live separately from her husband – or to be reconciled to him (7:10–11);
- it is OK for a believer to live with an unbelieving partner – or to let that partner go if he or she is determined to (7:12–16);
- it is OK for a widow to marry again – or to stay single (7:39–40).

2 There are other states of life which get similar treatment:

- it is OK to be a circumcised – or an uncircumcised – man (7:17–20);
- it is OK to be a slave – or to be free (7:21–4).

These are presented as ethical issues, but ones from which Paul is drawing the ethical sting. There are commands of God (7:19), and they are to be kept. But there is a whole series of areas (such as those he has handled) where there are no hard-and-fast rules, and where mature choices can and should be made. And the underlying further agenda are also there: that no one should erect an area of choice into an area of rule (which would be highly divisive), and no one should treat one kind of preference in areas of choice as morally or otherwise 'better' than another preference, which would also be divisive. The retention of a harmonious way of different people (with different perceptions and preferences) living together is an ultimate purpose in answering 'the matters you wrote about' (7:1).

For the present purposes we may also bracket 11:2–16 with

the above discussion. Paul is reverting to the 'traditions' (*'paradoseis'*) he has 'handed on' (*'paredoken'* – from the same 'handing on' stem) (11:2). In 11:3–10 he sets up a fairly strong differentiation between men and women, which has both a so-called 'subordinationist' origin (11:3, 7–9) and a practical outcome (4–5) – though even there the woman is assumed to be 'praying or prophesying', which looks more permissive than other instructions of Paul. Then in 11:11–15 he glosses both the doctrine (11–12) and the practical outcome (13–15) to reconcile the polarised position – so that men and women may live in complementary ways in the church, neither judging nor despising but valuing the differences between the two sexes and valuing each other across the differences. Finally, he sounds in verse 16 as though, having set up certain positions as the 'tradition', he will not take a strong stand on any of them in practice – once again being more concerned about the harmony of the local congregation (here 'churches' are most clearly in the plural) than about particular 'customs', which, we may infer, are not absolutely and exclusively derivable from his doctrinal starting-points, and therefore will be not such as to be defended in any and every circumstance. Paul will take a non-negotiable stance on primary matters – but he knows very well what is secondary, what is of 'custom', and when being yielding serves the unity of the local church in a situation, where being unyielding might severely damage it.

Fifthly we come to Chapter 12. This is of great consequence because of what modern charismatics and Pentecostalists have discovered in the chapter, and the uses then made of it for bolstering certain styles of church life. It is important in today's church not only as airing the concept of 'body' very thoroughly, but also as raising the issue of 'gifts'.* I offer therefore, as a way of getting close to the chapter, three overarching canons of interpretation.

---

*The word translated 'gift' is in Greek *charisma*, with the plural *charismata*. We are used in English to the (metaphorical) secular notion that a leader with flair or special attractiveness has 'charisma'. We are also used to the labelling of 'neo-Pentecostalism' as 'charismatic', as particularly in the title 'charismatic movement'. Now read on . . .

1   The aim is unity

Paul *takes for granted* that there are differences and distinctions among the Corinthians; and the direction of his argument about the body is an argument *from* those known vast differences of the various members *to* the unity and harmony of the body (which, at Corinth, could by no means be taken for granted). The chapter is *not*, therefore, about how, within a known unity of the body, we should be busy discovering, affirming and exercising particular individual 'gifts'.

2   No 'spiritual gifts'

Paul has no special spiritual category of 'gifts' at all! This stark and perhaps surprising proposition is based upon three considerations:

1   The word *'charismata'* is used much less frequently in the Greek than in most of the translations, and it is these which have helped to fix people's understanding of the relative importance of the concept. Thus a careful listing elicits solely the following occurrences:

- 12:1: 'Now concerning spiritual matters' (this heading to the chapter has no mention of 'gifts');
- 12:4: 'There are differences of gifts' ('gifts' is there);
- 12:9: 'gifts of healings' ('gifts' is there);
- 12:12–26: No use of 'gifts';
- 12:28: 'gifts of healings' ('gifts' is there);
- 12:28: 'administration' (or 'steering') ('gifts' is not there);
- 12:30: 'gifts of healings' ('gifts' is there);
- 12:31: 'Seek the greater gifts' ('gifts' is there).

Chapters 13 and 14 have no use of the word 'gifts' at all (though the NIV puts the word into the translated English text at 13:2; 14:1; 14:12 and, in effect, in 14:37). So we find, in those three chapters which have traditionally fixed in minds the concept of 'gifts', the word actually occurs five times in Chapter 12 and then not at all. Of those five uses, three occasions take the form 'gifts of healings' (5, 28 and 30), almost as though it were a conventional phraseology for 'healings'; thus all the other activities in the lists in verses 8–11 and in verse 28 are entered simply as, for example, 'prophecy' (10), and not 'gifts of prophecy'. So, in the use of

'*charismata*' as a general term, we are left with two occurrences only (12:4, 31) from which to create a doctrine. There
are uses elsewhere (notably in Romans 12:6 – and a comparable use in 1 Peter 4:10), but they are hardly such as to
produce a defined and distinctive doctrine.

2   In the first use of *charismata* in Chapter 12 (i.e. in verse
4), Paul is merely using a slightly rhetorical threefold way
of summarising the different activities of different people.
All, no doubt, have gifts; all have ministries (*diakoniai* –
kinds of service); all have ways of operating (*energemata*) –
but the sole point of setting the different ways out in lists
is to indicate that we already know how different people are
from each other (that, we remember, is conceded at the
outset) and then to remind them that, despite this, it is
the one God who is activating them in their different ways.
This is the starting-point of the argument *from* the differences *to* the unity. And, from that point of view, it does not
matter which three categories he uses, nor even whether he
uses more than one category at all, as the point of the
argument does not lie in his (purely illustrative) categories,
but in the general range of differences among the disciples.*
As far as 12:4 is concerned there is no more basis for creating
a delineated doctrine of 'gifts' than there is for creating an
equally delineated one of 'ministries' or 'operations' – they
are all clearly very general terms, with no sharp doctrinal
distinctiveness.

3   In the actual listings of the differences (12:8–11; 12:28)
there is no attempt either to say that these, as listed, are,
as a category, 'gifts', or to suggest that the lists are exhaustive of the category. They are merely illustrative of variety –
and are exactly comparable to the illustrations from the
parts of the body in 12:14–26, where 'knee' and 'elbow' would
serve just as well as 'ear' and 'eye'. If this point is taken,
then there is no way of distinguishing from this chapter
(let alone from the next two chapters, where 'gifts' are not

---

*Indeed, if we are to speculate, there is more reason to speculate
about 'Why three categories?' than about 'Why gifts, ministries and
operations?' It is tempting then to see the working of 'one Spirit'
(12:4), 'one Lord' (12:5), and 'the same God' (12:6) as another passing
instance of Paul's half-unconscious trinitarianism!

mentioned) what specific activities or abilities are to be classified as a 'gift'. It is true that in 12:8–11 the Spirit is said to 'give' these activities and abilities; thus it is inevitably true to say that all that is set before us by God to do, and all the ability to do what is set before us, is 'given by God'. But at this point the 'giving' of God has become so general, so universal, so much his ordinary way of working, that the recognition of it was clearly there before any 'charismatic movement' arose; and its generalness leaves the onus of proof on the charismatic to show that there is some distinctive extraordinary 'charisma' which is to mark off one believer from another, one congregation from another. If there is any hesitation about conceding this, then the pointer on unity (see p. 119) – that is, the discernment of 'the direction of Paul's argument' – needs revisiting. If Paul is taking differences between people as known and already conceded, then he is *not* arguing towards giving particular individuals particular affirmation or status or labelling; no, he is using them as illustrative of differences and as requiring both an initial awareness that such differentiation springs from 'the one Spirit', and a consequent determination of the different parts that they should work together as an harmonious whole. It all moves *from* the many *to* the one.

That only leaves the use in 12:31: 'Seek the greater *charismata*'. It would be odd indeed to build a doctrine on that. But it might be worth a fraction more investigation. It is perhaps typical of Paul, while he is making his rhetorical argument in 12:29–30 about how all members of the body are different and complementary, to start to break off into an exhortation *quite unlike anything he has said before in this chapter.* For the first time he is hinting that there might be a priority among the range of activities mentioned. He is not wanting simply to leave everyone fixed and static in and with the particular 'gift' or function each one currently has. He is concerned with training, growth and, in the best sense, spiritual ambition. His mind starts on a new tack (as happens in dozens of other places in his letters). And (as also happens elsewhere) he has no sooner started it than he realises that he must put the whole thing on a different canvas. If the

Corinthians are to 'seek' anything other than what they have, then they had better forget gifts or distinctive functions for the moment, not worry about what might be 'greater' tasks to fulfil, but first and above all get hold of the 'most excellent' way of functioning – and all the distinctive functions are then brought into perspective by being compared with the presence or absence of love. That does not rule out 'Seek the greater gifts', but it does contextualise it.

3   Comparison with Romans

All the discussion of the 'body' should be read in close relationship to the parallel discussion in Romans 12. At the very least we must remember that Romans was probably written no more than two years after 1 Corinthians, and that it was written from Corinth. It would be perverse if we were to treat either 1 Corinthians or Romans as standing quite independently of Corinth itself, such that Paul could, for instance, describe church life for the Romans with his eyes tight shut against church life where he was residing. As the discussion of the 'body' is so similar in Romans 12 and in 1 Corinthians 12, and as Romans 12:6 includes one those rare Pauline uses of '*charismata*', the two must be used to interpret each other. There is, however, one interesting difference between them – a difference which helps validate the point about unity on p. 119 – and it is this: in Romans 12, the direction of the argument is less demonstrably from the many to the one, and is in part from the one to the many. Paul is writing in this chapter to mobilise the Roman church into practical action, and therefore part of the argument terminates on the individuals 'doing their own thing'.

When we make the comparison we discover certain common points:

1   The reference to the 'body' seems to be – as far as these chapters standing on their own are concerned – to the local disciples seen as a unity.*

2   The 'body' is the body of Christ (1 Cor. 12:12; Rom. 12:5);

---

*This is not to abandon anything said earlier (see p. 46) about the first connotation of 'body', nor is it to concede general points about Paul's use of 'body' in 1 Corinthians, but it is to acknowledge the surface implication of 'body' in these two parallel chapters.

the body has many 'members' (*mele*, 'limbs' – frequently in both chapters); the members have 'functions' (*praxeis* – Rom. 12:4; cf. actual functions such as 'sense of hearing' and 'sense of smell' in 1 Cor. 12:17); and the functions may be called 'gifts' (*charismata* – 1 Cor. 12:4; Rom. 12. 6), or indeed 'ministries' (*diakoniai* – 1 Cor. 12:5) or 'ways of operating' (*energemata* – 1 Cor. 12:6) – but these are simply different titles for the concept of distinctive roles; the functions differ enormously from each other (frequently in both chapters); the differentiation is an inbuilt feature of being members of the body (Rom. 12:4–6; 1 Cor. 12:14–20); it is also part of God's purposing (1 Cor. 12:18); and the members are to work together as one body in a very practical visible way (1 Cor. 12:21–6; Romans 12:7–21); the members (e.g. 'eye' and 'ear') illustrate variety, and it is the members themselves who are listed at the beginning of the list in 1 Corinthians 12:28 (e.g. 'apostles', 'prophets'), but the list then tails into the functions (cf. 'sense of hearing', 'sense of smell', with 'miracles', 'helps', and 'kinds of languages'). In Romans 12 it is reasonably clear that the people are the members and that they have gifts or functions – and that 'gifts' are 'functions', and 'functions' 'gifts'.

At the same time, once we approach the actual listings of functions, then there are real differences. The illustrations of variety which come to Paul in 1 Corinthians 12 are at first sight a range of what we would be tempted to call ministerial functions – though they include 'helps' and 'administration'. Perhaps the greatest interest has focused on 'tongues' and 'prophecy'. But he is, at that point, illustrating variety. In Romans 12 he is concerned to ensure that certain functions do actually happen, so, although he is in a minor way still interested in illustrating variety, he is also deliberately naming tasks to be done, and his injunctions are no longer in an illustrative mood. They prove to be very practical, caring and also comprehensive. They run off into general exhortations (Rom. 12:9–21) which have quite lost sight of differentiated functions and are now the generalised tasks of all the disciples of Jesus, especially as to how they are to bear themselves and conduct themselves towards others. If, in the course of the naming tasks, he occasionally touches on one which looks to us 'ministerial', as, for example, in teaching (12:7) or leading (12:8), it does not feel out of place to Paul himself, for the functions are all part of a general listing of overlapping and unpolarised activities. What is certain is that he wants the church at Rome, through the efforts of its members, to be deeply bonded in love. And I think we can confidently state that, if that were to be happening, then the Holy Spirit would be rightly deemed to be deeply at work among them – for all that he has not been mentioned by name in the chapter, not even in connection with *charismata*.

In the light of these principles, we can enquire how the assembly of the local church should conduct itself, and in the process have particular reference to 'tongues' and 'prophecy' in Chapter 14. There are certain preliminary points to be made here.

1   As noted above, the word 'gifts' does not occur in Chapter 14, and in discussing the 'tongues' and 'prophecy' issue we could perfectly well restrict ourselves to 'functions'. However, that does perhaps raise the question of the meaning of *'ta pneumatika'* in 14:1. This presumably corresponds to the use of the same term (also without *charismata*, despite the translations!) in 12:1. While both of them certainly introduce chapters where individual functions (or 'gifts') are discussed, in each case the chapter actually has a wider purpose than merely that discussion. In Chapter 12 the first three verses are about confession of Jesus as Lord, and most of the rest of the chapter is about how individual functions contribute to the harmony of the whole body; and in Chapter 14, the first 25 verses involve the particular controversy, but 14:26–40 are about order in the assembly – a much wider handling of church life. While we ought not to think of Paul introducing *chapters* (for he had no such division, and might be surprised to find the divisions of his writings that we have), yet he was in each case opening up new areas of discussion. Could his *'ta pneumatika'* then have a wider meaning, which is in common between Chapters 12 and 14? Could it in fact mean 'spiritual agenda', 'the spiritual life of the church' or 'living corporately in the Spirit'?* I think there

---

*We ought also to work at a related translation of 14:12, where the NIV manages to get 'spiritual gifts' in once and a further 'gifts' as

is a real case for this, and the more so as, once the traditional translations of the phrase as 'spiritual gifts' has been dropped, there is no other place in the New Testament where the phrase 'spiritual gifts' or 'gifts of the Spirit' actually occurs at all. There is *no* technical phrase 'spiritual gifts', and we must not read into Scripture ill-based contemporary terminology!

2   We need to ask ourselves *why* Paul writes at this length about these two particular functions. I judge that it is not because he views them as of outstanding importance in themselves, but because they have proved a matter of dispute within the Corinthian church, and disputes *are*, simply by being disputes, of great importance, lest they rend the unity of the body (compare his handling of Paul versus Apollos (1 Cor. 1:10–12; 3:5–9, etc.), or of idol-meats versus no idol-meats (1 Cor. 8:1–13; 10:14–11:1)). Clearly some 'tongue-speaker' thinks his function is of greater importance than that of a 'prophet', and others may have rallied to one side or another, and Paul must now sort it out gently lest it rupture the unity of the church.

3   We ought to be very careful of the word 'tongues'. The Greek for this is *glossai*, and it would more naturally in modern English be translated as 'languages'. It so happens that 'unknown tongues' (with '*unknown*' in italics!) was used in the Authorised Version, and that version was still in universal use when, from the turn of this century onwards, the phenomenon known as 'tongues' became a normal and even normative feature of one strand of church life. Thus the English-language understanding of the New Testament has become relatively fixed in a framework of thought that distinguishes 'tongues' from 'languages', though that is a distinction impossible to sustain in Greek. Furthermore, there was a strong predilection conveyed by the AV's

---

well, when there are no *charismata* in the original. A more literal tranlation would be: 'So it is with you – as you are seekers after spirits, seek to abound in building up the church.' This might leave us uncertain as to the meaning of 'spirits', but it would lay the weight of understanding more heavily upon the interaction within the assembly, and less upon the exercise of one or more person's special functions.

'unknown' in favour of 'tongues' being unrecognisable bur-blings. Since the phenomenon of 'speaking in tongues' started to appear from the beginning of this century onwards, virtually all readers of 1 Corinthians 14 have been fairly sure what they were encountering in Corinth. In the process, the word 'tongues' has come to glow (like 'gifts') with special religious colours.* The process has been bolstered by an astonishing parallel which is closely linked with it, whereby the Greek stem *hermeneuo* has been rendered 'interpret' in the traditional English versions, when 'trans-late' would have done equally well, or even better. We thus have a further specially glowing religious concept – that of 'interpretation' – lurking in 1 Corinthians 14 (with an earlier mention in the lists in 12:30), a concept which is bound to have different overtones from 'translate', although it would be extremely hard to make the distinction when speaking the Greek of the New Testament.

4   While prophecy has reference back to the Old Testa-ment and is mentioned in the New Testament in a variety of ways and places, 'languages' as a characteristic of the life or lifestyle of believers is only found in Acts and in 1 Corinthians 12—14.** It does not appear as part of church life anywhere else in the New Testament. It may therefore be useful, in approaching 1 Corinthians, at least to note the uses in Acts.

• In Acts 2:6, 8, the word used is *dialectos*, meaning 'dialect' – though clearly in a very broad sense of

---

*Curiously, the most neutral (and therefore illuminating) use of *glossai* comes in Revelation, where it is used simply as categorising of all the nations on earth (e.g. in 5:9; 7:9; 10:11; 11:9; 13:7; and 14:6) and is regularly translated as 'languages'.

**I naturally exempt Mark 16:17, which charismatics regularly quote; as Mark 16:9–20 is clearly without textual justification and appears from internal evidence to be a later scribal attempt to give a coherent ending to a gospel which (whether by Mark's design or by some later accidental mishandling of a manuscript) apparently finished with 'for they were afraid' at verse 8 – which for a scribe who knew the gospel stories (and he did) was a bit hard to take as the authentic conclusion of the gospel. He refers of course to 'new languages' which was his own (valueless) gloss on *glossai* – valueless, as it has no parallel elsewhere in Scripture and it is exactly the question as to whether they were 'new' which is under consideration.

'dialect'. In 2:4, 11, the classic word *glossai* is used. A miracle is being asserted, of that there is no doubt. The crowd has been arrested, and they duly listen to Peter. But, in the light of later understanding of 'tongues', something very exceptional was happening, as the 'tongues' were their own 'interpretation', for they were already and identically the language of the hearers.

- In Acts 8:17, the Samaritans received the Spirit in some sufficiently dramatic way for the onlookers to know that they were different instantly – was it that they were 'speaking in tongues'? We can only guess by comparison with the next two citations.

- In Acts 10:46 the first Gentile converts received the Spirit, and they were known to have received the Spirit just because they were 'speaking in (different) languages and praising God'. When Peter describes the event to the Jerusalem church, he says 'the Holy Spirit fell upon them, as he had upon us at the beginning' (Acts 11:15); and this strongly suggests that the different languages they were using had some recognisable comparability to the disciples' experience on the day of Pentecost.

- In Acts 19:6, the (slightly mysterious) followers of the baptism of John received both baptism into Jesus and the laying on of hands with prayer, and the Holy Spirit came upon them and they then 'spoke in (different) languages and prophesied'.

That is the sum total. On three occasions (and possibly four) in the Acts narrative, those on whom the Spirit came in power spoke in languages, which was part of the evidence of the Spirit having come. On each occasion the speaking in such languages appears to be connected with that initial coming of the Spirit – though nowhere else in the New Testament is that connection made – and, by contrast, whatever was happening at Corinth was clearly an ongoing practice, not a once-for-all evidence of the coming of the Spirit. Furthermore the instances in Acts happened to *all* on whom the Spirit came, and happened almost involuntarily – that is, they apparently found themselves 'speaking in languages' without having first decided to do anything of the sort and, presumably, in the latter cases not even knowing whether anyone ever had done so before. In 1 Corinthians, on the other hand, the 'gift of languages' is one function among many within the body, and it is clearly to be controlled by those to whom it belongs and is only to be used in stated circumstances.

That still leaves a hatful of problems as to what 'languages' in 1 Corinthians might be. I have contented myself with a separate discussion as an appendix to this chapter (see pp. 299–309). For the moment, even with certain factors unknown, we return to learn what we can from the treatment of the matter about life in the local church in Corinth. The most distinctive incontrovertible feature of life in the assembly at Corinth was that, in principle, they were addressing each other. The rivalry between 'languages' and 'prophecy' is resolved by a higher principle – that is, that when anyone speaks in the assembly the words must communicate to the assembly. It is not sufficient for God to understand what is going on (14:2) – the people must too! This in turn means that prophecy is immediately relevant, as – by definition, it seems – it is delivered 'in clear', that is, in a language 'understanded of the people'. Other languages are not necessarily out of court, but they will need translation and will not be understood nor build anyone up if they are not translated, and should not therefore be used without translation. The form of such speech may be addressed, as prophecy normally would be, to the assembly, or it may be praise or thanksgiving addressed to God – which then should elicit an 'Amen' (14:16) from the assembly.

Paul himself uses languages privately more than the Corinthians do, but he will not say even a few words in the assembly if they will not be understood (14:18–19). So therefore, to return to the original argument, it is all right to speak in languages (given the right conditions), but speaking in the local vernacular is a far safer and more universalisable procedure. It is not crucial in relation to this particular discussion to know what the languages were: the only point Paul is making in relation to the building up of the church is that the languages should be translated. Once the point about understanding has been grasped, then the curtain goes up on some incidental evangelism: wonderfully for our latter-day church life, we have a passing glimpse of a stranger who, for reasons beyond our ken, has decided to go to church, and where all are prophesying, speaking in the vernacular, he will be convicted of his sin and be convinced that God is really among them (14:24–5).

If the assembly really is engaged in such interaction (and 'all prophesying' is fairly mind-blowing) then it will take some controlling. The requirement that all should understand what is being said is queered not only by the use of languages unknown to some or all of those present, but also by several persons talking at once. The use of languages should be one at a time, with translation (14:27–8), and similarly the prophets should also speak 'one at a time' (14:31) – they are perfectly well capable of controlling themselves (14:32). The picture of 14:26 is of a proactive group of people who 'come together' (Paul's semi-technical term for the church gathering) and have many contributions to share. But the implication of the need for them to be told to speak 'one at a time' is that the loquacious (whatever their speaking medium) could not wait actually to ensure they communicated with the assembly – people spoke simultaneously out of sheer self-indulgence or some spirit of competition. Neither of these would build up the church.

The two verses on the desired unproactive role of women should simply be noted, compared with other verses, and handled as constructively as possible. We find in them once again the words 'in church' (14:35), a phrase which has regularly meant 'in the assembly'.

One last glimpse of Chapter 14 is afforded in the provision that a 'revelation' may come to someone sitting down, and he has then the right – perhaps even the duty – to interrupt the man currently speaking (14:30). All this is to make for peace and good order (14:40). Every feature of the relationships between the various proactive persons, as also between them and the less proactive, is to instruct and to build up. There will be much in the way of spoken words, and they are to apply God's truth, perhaps even by 'revelation', to existing church life. Some of this will be known and prepared in advance; other features will emerge as the meeting proceeds. It looks as though the Holy Spirit might be viewed as 'in' that which is already ready when they first come together, just as much as 'in' the immediacy of a word being given directly. We also get a hint that psalms, if not hymns and spiritual songs, were part of the assembly's programme (14:26), so perhaps they sang (which provides a point of contact with Ephesians 5:19 and Colossians 3:16).

If we go back over these various features of church life which have emerged, we find that Paul has taught a foundation in the Gospel ('which you have received and in which you stand' – (15:1), and this is not only non-negotiable (e.g. in 1:18–25; 15:12–19), but something of which they need to be reminded (15:1). Baptism into Jesus has made them one body, organically belonging to each other (1:13–15; 12:12–26). For disciples of Jesus, living as a loving community, there are God-given constraints upon their behaviour (e.g. Chapters 5 and 6). However, there are also great other areas of church life where, in matters which we must deem secondary, disciples ought to defer to one another in the name of love – a constraint even on those who may have truth on their side. In the functions people perform, all are to be valued by each other for their extraordinarily different contributions. In the Lord's Supper they are actually to care practically for each other, and in that and in other meetings or gatherings (such as we might call 'times of worship') they are to take care that their words make sense to each other, and build up the church. Love is the first and great criterion for discovering how the church is to live in its nexus of internal relationships – and the weak and needy and marginalised are to be the first candidates for receiving love.

One doubly marvellous feature of church life there is that *we never read any reference to anyone in charge*.[9] All instructions, and we have seen there are many, are simply directed to the church corporately. They are together to implement it. And, although all Paul's instructions are directed to building up the church in love and peace, one wonders whether attempting, without visible responsible leaders, to respond to this letter may perhaps have put further strain upon their love.

(See Appendix 1, pp. 299–309, for a Note on tongues and languages, and pp. 309–11 for a Note on prophecy.)

Ministers of the local church

The lacuna about leaders in 1 Corinthians is a cue for a closer look at the whole New Testament. There is a very disparate picture.

Firstly, there are the twelve. They are called by Jesus, become his 'disciples', and are with him through his earthly ministry; they are taken into his confidence, entrusted with his message and mission and are witnesses to his resurrection. They are 'the apostles whom he had chosen' (Acts 1:2). It is they (minus Judas) who receive the various instructions of Jesus in his resurrection period; and they who are specifically listed again in Acts 1:13, and are distinguished from the other disciples. Among them Peter has a leading role. Matthias is added to them after the ascension, and on the day of Pentecost, although the 120 may all have been present, it was Galileans (whether twelve or more, but clearly encompassing the twelve) who spoke other languages (Acts 2:7), and there is the very clear phrase, 'Peter stood up with the eleven' (Acts 2:14). So they are a distinct group of 'apostles', who are still seen as distinct, for instance, in Acts 8:1; 8:14; 11:1.

To the twelve was in some respects added Paul. Paul himself claims to have 'seen the Lord' (1 Cor. 9:1; 15:8 – presumably on the road to Damascus), to have received a special revelation from God charging him with the task of apostleship (as, for example, in Galatians 1:15–17), to have been recognised and supported at a later stage by James, Peter and John as 'going to the Gentiles' (Gal. 2:8–10), and to have exercised his authority then towards Peter himself on behalf of Gentile believers and of the Gospel itself (Gal. 2:11–16). He gives a very strong impression of being a loner, for all that he usually had companions on his journeys. But he also has a sense of answerability and accountability to the Antioch church which first sent him out, and to the Jerusalem church which is in some sense the hub of the whole missionary expansion in which he is taking such a full part.

In both the Corinthian letters he spends some time defending his apostleship. When, some years later, he writes from Corinth to Rome, he relies upon the role he already has as apostle of the Gentiles, and tells the Romans how he has been working it out in practice in Greece (Rom. 15:14–22).

However, he also claims that this gives him authority in relation to the Romans themselves, although he has never yet been to Rome. At the beginning of the letter it takes this form: '[The gospel concerns the Son of God, Jesus Christ] through whom we have received grace and apostleship for bringing the obedience of faith among all the Gentiles, *among whom are you also* the called of Jesus Christ' (Rom. 1:5–7, italics mine).

But in one sense this illustrates the delicate sensitivity of the role of an apostle – Paul has to intrude his position very carefully into their consciousness, just as he has to in Corinth where, although he had first evangelised the Corinthians, it was by no means certain that they would either recognise him or take instructions and directions from him (1 Cor. 3—4; 2 Cor. 10—12). Later, from prison, he tiptoes into making the same claim towards the Colossians whom he has never visited (Col. 2:1–5). In some measure we are left to reckon that Paul's teachings in his letter had to ring irresistibly by the Spirit into the lives of the recipients, and that response was not wholly or very much dependent upon debates in the churches about the implications of his apostleship, but much more upon the burning character of what he wrote. For all we know, that might even have been the differentiating principle which determined which letters got saved and copied out – it was not simply that they were from the apostle, but was also the way in which they 'burned' into those who received them.

The concept of 'the apostles' is reasonably clear, though there are occasionally slightly uncertain limits as to who is on the list.* They held some responsibility for leadership of the mission, and for the oversight of the churches. They did not see themselves as acting on behalf of God or of the Church on

---

*People beyond the twelve-and-Paul are at intervals called 'apostles'. Thus Barnabas (who is distinguished from the twelve in Acts 4:36–7 and 9:27) is bracketed with Paul as 'apostles' in Acts 14:4; the letter from the Council of Jerusalem in Acts 15 is in the name of the 'apostles and elders', and it seems a fair guess that James, the Lord's brother, who had in some sense chaired the Council, was among the 'apostles' rather than the 'elders' (Paul seems to call him an apostle in Galatians 1:19, though that is not absolutely clear) – but he is nevertheless distinct from the twelve (1 Corinthians 15:5–8). There are other instances, such as Romans 16:7 – or even Philippians 2:25, where Epaphroditus is '*your*' apostle' (to minister to Paul).

their own; and both in Acts 6 and in Acts 15 they are found giving a lead, but associating the rest of the Church in some way with the decision-taking process.

Other ministers (as we would call them – but the word means 'servants') are found as follows:

- Acts 11:27: prophets came to Antioch.
- Acts 11:30: elders (*presbuteroi*) in Jerusalem.
- Acts 13:1: prophets and teachers in Antioch.
- Acts 14:23: elders in the Galatian churches.
- Acts 15:2; 15:6; 15:22; 16:4: apostles and elders in Jerusalem.
- Acts 15:22: leaders among the brothers.
- Acts 20:17: elders at Ephesus – also called bishops (*episkopoi*) and shepherds in 20:28.
- Acts 21:8: Philip the evangelist at Caesarea.
- Acts 21:10: prophet Agabus from Judaea.
- Acts 21:17: elders at Jerusalem.
- Romans 16:1: a woman deacon (*diakonos*) in Cenchrea.
- Romans 16:7: apostles in Rome (no distinct other officers in Acts 28 or in the letter to the Romans).
- In Corinth, apart from the apostles (and Apollos whose role is not defined), no local officers are mentioned in either of the two letters. The only possibility would be the illustrative 'apostles, prophets, teachers, workers of miracles, those with gifts of healing, those who help, administrators [*or* steerers]' in 1 Corinthians 12:28–30 – but there is no indication which, if any, of these actually functioned in Corinth.
- In the letter to the Galatian churches no local officers are mentioned.
- In the (perhaps general) letter to the Ephesians there are no greetings or messages to any local officers, but there is twice a reference to 'apostles and prophets' (2:20; 3:5); and there is a consolidated list in 4:11 of 'apostles, prophets, evangelists, pastors (*poimenes*), teachers'. Again, we do not know which of these officers were to be found in Ephesus, and, although they are very much related to the church and presumably very visible in it, they are a feature of the worldwide Church, and we do not know how they were in action in Ephesus.

- In Philippi, Paul greets the 'bishops and deacons' (1:1). But that is all.
- In the letter to the Colossians, Tychicus is not only a 'fellow-servant' but is also a 'faithful deacon' (4:7).
- In the letters to the Thessalonians there is no mention of any kind of office in the church, but there are 'those who are over you in the Lord and instruct you' (1 Thess. 5:12) – people whom the Thessalonians are to hold in high regard. And there are 'prophesyings' (5:20) which must be respected.
- 1 Timothy 2:7: Paul is 'herald, apostle . . . and teacher to the Gentiles'.
- 1 Timothy 3:1–7: the qualifications for a bishop's office.
- 1 Timothy 3:8–13: the qualifications for a deacon's office.
- 1 Timothy 4:14: Timothy is not to neglect the *charisma* which he has received through prophecy with the laying on of hands of the *presbyterion* (which is apparently a single collective noun for 'the eldership' or 'the presbyterate').
- 1 Timothy 5:1: an 'elder' is not to be abused – but he is contrasted with 'younger men', and may therefore be a literal elder, not the holder of an office.
- 1 Timothy 5:17–20: an acccount of the 'elders'.
- 1 Timothy 5:22: Timothy is not himself to be hasty laying on hands. Could this be connected with office?
- 2 Timothy 1:6: Timothy is to 'stir up' the *charisma* which is in him through the laying on of Paul's hands.
- 2 Timothy 1:11: Paul is again a 'herald and apostle and teacher'.
- 2 Timothy 4:5: Timothy is to do the work of an evangelist and fulfil his ministry (*diakonia*).
- Titus 1:5: Titus is to 'establish' (hardly 'ordain') elders in each city of Crete.
- Titus 1:6–9: the qualifications for an elder – but in 1:7 the elder has become a bishop.
- In the letter to the Hebrews the readers are told to 'remember your leaders' (13:7), who are 'those who keep watch over your lives' and should be obeyed (13:17).
- James 5:14: the sick should send for the elders of the church.

- 1 Peter 5:1: Peter is a 'fellow-elder' writing to the elders, who are to be shepherds (5:2) and bishops (5:2). As in 1 Timothy, the younger are to defer to the elders, which does suggest seniority (in years or in Christian standing) without reference to office (5:5).
- In 2 Peter there is much reference to false teachers and false prophets, and one call (3:2) to revert to the words of the 'holy prophets and the command of the Lord through your apostles'.
- In 2 John and 3 John the author describes himself as 'the elder' in verse 1 of each letter.
- Jude 17: readers are to remember what the apostles of Jesus Christ foretold.
- In Revelation there is an 'angel' of each of the seven churches in Asia; while there is later reference to 'twenty-four elders' (4:4; 5:8), the relevance of such detail to patterns of church life on earth is not easy to discern.

When all these scattered bits of evidence are put together, what general conclusions can be drawn? One has to reply to this that the conclusions do appear to depend *enormously* upon the context and the doctrinal priorities of those drawing them, and upon what is being read back from later stages of church life into these first century situations. With that health warning, here are those which strike one reader of the Bible as significant.

Firstly, it is doubtful whether we are encountering anything as fixed as the concept of 'office' at all. The most fixed category seems to be 'the apostles and prophets', but they are probably not contemporary church officers, but people who have in a once-for-all way shaped and established the foundation truths of the Gospel – this would seem to be the natural sense of Ephesians 2:20; 3:8; Wayne Grudem very convincingly propounds the case that these are one and the same set of people, i.e. 'apostles who are also prophets'.[10] This could well account for 'apostles' and 'prophets' coming first two in the lists in 1 Corinthians 12:28 and Ephesians 4:11, though it is clear that in those cases, two distinct sets of people are being listed. If its reference is as much to the message as to the human beings (which is particularly obvious in Ephesians 2:20 and 3:8), nevertheless it fits the other contexts, where the kinds of ministering, and the substance of what is ministered, is fairly close to the listing of people in both 1 Corinthians 12:28 and Ephesians 4:11.

Secondly, the 'elders' have a fair amount of attestation, though they are in the Pastoral epistles simply contrasted with the 'youngers', suggesting a mere contrast of ages, rather than any kind of appointment.* They are also called 'bishops' (Acts 20:28; Tit. 1:7; 1 Pet. 5:2), which may distinguish status (i.e. 'elder' denotes seniority) from function (i.e. oversight – *episkope*). And the John who wrote 2 and 3 John, certainly thought in the early Church to be *the* apostle John, apparently has no more problem in calling himself 'the elder' than Peter does in calling himself a 'fellow-elder'. There is the intriguing pointing in the 1 Timothy 5:17 passage to elders, 'especially those who labour at speaking and teaching' – which in Presbyterian circles has led by tacit inference to a development of the office of those who do *not* speak and teach – i.e. 'ruling elders'. But all in all it looks as though 'presbyters' had an honoured place in the first-century Church, even if they were not found everywhere (were the Philippian 'bishops' also presbyters?).

Thirdly, the list tails off into the indistinctive. There are 'brothers', 'fellow-workers', 'servants/deacons', and a host of others. Many quite senior people appear without any more distinctive office being attributed to them – including Silas in Acts and in 1 and 2 Thessalonians, Timothy in Acts, 1 and 2 Thessalonians, 1 Corinthians 16:10, Romans 16:21 and elsewhere, and Titus in Galatians 2:1–3 and 2 Corinthians 2:13; 7:6–16; 8:16–24; 12:18. The nearest approach to a visible office is in 'the deacons' at Philippi (Phil.1:1).**

---

*See the contrast (treating men and women alike!) set out in 1 Timothy 5:1–2, and (I would suggest) without a hint of 'office' in the church (unlike 5:17).

**One of the problems here is the generalised implications of the *diakonia* ('service') stem. Should those such as the seven in Acts 6 who were to 'serve tables' (*diakonein*) be for that reason labelled 'deacons', when, at this very inauguration of this 'diaconal' ministry, the apostles said that they were going to give themselves to the 'service' (*diakonia*) of the word and prayer? If Archippus (Col. 4:17) was to 'fulfil his *diakonia*', did that make him a deacon? And was Phoebe a deacon (or deaconess) at Cenchrea, or is the word so general

Fourthly, far more impressive than any of the specific mentions cited above is the plethora of instances which have a total absence of mentions. Whole congregations are being exhorted to sort themselves out before God, they are being told that Jewish believers must not discriminate against Gentile ones, they are being told how to run their assemblies (including when to speak and when not – and how to run the Lord's Supper), they are being encouraged to excommunicate the rebellious and immoral, they are being called on to give money for the saints in Jerusalem – and in it all there are hardly any references to any officers of the Church at all, and what there are are hardly noticeable passing mentions, with virtually nothing about their responsibility in leading the Church from its present immature (and often disrupted sinful) state into that anticipation of heaven which its life is supposed to be. Of course, somewhere in the offing, there are apostles. But they never seem to be present in the churches to whom Paul writes (nor indeed, his own self excepted, in the churches from which he writes), and general statements about their continuing role in the Church after most of them disappear from sight early on in Acts appear to be without good foundation. This does not, I tentatively suggest, mean that we abolish all church offices, but it is a warning against making the forms of them too autocratic, or too doctrinally exclusive, or in any way integral or essential to our doctrine of the Church itself.

Fifthly, we need to round up one false trail. Despite the range of titles used for 'ministers' of the Church, titles which involve some considerable overlapping of meaning, there is one word-stem which does not occur at all. This is of some significance, as it is the word translated into English as 'priest' – in Greek the *hiereus* stem. Its absence is no mere accident of the scattered use of titles for ministers, but is rather due to a

---

that the AV was correct to call her simply a 'servant'? And if it is unspecific, then who were 'the deacons' at Philippi and what made them so? After all, in Ephesians 4:12 those whom we today would call 'ministers' (that is, the various categories in Ephesians 4:11) are there 'to equip [*or* kit out] the saints for the work of *diakonia*.' With 'ministers/ministry' 'servants/service' deacons/diaconate' all being translations of the same word-stem, it is only too easy to come to conclusions in English which are undemonstrable in the Greek.

clear distinction in the theology of the New Testament – a distinction which, it would appear, was mirrored in the Church's linguistic usage even before the theology was laid out, as it duly was, in the letter to the Hebrews. No words from that stem are ever used of specific offices or officers within the life of the Church, and no doctrine which relies upon that terminology has any basis in the New Testament. (Appendix 1, pp. 311–16, sets out the doctrine in detail.)

Sixthly, wherein lay the continuity of the churches? If in Corinth they were not to divide themselves to follow specific different people by forming admiring clones of the like-minded, by what other means were they to sustain a stability of life? While Paul is prepared to aver that he has upon him daily 'the care of all the churches' (2 Cor. 11:28), in actual practice most local congregations must have functioned for months if not years on end without seeing an apostle, or an emissary of one, or receiving a letter from one. If we are to take the evidence of the New Testament seriously, unity and continuity in those circumstances derived first from the apostolic message of Jesus Christ, and secondly from the self-sacrificing love for each other within the body of Christ of the disciples. The life of the congregation centred round the threefold 'word of the Gospel': firstly, the Old Testament; secondly, the stories of Jesus ('Gospel'); thirdly, the letters and admonitions of the apostles (the slowly growing collection of apostolic letters). While in the first generation much of this must have been taught and learned orally, it was the fixing of it in people's hearts which guaranteed the Church holding together, both in the local setting and throughout the known world. There was a clear habit of gathering in a rhythm which, as a very minimum, included a meeting (probably the Lord's meal) on the first day of the week. While particular officers might be steering and administering such meetings, they were doing so as servants of the saints, and were forbidden to 'lord it over' the people (cf. Mark 10:35–49 (which must have been very live among the apostles and in local leaders); 1 Thess. 2:7; 1 Pet. 5:3).

However different the people were from each other, however divergent their hopes or plans for the witness and work and mutual care of their church, yet in Christ they belonged to each other, and constrained by their own baptism, by the message of

Jesus, and by their unity in the Spirit, and sometimes given extra seriousness by persecution from outside, the people of God lived on in each city as *the* expression locally of the body of Christ.

This does leave us, in the light of today's questions, to ask what kind of succession to the apostles is envisaged or adumbrated within the pages of the New Testament. I discern the following pointers:

1   Both from a 'college' in Jerusalem, and by individuals going around the Mediterranean, the apostles did exercise some authority of a teaching kind over the worldwide Church.

2   Nevertheless, evangelism by persons other than the apostles did bring churches into existence in various places where the apostles had not been, and the converts in those places, being baptised, were viewed as fully incorporated into the worldwide Church, and were holding fast to the apostles' teaching even if they had never seen an apostle or even hardly knew there were such people.

3   The latest New Testament documents we have, which may be the best witness to how the Church of the second and third generation viewed the question, give us the following picture:

- Of Paul to Timothy in 2 Timothy:*

  'Keep as a pattern of sound words what you have heard from me ... guard the the good deposit through the Holy Spirit' (2 Tim.1:13–14).

  'And what you have heard from me through many witnesses, commit to faithful men who will be able to teach others also' (2 Tim. 2:2).

  'For yourself, continue in the things you have learned and in which you are established, knowing from which people you learned them – and from being a child you have known the holy scriptures' (2 Tim. 3:14).

---

*If it is doubted whether Paul wrote 2 Timothy, then, paradoxically, on that very assumption, we have a somewhat later witness as to what the post-apostolic Church thought was their apostolic deposit – and it is arguably telling us exactly what we want to know – more exactly even than if Paul had written it. The same applies to the following quotations from 2 Peter and from the writings of John.

- Of Peter in 1 and 2 Peter:
  'In your hearts keep Christ holy as Lord; and be ready always to give an answer to anyone who asks you the reason for the hope that is in you' (1 Pet. 3:15).
  'So I will always remind you of these things, although you know them and are deeply grounded in the truth you have. But I judge that it is right, as long as I am in this tent [i.e. of the body], to rouse your memory; for I know that the putting off of this tent is coming soon, as our Lord Jesus Christ has shown me, and I will bend every effort to see that after my departure you will remember these things' (2 Pet. 1: 12–15).
- Of John in John's gospel and in 1 John:
  'These are written that you might believe that Jesus is the Christ the Son of God and that believing you might have life through his name' (John 20:31).
  'This is the disciple who testifies about these events and has written them down, and we know that his testimony is true' (John 21:24).
  'That which was from the beginning, which we have seen with our eyes, which we have looked on and our hands have handled – this concerns the Word of life; and the life was made visible and we have seen him and bear witness to him and announce to you the life eternal which was with the Father and appeared to us' (1 John 1:1–2).

I do not think we can see any sign whatsoever of the apostles handing on their office, though we shall look to see how the early Church itself understood that question. The evidence from the day of Pentecost to the death of the last apostle runs in line with the extracts above – that the great issue to the apostles themselves was the handing on of the witness to Jesus, handing on indeed the knowledge of Jesus, and ensuring that the Church remained loyal to that deposit of faith. From that standpoint, the apostles had no need or cause to hand on their office, for in the New Testament writings they were handing on their own witness, or, to put it another way, in the role that they had in the Church of the first century they have retained in action from that day to this, giving us the faith of Christ in normative form, and recalling each successive generation to living by the revealed truth of the Scriptures as the believers of each generation have show signs of sliding away from both apostolic faith and practice.

It is fair to say therefore that, however romantic or appealing the ideas woven round an 'apostolic succession' of bishops succeeding to offices held by the apostles, it cannot be demonstrated from the New Testament. The whole bequest of the apostles is summed up in the apostolic faith, and the deposit is available to us in the writings of the key apostles collected for us in the New Testament. Those initial apostles still hold authority on behalf of Jesus Christ in the Church today by their writings, and the Church of God is apostolic today in so far as it lives a corporate discipleship under that authority of the apostles. The Church may well have leaders in each generation, and even have good and godly ways of appointing them. But there does not appear to be an office of divine appointment which is the passing down, over the centuries, of the role of the apostles.

(See Appendix 1, pp. 311–16, for a Note on what priesthood has the ministry and pp. 321–8 for a Note on theories of orders.)

5 An Assessment of the Biblical Data

If we look back on the emerging profile of the New Testament Church, but start to ask some latter-day questions, how does the picture then look? I offer a brief summary which is then the point of comparison in the rest of the book.

1 The incarnation, ministry, death, resurrection and ascension of Jesus and the coming of the Holy Spirit have brought in a new era – indeed, the 'last times' – in which there will be a people of God thereafter to live in the light of this great intervention by God (as the Jews lived in the light of the escape from Egypt and the entry into the Promised Land).

2 The Old Testament people of God, the Jews, have been transformed by Jesus and the Spirit into a 'new Israel' of Jews and Gentiles alike – the Church.

3 The body is visible, is one, is alive in the Spirit, and is the instrument of God's mission on earth and the building of his kingdom.

4 The body is made visible by the entry rite of baptism which unites the vastly disparate persons (including parents and children) into one body. To be converted is to be baptised and incorporated into the Church; and the Church not so much comprises individual converts binding themselves together to form a company which is a logical construct from their individual conversion; rather, the Church itself is the object of God's love which is being built up as he adds people to it. In terms of classic discussion of this issue, therefore, the New Testament is 'organic' in its understanding of the Church, not 'voluntarist'. 'Voluntarism' is a product of Western Protestantism which, having seized upon a doctrine of individual justification through faith, then so enthrones that individualistic doctrine as to make all other scriptural

truths function as servants of it. But in the beginning it was not so.

5 This church lives in the light of the great works of Jesus and the giving of the Spirit by dependence upon the 'word' – always including the written Old Testament but also including that which was originally the oral accounts of Jesus (until they were written in definitive form) and the writings of the apostles, mostly Paul's letters, as they become more and more available through copying – and the task of the writings ('Scripture') is constantly to correct and recall the Church to the person, the love, the teachings and the standards of Jesus. This dynamic relationship continues all down time, as the same Scripture addresses each new generation of believers, and as they, richly endowed as they may be from their tradition, nevertheless open up themselves to be reformed by the authority of the original apostles, and their witness to Jesus.

6 The church of Jesus is the extension of his resurrection, as one worldwide body, with not only mutual belongingness but actual interlocking of the activities of all the members. This organic relationship joins together in Christ those who differ enormously from each other in colour, intelligence, class, ethnicity, culture and wealth. It transcends nationalisms, and creates an international community. But the interlockingness means that the differing members should *work* as a unity.

7 The body is sustained in its unity by the baptised rhythmically sharing the meal which Jesus gave to his disciples to be observed 'in commemoration' of him.

8 The sharing the meal is the test-case or paradigm for a life of mutual meeting and sharing.

9 The wider sharing includes support of the needy, works of service to others, and ministering the good news of Jesus and its application to life orally to each other when they meet.

10 There are various forms of ministers to be found within local congregations, as officers with tasks of leadership, teaching and pastoral care. But the forms are not set in concrete, and they exist to facilitate the 'ministry' (or service) of all the members.

It may also be useful, once the questions of a later period are allowed to engage with the scriptural account, to observe what is *not* manifest.

1   There is no set pattern of liturgical services (nor even much indication as to how frequently the Lord's meal should be held).

2   There is very little emphasis, if any, upon who should lead the church (universal or local), and certainly none upon who should or does succeed the apostles, let alone upon who should preside at the Lord's meal.

3   There is no possibility of the Church becoming denominations or locally gathered separate, independent congregations – and similarly there is no question of anyone 'leaving' a local church unless either moving to another city (with letters of commendation) or actually lapsing or apostasising from the faith; and, to take an extreme example, in the seven churches of Asia in Revelation 1—3, where whole churches were apparently lapsing into heresy or immorality or both, the 'few' who had not compromised themselves were to 'hold fast' rather than get out. Those who, on an organic understanding of the Church, had not become members by 'opting in' or 'joining' subsequent to conversion, could hardly, when things were difficult, 'opt out'.

4   There are no church buildings, no holy places, no pilgrimages or shrines – and most expositions of 'temple' or 'the dwelling-place of the Spirit' would locate these 'holy places' *in the people*, not in earthly buildings.

5   There is no distinctive priesthood attaching to Christian ministers.

Part II

The Early Church

6 The Authority of the Early Church

If we hold to the supreme authority of Scripture, and to the foundation point that it alone is non-negotiable as the word of God, then we might expect to find two different tendencies at work in the life of the post-apostolic Church. Firstly, we would expect deepening reflection upon Scripture, the distillation of apostolic teaching in a harmonious form from Scripture, and the learning of the disciplines of applying those teachings relevantly in succeeding generations. Secondly, however, we must expect not only the refining but also the corrupting of tradition to be taking effect. We are not therefore in any sense bound by the ways of 'the early Church'; and those who have claimed to be so have very often been highly selective in what they have embraced and what they have ignored from the patristic period. We go to that period to examine the formative effect of the centuries upon the *de facto* Church. But we do not have any preconceived assumption that they will have got it right to the extent that what developed was, by the mere fact that it developed, God's further revelation, or that mere proven antiquity will canonise a practice, a formula or an office. While we need a high doctrine of tradition (see below), each generation of Christians is supposed to be in closely locked dialogue with the original Scripture, and in each generation the life of the Church is to be recalled from lapsing, to be retooled doctrinally, and to be recharged spiritually by the power of the original written Scripture, working in that generation's believers by the power of the Holy Spirit.

Kenneth Woolcombe once issued a warning that we must not talk about the early Fathers as though they all lived in the same town in the same years and sat round the same table with each other.[1] Far from expounding an agreed set of patristic propositions, they are usually found wrestling with Scripture as if from scratch to find appropriate answers to new questions, unforeseen heresies, and pressing pastoral needs. They are spread over a thousand miles of the Mediterranean and its littoral territories; they are spread (on the most conservative count) over five centuries of time; they write in two main languages, Greek and Latin, and in various others also; and what they do not tell us is as important as what they do.

I believe this last point is worth illustrating. In Justin Martyr (mid second century) there is an account of Sunday worship in Rome, designed to reassure the emperor that Christians represented no threat to the safety of the empire. It is a detailed and fascinating account; it is the earliest such detailed account that we possess; and we can build quite a large set of inferences upon it.

But suppose, for the sake of argument, we approached the story from the other end – from what we do *not* know about Sunday worship. From the deaths of Peter and Paul to the time of Hippolytus (notable for the first substantial set of liturgical texts we possess) there are 150 years, and Justin's account tells us of customs at Rome about two-thirds of the way through that period. Within that same time, how many Christian congregations in the Mediterranean basin took part in Sunday worship? If there were, on average, around 300 congregations (surely a conservative guess?), then the 52 Sundays of the year would mean that in each year there were 15,600 Sunday worship events (even 'liturgies', but we must be careful about not pretending to know too much – for that is exactly what the enquiry is pursuing). Over the 150 years, this would add up to 2,340,000 worship events. If we then revert to Justin and ask how long a period at Rome his account might cover, we might presume that, as he tells of settled practice, his description of worship of a reasonably consistent kind would cover some hundreds of Sundays. We may conceivably allow that the Roman use would have extra prestige and be copied elsewhere – but that is technically an anachronism, and we should be wary of it. We may even allow also that practice after 215 throws light upon earlier developments (though in fact we have little reliable third-century evidence either); and again we must be very careful about that principle.

We may put together wisps of evidence from other writers apart from Justin. But, when all that is done, there are in those 150 years at least 2,500,000 Sunday worship assemblies of which we actually know nothing, and under 1000 of which we can learn anything at all. So do we actually know, or can we pretend to know, how the post-apostolic second-century Church worshipped on Sundays? Was it similiar in Egypt and in Spain? Or was it vastly different? Was it different when a place was under persecution? Was it different in one place simply through the cycle of the year? Or was it obstinately unchanging? Did it differ as different leaders arose? Or was there a programme which was more or less enduring under different leaders? Were there song-writers and musicians? Was there architecture and ceremonial? Was there preaching from the front, or varied contributions from the lay people? Were the Scriptures studied informally and interactively, or were they simply the subject of episcopal exposition? Were there *charismata*? What happened to the *agape*? We are completely at a loss. Even with Justin himself, we do not know how typical he was – and, though we may guess at the answer, we might yet find that in him we are on to something as rare as a lottery winner.

With that warning – that even apparently valuable evidence has to be seen as a minuscule and unquantifiable element among great tracts of the unknown – we return to look at some general characteristics of the early Church (as far as they can be ascertained), and in the process perhaps to do some re-angling of a few received traditions.

It will be immediately obvious that this reading of history is at odds with an often-asserted doctrine – that what developed in the early Church was by, the providence of God, part of his revealing himself to us, and is beyond appeal or correction. If this were credible, then the most detailed investigation of every early Father would be requisite, for the writings of each would have become part of a larger canon of Scripture, and we should be committed *a priori* to the expectation that the writings of the Fathers could be harmonised, that they would express a continuing revelation of God to his people, and that the developing pattern of doctrine and life which we detected as we watched that further self-revealing of God

would become binding on us. It is a big idea, and it has echoes
in the life of Eastern Orthodoxy. But, for reasons I now set
out, it is not my understanding of the status of early Church
history.

My central purpose in the relatively brief enquiry here is to
show that no such notion of the autonomy of Church tradition
is to be found in the early Fathers themselves. Scripture
remains supremely authoritative, and the witness of the
Fathers is of persons bending their energies to understand
Scripture and apply scriptural truth in their own generation.
We are free, on their principles as well as ours, to affirm
that they are subordinate to Scripture, and that that is the
controlling principle of their church life. To get the best sense
of this perspective of theirs, it is to the earliest Fathers, few
and scattered though they are, that this Part II of my book
refers.

7   Apostles and Apostolicity

We have already seen that the building of the apostolic Church
'upon the foundation of the apostles and prophets' refers primarily to the witness of the apostles to Jesus Christ and his
resurrection (as on pp. 53–4). We have also seen the relative
imprecision of the various offices within the Church, from the
passing references in the New Testament writings. And we
have seen that the apostles were, above all, concerned to pass
on their message to those who came after. This was achieved
in general terms by a kind of 'fading in' of the New Testament
as there came a 'fading out' of the apostles themselves. By
the turn of the first century there were collections of New
Testaments writings in regular use 'in church', and the concept
of 'the gospel' and 'the apostle' was already leading to a
drawing together of four gospels and of the various epistles
into two sets of authoritative 'Scriptures' (2 Pet. 3:16); and
that provision for reading in church still to this day governs
the order of the books of the New Testament.* When we open
our Bibles, we are looking directly at the way in which the
'writings/Scriptures' impressed themselves on the sub-
apostolic Church (and Acts and Revelation were fitted between
and after these two major collections).

How then did the authority of the apostles relate to the
contemporary leadership of the Church in succeeding gener-

---

*This 'liturgical' shaping of the collections of writings is delightfully
(if not totally convincingly) set out by Irenaeus: 'As there are four
zones of the world in which we live and four principal winds, while
the Church is dispersed throughout the world . . . it is fitting that she
should have four pillars . . . The Word . . . has given us the gospel
under four aspects' (Irenaeus, *Adv. Haereses* III.xi.8).

ations? There are various latterday accounts which lay out for our adherence the following scenario:

1 The apostles provided, by the laying on of hands, for a 'succession' of bishops down history, bishops who in some sense are living apostles in the life of the Church.

2 This succession antedates the settling of the canon of Scripture and in some sense stands over it to interpret it, especially as it was church leaders who decided what is canon.

3 The early Church 'Fathers' developed and defined the Christian faith in such a way as to provide an authoritative pattern of understanding of the Bible, a pattern which is therefore the coherent authority to which we ought to look back.

But there is a prior question – is this a fair reading of history?

Firstly, we note the developments in the ministry. From the very shadowy situation in the New Testament, we find the development almost immediately of a threefold pattern – bishops, presbyters and deacons. It does not appear universally identical – in the Didache in the early second century the presbyters are still also bishops (though the 'bishops and deacons' are supplemented or even upstaged, by itinerant 'apostles' and 'prophets' – who may well in turn, by overstaying their welcome, prove to be false).

There is a similar imprecision in a letter from Rome to the Corinthians in AD 96. Irenaeus, in the late second century, attributes this letter to the time of Clement, third bishop of Rome, and it is thus known as '1 Clement', though both the letter itself and the Irenaean account state only that it was sent by 'the church at Rome'. Rome, it seems, had a bishop, even if he did not actually initiate, write or sign the letter. But Corinth had no bishop! Or possibly it had no presbyters, for possibly its bishops were presbyters. At one point the author says: '[The apostles] appointed their first-fruits ... to be bishops and deacons for future believers ... and is it any wonder that those who in Christ were entrusted by God with such a work appointed the officials just mentioned?'[1]

The very point of the letter, that presbyters should not be dismissed from office, is reinforced by saying that they exercise 'the bishop's office'. Were the Corinthians presbyterians? Or were they embryonic 'high' churchmen? For in connection with 'offerings and services' the letter makes cryptic reference to (Old Testament) 'priestly' tasks: 'For to the high priest the proper services have been given, and to the priests the proper offices have been assigned, and upon the Levites the proper ministries have been imposed. The layman is bound by the layman's rules.'[2] This varies from the other references to ministers in that it does look remarkably like a threefold order of ministry with specific functions (possibly cultic or liturgical ones), and some limitations upon the layman. If so, it may also be significant for later developments by its citation of Old Testament Levitical offices as precedents, or at least as illustrations, for the distinctive ministries within the post-apostolic Church. However, the main impression of the letter is that it is steeped in Scripture, full of verbatim quotes and ready to refer to Paul's own first letter to the Corinthians as it demonstrates the Corinthian tendency – even 40 years previously, in Paul's time – to split into factions. Clearly, we should note, 1 Corinthians itself was perfectly well known in Rome; the collections of writings ('Scripture') were getting around.

All becomes clear – or nearly so – in Ignatius, bishop of Antioch, around the year 107. He is going to Rome to be martyred for his faith, and he writes to other churches in Asia and Europe as he goes, including a letter to Polycarp, bishop of Smyrna, and an advance letter to the Romans themselves. The threefold structure of bishop (singular), presbyters and deacons comes out very strongly in his letters. He views adherence to the bishop as crucial for good order and avoidance of schism, and for holding on to the truth. But there are certain things he does not say:

1   He never mentions any method of appointment (such as the laying on of hands).

2   Amazingly, he never mentions a bishop at Rome in his letter to the Romans.

3   Equally, he has the surprising doctrine that, as he is being removed from his church of Antioch, Jesus Christ will have to be their bishop. So it is difficult to trace anyone to succeed him – there is no mention of 'succession' anywhere in his writings.

4   He does not place the bishop in the position of the apos-

tles; if anything the bishop is in the place of God and the presbyters in the place of the apostles! This kind of reference comes at least three times and possibly more.[3] But it refers to the discipline of the good ordering of the local church. When it comes to the teaching authority of the apostles, he distances himself: 'Be subject to the precepts of the Lord and of the apostles'; and 'I do not give you orders like Peter and Paul; they were apostles, I am a convict'.[4] So, through all the emphasis on bishops, he never says they hold an apostolic office.

5　He does not use 'priestly' language of the threefold orders – instead he calls Jesus 'the high priest' in strict conformity to the letter to the Hebrews.[5]

6　He does not have anything like a pattern of diocesan oversight of many congregations – the most natural understanding of his role of the bishop is as a very local chief pastor, comparable to today's parish incumbent or at most to a team rector.[6]

Against these omissions, we also ought to note that Ignatius is full of Scripture, quoting it all through his letters, and assuming that his readers both know the Scriptures and share his total acceptance of their authority.

Other authors of the second century have no problem in referring to bishops. Polycarp was bishop of Smyrna from before Ignatius' time till after 155 (i.e. probably for more than 50 years). Justin has 'he who presides' as a reference to the bishop (once again there is no naming of the bishop of Rome!); but in his *Dialogue with Trypho* he makes an (erroneous) comparison between the 'twelve bells' of the high priest (in fact it was the names on the breastplate that were twelve), and these were 'a symbol of the twelve apostles, who depend on the power of Christ, the eternal priest; and through their voice it is that all the earth has been filled with the glory and grace of God and of his Christ'.[7] Once again there is a clear understanding that the bequest of the apostles is their message; and somehow he manages both his *Dialogue* and his *Apology* without reference (apart from 'he who presides' in worship) to leaders, bishops, other ministers of his own day (and he in Rome too), or to any principle of succession.

So the crucial witness after Ignatius is Irenaeus. It is he

who first gives us a concept of 'succession' – and his concept is so different from latter-day notions that we need to consider it carefully. Irenaeus was bishop of Lyons for roughly the last two decades of the second century; he came to Gaul from Smyrna, where he had in his youth sat at the feet of Polycarp; and he points out that Polycarp had known the apostle John. He was disturbed at the apparent virulence of heretical (often Gnostic) doctrines seeping into the life of the church in Rome, a city he visited in 177 shortly before he became the bishop in Lyons. And he thereafter made it almost his life's work to write five books *Against Heresies*.

His treatment of episcopal succession comes early in Book III. In Chapter ii he states that the 'tradition of the apostles' is preserved 'by means of the successions of the presbyters in the churches' – which is a slightly surprising concept to modern episcopalians. But in Chapter iii he gives an actual succession of bishops. He introduces his discussion by saying: 'We are in position to reckon up those who were by the apostles instituted as bishops in the churches', and '[men] whom they were leaving behind as their successors, delivering up their own place of government to these men'. As it would be 'tedious' to set out the successions in all the cities, he takes Rome as his archetypal illustration: he states that Peter and Paul 'committed into the hands of Linus' the episcopal office; he then names the succession (including Clement as number three) right down to Eleutherius (number 12) of his own day. The whole point of this succession, he ends, is to demonstrate that the truth held and taught by the apostles has been handed down to our own day.

Irenaeus also cites his own 'succession', in some ways more colourful and memorable than the account of the bishops at Rome – for Irenaeus learned from Polycarp, Polycarp ('appointed by apostles in Asia as bishop in Smyrna') from John, and John from Jesus. This is notable to us, as this historical linkage is *not* succession in a place, nor succession by the laying on of hands, nor even succession in an office – but succession *to a truth*. The receiving of the message by Polycarp and by Irenaeus in each case preceded their becoming bishops, and was in no sense tied to any such succession. They succeeded *to a truth*.

We have to be aware of the reason why Irenaeus was recounting successions. It was a far cry from the exercise the Anglican Churches of Britain and Ireland have gone through with the Lutheran Churches of the Baltic and Nordic countries in recent years. Our interest today is apparently in whether the episcopal ordinations were preserved intact in a tactual succession (and a point on that issue was kindly stretched in Denmark's favour). But Irenaeus' interest is in whether the *apostolic teaching* was preserved unchanged through the generations from the apostles. There is no mention of the laying on of hands. It is all part of his polemic against the Gnostic and other heretics who were threatening church life in his time. And the polemic, reinforced in Chapter iv, goes like this: there were no Valentinians before Valentinus (at the time of the ninth bishop of Rome); and there were no Marcionites before Marcion (at the time of the tenth bishop of Rome). These heretics are, through their latter-day provenance, clearly upstarts and thus self-evidently mere pretenders to the truth. They appear, he is saying, in sharp contrast to us, the orthodox, who have openly throughout the world held to the apostolic teachings since the days of the apostles – as can be shown by charting our succession of teachers.

Now this is not simply a case of saying: we have an open succession of teachers, and so you had better believe the bishop of Rome (or whomever) in our present day. Such a procedure would certainly lend itself to what we today would call 'Chinese whispers', in which a message passed secretly along 12 persons will emerge from the twelfth as rather different from the way it was fed into the chain by the first. No, quite the reverse: Irenaeus is placing the Scripture itself – the beginning of the chain of teaching – into the discussion, so that the current teaching can be, and should be, easily checked against the original revelation. There was a greater need in his time, it might be argued, than there is in ours to trust the leaders of the Church to get the Gospel right, for there were no printed Bibles and little or nothing of Bibles in private homes, so the bishop had to embody the truth of God, and proffer and deploy it on every possible occasion – and the average church member had to take it on trust from him. But that did not mean that the bishop's teaching was autonomous or unaccountable; no, it was always open to the test of Scripture, and the test was clearly envisaged as part of the dynamics of leadership.

Irenaeus even handles, in Chapter iv, two interesting test-cases – one hypothetical, one actual. The hypothetical one is this: 'How would it be if the apostles themselves had not left us writings? Would it not be necessary to follow the course of the tradition which they handed down to those to whom they did commit the Churches?' The logic of this is very clear: we do have the writings, we do receive our teaching straight from the writings, but, in, a hypothetical worst case, we would go back as far as we can (long before the Gnostics) to those who heard the word from the twelve. Fortunately, the writings (that is, the 'Scriptures') are in fact available to us and are, as the argument makes clear, the given prime source for what we are to believe.

The actual case he quotes is comparable, and runs on in sequence to the above: '[To this course of tradition] many nations of those barbarians who believe in Christ do assent . . . without paper or ink [and are highly orthodox]. Those who, in the absence of written documents, have believed this faith, are barbarians, so far as regards our language.' We should just note that 'barbarians' are not necessarily uncivilised, but they are without the benefit of Greek or Latin (their voices sound like 'bar-bar-bar'!). That is the point being made about their not understanding 'our language'. Irenaeus here is so evidently citing a necessary exception (as we might with a blind person without benefit of Braille) as to establish the norm that under-lies it – that the Church at large *has* recourse to the Scriptures and *can* check out from what was fed into the chain of witnesses the reliability of what comes out from it.

If we then return to the very beginning of Book III, we find Irenaeus setting up the whole principle of Scripture as the starting-point in dealing with heretics. In Chapter i he describes how the four gospels came to be (and we have to remember that the arch-heresiarch Marcion only allowed out of the four a truncated Luke into his canon); and then he begins Chapter ii thus:

When, however, they are confuted from the Scriptures, they turn round and accuse these same Scriptures, as if they were not correct, nor of authority, and [assert] that they are ambiguous, and that the truth cannot be extracted from them by those who are ignorant of tradition. For [they allege] the truth was not delivered by means of written documents, but viva voce.

Could an early Father speak more clearly to us? He is saying:

1 The truth was delivered to us directly from the apostles by written documents, the Scriptures.

2 These Scriptures are unambiguous to read and they convey their message clearly and authoritatively.

3 It is improper to suggest that a separate or superior unwritten tradition should be put forward over against the Scriptures.

It is only after that, and in exposition of that, that he gives his famous lists of succession in Chapter iii. It is frankly astonishing how the concept of 'succession' has been distorted by history from his scripturally based starting-point. And, to make assurance doubly sure, there is another passage in Book I, which appears to clinch the argument:

Since, therefore, the entire Scriptures, the prophets and the Gospels, can be clearly, unambiguously and harmoniously understood by all (though not all believe them); and since they proclaim that one only God . . . formed all things . . . as I have shown from the very words of Scripture . . . these persons will seem truly foolish who blind their eyes to such a clear demonstration.[8]

I therefore register a provisional protest against the (very gently propounded) exposition of Irenaeus that we find in Michael Ramsey: 'In the greatest of the anti-gnostic theologians, St Irenaeus, we find this twofold emphasis on Scripture and on the Apostolic succession. He is led to this twofold emphasis solely through his concern with the essential revelation.'[9] I would counter-contend that Irenaeus' 'Apostolic succession' is a consistency in holding apostolic teaching, and that his citing of the successive teachers of the faith is, in the context of his whole argument, a mere passing illustration of the importance and the unchanging character of what is taught.

It is interesting too to find that that great over-stater, Gregory Dix, is inevitably attracted to Irenaeus (to be frank, Irenaeus, with all the limitations we are seeing, is the best hope of finding anything much for a Dix to cling to). So he in turn writes: 'Thus the doctrine of the "Apostolic Succession" of bishops as it is advanced, for example by St Irenaeus, makes first and foremost a theological statement about bishops in the Church.'[10] To this we must retort with an alternative (and less loaded) finding: 'Thus the doctrine of the "Succession" of bishops as it is advanced, for example by St Irenaeus, makes first and foremost a theological statement about apostolic truth in the Church.'

This in no sense is to deny that there was a threefold order of ministers in the Church in Irenaeus' day (though we have seen that he, like some of his predecessors, quite unselfconsciously calls the bishops 'presbyters' when it pleases him to do so). It is to deny that the bishops were other than servants of the revealed word. Although the written evidence is very fragmentary, it does look as though by the end of the second century there were bishops, presbyters and deacons throughout the world, and that the episcopal structuring of the Church's life and oversight was taken for granted (it does not seem to have come into question).* It is, however, to say that the bishops were only in a very qualified way 'successors to the apostles', and that the original apostles had an authority in their writings to which all in following generations were to submit. The strongest general impression I have from reading the second-century authors is that they opened Scripture freely, assumed its meaning would be clear to others, and handled it freely, suggesting that, apart perhaps from slowly solidifying central quasi-credal statements, they were not bound by an interpretative tradition, let alone an hierarchically imposed one. From my own standpoint I think they made

---

*There is a certain openness, for instance, in Tertulllian's *De Baptismo* from North Africa in the last years of the second century. He does not particularly mind who officiates at baptism (though it should be the senior person around, and the permission of the bishop should be given – ch. xvii); and when he is describing the anointing and laying on of a hand after baptism, he does not indicate who anoints or whose hand it is that does it! (chs vii, viii).

mistakes and at intervals were frankly fanciful. But I am thereby all the more convinced that they were simply treating themselves as people subject to the written word.

Space does not permit a following through of this. But a comprehensive sweep of the later Fathers may still allow this kind of statement:

> Right down to the eighth century it was still possible for John of Damascus, the systematizer of Eastern theology, to refer to biblical revelation in general as 'the divine tradition', to claim the Bible as the sole channel of revelation, and to urge that nobody should try to inquire too curiously into matters of religion that fell outside its venerable limits (*fid. orth.* 1.1).[11]

What we totally lack from the second century is any emphasis upon forms of ordination, let alone an account or evaluation of tactual succession. Irenaeus uses untechnical words like 'appointed' or 'constituted' about the bringing into office of bishops. We lack not only liturgical forms (if such there were), but even a passing mention. A tactual succession is no doubt fairly likely – but it receives no treatment whatsoever, and might itself have been worked out in different ways. The laconic accounts of the succession of one bishop to another over a period of two centuries or more, as reported in Eusebius of Caesarea, emphasise the importance attached to the fact of a succession, but never mention the participation of other bishops, and frequently report a succession occurring (sometimes because of martyrdom) during a time of persecution; and the naturalness of the succession then reported suggests a purely local event. All this would be consistent with a bishop appointing his successor by naming him in his will, *or* with the local church meeting to elect (and thus appoint) from scratch after the death of the previous incumbent. This is very much in line with the evidence of Jerome in the fourth century, who states that at Alexandria, from the time of St Mark (the reputed first bishop) to the end of the second century, whenever a bishop died, the presbyters then chose one of themselves to succeed him. The first evidence of actual forms of ordination comes in Hippolytus, around 215 – and even then the text and its date and status are liable to all the qualifications which have been raised in respect of the apostolic tradition generally.[12] It looks, indeed, as though succession in the leading and teaching office was of much greater significance than the laying of episcopal hands on the head.* And succession itself occurred *after* a bishop died, without there being any suggestion of existing duly consecrated assistant (or coadjutor!) bishops waiting in the wings to succeed when the crucial decease occurred.

No one could deny that Cyprian in the mid third century takes the treatment further and begins to solidify the doctrine with, 'Where the bishop is, there is the catholic Church'. He has to deal with a major revolt against a bishop, and the strong reaction in turn bids up the doctrine. But the apostolic Church is by then already well down the line.

There is a further feature of the overstatement of the role of the episcopate with which I began this chapter. It has been conventional to say that the threefold order antedates the formation of the canon of Scripture, and in one sense guided and controlled that process, which is therefore a kind of paradigm of the authority of the bishops and tradition. To this there are three interrelated lines of answer:

(a) The church and/or its leaders did not at any point pick and choose books to form the canon of the New Testament as the description would suggest. It is rather that the Scriptures won their way by enforcing themselves upon the Church. We have already looked at the origins of the New Testament writings and, if the inferences drawn have any credibility, then it is not so much that a set of writings on a library shelf were pulled off by a bishop who said, 'We could make these the canon of Scripture'; rather, the books which impressed were immediately conserved, copied, and (within the normal limits of human sin) obeyed as the word of God virtually from the point when they were first written, despatched and received. If they were available (for example, on a library shelf) it was because they were *already* recognised as Scripture. I call an expert witness:

---

*The lack is sufficient for even a convinced 'Catholic' like Arthur Couratin to say: 'In the first centuries, it is bottoms on thrones that count more than hands on heads' (casual conversational piece).

But did not the church select the canon? And does not that mean that early catholicism is the norm rather than the NT as such? No! To say the church chose the canon is a misleading half-truth. A closer approximation would be to say that the church *recognized* the canon. That is to say, early catholicism recognized that there were certain documents which had been exercising authority within a widening circle of churches since they were delivered to their first readers. It was the fact that the Gospels and Paul were being acknowledged and were already functioning as 'canonical' more or less from the beginning which made it inevitable that they would be recognized as canonical when the idea of a closed canon became important . . . In a very real sense the major NT documents chose themselves; the NT canon chose itself![13]

If the effort to convey the idea that 'the church chose the canon' is undertaken in the interests of erecting an ecclesiastical authority, which sits over Scripture as a supreme interpreter and thus canonises church authority itself, what conclusions can be drawn from failure of that idea to convince? Surely that Scripture, having once asserted its authority over the Church, having demonstrated its character as an 'external' voice from God towards his Church, retains its supreme authority and must be allowed down history to address the Church with that authority, and to command, correct and empower us?

(b) But did the Church never take decisions about the New Testament canon? It is an interesting question, but, despite all the hassles arising from Marcion in the second century, and various queries until the fourth century about the standing of a tiny number of the books, the broadest answer to the question is, 'No'. This is in line with Dunn's judgement quoted above. Lectionary uses contributed (as noted earlier) the existing arrangement of gospels and epistles; Marcion provoked some more combative listing of the books; minor queries continued; but no definitive moment ever occurred of a general council defining the list. That did not happen until Trent (hardly a 'general' council) listed the books in the sixteenth century. The first listings which exactly coincide with our New Testament of today are dated from the fourth century, but the mind of the Church had been approaching that asymptotically for two centuries before.

(c) It is at least arguable that, once the premise of the control of Scripture by Church authority is granted, then both Roman and Eastern church structures fit the bill better than the inconsistent and erratic relating to tradition, which is as far as Anglicanism can go. I have argued elsewhere that, to take 'tradition' as supreme authority for the Church actually leads to a magisterium.

Perhaps we have an illustration of this process in the King James Bible. For hundreds of years it has been known as the 'Authorised Version' (AV). In printings as far back as most of us can trace, it has carried the legend on the title page 'Authorised to be read in churches'. It did have a minor authorisation in the 1662 Prayer Book, when the Puritans at the Savoy Conference asked that 'the new translation allowed by authority alone may be used', and the response was that the epistles and gospels were now printed 'according to the last translation'. But no order was made about readings at Morning and Evening Prayer, and no change was made in the Comfortable Words and other sentences of Scripture in the liturgical text; and therefore it is difficult to say that it had been 'authorised'. Perhaps the Puritan word 'allowed' is as far as we can go. But, whatever status, or inadequacies of status, monarchs or parliament gave to the version, it swept the board, drove out all previous translations and *asserted its own authority*. That is roughly how the canon of the New Testament came about.

8 The Universality of the Church

We have seen that in the New Testament the Church was a single entity – a body – across the known world. Much organisational responsibility might lie with the local gathering of the Church in any one town or city – and there were officers there to undertake it and to pastor the flock. Bishops arose in different cities. But the people of God shared 'one Lord, one faith, one baptism' – and one citizenship of the kingdom of God throughout the world. They moved freely from one place to another; they acknowledged no boundaries between their communities and virtually no special 'holy places'; and they were in regular correspondence with each other. The degree to which the persons of the apostles were part of that bonding eludes us, largely because we know so little of the apostles' role (apart from Paul). And we perhaps get the first hints in the New Testament, particularly in the role of Titus in Crete, of an 'oversight' by sub-apostolic persons which, at least in Crete itself, must have given a personal focus of unity within the island. But even that function of *episcope* cannot be shown to have continued as a normative practice through the second century.

We also learn of the concern of one part of the body for another, an extension of the enormous degree of mutual support offered in the post-Pentecost growth of the church in Jerusalem itself (Acts 2:41–7). We read of help from one place to another initially in the 'famine visit' of Barnabas and Saul from Antioch to Jerusalem (Acts 11:29–30), but later in the 'collection' for the 'saints in Jerusalem' which Paul was making on his third missionary journey some 15 years later. There is also evidence of the Philippians (as a particular instance) sending support to Paul, initially in the course of his second missionary journey, when he had gone on from Macedonia into Achaea (Phil. 4:14–16); but also later, when he was in prison, and Epaphroditus arrived with gifts from the church under persecution (Phil. 2:25–31). The mutual belongingness across the world must have been well recognised.

The same pattern is discernible in the post-apostolic writers. If the church of Rome wrote a corrective to the church at Corinth, or the bishop of Antioch wrote to combat Gnosticism in churches he would probably never visit, or the bishop of Smyrna wrote a letter to the Philippians – then they had a profound sense of a common citizenship in the kingdom of Christ.

This is graphically and memorably declared in the late second-century *Epistle to Diognetus*:

For Christians are not distinguished from the rest of humanity by country, language or custom. For nowhere do they live in cities of their own, nor do they speak some unusual dialect, nor do they practise an eccentric lifestyle. This teaching of theirs has not been discovered by the thought and reflection of ingenious men, nor do they promote any human doctrine, as some do. But while they live in both Greek and barbarian cities, as each one's lot was cast, and follow the local customs in dress and food and other aspects of life, at the same time they demonstrate the remarkable and admittedly unusual character of their own citizenship. They live in their own countries, but only as aliens; they participate in everything as citizens, and endure everything as foreigners. Every foreign land is their fatherland, and every fatherland is foreign. They marry like everyone else, and have children, but they do not expose their offspring. They share their food but not their wives. They are 'in the flesh' but they do not live 'according to the flesh'. They live on earth, but their citizenship is in heaven. They obey the established laws; indeed in their private lives they transcend the laws. They love everyone, and by everyone they are persecuted ... In a word, what the soul is to the body, Christians are to the world. The soul is dispersed through all the members of the body, and Christians dwell throughout the cities of the world. The soul dwells in the body, but is not of the body; likewise Christians dwell in the world, but are not of the world.[1]

But the story which begins in parallel to the development of episcopacy then starts to converge with it. The initial bonding had been in a shared baptism into Christ and in a common apostolic faith and teaching, but a degree of leadership authority emerges with the teaching and pastoring role of the bishops, who individually led their sees of the second century – and it is the persons of the bishops who confer to handle disputes and schisms. Polycarp travels to Rome, probably around 155, to discuss the date of Easter with the bishop of Rome, Anicetus. The Church in Gaul sent Irenaeus to Rome, as far as we can tell, to combat heresy there. The schismatics in Carthage appealed from Cyprian to Rome in the mid third century. Bishops in one province of the Roman empire meet together. And the stage is slowly being set for 'ecumenical councils', gatherings of bishops from the whole world.* We know a little of 'provincial' gatherings of bishops. We know of three bishops from Roman England present at the Council of Arles in 314. But the full-blown ecumenical councils were to come to pass after the Peace of Constantine in 313, and were occasioned by the rise of heresies about the nature of the Trinity and the incarnation. The first of these was the Council of Nicaea in 325. It was an instructive if saddening character-istic of the fourth century thereafter that all Christian believers still held to the indivisible unity of the worldwide Church, all were in principle ready to see this expressed in and through the persons of their bishops; but in fact, on the ground, bishops might be attacked within their own cities and in their own congregations for being insufficiently orthodox on sophisticated points of doctrine – and *Sanctiores aures plebis quam corda sunt sacerdotum* ('The ears of the laity are holier than the hearts of the clergy').[2] This oddity, while damaging to the notion that the bishops guard the purity of the faith and keep its expression biblical in each generation, helps (by frantic overstatement) to make the New Testament point that it is not simply that one portion of the Church teaches and

---

*Using 'ecumenical' in its original sense of 'covering the whole inhabited world' (as *oikoumene* in Luke 2:1).

another learns, but that the digesting, testing, conserving and deploying of the apostolic faith belong to the whole people of God together.

The worldwide nature of the Church also meant that, in our modern terms, the whole Church was in communion with itself. Sustaining a visible unity is viewed as vital by virtually all the post-apostolic writers, and Ignatius' injunctions to do nothing without the bishop are arguably a new way of ensuring this. On the whole, heretics tended to function outside the Church, and were therefore simply not of the Church; but the passing years brought danger-signs within the Church. Differences between one place and another were handled by conferencing and, it seems, remaining in communion. But Cyprian of Carthage in the mid third century had to face the most threatening split within the fabric of the church of which he was himself bishop. The details are not significant for these purposes (and they are complex), but he responded with an appalled horror that 'altar is set up against altar'. And, in short, his practical and doctrinal answer is that those who separate from him, the bishop, are not Church – and so far not Church that they cannot confer baptism. Cyprian's Council of Carthage specifically handled the question of those baptised in schism, and stated (over against Stephen, the bishop of Rome, who had been consulted) that those who had undergone a rite like baptism among separated groups but were being reconciled to the Church must be, not rebaptised, but baptised for the first time (as the rite they had undergone was not to be counted as baptism). So tightly was Cyprian ready to draw the boundaries around the worldwide Church. For any part of the Church to be out of communion with other parts was in fact for one or other part not to be the Church – and for Cyprian the test of that was the permanence of the bishop, and the need for the Church in each place to gather round its bishop.

It would be difficult to know what freedom of opinion remained after Cyprian's time. Was it legitimate for one person, or the church in one place, to think with Stephen, and for another person, or the church in another place, to think with Cyprian? The difficulty usually arose when acting on a principle became vital. So it took another century and a half

before Augustine of Hippo reversed the North African position
of the Council of Carthage and recognised (schismatic) Donatist baptism *as* baptism, and reckoned to reconcile Donatists
to the catholic Church as already baptised. The notion even
ran through to recognising Donatist ordinations as true ordinations, though performed by excommunicate persons not
reconciled to the catholic Church. This, as a feature of Western
theology, has in post-Reformation times allowed the question
as to whether Anglican ordinations, though conferred in total
separation from Rome, might not still be 'valid' on this Augus-
tinian basis; and it has also allowed or even promoted the rise
of lines of carefully validated successions of *episcopi vagantes*,
bishops with an impeccable dynastic pedigree but without
churches, congregations, or Christian credibility (see Appendix
1, pp. 336–9).

9 The Early Development of Sacraments

The word 'sacrament' is no doubt an anachronism for the very early Church.* It does not take on its full significance until the Middle Ages, and then it is revamped and reinterpreted by the Reformers. But, if we may allow ourselves the concept without necessarily invoking the terminology, it is clear that the actual uses of baptism – the 'sacrament' of entry – and of communion – the 'sacrament' of continuance and cohesion – are traceable from the New Testament into the second century with as much attestation as could ever be sought for any church practice, granted the already noted paucity of the total evidence.**

Baptism is mentioned in Ignatius, described in the Didache, mentioned briefly in the Epistle of Barnabas, described more fully in Justin, and becomes for the first time the subject of a monograph by Tertullian (the *De Baptismo*). Irenaeus has some passing references. Hippolytus gives a much fuller description of the rite than anything previously. The overall picture looks very similar to the New Testament one, so that we may infer that, although baptism is not mentioned every

---

*Its first occurrence in Latin is in Pliny's letter to Hadrian (usually dated around 112), where it was presumably carrying its normal Latin meaning of an 'oath' (unless Pliny had misunderstood Christian jargon!).
**I shall relaxedly use the term 'Eucharist', not only because I accept my own argument that terminology may lawfully depart from its own etymology (the etymology means 'thanksgiving'), but also because I find it used across the world without any sinister overtones; and, as a long-time teacher of liturgy, I found it alone yields the highly needful adjectival form – i.e. 'eucharistic' – which saves a troublesome periphrasis time and again in what may otherwise be a quite neutral or scholarly discussion.

time there is reference to evangelism or conversion, it is mentioned sufficiently often, and is sufficiently clearly taken for granted, for us to conclude that it was universally practised, was given once-for-all-for-life, and did indeed rule off the Church from the pagan world. There is a trend over the first two centuries for there to be preparation for the rite, leading in Hippolytus to a norm of a *three-year* catechumenate, though with some possibility of remission for promising growth in grace. A catechumenate is itself an innovation since apostolic times. It also appears that, with the institutionalising of the preparation, there arose a normal practice of baptising at Easter, and bringing the neophytes straight into the assembly to share the prayers, the greeting or kiss of peace and, as a climax, the Eucharist itself. The pinning of the actual baptism to Easter in this way gave institutionalised shape to the catechumenate (and, in time, to Lent), and even gave birth to queries about how Christian a catechumen is who dies, especially one who is martyred.

The question of infant baptism

There is a question as to the occurrence of infant baptism. In this respect the early authors are remarkably like the New Testament – that is, they take their practice for granted and neither describe it nor defend it – so, if infants were being baptised, then that can be read easily in the accounts in Didache and Justin, but if there were no such practice, that too is fairly consistent with the accounts. The kind of evidence that has to be evaluated is:

1   When Polycarp says at his martyrdom (?AD 156) that he has served the Lord 'for 86 years', does he count the years from his baptism? And, if he does count them from his baptism, is he now 86 (or possibly 87) years of age (and was baptised as an infant), or is he a centenarian who was baptised as a teenager? If his discipleship is counted from his baptism, then his baptism may have been around AD 70.
2   Justin states that he can produce 'many, both men and women, who have been discipled to Christ since childhood, and remain unstained at 60 or 70 years of age'.[1] The question here is whether to 'be discipled' refers to baptism (as it does elsewhere), and possibly also whether the 'childhood'

discipling might or might not connote younger teenager years or alternatively would go back to infancy – which in Justin's time would take the actual administration of infant baptism back well before AD 100.

3   Irenaeus, while remarking that Jesus passed through all the ages of the human race, states: 'He came to save all through means of himself – all, I say, who through him are born again to God – infants and children and boys and youths and old men. He therefore passed through every age' – and this reference to being 'born again' virtually certainly (from contemporary usage) implies baptism.[2]

4   Origen (in the East) writes (probably after 240): 'The Church received from the apostles the tradition of baptising infants also.'[3] While Origen's date is latish, he is describing that which has been 'handed down' – and his own parents were Christian, and presumably involved in the 'handing down', and, it would seem quite likely, would have had him himself baptised as an infant (in around 185?).

The hinge author in all this is Tertullian with his *De Baptismo* (from his orthodox days, probably before 200). He opposes infant baptism, which is the first absolutely explicit mention of it in Christian history. So that poses the question for us as to whether he is opposing a long-standing or a recently invented usage. There are two tiny wisps in the wind which blow in the direction of its being a long-standing practice:

1   Tertullian, who clearly thinks infant baptism *is* baptism but is undesirable, fails to nail it with what would have been the conclusive argument of his times – i.e. 'The apostles had no such practice'. Practice that was continuous from the apostles had high credibility in his time; a practice of which an opponent could say, 'But it is only of a few years' standing', was virtually self-condemned. If infant baptism was an innovation, why does Tertullian fail to make the point?

2   There is a plausible answer closely related to Tertullian's own understanding of the rationale for infant baptism – that is, that it apparently depends upon sponsors 'going bail' for the candidates. If the children then grow up in rebellion or in vicious ways, the sponsors are answerable to God for them; and that is thrusting them into unnecessary danger.[4]

It seems consistent to interpret this approach as implying that Tertullian was wrestling not with a new practice of infant baptism, but with a relatively new rationale for it – a rationale which, if accepted, was pastorally undesirable. He does not so much seem to be saying that infants are improper candidates, but that sponsoring becomes hazardous if you take on infants, and the sponsors need protecting.

If Tertullian is a witness for the existence of infant baptism, Hippolytus is the first to describe how infants are baptised. He reports that a parent or someone else answers for the child who then goes through the same rite as adults, culminating, it would seem, in receiving communion.

The question of post-baptismal ceremonies

Another issue about the early centuries is whether there was a post-baptismal laying on of hands or anointing. This issue runs within a similar time-frame to the infant baptism issue, though with the opposite inference – that is, that the silence of the witnesses this time implies the absence of the ceremony. The contrast between the evidence for two practices in the period between the New Testament and the end of the second century is this: *any* evidence that infants were baptised would demonstrate it was a *possible* practice, while, for a post-baptismal laying on of hands or anointing, the only evidence that would bear weightily on the issue is that which would demonstrate its *universal necessity*. The silences of the authors need not therefore imply a total absence from history (that would be asking them to prove a most massive negative); but the evidence is sufficient to show that such a post-baptismal rite was neither universal nor 'generally necessary' – and that is more easily demonstrated The same authors as with infant baptism close off the silent period (Tertullian in *De Baptismo* and Hippolytus in *The Apostolic Tradition*), each, as with infant baptism, giving the earliest positive evidence we possess of the particular usage.

We have seen above the oddity of the two occasions in the Acts of the Apostles where a post-baptismal rite is administered (see p. 89). The other baptismal references in the New Testament give no hint of a 'second half' to baptism, and the single and simple rite of water-baptism appears to be complete sacramental initiation. The passing references in Ignatius and the Epistle of Barnabas give no hint of a rite following baptism, and the actual descriptions of baptism in the Didache (in the East) and in Justin (in the West), both of which have an element of blow-by-blow detail about them, signally omit the point. In Justin Martyr it is almost impossible to conceive that there was such a laying on of hands, as the candidate is brought from baptism into the assembly, for the detail given is exact – the newly baptised is incorporated into the prayers, welcomed with the kiss of peace, and shares in the communion.

The evidence of a 'second half' begins with Tertullian. The *De Baptismo* gives a pattern which, from our paucity of evidence, appears to be unprecedented. There is not only a two-stage ritual – there is also a two-stage inner spiritual renewal associated with the two outward parts.

Firstly, there is the water-baptism. This frees us from sin and washes us 'in preparation' for the coming of the Spirit – wonderfully compared by Tertullian to John the Baptist's baptism which was to 'prepare' the way of the Lord.[5] Of the Spirit himself we are told, *'Sed non in aquis'* ('But it is not in the waters [that we receive the Spirit]'). There is then an anointing, which he traces to the anointing of the Aaronic priesthood, but particularly relates to our becoming 'Christ's', with a play on the name 'Christ' itself as meaning 'anointed'. But the climax is the laying on of a hand 'invoking and inviting the Holy Spirit'.[6] A complete change has happened in the single-stage pattern – and, because of that paucity of evidence, we do not know when or where or why it happened. It would be possible, for instance, to opine that this two-stage pattern had been in operation in North Africa from the times of Paul and Luke – and there is no contrary evidence. But it appears more consonant with the evidence of Scripture and the other early references in East and West to conclude that a simple ceremony of baptism has been augmented (and in the process curiously diminished) by a recent addition towards the end of the second century.

This passage in Tertullian remains, however, a very undeveloped account. From a latter-day standpoint we may be

genuinely surprised that there is no mention at this point of
who lays on the hand. Indeed, if these chapters about the
administration of the water, the oil, and the laying on a hand
are read with Chapter XVII about the minister of baptism, we
find that bishop, presbyter, deacon or layman could officiate at
baptism, and that would seem to drive us to two perhaps
unwelcome alternatives in respect of the laying on the hand:
either this too was performed by the minister of baptism (be
he bishop or layman); *or* the laying on of the hand was done
by the bishop, but at a later point than the baptism, when the
bishop could be available. If we prefer the first alternative,
then there is nothing distinctively 'episcopal' (or 'coming into
relationship with the bishop') about the laying on of the hand;
and if we prefer the second, then the earliest historical
example of what has been called the 'primitive integrated rite'
was itself not necessarily 'integrated', but came in highly separable parts. The alternatives are uncomfortable for latter-day
Anglicans who would have difficulty in describing the
initiation without mentioning the role of the bishop – yet Tertullian completely forgets to do so. He also, we note in passing,
omits the greeting of the kiss of peace and the entry into the
Eucharist.

We must inevitably ask why, if we take the dating of Tertullian and the lack of earlier evidence at its face value, the laying
on of the hand was added to baptism in the late second century.
The most plausible answer I have encountered is Geoffrey
Lampe's suggestion that, since the Church had to define itself
over against Marcion in the second half of the second century,
there was a rising interest in the canon of Scripture, and thus
a renewed valuing of the Acts of the Apostles, which was not
previously being read in Church (being neither 'gospel' nor
'apostle') and had thus not been in the forefront of attention.
Now, as Acts came higher on to the agenda, a piecemeal
approach to its accounts of baptism might well have the
Church in one place or another saying from Acts 8 and Acts
19, 'But see how they laid on hands post-baptismally for the
conveying of the Holy Spirit' – and, once imitated, the practice
became general, at least in the West. That is speculation; but
it meets the point that the crucial question is not so much why

a new practice started as whether (and why) it started at this particular date in the late second century.

In Hippolytus, the candidates are baptised outside the assembly (as in Justin) and are then brought in. The difference is that they are then immediately welcomed by the bishop laying his hand on them, and praying a prayer that makes reference to the coming of the Spirit. (There is doubt about the text here: Dix naturally prefers the reading which prays for the coming of the Spirit; Lampe, Cuming and Whitaker accept the reading which suggests they have already received the Spirit. But in any case it is this Hippolytan text which is normally in view in the modern writings of the last half-century or so which claim there was a 'primitive integrated rite of initiation'. But that is *not* what we learn from the truly primitive authors who preceded Hippolytus. Then there was simple baptism *simpliciter*.)

In the East, however, it did not develop in this way. We have to go on to the fourth century before we discover a generally used practice of a post-baptismal sort. When it came it took the form of an anointing, which might well be administered by a presbyter and did not need a bishop.

Communion

It is fairly clear that, in the New Testament, the 'sacrament' of communion was used within the context of a meal, the *agape* or 'love-feast'. There are somewhat inconclusive arguments for thinking that the communion was in the first century observed every week in all Christian communities, for the evidence is slender. But it looks as though, at least by the middle of the second century, this was the practice in Rome, and very probably elsewhere as well. It is associated with the first day of the week in Acts 20:7, in the Didache, and in Justin. But issues other than frequency may concern us more.

The '*agape*' is a title found in the letter of Jude (see pp. 112–13), in Ignatius of Antioch,[7] and also in Tertullian, who actually explains its name to the Roman authorities: '[You put up with lavish feasts of all sorts of the mystery religions.] Yet about the modest supper-room of the Christians alone a great ado is made. Our feast explains itself by its name. The Greeks call it *agape*, the name for "love".'[8] However, it is unlikely that the provision of the sacrament within the meal ran as late as Tertullian's time, and it is probable that Ignatius in 107 or thereabouts can use the terms 'Eucharist' and *'agape'* (as he does within a few lines of each other) interchangeably, and that, by the middle of the second century, Justin is describing a use of bread and wine independently of a larger meal. We cannot trace how the meal context fell away during the second century, but it is at least likely that it was one of the effects of persecution; for under persecution the primary, commanded ordinance – the eating bread and drinking wine of which Jesus had said 'Do this' – still had to be observed, even if flanking and less crucial matters were to be allowed to drop. When dropped from the basic Sunday liturgy, they might still run on, if we read Tertullian aright, as subsidiary forms of Christian bonding and fellowship.

What seems reasonably clear in church-life terms is that only the baptised were admitted to communion; that the faithful were expected to follow a disciplined life of participation (even when under persecution); and that the great penalty for improper behaviour was ex-communication. In Ignatius there is great emphasis upon the unity of the Church implied and mediated in the 'one Eucharist . . . one flesh of our Lord Jesus Christ . . . one cup . . . one altar . . . one bishop'.[9] In Justin the president gives a teaching exhortation and articulates the 'great thanksgiving', but the people generally join in the prayers, share the kiss of peace and receive communion in both kinds.* It was clearly a structured congregational event, the focal bonding-point of the local church. Sharing the prayers and the kiss of peace were marks of inclusion almost as strong as receiving the bread and wine.

For the sake of understanding church history we also note some disquieting signs which begin to appear in relation to the Eucharist in the first two centuries. These are:

Firstly, there is very strong 'realist' language used from a very early date. Ignatius takes the Gnostics to task, as they refuse the Eucharist 'because they refuse to acknowledge the Eucharist is the flesh of our Saviour Jesus Christ, which suf-

---

*There is a clear contrast between the 'we' who offer the intercessory prayers and the 'president' who articulates the eucharistic prayer.

fered for our sins, and which the Father . . . raised up'.[10] Justin, in a passage difficult to translate, says (to the pagan authorities) that 'the food which is blessed . . . from which our flesh and blood . . . are nourished, is the flesh and blood of Jesus who was made flesh'.[11] While the language of the New Testament is not to be evaded, it is rather to be carefully interpreted than to be allowed to become a starting-point, as here, of the kind of linguistic auction which ultimately ended in transubstantiation.

Secondly, there are the first hints in the first two centuries of a relapse into the language of the Levitical priesthood. It is not very strong; it is surely innocent in its intentions, and certainly unguarded. But it begins. In the letter of Clement of Rome to the Corinthians we saw at one point a hint of distributed cultic roles which are differentiated from each other by the use of Levitical titles (see p. 153). In the same letter the people who are in danger of being dismissed from their ministerial posts are those who have 'offered the gifts', which, in the light of later usage, looks like a way of saying that they have 'presided at the Lord's Supper'. The New Testament has no such language of 'offering' in connection with the Eucharist, and this looks like a slightly wrong turn.

In the second century there becomes current a famous exposition of a verse from the prophet Malachi to reinforce the superiority of Christianity over Judaism. Malachi wrote (as being the mouthpiece at this point of God):

> '[You Jews are bringing me polluted sacrifices] . . . I am not pleased with you', says the Lord Almighty, 'and I will accept no offering from your hands. For my name will be great among the Gentiles; and from the East to the West in every place incense and pure offerings will be made to my name, for my name will be great among the Gentiles', says the Lord Almighty. (Mal. 1:10–11)

I doubt if one expositor in a hundred tackling this text today would think of referring it to the Eucharist. But in the second century, when Christians needed to distinguish themselves from Jews, they failed to say that all sacrifices and similar offerings had ceased, being fulfilled in Jesus, but instead took refuge in this text from Malachi, as demonstrating that Christ-

ians have *superior* offerings as compared with the Jews,
namely the Eucharist. This reference is found first in the
Didache, where it has no direct anti-Jewish reference, but calls
for Christians to be reconciled to each other 'so that your
sacrifice may not be defiled [but instead may be pure]' – and
the Eucharist is now 'your sacrifice'.[12] In Justin it is used as a
lever upon Trypho the Jew, and is actually quoted in three
places.[13] His exposition includes, in Chapter XLI:

[The offering of fine flour offered by the cleansed leper] was
a type of the bread of the Eucharist ... Hence God speaks
by the mouth of Malachi ... about the sacrifices at that
time presented by you: 'I have no pleasure in you ... [Mal.
1:10–12] ... but you profane my name.' He then speaks of
those Gentiles, namely us, who in every place offer sacrifices
to him, i.e. the bread of the Eucharist and also the cup of
the Eucharist.

Clearly it is unsurprising that the Eucharist became known
as the 'offering' or the 'oblation' or even 'the Christian sacrifice'.
And a similar pattern is found at the end of the second century
in Irenaeus, who draws from it that we offer to God the bread
and wine as the first-fruits of his creation, as the 'pure sacrifice', a thankoffering to God which the Jews cannot match.[14]

By a curious historical coincidence, at the very time this
terminology (and consequent doctrinal cast of mind) was
taking root in the early Church, there was also a drift towards
fixing the language of the Old Testament priesthood upon
Christian ministers, the very people who were responsible for
presiding at the Eucharist. The beginnings of it seem to have
been with a view to good order (see the quotation from 1
Clement on p. 153). The continuing of it certainly included
both an element of bolstering the authority carried by the
bishop and the proper respect due to him. Tertullian calls
the bishop 'the high priest' (though he will also call all the
laity 'priests'). Hippolytus' ordination prayer for the making
of a bishop says that the man has been chosen 'to exercise the
high-priesthood', and it looks as though this implies a cultic
or liturgical role as well as a ruling and honorific one. And
by the middle of the third century, Cyprian could compare a
challenge to his authority to the sin of Korah, who set up an

unsanctioned priesthood in opposition to Aaron – and the ground opened up and swallowed him. In the words of his biographer: 'The Jewish Priesthood at last became "a name and a shade" on the day when it crucified Christ. *Its reality passed on to the Christian bishop*'.[15] The high priest (the title of 'priest' took some time longer to pass regularly to the presbyter) was now presiding at a Eucharist where the elements were offered to God (as in the anamnesis paragraph in Hippolytus' eucharistic prayer), where a standard exposition (which also found its way into the anamnesis text of the Western rite) was that this was the 'pure sacrifice' prophesied by Malachi, and where in the Eucharist the Church might even be offering Christ himself to the Father, a concept first articulated by Cyprian. All the parts were in place for a developed later doctrine of Mass sacrifice.

In one sense this trend was totally unconscious. It is a good example of Chinese whispers. Each generation believes itself to be consonant with Scripture, but the content is steadily moving away from Scripture, and the persons of each generation are so trapped in their own generation's liturgical and devotional understandings of the Eucharist that they are only with the greatest difficulty able to stand outside those understandings and criticise them. The matter only comes to a head in the sixteenth century.

On one point, however, the relationship of Eucharist and Church was preserved in a relatively stable form. Until the Reformation the central worship of the Church (East and West) was eucharistic, and the members of the Church were in principle 'communicants', even if over the centuries they actually received communion less and less often. Thus to be 'ex-communicated' was to be cut off from the Church, and the boundaries of visible Church and community of communicants remained coterminous.

10   The Unity of the Church

The Christian Church entered the second century knowing itself to be one body across the earth as confidently as Paul had when he wrote Ephesians. Various stresses upon its fabric arose during the next two centuries – a period in which it was not only liable to be persecuted, but actually suffered from persecution, and often had to resolve issues in a local or even fragmentary way – for the great age of the universal councils of the Church awaited the Decree of Constantine before it could be contemplated. It was often not at all clear whether a particular division of opinion was a difference within the life of the Church, or whether one side in such a division was thought by the other to be teaching so prejudicial a doctrine as to require the other side to excommunicate them; and we ourselves, while now having the useful vantage-point of hindsight and thus knowing which side actually prevailed and thus emerged as orthodox, must surely confess that we might well have been hard put to it to distinguish truth from error, if we had been living within the strains of such a division.

Several of the deviations which threatened to disrupt or rend the 'catholic' body seem to be clear-cut. The most obvious early one is the group broadly dubbed 'Gnostic' – a group which is addressed confrontationally in several New Testament writings, including the Johannine writings, Paul's letter to the Colossians, and quite probably 1 and 2 Peter, Jude and some of the letters to the seven churches at the beginning of Revelation. They recur as opponents in Ignatius, and are traceable through the second century, and are a major target of Irenaeus. They are classified as 'heretics'. False teaching was always trying to take over the Church and change it, and the authorities of the Church always had to guard against them.

There was however some uncertainty in the second century as to how serious an error must be before it became a threat to the nature of the Church, and the whole Quartodeciman controversy illustrates this. When Polycarp visited Rome (around 155) to make the Eastern case that Easter should be celebrated on the Jewish passover (i.e. on Nisan 14, whichever day of the week that might be), the bishop of Rome, Anicetus, received him respectfully, invited him to preside at communion, and agreed to differ on the point at issue. From his point of view, we may judge, this issue could not rank with Gnosticism as a threat to the Church, and a difference might be tolerated without touching on the central beliefs. There is little doubt that the tolerance arose in part from the eminence of Polycarp, and his advanced old age (he must have been well into his eighties). It may also have been that a difference observed as between two different geographical regions was viewed as less serious than one which threatened stability or authority in any one place. It is at least possible (though not explicit) that Anicetus had some sense of what today would be called a 'hierarchy of truths', and deemed this particular difference as of very minor importance. In other liturgical respects, East and West developed on somewhat different lines, and travellers went from one to another, and noted differences, but rarely in the first 500 years thought that the two had to be identical. Historians are also left to wonder how much international authority Anicetus thought himself to possess – it looks as though Polycarp had come for a conference of equals, though he also may have recognised the power of the see at the heart of the Roman Empire, and may even have felt some pressures from the West to conform to their practice. We might well applaud the good sense concerned in the decision, were it not that within a few years the issue was much sharper and Victor at Rome was high-handedly trying to bring the East into conformity by excommunication. The issue could not be settled by straightforward appeal to Scripture, and therefore, as soon as it was perceived as a threat to the unity of the Church, the appeal was instead to contemporary authority – a thin end of the wedge which would, over the centuries, step up the claims to authority of the great sees.

There were dozens of other tensions straining the unity of

the Church over the early centuries. Quite apart from the major questions of Trinity and incarnation, to which the first four general councils gave definitive answers in the fourth and fifth centuries, there were a series of doctrinal disputes, and also schisms (such as the Donatist one) where the contenders were agreed on many central doctrines, but thought it crucial to separate. Arguably heretics were trying to infiltrate and take over the catholic Church while schismatics were trying to leave and refound it. But issues of, say, personality (technically leading to schism not heresy) might yet be represented as heresy (for example, the challenging of the God-given authority of a particular bishop), so that the two causes of strain were not always separable from each other.

At this point it might well be argued that the mere recourse to the Scriptures was not an adequate protection of the unity of the Church. There are, no doubt, good examples of the effect of this methodology, and, if we do not look too closely, those first four councils of the fourth and fifh centuries might be viewed as such good examples. An issue is disputed; the leaders from round the world get together; they comb through the Scriptures, seeking firstly agreement in substance and secondly careful wording which will protect the Church from error; and they then bind themselves and thus their churches and their successors to this credal exposition.

This was, however, a developed practice which was not so easy to adopt under persecution, and could in any case only be done when all sides in a dispute agreed that this was the way to do it, and agreed (at least implicitly) that they would accept the council's findings. It has been a near-miracle that the creeds of those first four councils have endured down the centuries since. But some other disputes might also be instructive for our purposes. What, for instance, was Cyprian to do in Carthage when men respected for their readiness to go to prison for their faith began to seize authority in the Church (including that of reconciling the remiss) over against him? In more general terms, what was a bishop to do anywhere if his position was challenged, either because, like Cyprian, he lacked the credibility as leader that others had (that is, he had evaded going to prison!), or because, as happened at the beginning of the Donatist schism, there was opposition to his appointment in the first place?

One obvious answer was to hold conference, and seek agreement. This sounds Christian, but to insecure leaders it was to connive at assaults on their authority, and counterattack was more tempting. This was generally effected through excommunication – a simple retention of the unity of the Church by cutting off those who threatened its peace. Those who were thus cut off might perish from the earth, but they might, like the Donatists, endure for a long period. They in turn would claim to be *the* true Church. Both sides held strongly to the notion that the Church was in total communion with itself, and anyone outside it could not be in communion with it – the scene was very unlike the latter-day situation in England where denominations or congregations gladly welcome to communion visitors from other churches, and where the Church of Rome, which still exhibits the early Church discipline in this respect, is under constant pressure to allow its communicants to be a different set of persons from its members.

However, disputes were not always settled locally by either conciliation or excommunication. There was a third way through, and it was tempting. General councils may not have been on the agenda in Cyprian's time, but getting support from elsewhere was. Regional or provincial gatherings were one possibility but appeals to Rome were another. It is clear that Cyprian, when he appealed to the Church of Rome, was only seeking moral support, almost certainly because of its position at the capital of the Roman empire, and not because he had any thought that the bishop of Rome would give a definitive and authoritative answer to which he would necessarily have to submit. Getting the wrong answer from Stephen actually complicated the matter for Cyprian, and opened up disputes on two fronts, for the truth was slowly emerging that, without agreed authorities for settling issues, division and internal struggle might well become endemic. The ending of persecution and the establishment of Christianity as lawful within the Roman empire in the fourth century arguably provided an escape from this dilemma, as powerful outside forces like the emperor showed an interest in bringing ecumenical councils together and enforcing their outcome. It is also apparent that it was important for disputants to demonstrate continuity with the past and the relatively innovatory character of the beliefs or practices of opponents.

In the light of history there is a real dilemma here. We today accept the findings of those first four councils as being in accordance with the teaching of Scripture. We are less convinced by the findings of later councils, and are heirs of the dictum, 'General councils . . . may err and have erred'. We are children of the Reformation which asserted scriptural authority over the traditions of the Church, and took its chance on being excommunicated by the larger part of the then prevalent Western Church and its authorities. So we return to the historical dilemma, and restate it thus:

1   If the Church is to live under the supreme authority of Scripture, how is it both to handle disputes and retain a visible unity?

2   If the Church is to live under the supreme authority of a magisterium (whether local or worldwide), how is it to challenge error within that constituted leadership?

There could of course be a limp third possibility: can the Church take Scripture and tradition and unity (and episcopacy) fairly seriously without being definitive about the status of any of them, or clear about their relationship to each other? Anglicans may have an instinct (their classic fudging instinct) to settle for this kind of a possibility, but it is not only improper to decide the basis for theology on the supremacy or at least autonomy of Anglican instincts, but it is also unlikely that such a possibility will of itself provide any charter for policies for the future, or for the handling of actual disputes.

If we set that aside and return to the starkness of the original dilemma, then it is clear that we must settle for the first horn of that dilemma, and adjust ourselves to its discomfort. For the principle stated in it can only keep unity while sustaining disputes if there is much elasticity in practice. If we believe in worldwide visible unity, we can only be driven to division or excommunication by the most sharp-edged examples of heresy, immorality, or personal headstrongness. Our higher priority is to get various disputing parties together and work at finding agreement under the authority of Scripture; we may be short on heresy trials, disciplinary proceedings and settling issues by hierarchical authority; but we have not quite settled for the notion that anyone can set up in business as a Christian Church anywhere he or she chooses without reference to the historic character of the existing institution. We want to keep people together, Jew and Gentile alike, and to keep them Christianly in communion with each other seeking resolutions of difficulties. It is not easy, as the second and third centuries illustrate. But it is truer to the revelation of God in Scripture than the other horn of the dilemma – for that can only take us to Rome, and to the vast problem of being required by the magisterium to believe what is not in Scripture nor even in the early Church, and to be held in visible unity by that requirement, and thus to build our lives of discipleship upon that yawning gap. There would seem to be scriptural precedent for arguing the way through controversies: 'Speaking the truth in love, let us grow up in all things into him that is the head' (Eph. 4:15).

Part III

The Church of England Then and Now

11   The Reformation

The Church of England's separation from Rome in 1533–4, with which this book began, ushered in for that Church a totally different path through subsequent history from that which the Church of Rome was to follow. At the outset the separation hardly changed the face of the average parish: from 1534 to 1547 the same priest might well still be the vicar, his patrons would also still be in place, and he would almost certainly be providing virtually the same liturgical programme – still in Latin – as he had provided before, still functioning in the same building with the same vestments, ornaments and ceremonial. (If he was a bold spirit, he might at one point have acquired a wife, but then at another point he would have had to pretend he had not.) At a higher level, the same bishop was in the same palace (save in Rochester, where John Fisher died for the papal supremacy), the same bishops were still lords spiritual in parliament, and, although monasteries had been uprooted, the cathedrals retained much of their former glory (a notable exception was Canterbury, where the shrine of Becket gave a very ambiguous message in the newly royalised Church; the shrine was broken up and pilgrimages to it were prohibited).

However, the external appearance belied the underlying truth – the fount of authority had completely changed. The pope had lost all say-so in the English Church, the monarch had become 'head on earth of the Church of England', and the Church of England, instead of being a local branch of a transnational company, was now a department of state under the unfettered autonomy of its royal supreme head. If the outward face of the Church of England remained unchanged, then that was solely because the king's whim was that it should be so – he had taken power to do with it what he willed, and the clergy had bowed the knee, had accepted his and their new role, and, with every form of whip-and-carrot encouragement, had started to theologise about the divine right of kings.

I have suggested at the beginning of Part I that there was a kind of archetypal citing of the supreme authority of Scripture in the original questioning of the pope's right to dispense from (what were thought to be) God's rulings in Scripture. While the official position after 1534 was arguably that Henry would rule arbitrarily as he saw fit, it is clear that Cranmer, who was archbishop of Canterbury from 1533 onwards, was coming to a 'reformed' mind on the authority of Scripture. In its most explicit form this mind wrote as follows:

> Let us diligently search for the well of life in the books of the New and Old Testament, and not run to the stinking puddles of men's traditions, devised by man's imagination, for our justification and salvation . . . These books therefore ought to be much in our hands, in our eyes, in our ears, in our mouths, but most of all in our hearts.[1]

Here is a total disjunction: Scripture – life-givingly good; men's traditions – stinkingly bad. The Reformation choices actually seemed at root as simple as that. The received traditions of Roman Catholicism included not only the self-authenticating authority of the bishop of Rome, but a vast series of specific adjustments and subtle alterations of the faith which the medieval Western Church had canonised, and which the first generation of Reformers had themselves imbibed with their mother's milk – and now wished to reverse. So the prime principle of the Reformation is that Scripture is to sit in judgement on the whole received church system. In the reign of Edward VI, this principle was enforced by legal enactments bringing in vast changes to give expression to the supreme authority of Scripture. The supremacy and relative perspicuity of Scripture, which is the starting-point for Part I above, is then duly to be found enshrined in the English Reformation Settlement as follows:

1   In the liturgical reformation (which preceded the systematic doctrinal formulation), these steps were taken from 1547 onwards, more or less in the order shown:

a Vernacular language was used (on the basis of a citation of 1 Corinthians 14 against the use of unknown tongues).
b The cup was restored to the laity (citing the Lord's institution).
c The daily offices were simplified, providing for a sequential reading of Scripture.
d The forms of prayer were expurgated, removing all reverence or near-worship to the Virgin Mary, all invocation of saints or angels, and all petitions for souls in purgatory.
e The communion service was totally remade as follows:

- There would be an ante-communion including Scripture, preaching, intercession, and almsgiving;
- There would be no communion without communicants;
- There would be a corporate expression of penitence (and provision for private reconciliation in advance of any warring parties);
- There would be an end of any description of the elements of bread and wine as 'offerings' or the action of the presbyter as 'offering';
- The focus of the communion would be the 'full, perfect and sufficient' sacrifice of the Son of God on the cross;
- There would be emphasis upon the giving and receiving of the bread and wine as both the essential action of the sacrament and the context for describing the elements as 'the body and blood of Christ' – indeed 'giving and receiving' would be the whole sacramental action;[2]
- There would be an end of an objective (and ceremonial) 'consecration' of the elements;
- There would be an elimination of over-luxuriant dress, ornament and ceremonial, and an end of reservation and revering of the 'consecrated' elements.

f The occasional services would be pruned and made more biblical in similar ways.
g The ordination rites, in conformity with the communion, would eliminate all references to the priest offering sacrifices, would centre upon making 'ministers of word and sacraments', and, in place of the medieval handing over of paten and chalice to the new priests (with the injunction

to receive authority to offer sacrifice for the living and the dead), would have the delivery of a Bible;*

h A biblically based set of homilies would be provided to reform the preaching of a reluctant set of clergy.

All kinds of loose ends were left, but the procedure and the direction of change were very clear and in the six short years of Edward's reign a very fast rate of practical reform was established.

2 The doctrinal reformulation followed, in the Forty-Two Articles of 1553 and the marginally retouched Thirty-Nine Articles of 1571, which are cited in the list below:

- Articles I–V conserve Chalcedonian orthodoxy about the Trinity and Incarnation.
- Article VI is 'Of the sufficiency of the holy Scriptures for salvation' and is very comparable to the question and answer in the interrogation of the candidates for the presbyterate in the ordination rites. There is a listing of the canonical books of the Bible, and an exclusion of the Apocrypha from the canon.
- Article VII, 'Of the Old Testament', holds Old and New Testaments together for the purposes of Christian understanding.
- Article VIII, 'Of the Three Creeds', locates the authority for the creeds in 'most certain warrants of holy Scripture' (see p. 30).
- Articles IX–XVI concern sin and salvation, and, without usually citing Scripture specifically, are scripturally based and include passing quotations from Scripture.
- Article XVII, in avoiding the most difficult logic of 'double predestination' says in its last paragraph: 'We must receive God's promises in such wise, as they be generally set forth to us in holy Scripture'.
- Article XVIII is based upon its own last sentence: 'Holy Scripture doth set out unto us only the Name of Jesus Christ, whereby men must be saved'.

---

*The candidates' adherence to the text and the supremacy of Scripture in the ordination rites is set out at the beginning of Part I above.

- Article XIX makes the first 'note' of the visible Church that 'in which the pure Word of God is preached'.
- Article XX allows the Church to make rules in areas not covered in detail by Scripture, but subject to various constraints arising from the supremacy and inviolability of Scripture.
- Article XXI, 'Of the Authority of General Councils', states that in general councils 'all be not governed with the Spirit and Word of God' – and consequently may err, and sometimes have erred; and nothing ordered by councils (touching our salvation) has any 'strength or authority' unless it is demonstrably drawn from Scripture.
- Article XXII rejects purgatory as 'repugnant to the Word of God'.
- Article XXV reduces the seven sacraments of the medieval system to the two 'ordained of Christ our Lord in the Gospel'. The other five include those which arise 'of the corrupt following of the apostles' – a clear appeal from later practice back to the original Scripture. Similarly the sacraments are to be used as Christ ordained ('not to be gazed upon, or to be carried about'), and those who receive them 'unworthily' are condemned, 'as Saint Paul saith'.
- Article XXVIII deals with the Lord's Supper. Transubstantiation not only 'cannot be proved by holy Writ' but is 'repugnant to the plain words of Scripture'. And there is a reference to 'Christ's ordinance' in contradistinction to reservation and kindred devotions.
- Article XXXII allows ministers to marry, as they 'are not commanded by God's Law' to be single.
- Article XXXIV allows diversities of ceremonies to be ordered in different places and times 'so [i.e. provided] that nothing be ordained against God's Word'. The ceremonies which are ordered 'only by man's authority' can be changed by authority.
- Article XXXVII, 'Of the Civil Magistrates', refers to 'that only prerogative, which we see to have been

given always to all godly Princes in holy Scriptures
by God himself'.

The case here is that, although some features of the faith are
set out in the Articles simply as declarations (as we find, for
instance, in a scriptural declaration like the Apostles' Creed),
the scriptural foundation of the Articles is axiomatic, and sufficiently frequently shows through as to set up a consistent
pattern. It is very clear that the doctrinal reformation of the
Church of England was carried through on the assertion of
the supremacy (and perspicuity) of Scripture. It also, in principle, means that the Church of England ought to be open
constantly to further reform on the same basis.

What would constant reform then look like? It does not
appear to me that it would be constantly backward-looking,
engaged in trying to refine existing doctrinal texts. In a fast-
changing world, being 'scriptural' as a Church may well mean
being 'incarnational'.* A Church which is culturally of its own
times will use language, architecture, dress and ceremonial of
its own times. It will address the varying ethical issues
of differing generations. It will orientate its mission to the
actual life-patterns of the people around it. It will look at
the priorities for its resources, it will prophesy to an unbelieving society, it will adapt to the needs of the broken reeds
of the present generation – not those of the last. To live under
the supremacy of Scripture is the reverse of a retreat into a
semi-private stained-glass window world of a unique culture
adapted most closely to the nostalgic taste of those in it; to
live under the supremacy of Scripture is to question, test and
reform all received traditions, conventions and cultural safety-
nets; to live under the supremacy of Scripture is to seek an
eschatological goal of perfection in belief and behaviour, rather
than to set up a supposed past golden age and to seek to return
to that.

---

*I use 'incarnational' in its received popular sense, though, as a
matter of doctrinal ideals, I suggest elsewhere that the Church is the
extension of the resurrection more than of the incarnation.

12   Scripture and Tradition

It will be very clear from the above account that a Church of the Reformation is inevitably asserting the supreme authority of holy Scripture. That is the formal position of the Church of England. However, if that supreme authority were solely contrasted with 'tradition' as it is portrayed in Chapter 11 in the quotation from Cranmer's homily (p. 190), then there would be no further complex questions to solve. But in fact at the Reformation 'men's traditions' were not put aside that easily – and it is wholly arguable that it would actually have been both inadvisable and wrong to have wished or to have attempted to abolish them that easily. For the Reformation principle at stake is not, and ought not to be rendered as, *'sola scriptura'*, but rather it is *'suprema scriptura'*. How then are we to identify and allocate the appropriate status for 'tradition'?

'Tradition' may mean the 'handing down' or 'handing over' process – though it more usually indicates the content of what is handed down. This is the 'men's traditions'. And it runs strongly in the Church – we receive 'by tradition' and 'as traditions' creeds, calendar, rituals, hymnody, ceremonial and a host of specific uses. This is simply a neutral fact and neither good nor bad in itself.

In general, however, Christian traditions start with a presumption in their favour. If *this* is what the Church did (or said) last year or the year before, or long years before that, and still does, then that *'this'* is part of what the Church now is. Most of us, then, have to take on trust most of what the Church now is and most of the ways it expresses its faith – though that trust is only being exercised in an interim way. The way in which the Church at large comes to believe in the Trinity gives a model illustration of this.

The Church has credal statements about the Trinity, so we, when we are new converts, join in them. Yet the formulated doctrine of the Trinity, whether in the simple form – 'We believe in one God, Father Son and Holy Spirit' – or in its full Chalcedonian rigour of complexity and even calculated self-contradiction, is well beyond the terminology of Scripture. It is handed to us by tradition; it is reinforced in us by our use of liturgical forms like the trinitarian blessing and three-verse hymns; it presents itself to us as what the Church believes – but it is a traditional formulation brought to us by a handing-down process. Is, then, the formulation of trinitarian belief the well of life or a stinking puddle?

The Roman Catholic answer at the Reformation would have been, 'This is the tradition of the Church' – and that would have settled it for Catholics. However, the answer in the Thirty-Nine Articles is, as we have seen, rather different: that the creeds (which contain the Chalcedonian formulations) 'may be proved by most certain warrants of holy Scripture'. That does not necessarily mean that all believers will be able to do the necessary thorough check in Scripture; nor does it mean that the formulation of the doctrine of the Trinity must be refused unless or until the individual has done that weighing by Scripture. Rather it provides four interconnected principles of faith:

1 that the fifth-century formulation of the doctrine of the Trinity (or any other still current formulation from Christian history) has a 'first blush' claim upon our adherence, simply because it is in our 'tradition';

2 that the Church and the individual (in so far as he or she is able) has in each generation the task of reassessing the stated scriptural foundation for such formulation;

3 that if necessary, after such reassessing, the formulation should be retouched or even reformulated;

4 that even a retouched formula has still its own provisionality, and is handed on to next generations as inviting further assessment and reformulation.

We conclude from this that Scripture alone is non-negotiable in its textual formulation, but that Christian traditions, negotiable and reformable as they are, should also be expected in principle to convey the word of God. This includes creeds, liturgies, songs, devotional traditions, homiletical traditions, and oral and written (and pictorial, symbolic and video) material of a thousand different sorts. Unbelievers will very often come to a knowledge of the Christian faith not by picking up a Gideon Bible in an hotel bedroom nor by being given a biblical tract by a street-corner evangelist, but through knowing believers, who will tell them the faith in their own terms, and introduce them to Christian worship which has its own terms. Similarly the young child of a Christian home will be learning the knowledge of God from simple prayers and songs, as well as Bible stories, long before he or she can read – and the child too enters into a handing-down process which is using its own terms. In each case the checking out from Scripture as to whether these terms are accurate is a sophisticated later task, which many may never do thoroughly. But it is the traditional formulation – one in which the Church rightly has confidence – which has brought the knowledge of God to the individual, rather than simple doses or neat chunks of Scripture.

From this we must conclude that we need a high doctrine of tradition as the vehicle of God's truth. It is that which enables us actually to have a programme of worship or teaching when we meet – for otherwise we would meet with open Bibles but no programme, no expectations and deliberately blank minds each week. But, even so, we must still insist that each strand, each feature, of how we speak the faith, and how we practise it, is always open to reform in the light of Scripture, and must never become autonomous. There may be hallowed traditions, but no tradition is so hallowed as not to be up for question in each generation. We are encouraged to have a positive high doctrine of tradition – but the doctrine of Scripture *must* be higher; and that is the thrust of the Reformation formularies. That is why we should insist on the 'supreme' authority of Scripture, rather than its 'sole' authority. And the outworking of this can be seen in the methodology of the Reformation itself: the procedures may have moved very fast in Edward's reign, but the process was one of provisionally accepting what was received by tradition, bringing it to the test of Scripture, and then reforming it where that was needed. Thus the liturgical texts of the Church of England can be traced in a succession from the Sarum (Latin) uses through to Cranmer's second Book of Common Prayer (and on to its 1662 offspring), with each change at each stage having a comprehensibility of its own in the light of the scriptural principles on which the Reformers were working.

Of course, there are many areas of church life in which we choose to behave or act in one way, where it might well still be in accord with Scripture to act in another. An obvious example is in the worlds of hymnody and liturgy. A choice of hymnody in worship is never viewed as more than a *choice*, and it is determined partly by issues like the theme of the liturgy, but partly by subjective issues, such as poetic taste or a sense that 'this one speaks to me', rather than by direct and insistent revelation of God. Similarly, if the Church has a broadly accepted way of celebrating communion, we go with it, at least in an interim way. Article XX says that the Church 'hath power to decree Rites or Ceremonies', and that would seem plain sense.* It is obvious that in a hundred other areas of decision-taking, two or more of any courses of action or directions of movement may be equally compatible with the scriptural revelation, and in principle the decision will have to be taken by the competent person or persons, the appropriate 'authority', on secondary grounds, but subject to the limits of action set by the Scriptures.

This appears to me to be fully in accord with all that we have seen of the second century. The appeal then was to the writings of the apostles over against errors of various sorts which were worming their way into the life of the Church. While great importance was attached to the oral handing on of apostolic truth in days before printing was invented, in principle the same dynamic was at work as in the argument I have set out above: the teachers of the faith claim to be handing on what the apostles had taught; and that received

---

*There may be controversy about who are 'the Church' which has this power – but even on a doctrine of total congregational independency (which, as we shall see below, is not the thrust of this book nor of Anglicanism itself), yet then 'the church', *being the local congregation*, clearly has the power. If there is controversy behind or around this Article it is a controversy more about the nature of 'the Church' than about its powers and duties.

body of teaching, with high credibility simply because it was the Christian tradition, could nevertheless be checked, yes, and could in principle be corrected, from the writings of the apostles themselves at any point.

However, this kind of doctrine requires us to evaluate three latter-day alternative statements about Scripture and tradition:

1 The rejection of tradition

Firstly, there is the Puritan denial of any positive value in tradition at all. *Sola scriptura* in its purest form can only function with Scripture and only value Scripture, and thus can only approach Church traditions with the gravest suspicion. This was the storm-centre of the conflict between churchmen and Puritans in the reigns of Elizabeth and the Stuart kings. The Puritans were incensed by the mandatory retention of any pre-Reformation ceremonies in the liturgy, and objected that the Settlement must not impose the 'excepted ceremonies' (see footnote on p. 259), as these were not of commandment in Scripture. Notable latter-day practitioners of this same *'sola'* principle have been the Christian Brethren (who in theory have no formulations of doctrine, no requirements of patterns in worship, no ministers or other officers – and no traditions). It is arguably the position of many 'new Churches' today – though in their case there is always also the suspicion that they may accord such *de facto* authority to the leading and presence of the Holy Spirit as in practice to override Scripture, and in any case there seems to be a lack of formulated statements (including creeds) which would either express or define the role and status of tradition within them.*
The same position surfaced in the anguished protest of the Methodist dissenters from the Report of the Conversations between the Church of England and the Methodist Church in 1963: 'In a word, tradition represents the wordliness of the Church, Scripture points to its supernatural origin and basis'.[1] This cannot but be too strong a protest; though, to be fair, it

---

*This is a provisional and even untutored statement. It arises from my being involved in theological dialogue with at least some leaders and theologians of these networks; but I would be very ready to be corrected.

arose from a conviction that there was too great a divinising of tradition by the Methodist majority within those Conversations.

2 Are Scripture and tradition equal and in double harness?

Secondly, there is the 'twin source' theory of the Church of Rome. While Roman Catholic theologians would have been clear throughout the Middle Ages that Rome taught only what the apostles had taught the Church, when pressed at the time of the Reformation, they stated that not all that the apostles taught was actually to be found explicitly in Scripture, but that there had been a live oral apostolic tradition in the Church which supplemented the revelation contained in Scripture. This meant that absolutely any doctrine taught by the Church in the late Middle Ages (such as purgatory or the intercession of the saints) could be traced confidently and unerringly to the apostles. Thus technically the Church of Rome at the Council of Trent was enunciating not exactly a twin-source theory, but a single-source-conveyed-to-us-by-twin-means doctrine:

> [This Council] following the example of the orthodox Fathers, receives and venerates with an equal affection of piety and reverence all the books both of the Old and New Testament . . . as also the said [unwritten] traditions, those relating to faith as well as to morals, as having been dictated either by Christ's own word of mouth, or by the Holy Spirit, and preserved in the Catholic Church by a continuous succession.[2]

For all practical purposes this decree locates authority for belief in the magisterium of the contemporary Church – for on this basis almost anything can be promulged in a later generation as an unwritten tradition stemming from the apostles; and obviously there can be no appeal from such 'unwritten tradition' to the written Scriptures, for by definition the unwritten is as 'apostolic' and as authoritative as the written. Yet there are at sight many apparent clashes, so an official interpretation and reconciliation is needed. Thus the 'twin means' in fact remove all power of interpretation from the ordinary reader and deliver it over to the contemporary teaching authority in the Church.* The historic cartoon of a Roman Catholic teacher is of an authority figure saying, 'Yes, the Bible is the word of God; but it is difficult and you won't understand it, so I/we will explain it to you, and *then* you will know what to believe.' A Church taking such a stance is taking certain risks once it encourages lay people to study the Scriptures on their own . . .

The best defence of this kind of Catholic approach is to make the following propositions:

1   The Church preceded Scripture and has authority over it;
2   Oral tradition conveyed the Gospel from the start – and it was a random, or at least selective, matter as to which parts of the oral tradition happened to find written expression in Scripture; plenty did not, but, orally conveyed, they are no less apostolic;
3   The Church itself then defined the canon of Scripture.

I hope my opening chapters have sufficiently answered these points for present purposes. For the moment I reverse each one of these propositions and briefly counter-suggest:

1   The word of God (in the Old Testament and in live testimony to Jesus) created the Church;
2   That word, written down as the New Testament writings, was not so much an urbane product of the Church's internal teachings as God's fiery prophetic word to correct, continue and establish the Church, which his word had originally formed;
3   The Church did not arbitrarily define the canon, but rather, finding the apostolic corpus of writings within itself, acknowledged the canon's authority and submitted to it.
4   The difficult onus of proof is on any unscriptural latter-day belief which claims to have come unwritten from the apostles.

It is important too to recognise that, in the second century, the authors whom we possess revert constantly to the apostles'

---

*It has to be added that the bishops at the Council of Trent obviously thought they were defending apostolic teaching. There had not at that time been any concept of the 'development' of Christian doctrine, and the issue between Protestants and Roman Catholic was largely one as to how it is to be established that this or that formulation is truly apostolic.

writings, and fail to affirm that they are guardians of a trans-
mitted (but unwritten) parallel and complementary word of
God.

3 Has Rome changed?

George Carey (in a pre-episcopal writing) suggests that the
second Vatican council rejected this 'two-source concept'.[3] I
do not myself read the Constitution on Revelation that way.[4]
However, he is on better ground when he quotes from *The
Final Report* of ARCIC I:

> The person and work of Jesus Christ, preached by the apos-
> tles and set forth and interpreted in the New Testament
> writings, through the inspiration of the Holy Spirit, are
> the primary norm for Christian faith and life ... since the
> Scriptures are the uniquely inspired witness to divine revel-
> ation, the Church's expression of that revelation must be
> tested by its consonance with Scripture.'[5]

This looks as though the Roman Catholics on the Commission
have moved quite some distance, but one is left with a distinct
impression that Rome itself has not moved like that (and
actually cannot – how can the Marian decrees be squared with
this principle?). Certainly the documents of ARCIC I received
a less than enthusiastic welcome from the Vatican; and two
recent documents suggest a less flexible Roman response. The
first of these is in a far less satisfactory document from
ARCIC II:

> A distinction needs to be drawn between what Jesus is
> recorded as saying and doing, and his implicit intentions
> which may not have received explicit formulation till after
> the Resurrection, either in the words of the risen Lord
> himself or through his Holy Spirit instructing the primitive
> community. 'All this I have spoken while still with you. But
> the Counsellor ... will teach you all things.'[6]

It would be *just* possible to expound Jesus' 'implicit intentions'
as the revelation which is found in the Acts, the epistles and
Revelation – i.e. in the rest of the canon of the New Testament
over and above the gospels. But it is only just possible, and it
looks as though the text was drafted to reassure the pope

(for whose eyes chiefly, by an odd procedural deviation, the document was written). He would naturally read the text, I take it, as giving a strong boost to the 'unwritten traditions'.

Certainly when the present pope speaks, even in a document of extremely irenic spirit, we are left in little doubt:

> The examination of such disagreements [i.e. disagreements about the faith between different Christian bodies] has two essential points of reference: Sacred Scripture and the Great Tradition of the Church. Catholics have the help of the Church's living Magisterium . . .

> At the same time, however, they [post-Reformation Churches] 'think differently from us . . . about the relationship between the Scriptures and the Church. In the Church, according to Catholic belief, an authentic teaching office plays a special role in the explanation and proclamation of the written word of God' . . .

> It is already possible to identify the areas in need of fuller study before a true consensus of faith can be achieved: the relationship betwen Sacred Scripture, the highest authority in matters of faith, and Sacred Tradition as indispensable to the interpretation of the Word of God.[7]

While each of these three quotations expresses the problem, and sets out the Roman position which creates the problem, the third of the three is the most telling. It asserts the primacy of Scripture; it then negates it. An 'indispensable interpreter' is both an infallible controller of that which he interprets, and a paternalistic controller of those to whom he interprets.

4 Can Anglicans entrench a twin-means concept?

Anglicans at the time of the Reformation invoked 'tradition' on two different fronts at once. They were accustomed to invoking the 'early Church' for two purposes: firstly, selectively, whenever an apt quotation from Ambrose or Augustine or John Chrysostom sounded like backing for some principle which they had in fact derived from their reading of Scripture;[8] and, secondly, when they wanted to nail a Roman apologist with the inconsistency between sixteenth-century Rome and the

Fathers to whom Rome was bound by its own stance – an *ad hominem* argument.[9] They were also ready to urge a limited continuity with the pre-Reformation Church to the Puritans, though only in a context of a need for reformation of those things which actually needed reformation, and a continuity of those things which did not. (The Puritans thought that everything needed reformation . . .) Each of these limited uses of different parts of Church history was by definition subject to the supreme authority of Scripture, and none violated the general relationship between Scripture and tradition which we have examined above. At times a very high (and even romantic) view of the early Church was to be found among churchmen of the seventeenth century. Some of this admittedly went to further lengths in the non-jurors of the eighteenth century; but the Church of England itself was in that century in more danger of Latitudinarianism, rationalism or even Socinianism – of believing less than the scriptural revelation rather than more. Its scripturally-based framework remained in place throughout, and was perfectly capable, as far as doctrine was concerned, of retaining the Evangelical Revival (though Wesley and Fletcher were perhaps a little adrift of the Articles in respect of free will); the separation of the Methodists arose over different issues – of good order on the one hand, and of 'enthusiasm' on the other. The supremacy of Scripture was in theory a shared value across any divide about 'enthusiasm',* not of itself a divisive principle. The difference between Evangelicals (whether conforming Anglicans or separating Methodists) and most of the rest was not strictly doctrinal at all: it was simply that the Evangelicals *really* believed all the faith, and were staking their lives on it, and experiencing the power of the Spirit – they were 'enthusiasts' – while much of the rest of the Church of England was in that century fairly nominal in its profession of supernaturalism.

Shared doctrine did not, however, mark the relationship of the Tractarians of the next century to the rest of the Church of England. Now there was a sectional reassertion within an Anglican framework of something like a twin-source concept

---

*The word meant, in the Greek mysteries, 'God-inside-them' (*en-the-ousia*) and was used by opponents as a highly pejorative label.

of authority for belief. Newman was ready, in the early stages, to believe that Rome had apostasised, and he sought a '*via media*'. But the heart of this 'middle way' was that 'the Church' teaches, and the Bible is invoked to 'prove'. While he allowed in principle that traditions may be shown to be at odds with the Bible, in fact his doctrine made the teachings of 'the Church' supreme, and thus hardly open to criticism. But a great difficulty for him – one which is still present for those who would tread the same path – lay in defining the limits of what 'the Church' might teach. Initially it was the creeds and catechism, both safely in the Prayer Book, but he also reckoned that the Church taught apostolic succession, even if here it would have entailed 'the Tracts to prove'! Within a little while 'the Church' was also 'teaching' auricular confession, transubstantiation, purgatory, the transferable merits of the saints, and eucharistic sacrifice – far, far beyond the teachings of the 1662 Prayer Book, though, no doubt, the odd isolated text in the Bible could be cited to 'prove' them. But it is fairly obvious that an autonomous unaccountable system was being built. And the phrase, 'the Church to teach, the Bible to prove', was still around among Anglican Catholics when I was an undergraduate. It is a covert claim to an infallibility or near-infallibility lying elsewhere than in the Scriptures.* The difficulty for Anglicans who hold to it is not only that it is in destructive conflict with the supremacy of Scripture, but also that, once one has gone beyond Scripture, there remains a cluster of problems: firstly in locating anything with clear limits which 'the Church' is, as a Church, to teach; secondly and interconnectedly in defining who is the Church which is to set these limits and teach within them; and thirdly in

---

*It is also, in my experience, the characteristic feature of false sects. Their system of instruction is usually to have a book or body of doctrine, enshrining all their distinctive, bizarre or even dangerous doctrines, with some biblical references in the margin or at the foot of the page, so that individual biblical texts may be consulted which appear to buttress the overall teaching. It is, of course, this sort of use of the Bible which leads cynics to say 'you can prove anything from the Bible'. Christian teachers need to be very wary of a similar approach – even Chalcedonian teaching on the Trinity must demonstrate from the Bible that it is the best handling of the scattered biblical evidence that we know.

knowing how anyone can then test or challenge any teaching which may appear to go outside Scripture.

As with so many other Tractarian principles, this one secured a half-victory in the life of the Church of England, and has planted in many minds the notion that 'tradition' has unassailable authority among us, sometimes backed by the loaded modern interpretation which sees the Reformation as 'trying to get back to the life of the early Church' – or, more frequently, which supposes that we ourselves can get back 'behind the Reformation' to the supposedly serene, undivided, and fully chartable model of the early Church. The argument until quite recently, then, proceeded on the basis that the Reformers had insufficient knowledge to do this properly, while new knowledge would enable us to do it confidently today. To this one must reply not only that the Reformers never gave antiquity quite that status, but that the evidence we have of the earliest centuries is still very scanty indeed, and cannot even be securely dubbed 'typical'; but, if it is of value, it points consistently to the supremacy of Scripture in the thoughts and lives of those Fathers (see Chapters 6–7 above). If the Fathers are to be viewed as in some sense repositories of God's truth, it is not through their discovering or creating a faith at variance with that of the New Testament or deliberately twisting that which they read in the New Testament, but rather through their striving to reproduce the apostolic (that is, the New Testament) faith and to commend it to their own times.

One serious attempt to write a twin-source notion into a Church of England which had never before entrenched it came with the post-war revision of the canons. The original Canon Law Commission, which reported in 1947, recommended a draft Canon V which would have read:

> The doctrine of the Church of England is grounded in the Holy Scriptures and in the teaching of the Fathers and Councils of the Church, and is particularly contained in the Thirty-Nine Articles of Religion, the Book of Common Prayer, and the Ordinal.[10]

This looks fairly innocuous, and, if the councils are viewed solely as the formulators of the creeds (which is not what the draft says, but might be a disarming way of expounding it), then that 'core' teaching might in fact be close to Scripture.

Closer inspection, however, shows that there was being written in effect a second, independent source (or at least channel) of revelation in the way the 'teaching of the Fathers and Councils' is presented. That would have shifted the position of the Church of England considerably.

However, in the event, the Church Assembly, in its debates upon the report of the Commission, and in its revising of the draft texts of the canons, listened to opponents of this formulation and came up with the canon we have today:

A.5 The doctrine of the Church of England is grounded in the Holy Scriptures and in such teaching as the Fathers and Councils have collected from the said Scriptures, and is particularly contained in the Thirty-Nine Articles of Religion, the Book of Common Prayer, and the Ordinal.

This makes all of the difference. The early Church writers are not now a separate source of revelation, but they are commentators on Scripture whose work is only accepted when it can be seen to be 'collected' from Scripture. The canon hints at some status for the creeds, but in essence make the derivative formulations genuinely derivative and secondary. The same distinction is found in the current Declaration of Assent:

The Church of England ... professes the faith uniquely revealed in the holy Scriptures and set forth in the catholic creeds ... Led by the Holy Spirit, it has borne witness to Christian truth in its historic formularies, the Thirty-Nine Articles of Religion, the Book of Common Prayer, and the Ordering of Bishops, Priests and Deacons ...

We thus get:
- a unique revelation;
- a derivative summary;
- an historic witness.

Quite apart from the actual nature of Scripture and the earlier quotations from the Ordinal and the Articles, the current canon and this Declaration leave the supremacy of Scripture still in place in the Church of England, and very clearly affirmed.

5   Can Scripture and tradition be equated?

There exists on the breeze a notion that 'Montreal' solved the problem of Scripture and tradition. The reference is to the Montreal Faith and Order Conference of 1963, and to its section of 'Scripture, Tradition and Traditions'. A sample quotation will give the flavour of this statement:

> ... We wish to propose the following statement as a fruitful way of reformulating the question. Our starting-point is that we are all living in a tradition which goes back to our Lord and has its roots in the Old Testament, and are all indebted to that tradition inasmuch as we have received the revealed truth, the Gospel, through its being transmitted from one generation to another. Thus we can say that we exist as Christians by the Tradition of the Gospel ... testified in Scripture, transmitted in and by the Church through the power of the Holy Spirit. Tradition taken in this sense is actualized in the preaching of the Word, in the administration of the Sacraments and worship, in Christian teaching and theology, and in mission and witness to Christ by the lives of the members of the Church.[11]

This kind of statement, hailed as a breakthrough, is matched by the majority report of the Anglican–Methodist Conversationalists earlier the same year. The actual wording there is: 'Now we are coming to see that Scripture and tradition ought not to be put over against each other. Both are gifts and instruments of the Holy Spirit within the Church.'[12]

I do not believe these verdicts can stand. However attractively put, they make historical developments in the Church the fruit of the Holy Spirit, simply because they are historical developments. Scripture is then a slightly earlier form of historical development, but if it has been overlaid with deviations (as clearly happened during the Middle Ages), then the deviations are classified simply as 'tradition' which has been shaped by the Holy Spirit. I cannot see how a deviating church life (or even individual Christian life) can be judged and corrected by Scripture if at any point it is accurate to say (with Montreal), 'Scripture bears a testimony, but the transmission down history has rightly put another slant on it', or (with the Conversationalists), 'The historical developments which we inherit are not to be set over against Scripture, but must be true outworkings of that all-embracing tradition which includes the Scripture.'

To be fair the Conversationalists themselves acknowledge the problem: 'By itself, however, tradition in this wide sense exercises no authority, gives no answer to the problem acutely raised in many critical periods of Church history, how to diagnose virus, poison in the blood stream, and what are the remedies and safeguards against it.'[13]

The whole point of the supremacy of Scripture is not simply that it is a useful quarry for discovering information about the faith, but that it provides a norm of faith and life to be set over against existent church life, and by which the latter can be corrected and, ideally, reinvigorated, as the unique revelation in Scripture judges the points of actual practice we have reached in particular church life. I see no way out of the proper dynamics of the Scripture recalling the Church to God's standards, save in asserting and practising the supremacy of Scripture over against tradition.* To put this at its starkest and clearest, we must say that there is no Jesus but the Jesus meeting us from Scripture, no Holy Spirit but the Holy Spirit revealed to us in Scripture.[14]

There is a run-on from that Anglican–Methodist report in England. When the developed *Scheme* was published in 1968, with a slightly different team handling the issues, it gave more space to the issue. It endeavoured to report that the 1963 material had sufficiently established 'holy Scripture as the sole

---

*I do not stay on the variant about authority which is sometimes around, and lurks behind the Montreal Statement – i.e. the insistence that the true fount of authority in the Church is not Scripture but the living Christ (or even the Holy Spirit). This sounds admirable – and spiritual, and even spiritually superior. But we still have to learn the mind of Christ by some means or another, and we shall either be left with the wholly subjective (a persuasion that, whatever we are doing or believing, that is the will of Christ) or we shall be driven to Scripture (or less reliable authorities) to know the mind of Christ, indeed to know the true Christ at all. This contrast between Christ and the Scriptures is sometimes reinforced by the raising of a spectre of bibliolatry, as the natural trap into which Scriptures-lovers may fall; but it is a nonsense, for those who love the text of Scripture are inevitably pointed by it to the ascended Christ.

and authoritative source of "all doctrine required of necessity to eternal salvation", and as the norm and standard of doctrinal and ethical teaching, of worship, and of practice for the Church in every age.'[15] However, the team went on to quote the passage above which says that tradition of itself 'exercises no authority'. They then went not to the majority report of 1963, but to the minority one and quoted approvingly from the four Methodist dissenters in that report: 'All Christians have much to learn from the past, but it is their perpetual obligation to bring their inherited customs, institutions and traditions to the bar of Scripture, by which Christ rules his Church.'[16]

Clarity was beginning to re-emerge from the murk. A final stage, in which Jim Packer provided continuity with *The Scheme*, came with *Growing into Union* in 1970. After a careful discussion of the ways in which tradition and Scripture can and should stand close to each other, the argument concludes:

> Tradition, however venerable, is not infallible as a mode of transmission, and needs constantly to be tested by the Scriptures whose witness to Christ it seeks to convey. Scripture, however inspired, was not meant to be self-sufficient as a means of instruction and life, but to operate within the common life of the Christian community by way of preaching, sacrament, fellowship and prayers.[17]

6 Any mileage in 'Scripture, tradition and reason'?

There is a convention that Anglicanism derives from a three-fold authority of 'Scripture, tradition and reasons'. These are regularly juxtaposed, and occasionally sound as though they are the 'received wisdom' of Anglicanism. An associated (though not identical nor sufficiently explicatory) phrase is 'dispersed authority'. This appears to have originated in a Committee report of the 1948 Lambeth Conference:

> Authority, as inherited by the Anglican Communion from the undivided Church of the early centuries of the Christian era, is single in that it is derived from a single Divine source, and reflects within itself the richness and historicity of the divine Revelation, the authority of the eternal Father, the incarnate Son, and the life-giving Spirit. It is distributed

among Scripture, Tradition, Creeds, the Ministry of the Word and Sacraments, the witness of the saints, and the *consensus fidelium*, which is the continuing experience of the Holy Spirit through His faithful people in the Church. It is thus a dispersed rather than a centralized authority having many elements which combine, interact with, and check each other . . . It may be said that authority of this kind is much harder to understand and obey than authority of a more imperious character.[18]

Some of these ways of formulating Anglican principles of authority run specifically counter to the monolithic-looking centralised Roman authority. They seem then to have been influenced by a fear of treating the Scriptures as having supreme authority, lest that would be to sell out to some obscurantist fundamentalism. The post-war atmosphere of Anglicanism has undoubtedly been affected by a liberal cry that too many people are looking for the solid ground of either an infallible pope or an infallible Bible, whereas in fact mature and critical faith requires a more cautious path towards certainty than can ever be allowed by such plumping for one or other authority offering instant assurance. My own former boss, Hugh Montefiore, puts it now in terms of *four* authorities: Scripture, tradition, reason and experience.[19] However, at this stage a confusion is starting to set in: it is fair to say that the external attestation that leads a man or woman to accept some article of faith is bound to have some responding internal element of experienced conviction motivating the acceptance, but we note that to adopt such an analysis is almost ceasing to think ecclesially and is only asking about the individual. Our question is about authority for belief within the Church, about the basis of doctrinal formularies adopted or imposed within the Church.

We therefore return to address the triad of Scripture, tradition and reason to see whether the three sources do provide a genuine three-legged stool on which to sit, a stool, that is, whose three legs are of equal length and equal strength and rest equally on level ground of truth. We find that history (as well as the already quoted classic formularies) is against this delightful fantasy of three-sources-in-harmony. The whole point of the Reformation was that Scripture was being invoked *over against* Church tradition. The issue of what to believe when they coincide (as, for instance, in respect of the Trinity or the creeds) was of only passing interest; the crucial issue, the one over which blood might be spilled or nations divided, was which source was to prevail when Scripture and tradition clashed.

We might say the same in respect of reason. Is the resurrection of Jesus, so clearly attested in Scripture, *reasonable*? Reason is likely to approach such an issue from assumptions; and, if the assumption is that 'dead men don't rise', then reason will obliterate all Scripture witness on the subject and decree it an invention, and reason is lording it over Scripture. If, on the other hand, reason functions in an open enquiring way to learn and accept what Scripture says, then it has become the servant of Scripture. If 'liberalism' means retaining the right to accept or reject existing articles of faith on the basis of their inherent probability, then the belief in the resurrection becomes purely an arbitrary personal decision, and, as it is *not* inherently probable, it is hard to see what justification there would be for including it in the Church's creed. Thus the assertion that Scripture has supreme authority within the life of the Church does indeed demand that reason become its handmaid. This is far from a rejection of reason, which is clearly one of God's highest gifts to the human race. It is simply the Church saying that its members are to bring their reason into the service of God and of his word.

We thus conclude that Scripture, tradition and reason cannot be treated as three independent if complementary sources of Christian truth. Instead, Scripture remains supreme as the normative and irreformable expression of the word of God, tradition should convey the word of God but must be tested and reformed by it, and reason should be devoted to receiving and understanding the same word of God and applying it to each generation. The Church must still live 'under' the scriptural revelation. The historic formularies of the Church of England do assert this; and the modern Declaration repeats it.

13 The New Testament Church and the Church of England

If we return to the New Testament teaching about the Church, then we have a vision of a worldwide fellowship, bonded into a single nation, one body of Christ, made visible in the baptism of all its members, and in their conscious faith in Christ, their obedience to his word and their regular gathering in every locality across the face of the earth in obedience to their Lord's command, 'Do this in remembrance of me'. This Church proclaims one Jesus Christ as Lord and God, and witnesses to his coming kingdom throughout the world, and people are baptised into him as they come to faith in him. Its life is communal and is lived in deliberate obedience to the revelation of God in the scriptures. The Spirit transforms them as they live out this obedience.

How then does the *de facto* Church of England measure up against this standard?

1 Separation from Rome
This book begins with the separation from Rome – the point of decision which, as history unfolded in a highly unpredictable way, proved with hindsight to have been the point of origin of a wholly separated and distinctive brand of Christianity, Anglicanism, which has spread across the earth's surface to the extent of collecting roughly 800 bishops at the 1998 Lambeth Conference.

Until the 1520s, when the first winds of the Reformation began to blow on the Continent, the Western Church had always in theory been a single communion, living under a common patriarch, the bishop of Rome, and conforming to a common canon law. It was complex and diverse and not without internal theological debate. It was also superstitious and priest-ridden. At times its leaders were rapacious and immoral. Its doctrines had developed within an autonomous tradition until they were far distant from Scripture. It exercised an improper control over people's lives. But it was a single communion, bounded by a common baptism, and fully in communion with itself.*

Henry VIII reckoned to retain most of the features of this list. But in order to be done with the power of the bishop of Rome (and thus be free to marry Anne Boleyn), he was ready to risk the sundering of the single communion. What were the realities in his risk-taking?

Firstly, there was a conviction that there existed a definable 'Church of England' (as there had been, for instance, in Magna Carta). From Henry's point of view this was what the Articles later called a 'particular or national Church', an entity which was distinguishable from the Church of Rome and the jurisdiction of the bishop of Rome, and might take separate decisions about its life; which, in so doing, might be engaged in brinkmanship, but was not itself particularly seeking actually to break bonds of communion. Over the previous centuries there had been comings and goings about the distribution of powers patronage and jurisdiction with the pope (and there had even been a time with two popes, one in Avignon), but these had all sorted themselves out without ending the belonging to the pope – so now there was little expectation that Henry's quarrel was such as to be creating an irreparable breach.

Secondly, this Church of England was in principle coextensive with the citizenry of England, and their religious loyalty and their duties as citizens were not, in Henry's view, to be pulled in two opposite directions – the Church of England must therefore acknowledge the divinely appointed head of state as head of the Church. This was bound to bear hard upon the clergy, for they were in many senses the direct servants of Rome, a role from which they had to be deliberately detached. But it was bound to bear extremely hard indeed upon any persons, clergy or lay, who believed as an article of faith that

---

*This is not to ignore the existence of a Christian East, of which the sixteenth century was well aware. East and West were 'out of communion' with each other. But Western Europe was still an enormous ecclesiastical entity, to which England belonged.

the pope had a God-given universal jurisdiction, and who wanted to continue to live at ease in England in accord with that belief.

In the longer run, of course, Henry's actions 'nationalised' the Church of England, and in effect made it a department of state. It became a convention to look in justification for this to the models of Old Testament kingship (where, in Judah, kings ruled on behalf of God over a religio-politico entity in a unitary way).* It also meant that religious dissenters (whether unreformed papist or would-be reforming Protestant) were *ipso facto* political rebels. The people of England would constitute the royalist Church of England, and they would have little option but to take their religion the way they were given it – from one point of view, no new thing at all, for the pope had also made absolute requirements; but from another point of view highly disruptive, as they now had to see the matter differently from the way they had been brought up to see it; and it turned out that, when Edward succeeded his father, they had to learn almost a new religion – and in each case had to make the change under pain of prosecution overnight, or be in peril in the morning.

Thirdly, the separation from Rome included an assertion that the pope was in error. As we have seen, the case began from the belief that, if God had made a law (about marriage to a deceased brother's wife), then the pope could not dispense from that law. Henry obviously believed that the pope should not interfere in appointments in England, and, after the break, took severe umbrage at the pope's sentence of excommunication and his presumed favouring of rebels within England. Stories about the immorality, deceitfulness and self-aggrandisement of the popes received much encouragement in the remaining years of Henry's reign. Thus, even while so much of the medieval Latin worship was still in place, Henry's view of the pope was canonised in Cranmer's first English-language litany in 1544: 'From the tyranny of the Bishop of Rome and all his detestable enormities, Good Lord, deliver us.'

---

*In the Old Testament this kingship did not give to the kings roles in the temple worship, and a severe warning in the fate of Uzziah (2 Chron. 26:16–23) was duly noted, and eventually found its outworking in Article XXXVII of the Thirty-Nine.

While these years were passing, forces were preparing in various ways for the succession. The role of the monarchy itself (and the divine right of kings) was not in question, but special factors were arising such as to provide a very special opportunity for a theological change:

1 The monarch as head of the Church of England had now great freedom to impose change (usually, but not invariably, by working through parliament, as with the original breach with Rome);

2 The male heir to the throne, Edward, was only born in 1537, and would not come of age till far beyond the likely death of his father (who was clearly declining during the 1540s) – which would mean a Regency Council;

3 The actual power of guardianship as Lord Protector was to pass to Edward Seymour, the Duke of Somerset, brother of Jane Seymour and a convinced Protestant;

4 The archbishop of Canterbury, Thomas Cranmer, a vital member of the Council, was discreetly coming to a thoroughly Protestant set of doctrinal convictions – and some first signs of his influence in this direction were afoot, notably the provision in 1537 to set up an English Bible in each parish church.

So it came to pass. Henry died in January 1547, and the Council went about reforming the Church of England by imposed law (and daunting penalties) at breakneck speed. In the six and a half years which ensued there were injunctions, homilies, acts of parliament, two complete prayer books and two ordinals, a draft reform of canon law, and a vast amount of writings, controversies, consulting with Continental Protestants, and dealing with recalcitrants around the dioceses.

Mary's reign (1553–8) put everything into reverse. It was anomalous indeed that a Roman Catholic monarch could inherit a nation and the 'headship' of a Church in formal separation from Rome and by now deep into Protestant heresy. She set out to correct the anomaly. She burned some bishops, abused Bucer's bones, and led the nation in resubmitting to the pope. She also married Philip of Spain and thus alienated her own people, to whom Spain was *the* great political enemy; so, when she herself died childless in 1558, the country was much more ready to embrace Protestantism under her half-sister Elizabeth than it ever had been with previous monarchs. A new (1559) Act of Uniformity abolished the Latin uses, restored most of the provisions which were in force when Edward died, and set a course which would determine the general character of the Church of England for three centuries ahead.

There is no doubt this was a 'top down' Reformation and it produced a 'top down' Church. The Church of England would be governed by the queen in parliament, and Elizabeth was restive and unhappy about separate meetings of Convocation. Even archbishops were supposed simply to do what the queen demanded (Grindal was for many years under her majesty's displeasure for taking an initiative of which she disapproved). Bishops were there to support the monarch, and this became a cardinal feature in turn of the Stuart dynasty, and was arguably determinative of Charles I's readiness to die rather than surrender episcopacy.

Until 1689 the government's policy (except under the Commonwealth) was to keep the whole country under a unity of organisation, and a uniformity of forms of worship. Deviations were forbidden, and dissenters coerced into line. Roman Catholics were not simply dissenting but also, because of the 1570 papal bull dethroning Elizabeth, were technically traitors. They inevitably functioned underground, and the parish clergy were required by the 1604 canons to seek out 'recusants'. The whole attempt to get the whole citizenry to be but one Church is perhaps most strongly indicated by the provision in Elizabeth's reign of a fine for those who did not attend public worship on a Sunday; but the need for a fine (which was, we are told, rarely actually imposed) suggests that absenteeism was already rife.

2 Reactionary (papal) dissent

From the point of view of Roman Catholics of Elizabeth's reign and after, the Catholic Church which had once been in possession in England had been turned out of the church buildings of each parish and driven underground – and that was where the continuity of the Church was to be found. There is but 'One Holy Catholic and Apostolic Church' and they were it – and might have to be martyred for being faithful to it. The usurping royalist 'Church' was no Church, but an heretical sect, and they would not seek nor accept its ministrations. They would live as peaceably as they could as citizens, but in religious terms they would have to keep their heads well down.

From the point of view of the Church of England, Rome was now an enemy – literally so when she countenanced rebellion against Elizabeth or backed Philip of Spain's Armada, but spiritually so in any case. Rome barely met the new criteria for the 'notes' of the Church ('where the pure word of God is preached and the sacraments are duly ministered according to Christ's ordinance'), so it was questionable whether it really ranked as a Church at all; and it was by the providence of God, and the blood of the martyrs (Foxe's *Acts and Monuments*, commonly known as the *Book of Martyrs*, sold like hot cakes during Elizabeth's reign), that the Church of England had been delivered from the pope's thrall.

3   Reforming dissent

During Elizabeth's reign, there was a great upsurge of Puritan energies and initiatives within the Church of England. The basic principle of the Puritans' thought was that the Reformation had not proceeded to its proper conclusion, but had been stopped short well before the end was reached – and therefore now ought to be pursued relentlessly. Their programme included the dropping (or at least making optional) of the 'excepted ceremonies', the provision for preaching conferences ('prophesyings' as they were known), the end of versicles and responses (or any active congregational participation), the loosening of the requirement of a set liturgy, a virtual Presbyterianism (though they were prepared to call it 'primitive episcopacy') and a host of other demands. They lived within the Church of England uncomfortably, and were incessant in their demands. They built up hopes of James I as it became clear that he would inherit, for he had been brought up under Presbyterianism in Scotland; and thus, when he inherited, they duly met him on his way south with their 'Millenary Petition', a document signed by a thousand petitioners, setting out the redresses they desired. However, they got no change from the not-so-Presbyterian monarch, save the convening of the Hampton Court Conference (and thus in turn the 'King James Bible').*

Beyond the normal puritans were Anabaptists, much feared in England because of their democratic spirit and the rumours of their excesses on the Continent. The configuration they took in England was to form conventicles, semi-underground independent assemblies, often supported by the motto, 'Reformation, without tarrying for *any*' (my italics). There was thus a double struggle in the seventeenth century in this form:

1   a Church of England with a given form under a given management, arising from the Elizabethan Settlement, wishing to encompass the whole people of England in a single body, but on the imposed terms of the monarchy and the Settlement;

2   within that Church of England, but not usually in positions of power (until the time came when they were strong in parliament), a vocal and proactive Puritan force that wished to keep a single Church of England, but to have it fully reformed and to impose their own particular discipline in every parish;

3   over against that Church of England, independents who wanted to form pure conventicles at will, and could rarely be coerced into even minimal adherence to the parish church.

Groups 2 and 3 were, of course, fairly embattled, and rarely in a mood for compromise. Group 1, for political and monarchical reasons – as well as various mixtures of inertia, stupidity and/ or religious conviction – were also unlikely to compromise. Thus it was that groups 2 and 3 (who had vastly different religious aims) were driven together into a combined force to fight and win a civil war, run out Group 1, put a king to death, and, in a ramshackle and often irreverent or clumsy way, take over the parishes of the Church of England during the Commonwealth period.

The last attempts to keep all the citizenry of England in one Church came with the Restoration. The Savoy Conference between bishops and Presbyterian-type Puritans in early 1661 proceeded on the basis of a discussion of, 'What will the Church

---

*James said: 'Presbytery agreeth with monarchy as the Church of God agreeth with the devil'; and, 'No bishop, no king'.

of England be like henceforward?' (and of course the independents were not there). It is a matter of history that the
churchmen held all the cards and won all the tricks. Then
the 1662 Act of Uniformity, and the Prayer Book annexed to it,
functioned on the mythical assumption that the whole country
would conform, and that each parish would be wholly
Christian, wholly Protestant, and wholly 'C/E', and the unitary
concept of the Elizabethan Settlement would be restored. As
the Act required those clergy who had not been episcopally
ordained, as well as those who had been but were not prepared
to conform under such conditions, to leave their cures by 24
August 1662, it was actually highly unlikely that there would
be no dissenters – and in the event, there were above 1000
ministers and large numbers of laity. Legal account was soon
taken of them, and they were harried by the Clarendon Code –
the Penal Laws of the Corporation Act, the Five-Mile Act,
and the Conventicle Act. Clearly the assumptions of the Act of
Uniformity were myths, and the Church of England has lived
with a myth about its inclusion of the whole people of England
from that day to this.

Presbyterian-type Puritans who left the Church of England
(not a few stayed) were not only harried by the Penal Laws,
but were (paradoxically) often in conscience not wanting to set
up structures in opposition to the Church of England – and at
times lapsed (or advanced) into some kind of communion with
their parish churches, or the 'occasional conformity' which
Richard Baxter, the great leader of their type, himself
practised.

From 1685 to 1688 there was again a papist 'supreme governor' of the Church of England, a contradiction in terms if
ever there was one. James II was also extremely foolish, and
was duly run off the throne. In 1689, after the Glorious Revolution, the Church of England leaders had the option of going
for a more 'comprehensive' Church, which would have been
more truly the Church of the nation. Instead they took the
view that there was an Anglican 'churchmanship' (particularly
focused in monarchical episcopacy and the Book of Common
Prayer) which they could not compromise. So they discharged
their debt to the Nonconformists, who had assisted them in
resisting James, by providing not for inclusion or comprehen-

sion but for 'toleration' – conventicles were no longer banned but could flourish. Their adherents could not attend the ancient universities and could not hold public office under the crown, but were otherwise totally free (if licensed) to congregate and worship as they saw fit.

The story of the multiplication of denominations in England from 1689 to the present day is arguably the story of rushing enthusiasm among this group in one generation and that group in another, each such outburst leading to their forming conventicles – often helped on their way by the Church of England's disdainful inability to 'comprehend' them. The march of time very often reveals the present-day successors to the original enthusiasts as still in possession of the inherited buildings, constitutions and church structures. Yet there is also the anomaly that they are so often now sustaining a static or flagging tradition which remains in formal separation from those from whom they originally seceded, without their having the original reason of a burning Christian fervour to account for their separate existence. I offer a hop-skip-and-jump view of this phenomenon.

*a   The originals: Baptists, Congregationalists, Presbyterians**
These were the main groups in existence in 1689 – the first two being the major division of independents (being divided from each other over the question of infant baptism), the third being in principle keen to be in the national Church, but seeing the opportunity fleeing from them. The independents had no problems in establishing conventicles – they actually wanted to do so, and saw no difficulty in a multiplication of them. All three groups tended to fade in their enthusiasm in the eighteenth century. In 1972 the large proportion of Congregationalist and Presbyterian congregations joined with each other into the United Reformed Church, in which the full independency of Congregationalism was surrendered for the sake of joining a loosely connexionalist body. The Baptists saw

---

*I confess I have not attempted to work the Quakers (who also originated in the seventeenth century) into this scheme. They seem to be both so inclusive (having no standards or tests) and so exclusive (having so inflexible a style of communal life) as to defy categorisation.

a great expansion in the nineteenth century, have generally remained fairly zealously evangelical, and retain their formal independency of congregations. As between congregations their key word is 'association', a word which both betrays the originating principle of independency and yet qualifies it with a secondary principle of some mutual belongingness.

b   The Methodists

The Evangelical Revival is usually traced to the preaching of the Wesleys and George Whitefield from 1737 onwards. John Wesley lived on till 1791, and presided over a great chain of Methodist 'societies' which had sprung up in the wake of the preaching and the consequent organising into 'classes'. Wesley himself, being an Anglican presbyter, took the view that his converts belonged to their parish churches, and would only meet out of the time of church services, and then only as a 'society' for mutual encouragement, teaching and care. The converts themselves usually took a different view – that they were unwanted by the parish churches, that the sentiment was mutual, and that they belonged where they had heard and received the Gospel, and where they had experienced Christian love rather than a cold shoulder. At a late stage Wesley found himself forced to register the 'meeting houses' of 'the people called Methodists' as dissenting chapels, and in his last years he even ordained ministers to serve these people – something he had earlier done for Methodists in other countries, but would not do until that late stage in England. The moment he died, there was a denomination ready-made to assert its independence – though it contained within itself both the central grip, that Wesley had exercised and had bequeathed to his 'Legal Hundred', and the local autonomy which was inevitable with the relative self-sufficiency of each society or circuit. In the nineteenth century these emerged as the Wesleyan Methodists (the connexion with a strong central 'Conference'), the Primitive Methodists (who were nearer to being independents), and the Bible Christians, who, after some unions, further emerged into this century as the United Methodists (who were most strongly not only near-independent, but also somewhat anti-clericalist). These three strands united with each other in 1932.

c   The Brethren movement

In the 1830s some Anglicans in Dublin, led by an ordained presbyter, J. N. Darby, left the Church of Ireland and formed a congregation of their own, calling themselves 'Christian brethren', and seeking biblical holiness. The movement spread and multiplied, and it was sometimes called the 'Plymouth Brethren'. There were no ministers, and, for many of their meetings, no leadership of any sort – all could contribute (except, of course, the women). The movement had no principle of mutual belongingness, and assemblies have tended to divide rather than have internal disagreements – and their keen interest in eschatology has been a fertile breeding-ground for the disagreements which have led to such dividing. In effect there is no doctrine of the visible Church at all – only a slightly frail getting together of those who know themselves to be like-minded. At a later stage in the nineteenth century a clear distinction arose between the 'Open' and the 'Exclusive' Brethren. The Open Brethren have functioned not unlike a lay independent assembly, the key point being the readiness to admit to communion those who profess faith in Christ; whereas the Exclusive Brethren need to have baptised a person themselves, or to have letters of commendation from an assembly of their own sort which has done the baptism, before they admit such a person to communion.

d   The Salvation Army

General Booth went into 'darkest London' in the 1880s 'to save to the guttermost' those who were at the bottom of the heap in society. He found the brass band, which has been characteristic of the Army since, a potent interest-stirrer in the streets and squares. He opened halls (or 'citadels') where enquirers and those in need (especially drunks and prostitutes) could be succoured and converted – but, rather like Wesley with his converts, hesitated to become a 'Church'. The Army has continued with a very tight, well-drilled life of its own, strong in both faith and good works, yet not only celebrating no sacraments, but unsure how to relate to the rest of the Christian Churches.

e   Independent Evangelical Churches

At intervals from the second half of the nineteenth century onwards, two or three meeting in the Lord's name have decided to form their own Church, and many such independent congregations have dubbed themselves 'Independent Evangelical Churches'. There exists a Federation of them (the FIEC), but it is not at all clear how many have federated – certainly many have not. Where such churches employ recognised pastors they tend towards being seen as Baptists (usually Baptists which have not joined the Baptist Union); where they have no such pastors they tend to look like Brethren assemblies.

f   The Pentecostalist Churches

At the turn of the century Pentecostalism broke surface in both Britain and America, and formed distinctive congregations – traditionally identified as people 'baptised in the Spirit' and consequently 'speaking in tongues'. There exist two major networks in Britain – the Elim Churches and the Assemblies of God – and a great variety of smaller groupings or independent congregations. Until the early 1960s it was assumed that anyone in a 'mainline' or 'historic' denomination who began speaking in tongues would naturally expect to leave and join a Pentecostalist Church. That, however, has not been the case during the last 35 years.

g   The 'New Churches' (house church, or restorationist, movement)

With the rise of the charismatic movement in the mainstream Churches of England in the 1960s, there also arose a secession from them which did not depart to the long-standing Pentecostalists, but instead formed new groupings, which, to the persons concerned, had a sense of crossing from an old world of Churches into a new one. There have been various networks of such congregations, and a large church-planting thrust, and they showed enormous growth during the 1980s (tested by two Church censuses). Their ecclesiology is still largely undeveloped.

h   The 'black-led' or 'black-majority' Churches

Since the immigration from the West Indies started in Britain in the 1940s, there has been a rise in what were for a period known as 'West Indian Pentecostalist Churches'. These often include people who had been Anglican (or of another main-stream denomination) in the Caribbean, but who found themselves cold-shouldered by white Christians when they came here, and made welcome by black Churches in the area. There are some national (or, more accurately, international) networks, such as the New Testament Church of God and the Church of God of Prophecy, but also many independent congregations, some affiliated to the Council of Afro-Caribbean Churches or the International Ministerial Council of Great Britain. Not all members of black-led Churches are predomi-nantly Caribbean in their place of origin of the families; there are also thriving congregations of West African Christians, and they too have networks, such as the Church of the Cherubim and Seraphim, originally a Nigerian grouping. There are also Asian, Chinese, Korean and other ethnic or language-based groupings in and around London. These assemblings of people from a minority ethnic or language group may have extra values for them if they believe them-selves to be marginalised or even unwanted in English society, for then gatherings of like-minded persons in the same social conditions are reassuring and supportive. On the other hand, they do tend to fall short of the New Testament fullness entailed in 'neither Jew nor Gentile, bond nor free'; and a particular responsibility falls upon those committed to cath-olicity to seek ways of converging and integrating with them.

This listing provides eight separate historic groupings, apart the Church of England and the 'historic' Churches of Rome and of Eastern Orthodoxy. It is perhaps worth noting that groups a, b, d and h, but not the other four, have joined in the 'ecumenical instruments' in England. What are we to make of all this?

4 Apologia towards Rome

Firstly, we need an Anglican apologia towards Rome. Rome has the claims of history, of numbers and of a profound under-standing of the worldwide organic unity of the Church of God. We left this Church; and it is obviously part of the biblical exposition earlier in this book to say that 'leaving' or 'seceding' or 'going into schism' is without biblical warrant. Those who share 'one Lord, one faith, one baptism' should belong visibly to each other.

The only defensible reason for the English to have been Anglican rather than Roman Catholic is that Rome is wrong, and that this error is not incidental in the framing of an article of faith, but is fundamental in establishing improper authorities for belief. This can be illustrated from particular doctrines, but it is not in them that the fundamental differences lie. Particular doctrines will only illustrate the issue, but it may be helpful to begin with such an illustration.

So we consider the issue of the Blessed Virgin Mary. No one who draws a pattern of beliefs from the New Testament would ever arrive at the Roman doctrines of Mary – none of the Evangelical Churches which claims Scripture as the primary authority for faith has ever done so or is ever likely to. Furthermore, none of the second-century and third-century authors, whose primary authority was Scripture (those who are considered in Part II above), ever did so. So it is up to an Evangelical today to urge that the doctrines about Mary both ask us to believe in unbiblical, unknown, uncharted miracles asserted about Mary and also disturb the unique mediatorship of Jesus.

But this illustrates that the issue is in fact much deeper than particular teachings about Mary. It is an issue of 'On what authority?' Certainly Pius IX in 1854 and Pius XII in 1950, the two popes who respectively defined the doctrines of the Immaculate Conception and the Bodily Assumption of Mary, did not invent the ideas out of their own heads – no, they were articulating and entrenching deep and widespread devotional traditions within their Church. But it is clear that those traditions had not grown and developed in accord with the teachings of Scripture – nor, for what it is worth, with the early Fathers – but through a kind of internal devotional auction within the life of the Roman Catholic Church, largely in the second millennium of its existence. The promulgation of the definitions exactly illustrates the different positions taken by Rome and by us on authority for belief – and illustrates that 'unwritten traditions' naturally resolve themselves into the voice of a contemporary magisterium (see p. 200).

Indeed, an Evangelical approaching the development of such traditions within the Church would have to be saying just the opposite of the popes: they, it seems, asked themselves, 'How can I define and entrench within the future life of the Church this valuable devotional belief which has been steadily growing over the centuries and is now in full bloom?' But we, if we discovered such teaching in our Church (and actually we can), would be asking, 'How can we bring this exaggerated set of beliefs about Mary to the test of holy Scripture and confine ourselves in relation to her to the role in the Christian faith that holy Scripture gives her?'*

It is as simple as that. We do not excommunicate the Church of Rome; but, by historical accident, and through some not-altogether-lovely persons of the sixteenth century and, we submit, the providence of God, we, who historically were part of the Roman fabric, have freed ourselves from Rome's principles of belief and reverted to the biblical faith. We think Rome is wrong; we are glad to have dialogue about the Christian faith to see if we can reduce the gap between us; and we do not excommunicate Rome. It is Rome who has excommunicated us.

I should add that I am enormously appreciative of all that Vatican II has brought in. I can recall sharing seminars in the 1950s as an undergraduate with a godly Roman Catholic; but he could not attend a service of worship in a Protestant context, and he was forbidden to say the Lord's Prayer with me. We could just manage to discuss the Greek text of the New Testament together, as we were studying classics! But Vatican II has since unleashed in Rome the Bible, the laity, and a view of other Christians in ways that can never now be reversed. The issue which is difficult to address is the extent to which the 'traditions' of the Church of Rome are sacrosanct,

---

*An Anglican who holds to some autonomy for 'tradition' is in some trouble here, for, without an authoritative magisterium, it is difficult to know what status particular traditions should have. It is doubly difficult if a doctrine has been defined by Rome in the last century and a half, so that it never was part of, say, the pre-Reformation tradition. And it is not helped by an individual semi-private decision to take on some (though clearly not all) beliefs on the pope's say-so, even though remaining within the fabric of a Church which rejects the basis of such definitions.

and the extent to which they can be gently re-interpreted (I do not here address the issue of papal authority and infallibility).

I put this in fairly stark and adversarial tones not in order to provoke, but in order to clarify. The organic unity of Christ's Church on earth is such that nothing but the most serious issues of truth and error would ever justify our separation. This is not simply a matter of choice, taste, upbringing or preference – we are separate only through having been driven from Rome by its principles. It is a separation which is hurtful in the extreme, a separation which both sides ought to mitigate by as much Christian sharing, dialogue and joint action as possible.

5 Policy towards 'dissent'

Many of the denominations listed under my eight categories above were founded upon a principle of 'We will split away from existing Christians to give especial force to a doctrine or a fervour that they have neglected'. Often, in England, their very existence is a condemnation of the dryness, social airs, cultural exclusiveness, pastoral insensitivity or sheer lack of Christianity in the Church of England at the time of their origin. We can today look back to those various points of origin and lament the errors of our spiritual forebears, and applaud the spiritual power of those who seceded. Incidentally, however, it is likely that very few foundings of new groupings or connections were actually done in protest against episcopacy. Most anti-Anglican moves in history have been opposing 'uniformity', or the liturgy, or the spiritual deadness of the parish church, or the state connection, or the upper-middle-class ethos, or particular incumbents or churchwardens of unlovely character. A distrust of episcopacy, or a dislike of the way it manifests itself in the Church of England, may have been later added to the original rationale, but it is rarely the single or central precipitating factor in the original secession.

However, we now face an extraordinary problem. All the products of the succeeding centuries, as listed above, are still with us today, and, as often as not, they have forgotten why they stood separate. A good proportion of lay people either belong to a local congregation for traditional denominational reasons ('I've always been a Methodist') or for reasons to do with the choices in the particular locality ('I come here because I can walk here on Sundays', or 'I come here because my neighbour brings me', or 'I come here because you know where you are in the service'). The result may be up to seven church buildings within a few hundred metres of each other, all or most technically belonging to different wider national bodies, with very little connection with each other.* It is all the odder and sadder if in fact they profess a virtually identical faith, but are still out of relationship with each other. And it is sadder beyond that if on balance they are in gentle decline.

The tendency nowadays is to rationalise such proliferation. There are those who say 'the more the merrier', those who want people to have a choice (as in supermarkets or football clubs), those who argue that when revival comes we shall need every possible building and congregation which we currently possess, and those who see no need to defend the multiplicities because they have failed to see any problem about them anyway. Outside 'Catholic' circles the concept of organic and structural unity is hard to find as an actual driving force in church life. There may occasionally be those in particular denominations who believe they are right and everybody else is wrong – but that is rare (outside of Rome and Eastern Orthodoxy). There may be those who, without going quite so far, believe their denomination ought to persist into the future to give witness to some specially valued portion of truth which other denominations are thought incapable of providing, or providing adequately. All institutions – especially gently fading ones – are caught in an institutional inertia which would rather leave things as they are this year, and reckon perhaps to address any growing problems next year. So, as a general rule, denominations, even those which profess a distant goal of organic unity, nevertheless justify their separate existence by some form of rationalising. And all denominations are caught in the immediate necessity of

---

*The 'seven' is deliberately conservative, though close to my experience as an incumbent in the Medway towns in recent years. After the riots in Handsworth in September 1985, I discovered that there were 57 Christian congregations located in about a square mile of inner-city Birmingham – in the very area that had been torn apart and combusted by the riots.

keeping congregations going to provide finance to keep ministers in action to keep congregations going to provide finance . . . and so *ad infinitum*.

The result is totally unlike anything to be found in the New Testament. I list the more obvious unbiblical outcomes:

1   People are indeed being offered a choice. They are being told *sotto voce* (or even openly) that individually being a Christian is one thing, and finding the right church is another. They are usually told that they ought to belong to some church or another, but which that should be is clearly a personal choice which comes logically and chronologically, and presumably theologically, in separation from, and subsequent to, being converted. Once the choice is made, then a particular congregation will hope it will stick – that the attender will become a joiner and will say, 'Yes, I am a member of St Luke's' (and pay a proportionate share of the necessary finance). But it is only a subjective hope, and attenders may stay on the fringe, or run well for a time, or even sign up now, and then stump out later when a new minister or organist or greeter does not please him or her. There is no such deep bonding to the structure of the Church of God as is implied in the New Testament doctrines of the 'body' and the 'temple'.*

One of the most unbiblical features of this 'choosing' is that, in effect, all are being invited to belong where they 'fit', where there are like-minded people. That is exactly comparable to Peter choosing only to eat with Jewish Christians in Antioch (Gal. 2:11–16, and see p. 97). It creates a notion of 'fellowship' as 'having like-minded people round me whom I naturally like and with whom I interact easily'. This is exactly the opposite of the fellowship in Christ in the New Testament, where there is neither Jew nor Greek, bond nor free, male nor female, black nor white etc. We are over a barrel: of course we want to entice the half-believer or might-be-believer to attend a congregation where he or she

---

*That does not mean that this language is avoided: quite the reverse – the more determinedly subjective and voluntarist people are in their adherence to their local congregation, the more they talk about 'body-life', and being 'one in the body of Christ', and the more they see 'subjective' fellowship as that sharing and unity in the body.

will 'naturally' feel 'at home', and yet the very challenge of Christian fellowship ought radically to change the natural idea of 'home'. Christian congregations ought to be where the unlike are bonded with the unlike.

2   The ministers are hired to build up their particular congregations. No minister can say to the leading lay persons of his or her own congregation, 'I have been advising newcomers to go down the road to the High Street church, as I am persuaded they have a better chance of being built up in Christ there.' The lay leaders are bound to respond: 'But you have been hired to believe that we here offer the best possible pattern of Christian nurture, church life and witness, and you have been hired to bring people in on that basis, and to encourage us to do the same; if you don't believe that, and aren't prepared to act in that way, then you are our death-knell and the sooner you leave the better.' So, however courteous ministers may be to each other, even praying together for the building up of each other's congregations, at root they are in unspoken fierce competition (and are open also to both the smugness, or self-congratulation, of those who win a competition and the aching sorrow and erosion of self-confidence of those who are losing it).

3   In general any sense of the Church of God being incarnated in an area is lost. The best rationale for a territorial parish would be if the believers down one street knew each other, prayed with each other, worshipped with each other on Sundays, and took joint responsibility for evangelising and giving practical care to the needy within their street. But the reality of urban church life is that the tiny percentage of the population who attend Christian worship on a Sunday all emerge from their homes at different times and go by different forms of transport, of which the car is most prominent, to chosen places of worship which may or may not be local. Any interrelatedness between them, arising from being brothers and sisters in Christ, is excluded by their being largely unaware of each other's existence; and, if they do become aware of that, by their still being largely separated from each other by different routines, by different belongingnesses, and even by that half-suppressed sense of competition.

4   Denominationalism means that we have lost all sense of visible unity. If four congregations face each other at the four corners of a crossroads, the issue is not whether their communion-tables are open to each other, but how it is that the Church of God has four different communion-tables within that short distance. What would Paul – or Cyprian – have said? In one sense, to excommunicate all others, and thus declare them 'not-Church', might be a more consistent and logical response to that situation than simply to say, 'We receive them all without making a distinction'. Both are attempts to make rational sense of an irrationally bad situation, and the judgement should be levelled against the situation, not against the remedies.

5   A further upshot is that there is no traceable doctrine of schism! If half a congregation decide to walk out from the rest and to set up another grouping for worship round the corner, there is no doctrinal come-back, no biblical argument to dissuade them. If that congregation was formed by people exercising their 'right to choose' in the first place, then people have an equal right to choose to walk out, not only singly but also *en bloc*, whenever they wish. They have associated with each other voluntarily; they may later dissociate from each other equally voluntarily.

6   A corollary of all the above is a steady collapse of discipline. If a man walks out on his wife, he may feel uncomfortable at being in the same congregation; but let him go round the corner to a place where he does not have to meet her, and he may start again, and even in due course contract respectable matrimony there without any question of his past being raised. If there is reason to ask a person to withdraw from communion because of some public scandal in one congregation, he or she may travel a mile or two and begin again without the matter being addressed. Pastors in turn find it expedient to be wary of being too confrontational with people's sins and faults, as the pastored may simply snap their fingers, walk out and begin again.

7   The overall upshot is a desperate duplication of resources, a flush of buildings far beyond any realistic needs of a properly organised church, and often a shortage of ministers who rush about in each other's footsteps without even

realising it, each entrapped in a particular denomination's walls, with its programme, priorities, and people making incessant demands, so that the whole-Church scene is never viewed. No congregation must ever contemplate its own voluntary demise by uniting with another; no denomination can afford to let go any grouping or role which belongs to them; and all believers find themselves being asked for greater and greater financial contributions, either to spend on themselves (their buildings and ministers) while kidding themselves they are 'giving to God', or to give to their denomination's central funds, when it is not entirely clear why they are of that denomination anyway or what its special *raison d'être* may be.

8 All the above cover the local congregations. But at a regional or national level the problem is also intense and painful. Boundaries are different for each denomination, so each functions with a totally different map (which affects the mind-set). Decision-taking bodies function at different levels from each other and on different timetables from each other. Leaders cannot find time to spend with each other or even attempt co-ordination. And more and more resources are spent in parallel, as though we all had bottomless purses, and as though there were nothing better to do with our money than spend it on ourselves.

I do not see how this situation can be defended as anything near to the biblical or even sensible. I have heard people saying, 'We are all separate battalions in the Lord's army' – but no army would operate by placing various independent infantry battalions on the same piece of ground and telling them to pursue a campaign against an enemy without worrying who else was fighting over the same patch. The classic dissenting cry is, 'Unity without uniformity', and that is thought to justify any number of proliferated congregations living their often struggling lives separately from each other while being geographically close. There is of course a genuine point behind the cry – the 'uniformity' and compelled conformity of the Restoration Church of England was such as to create a very strong reaction. But the cry now means, 'We will retain our separate life, and we will call that being in unity with you, and it is so in a spiritual sense, so do not press us any further.'

What shall we say to these things? Well, we can start with the biblical imagery of the body. When J. D. G. Dunn was speaking from Romans 8–14 at the assembly of the Council of Churches of Britain and Ireland in February 1996, he was handling the issue of 'diversity'.[1] He was offered from the floor the slogan 'Unity in Diversity', but he responded tellingly with 'Co-ordinated Diversity'. And this exactly condemns our present church scene in England – there is today an unco-ordinated diversity, one which has in it few evidences of actual unity, though some lip-service is paid to 'unity'. But this 'unity' is self-preserving, and apparently involves no merging of identities, no surrender of buildings, no harmonising of the work of ministers, no seeking what a common and shared mission to the nation and to the world would be.

Are there first steps which can be taken? I would suggest the following:

1   Let each denomination centrally state whether it is interested in a unity which includes 'co-ordinated diversity'. (Perhaps some of this is under way at the present time in the 'Called to be One' process.)*

2   Let each denomination centrally state what are its distinctive features of Christianity which would be lost to England's church life if that denomination did not exist. Let this statement be backed by a listing of features of their distinctive life which are so valuable – and so lacking in other denominations – that they deem it more important to be a separate denomination than to risk the loss of those features.

3   Let each denomination centrally make a responsive statement, stating what it cannot accept of those features which other denominations cannot let go.

4   In parallel with the above, let each denomination urge its 'intermediate' or regional authorities no longer to exist primarily for the pastoral care and upbuilding of their own

---

*A process initiated by Churches Together in England to prod the various constituent bodies into stating how they understand 'visible', 'unity', and 'Church'. I am writing this in the midst of the process, so do not know how it will eventuate.

denominational congregations and structures, but to reorganise priorities to seek visible local unity with the other denominations around – even if this means that some people lose their jobs.

In such a case the Church of England might be found saying:

1   We are a biblical Church, standing for a principle of 'one holy catholic and apostolic Church', and seeking organic unity (even at a high price to ourselves) as God's revealed way for his Church. The Bible must have supreme authority within the life of the Church.

2   We believe we have a historic calling to function territorially, so that, as far as we can manage, there is a credible parish system running throughout the country. We know it is greatly distorted, and in some areas totally ignored by the lay people, and in many places very thinly staffed with stipendiary ministers, but we would hope that a healthy reunion would enable resources to strengthen this territorial concept rather than weaken it.

3   We are a liturgical Church, though our freedom in relation to liturgical forms has grown rapidly recently. We believe it is of great importance for sacramental liturgy to have a publicly recognisable shape, and for a ministry of the word to run through all worship events.

4   We are an episcopal Church, and value (without pretending too much) the 'historic episcopate'. We look for a reform of the structures of episcopacy, to make them credible and effective. But we would hope for both the recognition and uniting with us of existing ministries of non-episcopal Churches and also the continuity of this historic episcopate.

5   We are a synodical Church (and, at our best, not a prelatical one). We believe in the whole Church – bishops, presbyters, and laity – taking decisions through representatives at each level, with provision for major decisions to be referred to local units of decision-taking prior to final decisions.

6   We are currently an established Church. We would be ready to abandon the subordination to the machinery of state if the Free Churches value their existing freedom. (See Appendix 3, p. 349.)

7   We are a (relatively) wealthy Church, with accumulated

historic resources. We long to pool resources with Churches with which we unite.

8   We are a completely cuckoo Church as far as the methods of appointment to ministerial offices are concerned. We are ready for a serious critique from others and a careful provision of new methods of appointment.

9   We are a flexible Church. We can go a long way in forming Local Ecumenical Partnerships and similar ventures, if the will is there. We want to be pushed in this direction.

10   We are a multi-ethnic Church and wish to be free of any notion that we are simply 'old white', let alone in any way exclusive.

11   We are *de facto* a somewhat comprehensive and diverse Church, and we make a half-virtue out of this extraordinary contemporary feature of a Church once bounded by extraordinary uniformity. We would be ready to talk through the implications of this for uniting with any other body. But we do function with doctrinal standards, and have a practice of seeking eschatologically to improve both their formulation and their authority.

The case of the relationship to ethnic-minority Churches warrants careful attention. Because, as noted earlier, their ecclesial identity often reflects and sustains a minority culture (including language, affinity and customs) which is part of their personal and corporate identity – and because they are often short of buildings, finance and other earthly resources – approaches towards them on behalf of co-operation, convergence or uniting may be experienced as more like empire-building or marginalisation.

At the same time, we would have to express our responses to others. There is an element of shadow-boxing in anticipating what others might say, but our responses might have to include:

1   We cannot say that infant baptism is not baptism – but we can look at ways in which its administration can be guided by biblical principles in a missionary Church, and we can look at ways in which two different disciplines of baptism can live with each other in one framework.

2   We cannot abandon all connexionalism and buy into total independency – but we can look at ways in which congre-

gational decision-taking can have a greater part than it has in our present structures.

3   We are seriously interested in organic union, and are prepared to jettison many of our inherited ways for the sake of it – indeed, to put ourselves and our ways of corporate life and worship on the line, with a view to mutual reform to gain that end.

At the time of writing it is likely that new talks between the Church of England and the Methodist Church, and some less formal three-sided ones involving the United Reformed Church also, are about to begin. This specific opportunity may reduce the need for a stated public stance as advocated above. Certainly such talks must not stop short of any scriptural goal. But whatever approach to the uniting of believers in this land is advocated or employed, the difficulty for the Church of England is not so much doctrinal as inertial – the overwhelming orientation of our resources, priorities and interest is towards taking care of ourselves and sustaining our own institutional life; and the prevailing rationale for this (though not the inevitable outcome) is that we are engaged in a mission, in the fullest sense of that word, to the nation. 'Mission' and 'unity' are often linked in our terminology, but the link is desperately lacking in our practice.

14   A Sacramental Church

The issue of sacraments was central to the Reformation. The Reformers had to grapple, in the light of Scripture, with the definition of sacraments, the related issue of the number of sacraments, the efficacy of sacraments, the doctrinal formulas and liturgical texts for sacraments, and the status to be attributed to those rites which were not now being counted as sacraments. In essence they inherited a mystical scheme of seven sacraments, a scheme derived from Peter Lombard in the thirteenth century, and they had to recreate a whole sacramental theology, and recreate it in relation to both soteriology and ecclesiology. The issues were fought through by stages, and a good indication of a mature restatement comes in Article XXVI of the Forty-Two Articles of 1553:*

> Our Lord Jesus Christ hath knit together a company of new people with Sacraments, most few in number, most easy to be kept, most excellent in signification, as is baptism and the Lord's Supper.

This statement delightfully unites the two sacraments with each other in an ecclesially related confession. In a period when a large amount of debate on the sacraments concerned the quantity of benefit to the individual recipient, the ecclesial

---

*See pp. 192–3. The small changes from one version to the next touched most closely on Articles concerning sacraments and ecclesiology. Thus the 1553 extract quoted above did not reappear later (for reasons we cannot securely trace), but the whole of Article XXIX ('Of the wicked which eat not the body of Christ in the Lord's Supper') was incorporated in 1571. The texts (including the parallel and equally authoritative Latin version) are set out in Hardwick, *A History of the Articles* (various nineteenth-century editions).

frame is crucial. But the extract also gives us the following
further clues:

1 It traces the concept of a sacrament to the institution
of Christ, and from Edward VI's reign onwards it became
standard Anglican exposition, thus:

- 'There are two Sacraments ordained of Christ our Lord
  in the Gospel, that is to say, baptism and the Supper of
  the Lord' (Article XXV of 1571);

- 'How many Sacraments hath Christ ordained in his
  Church? *Answer*: Two only, as generally necessary to
  salvation; that is to say, baptism and the Supper of
  the Lord' (catechism section added to Book of Common
  Prayer in 1604).

2 It sets the two in juxtaposition and relationship to each
other: as we have seen in the New Testament, baptism is
the sacrament of once-and-for-all admission to the people of
God, and the Lord's Supper the sacrament of continuance in
them (see Chapter 4). Both are the Lord's way of knitting
together his new people; both are strongly ecclesial. But the
Reformers also saw the two as mutually interpretative. Thus
baptism gave a major clue about the Eucharist, for no one
thinks that there is any sacrament of baptism save in the
administration of water on the candidate, and this was used
as an example from which to understand the Eucharist –
that there is no sacrament in the 'consecrated' elements
independent of proper reception of them, and all liturgical
usage must move towards reception, and all spiritual benefits are to be found in the 'worthy' (i.e. penitent and
believing) recipient.[1] Conversely, once it is established from
the doctrine of communion that it is worthy reception which
conveys the benefits of the sacrament, rather than mere
outwardly correct administration (*ex opere operato*), then
that becomes the key for understanding baptismal regeneration as well as eucharistic fruitfulness.[2]

3 The phrase 'most excellent in signification' shows that
the Reformers intended the sacraments to play a major part
in church life. While being driven to protest against the
superstitions which the medievals had attached to their sacramental system, they wished to live churchwise by a
positive sacramentalism, not by mere denials. Their 'test' or

definition of the 'visible church' in Article XIX included the phrase, '[the visible church is a congregation] in the which ... the Sacraments be duly ministered according to Christ's ordinance'. They saw the sacraments as conveying saving grace, and one of their earliest changes in the liturgical round of the average parish was an attempt not only to have the Lord's Supper ministered in both bread and wine, but to bring the people to be regular recipients – ideally, weekly recipients – of that sacrament. It is a matter of history that the long centuries of the Dark and Middle Ages had so accustomed the people to receiving the elements no more than once a year that the Reformers were unable to change the people's devotional habits by Acts of Parliament.

Baptism

While the Reformers retained and enjoined infant baptism, it is arguable that they were thin in their public pronouncements on the subject. For an Anabaptist to read in Article XXVII that the baptism of infants is to be retained 'as being most agreeable to the institution of Christ' is hardly compelling; and to find in the liturgy for infant baptism of 1549, 1552 and 1662 that Cranmer both thought on the one hand that a kind of apologia for infant baptism could be helpfully provided in a three-minute exhortation on the gospel, and on the other that the chosen gospel passage for this heroic exposition was to be Mark 10:13–16, is almost mind-blowing in its futility. The actual rationale offered ('he favourably alloweth this charitable work of ours in bringing this child to holy baptism') would never convince a Baptist and ought not to convince an Anglican. Yet infant baptism was more than just allowed – it was virtually enforced. The rubrics of the 'private baptism of infants' and the canons of 1604 required the presbyter to hunt out all infants born in his parish and bring them to baptism. The presupposition, easily forgotten today, is that England was a rural nation, and the incumbent knew all the families, and could not but know all the pregnancies also. However, the political reasoning behind the requirements, at least in the years down to 1645, was:

- that the whole parish must belong to the Church of England in true uniformity;

- that any family unwilling to bring a child to baptism must be either an 'Anabaptist' or a secret Roman Catholic – the former not wanting their child baptised at all, and the latter only wanting baptism performed by an (underground) recusant Roman Catholic priest.

The Church of England's energies were to be engaged in getting both sets to conform. The possibility that an evasive family was actually unbelieving or godless was not given much space or credibility.

Although the reasoning given for the administration of infant baptism was thin, and the gospel passage on which it was based arguably irrelevant, the rite itself overall expressed liturgically a true theology of baptism. The Church of England's baptismal liturgies have been criticised in the past for being developed in a cart-before-the horse way, with the infant rite coming first (i.e. in 1549), and the adult (strictly 'riper years') rite being developed from it in 1662. This would be a fair criticism if the 1549 rite had been distorted through being written for infants. However, Cranmer, while he presumably never saw an adult baptised in his whole lifetime, was perfectly capable of distinguishing the general nature of baptism from the particularities attaching to baptising infants. In principle, therefore, the candidates came as unregenerate, then expressed their repentance and adherence to the Apostles' Creed, received baptism and were duly declared to be received into the 'congregation of Christ's flock', and to be born again of the Spirit. The formal structure was embellished with prayer, exhortation, and the signing with the sign of the cross – items which were moved about within the structure in the changes from 1549 to 1552. But the requisite adaptation of that formal sacramental structure to enable infants to respond by proxies (i.e. by the mouth of godparents)* was minimal; and

---

*Godparents have figured in history in various roles, and were retained at the Reformation to speak as proxies on behalf of infants. The 1604 canons (and the modern ones) require godparents to be confirmed – the original purpose being to ensure that young children were not eligible for the role. There are two early sources for the concept of godparents – a maximising one in Tertullian's *De Baptismo*, in which the godparents are held answerable to God for the behaviour (and especially the misbehaviour) of the child as he or she grows; and a minimalising one in Hippolytus' *Apostolic Tradition*, where all that

the formal structure itself is still easily discernible. Hence in turn it was not difficult in the next century to remove that minimal adaptation, to enable candidates of sufficient age to respond in their own persons, when the riper-years rite was produced in 1662. Paradoxically, if predictably, it was Mark 10 (and the exhortation on it) which had to be eliminated for the riper-years rite – it was not in the first place an adaptation of a text about baptism, and therefore was not amenable to a reversing of adaptations in order to provide a rite for adults.

The retention of infant baptism through the Reformation without adequate rationale has left the Church of England with other issues to handle apart from the liturgical text. There are four prominent ones, each with a cluster of sub-issues:

1   Have we a *biblical* basis for baptising infants? The lack of argumentation about this during the Reformation controversies left us with a suspicion of a practice that had no biblical foundations – and, as Baptists and Anabaptists grew in strength in England in the seventeenth century, it became ever easier to urge that the Church of England only practised infant baptism through uncritical adherence to a pre-Reformation tradition, and not through biblical conviction. This understanding of Church tradition as the basis for infant baptism was reinforced in the nineteenth century by the Anglo-Catholic teaching that such tradition was self-authenticating, sufficient and authoritative – and this was an apologia for infant baptism that virtually admitted it was not based in Scripture. As the Catholic tendency has always also been to relate infant baptism to an invariable,

---

is needed is a voice to articulate the baptismal profession on behalf of the infant or child too young to profess it himself or herself, without any apparent forward-looking moral implications for the godparent in his or her own person. The concept of proxy articulation (often questioned in recent years) is important if the 'one common baptism' is to be visibly retained – the proxy declarations provide a set of statements on repentance and faith *which belong to the candidate*, thus ensuring that 'baptismal obligations' are the same for all candidates, whether they were baptised as infants or as adults. Statements by parents or godparents about their own faith may have a part to play in the liturgy, but they cannot be the central baptismal vows, declarations or obligations.

almost automatic, remission of original sin (which is, crudely, how it has come to us from Augustine), the reliance upon tradition as the basis has not only suggested that the Bible gave no warrant for infant baptism, but that tradition taught that infant baptism could and should be administered indiscriminately.

Over against that, careful investigation of Scripture points to an origin of infant baptism in the very origins of the Church, with roots in the Old Testament. (This is reviewed in Chapter 4 above, with a survey also of early Church evidence in Chapter 9.) Anglicans today are in a position to say that, even if a superficial reading of the Reformation period might suggest that the tradition was sustained without sufficient critical scrutiny, it is no mere accident of history, but scriptural conviction, which makes us ready in principle to baptise infants today.

2   Do we believe in invariable regeneration in baptism? The language of all our baptismal rites has always been categorical – that is, those who are baptised (infant or adult) are, after baptism, declared to be regenerate, or born again, or adopted into the family of God. So strong has this categorical language been that Evangelicals have at times been tempted into denouncing it, while non-Evangelicals have been tempted into trying to expound it as universally true, at least for infants, at whatever cost that might involve for any doctrine of regeneration. But the categorical language would seem to be true to the New Testament allusions to baptism (as shown in Part I above), and true to the liturgical structure of the baptism service, where a once-for-all passage from darkness to light, or death to life, is being worked through. The presence of such categorical language would not, however, of itself determine that the benefit of regeneration was always (let alone automatically) conferred. The emphasis in Article XXV upon right reception of sacraments, and the particular choice in Article XXVII of the phrase, 'those who receive baptism rightly [*recte*]', suggest that a cautious approach may be advisable.

The whole issue was brought to a head, and to a judicial verdict, in the famous Gorham Controversy between 1847 and 1850. In 1847 George Gorham, the Evangelical vicar of

St Just-in-Penwith in Cornwall, was nominated by the lord chancellor to be vicar of Brampford Speke near Exeter. Both parishes were in those days in the diocese of Exeter, of whom the bishop then was Henry Philpotts, a pre-Tractarian high churchman of a peppery temperament, who had conceived an antipathy to Gorham. When he received the nomination, he sent for Gorham and interrogated him for eight separate days on his doctrine of baptismal regeneration. At the end of this process, he declared him heretical, on the grounds that he did not believe in the invariable regeneration of infants in baptism, and he declined to institute him as vicar. Gorham then became plaintiff in an ecclesiastical case before the Provincial (i.e. Canterbury) Court of Arches, in which he sought an injunction requiring the bishop to institute him. The bishop's defence was that he had discovered Gorham to be a heretic. Clearly it was Gorham's doctrine which was actually on trial – and the verdict of the Court of Arches in 1849 was that Gorham was indeed heretical, that all baptised infants have been regenerated in their baptism, and that the bishop was right therefore not to institute him. Gorham appealed from this verdict to the highest court in ecclesiastical cases, the Judicial Committee of the Privy Council. In the intervening months, before the appeal was heard, William Goode, the dean of Ripon, published a massive book entitled *The Effects of Infant Baptism*. This demonstrated that Gorham's doctrine was that held by all the leading Anglican theologians of the sixteenth and seventeenth centuries and was the most consistent understanding of the formularies also; it also showed that Philpotts' doctrine could probably be traced no earlier than the teaching of Bishop Mant in his Bampton Lectures published in 1816, little more than 30 years earlier. While there was a vast outpouring of tracts and other publications from both standpoints during these same months, it looks as though Goode's book was decisive. On appeal the Judicial Committee found in March 1850 that Gorham's teaching was consistent with the Church of England's formularies, and stated his doctrine in these terms:

That Baptism is a Sacrament generally necessary to sal-

vation, but that the grace of regeneration does not so
necessarily accompany the act of Baptism that regeneration
invariably takes place in Baptism; that the grace may be
granted before, in or after baptism; that Baptism is an effectual sign of grace, by which God works invisibly in us, but
only in such as worthily receive it, – in them alone it has a
wholesome effect.[3]

The finding did not positively show Philpotts to be in error;
it merely allowed that both his position *and* Gorham's were
equally compatible with the formularies, and that neither
could establish an exclusive claim to be *the* position of the
Church of England.* However, the Judgement remains to
this day the most authoritative exposition of the position of
the Church of England on baptismal regeneration, and thus
has ensured that those who held to Gorham's doctrine have
a wholly lawful part in the life of our Church.

It is worth noting points at which these two theological
antagonists actually shared common presuppositions:

- both were wholly accepting of the categorical language
  of the rites;
- both assumed that all infants born in England would
  be, or at least might be, baptised;
- both argued the issue in individualistic terms (i.e. in
  relation to the benefits to the individual), not only
  because the dispute was focused in that area, but also
  because, when the invariable practice of infant baptism
  is taken for granted across the land, ecclesial issues did
  not bulk large in the discussion. When all are baptised
  and are thus 'members of the Church', membership and
  being Church count for little, and that issue did not
  therefore present itself strongly to the disputants. They
  might well have agreed with each other that baptism
  does admit to the visible church, though Gorham might
  have added qualifications to that bald statement.

---

*This finding caused great dismay to Anglo-Catholics, an anguish
only partly ameliorated by a disinclination to recognise the jurisdiction of the Judicial Committee. The second wave of secessions to
Rome (following Ward and Newman in 1845) was triggered directly
by this finding, usually called the 'Gorham Judgement', and the
seceders were led by Robert Wilberforce and Henry Manning.

3   Are there any limits as to *which* infants qualify for
baptism? Clearly, in the New Testament, only the infants of
believers would qualify. Equally clearly, in the Christendom
of Western Europe from 500 to 1500, the practice was
invariable, and it was reinforced in its absolute requisite-
ness by the teaching of Augustine (see pp. 75 and 243). While
the Reformers may have had shifts in their understanding
of how sacraments convey their stated effects, and were
quite clear that 'unworthy reception' did not convey the
effects, they did not attempt to alter the Christendom practice whereby all infants in the parish were to be baptised.
Indeed, both the rubrics of the Book of Common Prayer and
the canons of 1604 bind the clergy to 'seek out' the unbaptised and bring them to baptism. This requirement from
Reformation and Stuart times sprang not simply from continuing a medieval tradition, but rather expressed in fierce
form the slowly collapsing attempts to hold the whole
country to an Anglican uniformity. Families who did not
bring infants for baptism were under suspicion of being
either secret Roman Catholics or more open Anabaptists –
two groups of people suspected of political rebellion as well
as religious deviation.

We face a somewhat different situation today, where
around 90 per cent of the nation never attend worship,
but around 25 per cent of parents seek baptism for newborn
children. If we grant baptism on request, we trivialise the
Lord's provision, lead parents into declarations which mean
nothing to them, and often precipitate a reaction against
infant baptism by strong believers whom we thus lose to
Anabaptists. There are, however, some signs of a gradual
learning of the missionary nature of this sacrament, and
there has been a slowly growing concern within the Church
of England to make infant baptism credible. The canons of
1969 require preparation of parents, confirmed godparents,
observance of parish boundaries, and a service of baptism
within a main Sunday service; and the rites of infant
baptism in the ASB (1980) and the new rites (1998) lay
emphasis upon the duties of parents to bring up children
within the worshipping life of the Church. There is also
provision for a rite for the thanksgiving for the birth of a

child, a service which is not a baptism, does not require affirmations of faith or undertakings in respect of the child, and may be more appropriate to some families than is baptism. As the scriptural basis of infant baptism relates so strongly to the faith of parents and the 'household' concept, there are serious questions to be asked about administering baptism where there is little evidence of parental faith.[4]

4   How do we handle requests for a 'second' baptism from those who have been baptised as infants? The Church of England, by its confident practice of infant baptism, and its strong assertion that the definition of a baptism is objective and not dependent upon the reported state of heart or mind of the candidate, must insist on the validity of infant baptism, or any baptism, once it has been given. It is clear that Paul, in his citations of baptism, is appealing not to individuals' memory of their baptisms, nor even to some spiritual experience which accompanied the giving of the sacrament, but to the significance of *being* a baptised person here and now. He takes the fact of baptism present in his readers' lives (as we might say, 'But you're a married man' – with implications for behaviour, but without special recollection of the past); and he then places the lever of the word upon the fulcrum of the given baptism, and by the lever moves his readers forwards to 'walk in newness of life'.[5] The Church of England may provide for renewal of baptismal vows (the first occurrence of this should be at confirmation), and even add significant ceremonies to that renewal, but it cannot take any steps which would call in doubt the propriety of an ordinary use of infant baptism.[6]

Communion

The Reformation centred controversially upon the sacrament of holy communion. The Reformers' own views (for which the leaders paid with their lives) are summarised in the paragraph added to Article XXV in 1571: 'The sacraments were not ordained of Christ to be gazed upon, or to be carried about, but that we should duly use them'. Before the Reformation, lay people had to be present at Mass on Sundays, and to miss that was to be in mortal sin. But they did not receive the bread and wine, and their function was to be present for the

consecration, by which transubtantiation was effected. 'This is
my body' was taken to mean precisely that – indeed, under
the definition of transubstantiation, it had ceased to be bread.
The priest elevated the consecrated wafer, and he and the
people adored Christ thus 'substantially' present. The eucharistic action included the offering of the Mass sacrifice by the
priest, and this had actual power with God to achieve or win
certain results, hence Masses for the repose of souls (who,
medieval doctrine taught, were going uncomfortably through
the spring-cleaning functions of purgatory). Only at Easter
would the lay people receive communion, and then only the
wafer. Children under seven were not able to receive at all.*

Cranmer reformed the understanding of communion by
changing practice, by changing the liturgy, by changing the
formularies, by controversial writings, and by dying for his
convictions (it was specifically for his beliefs and teaching on
the Lord's Supper that he was put on trial). The large part
of the debate centred on the relationship of the inward to
the outward (the transubstantiation issue); and here Cranmer
linked baptism and the Lord's Supper as the only two sacraments deserving the title 'sacraments'. He could thus teach
that the whole action of a sacrament lay in the giving and
receiving of the relevant element, and, by parallelism of
reasoning, that, just as the water of baptism is not of itself
a sacrament, but the sacrament consists specifically in the
administration of the water on to the candidate, so the bread
and wine of communion are not to be exalted as special or

---

*For the first millennium it had been axiomatic (as it still is in the
Eastern Churches) that infants could receive communion from the
the time of their baptism; but soon after 1200 (and the rise of
the defined doctrine of transubstantiation) the cup was withdrawn
from the laity in the West, and thus the drops of wine, by which the
child before weaning had previously been communicated, were not
now available. The medieval Church, rationalising a delay prior to
admission, made a virtue of it instead, insisted that a child should
know, for example, the Lord's Prayer and the Hail Mary, and be
instructed for first confession at the age of seven before receiving
communion. That pattern (which does not of itself involve the
necessity of confirmation at any one particular age) endures to
the present day in the Roman Catholic Church, though considerable
rethinking and some experimentation has followed the second Vatican
council.

supernatural in and of themselves and independently of reception – and the only 'sacramental action' is the administration of them to the participants. This is brought out very precisely in his 1552 revision of the epiclesis in the eucharistic rite. The text then became: 'Grant that we, receiving these thy creatures of bread and wine . . . may be partakers of his most blessed body and blood'. The 'consecration' (a term he scrupulously avoided in 1552) was located in the actual giving and receiving.* While it is true that later generations restored the 'consecration' which he had avowedly abolished in that 1552 communion rite, it is clear that that later 'setting apart' of the elements in readiness for the administration hardly touched or nullified the central doctrine he was purveying.

In terms of the ecclesial significance of the Eucharist, there are passing indications of his understanding that 'we who are many are one body, because we all share the one bread'. The Lord's Supper is (among other things) 'a sign of the love that Christians ought to have among themselves one to another' (Article XXVIII of 1571); if two parishioners cannot be reconciled before coming to communion, they must be restrained from coming (opening rubrics of the rite); and they are exhorted during the rite that they must be 'in love and charity with your neighbours'; and there is assurance in the rite 'that we are very members incorporate in the mystical body of thy Son, which is the blessed company of all faithful people'.

This is not the place to trace all the subsequent developments in the doctrine and liturgy of the Eucharist, not least because, even as I write, the texts are in a state of fluidity and it is unknown in what shape they will emerge. But the following brief headings are worth noting:

1   The Church of England is a sacramental and eucharistic Church. While there have been variants of practice from the Reformation until now, the groundwork was laid then for a weekly main celebration of communion, which was clearly what Cranmer himself wanted. In the event, the people were

---

*This point is reinforced by many other features of the rite and of Cranmer's other writings, one of the most obvious being that there is no provision for consuming 'consecrated remains', as, by definition, any bread or wine that remained was not 'consecrated'. So the minister could take it home for ordinary household use.

determinedly non-communicating (a relic of pre-Reformation traditions) and could not be cudgelled or levered out of their ways, and the principles of the Reformers would not allow them to provide celebrations of communion at which none but the presbyter communicated. In the nineteenth century, the Anglo-Catholic movement gave a new and much-blazoned centrality to the Eucharist, but, because most of their models were Roman, they laid more emphasis on the celebration in itself, and not only did not press people to receive, but actually taught for 100 years that communion was to be received fasting, that it should be preceded by auricular confession, that high Mass was complete in itself if the people did not receive, that celebrations of the Eucharist could not be held after noon, and that, in a variety of situations, it might well be better to receive a wafer from a 'reserved' stock of consecrated elements than to receive within the context of the liturgy. All this has, however, been modified beyond recognition by a combination of the Parish Communion movement, the impact of the (Roman Catholic) Continental Liturgical Movement, and the changes set in hand by Vatican II and its Constitution on the Sacred Liturgy (1963), so many of which ran near to the Reformers' principles.

2 Revision of the eucharistic rites in the recent decades has always been inspired or led by the Catholic party in the life of the Church of England. The reasons are twofold: firstly, because they have dominated the field of liturgical scholarship; and, secondly, because they have come to believe over the decades that the 1662 eucharistic rite is not after all for them. In addition to this, they have usually known what models – ancient (as Hippolytus) or modern (as Paul VI) – they wished to follow or adapt. In the process there has been thrown up for the Church of England (and also for the whole Anglican Communion) a series of problems in eucharistic theology – the nature of consecration, the content of an anamnesis paragraph, the appropriateness of 'eucharistic sacrifice', the position and character of an epiclesis. Evangelicals have had to be defensive, as if playing second on a chessboard where the first player has made a brilliant gambit; but they have produced two minor initiatives of

their own – lay presidency and the *agape* (see pp. 339–43 and pp. 112–13, 175–6 respectively).

3 Along with the doctrine of the Catholic revival, there have also come the ornaments and ceremonial. Much of this is now taken for granted as 'ordinary' Anglicanism, some is still somewhat connoisseur in character. Eucharistic vestments, stoles, mitres, frontals, candles, crucifixes, statues, aumbries, pyxes, tabernacles, thuribles, stations of the cross, stone altars, wafers, oils, ashes, genuflection, crossing oneself, elaborate ablutions, and a host of others have changed the face of the Church of England. Much of these are used specifically in connection with the eucharistic elements, and quite a few with the reservation of those elements. Such reserved elements are also used in 'exposition', in Corpus Christi processions, and in the wholly Roman (and surely passé Roman?) service of Benediction with the Blessed Sacrament.

4 There have also been explorations in new ways of stating eucharistic theology without imitating Rome directly. One such has been the recurrent attempt to 'get behind the disputes of the Reformation' and find early Church explanations of the Eucharist. These, however, tend to run towards texts about offering the elements to God, texts which were innocent enough in the second and third centuries, but which can hardly regain their innocence now (just as pre-Nicene statements about the Trinity do not actually get behind fourth-century and fifth-century disputes, but instead land us with material which, however innocent of heresy when first compiled, leads straight into heterodoxy today). 'Getting behind' controversies is almost certainly a methodological mistake.

Another approach is to be found in the work of the successive Anglican–Roman Catholic International Commissions (ARCIC). The first publication of ARCIC I in 1971 was the Statement on the Eucharist. It showed considerable promise, and at most points used terminology which Cranmer might well have managed to sign, but his accusers almost certainly would not have.[7]

5 One of the changes brought about through the Liturgical Movement but reinforced in textual revision has been the

reintroduction of the Peace. While the context of the 'holy kiss' in the New Testament letters is slightly opaque, in liturgical history it became at an early date the point at which the newly baptised were welcomed, and the people of God identified each other as united in Christ as they approached the Lord's Table. It fell out of congregational use as the rite became more clericalised in the Dark Ages, and was confined to the ministers of the 'sanctuary'. But its restoration has not only taught the members of Christ that they do belong to each other in Christ, but has also given the congregation faces, in which people see each other as people, and not as merely the back view of stuffed dummies.

6   The Church of England (along with Anglicans elsewhere) has also become less and less protective of 'our' communion service, recognising that in truth it is not 'ours'. While in law there never was a need to exclude the unconfirmed of other denominations, if they were communicants in their own denominations, since the 1870s the general culture and near-consensus of Anglicanism has been to read the 'confirmation rubric' absolutely literally and to debar the unconfirmed.[8] However, the canon on admission to communion was changed in 1971–2 to allow communicants of other denominations to share with us as guests without being confirmed; and in early 1997 the House of Bishops finally approved guidelines for the admission of baptised children to communion before the age of confirmation. We now have a situation where the communion table is very open to the baptised of all ages, denominations and situations, but a very formal notion is still maintained as to whether or not the Church of England is 'in communion with' other Churches. This still hangs upon the acceptability and interchangeability of their ministers, not directly upon rulings about the validity of the Eucharist within their structures.

7   A question has arisen as to whether, if we are seeking to build up the Church, to have communion as the main (and sometimes the only) service of a Sunday serves the mission of the Church. It has certainly at times seemed odd in the early days of the Parish Communion movement, where the devotees have been simultaneously saying, 'We are the

Church for the nation', and, 'even if you come to church, you will be excluded from the very purpose of our meeting'. On the other hand, as Christendom fades away around us, the very rhythm of obeying Christ's command week by week and joining in communion may well be argued as vital to the sustaining of a missionary Church in an unbelieving society; and similarly, when the unbeliever does have an urge to go into a worship assembly (and in the towns that is a regular phenomenon), in many areas hymns, prayers and reading the Bible are almost as strange and inaccessible as communion itself; and even those congregations which have communion as a main service only once a month may still find that the drifting unbeliever or half-believer has not stopped to ask which Sunday of the month it is before responding to some felt need.

But the communion should still be the point of arrival for the newly baptised (even infants!), for the restoration of the lapsed, for the visible perseverance of the body of Christ, and for the foreshadowing of the kingdom of God. The mission of the Church should flow from it as God's people are renewed in love within it; and the mission of the Church should also lead to it, and men and women in an unbelieving society should find there love and belongingness on God's behalf and the echo of that same love and belongingness, conveyed on his behalf by his company sharing together at his table.

(See Appendix 1, pp. 316–21, for a Note on sacraments.)

15 The Ordained Ministry

Whatever local and personal distortions of New Testament teaching about the Church may have affected the Reformation, there was never any doubt about its connexionalism. Over against the pattern of a single worldwide Church in the New Testament, a pattern displayed in its own distorted form by the Church of Rome, the Church of England by its various means asserted a 'national Church' independence, and tended to appeal to Old Testament models of the unitary religio-political state community. (The Reformers loved calling Edward VI 'our young Josiah'.) There was little practical alternative, and the Reformers, if pressed, would have said it was not they but the pope, and in due course the Council of Trent, which were breaking the unity of the Western Church – indeed, on the formal point of excommunication, they took no action against Roman Catholics; it was the pope who excommunicated Henry, Edward and Elizabeth, while the Church of England was doing its best to get papists (called in Elizabeth's reign and the Stuart period 'recusants') to conform. From that point of view, the Church of England took no steps to disunite Christendom. But from a structural standpoint the Church of England had denounced the concept of a 'universal pastor', and had denied to the bishop of Rome the universal jurisdiction and control which betokened Rome's 'Catholicism'.

But within the nation the monarch in parliament had total control of the Church, for the Church was the same people as the nation, and a single political will and organ of government covered both the civic and religious aspects of life, treating what we would call religious matters as equally political, and what we would call political matters as equally religious. Within such a structure diocesan episcopacy was retained as a very positive and forceful agent of the monarch in parliament's will, and thus, in Edward's and Elizabeth's reigns, not only of the doctrinal Reformation, but also of the divinely appointed monarchy. This in turn accounts for many of the staunch justifications of episcopacy in the sixteenth and seventeenth centuries – bishops were perceived as the natural concomitant and defence of monarchy.

The loss of the internationalism previously given by the Roman Catholic Church, along with the enforced rallying to the monarchical colours, inevitably produced a very nationalistic institution; and from the standpoint of a truly catholic connexionalism the single visible Church of Christ was being fragmented, or (to use a term anachronistically) balkanised, when Henry's legislation, the apologists and the Thirty-Nine Articles started treating 'particular or national Churches' as wholly autonomous separable units. However, it was very clear during the Reformation that within the nation there would be no comparable opportunity for separate parts, parishes or persons to act independently. The Church of England would move as a single entity or it would not move at all. The parishes would do what they were told. The liberty which the national Church claimed in relation to other national Churches or to Rome was not a liberty that could be granted on to smaller subunits within the Church of England – sauce for the national goose was not sauce for the diocesan or parochial gander.

Accepting that 'national Church' framework, we may still make a case for diocesan episcopacy. If congregations are not independent, but belong to each other interdependently, then there is a case for supra-parochial chief pastors. The case is not directly derivable from any one example or command in Scripture, though it may have some elements in common with Paul's 'the care of all churches' and with his command to Titus to appoint elders in the cities of Crete.* It is rather a case

---

*2 Corinthians 11:28 and Titus 1:5. It has been pointed out that Titus was to appoint elders *in the cities* (rather than in the churches), but the role the elders were to fulfil was clearly church-related. The passing emphasis upon 'cities' may reflect either that it was in populous places that the church had grown most and needed most care, or that it was in the cities that the potential lay (in accordance with Paul's general strategy) for the evangelisation of the countryside if the resources were rightly marshalled.

constructed from the connexionalist character of the worldwide Church, and the consequent appropriateness of chief pastors and supra-parochial overseers within it. The case may, in some parts of the world and some periods of history, be extended into the creation of specifically 'missionary bishoprics'.* The mere statement, however, that a particular Church 'is episcopal' or 'has bishops' does not of itself say much about the powers or roles of the bishops. In history the powers have varied: at one end of the spectrum was the Celtic Church, which is reported as keeping its bishops in monasteries as ordinary monks, while the priors or some such persons ran the dioceses – the bishop was simply wheeled out at intervals to perform ordinations at a particular prior's behest; and at the other end have been those bishops who have combined the arbitrary powers of a petty dictator with the constitutionally absolute powers of a colonial officer. Powers have also varied with the size of dioceses and the ease of communications within them – the bishop of a city in the Roman empire, such as the second-century bishops we have seen in Part II above, might have several congregations or groups to oversee, but he was constantly present with them. However, in England's Middle Ages, the bishop of Lincoln, whose diocese extended from the Humber to the Thames and was full of highwaymen and cutthroats, would not see his clergy so frequently or easily – and the first Anglican bishop of Calcutta in 1814, whose diocese included the whole of the Indian subcontinent, eastern Asia, Australia and New Zealand, was clearly not going to get within shouting distance of most of his scattered flocks. To this day the powers of an Anglican bishop within his (or her) diocese are usually defined by a provincial (sometimes by a diocesan) constitution; and the result is that those powers vary greatly from one province to another. Apart from providing the actual acts of ordination and confirmation and, if a diocesan, of being president of a diocesan synod, there are few powers held in common by all bishops of the Anglican Communion.

Anglicans have historically been over-fascinated by the many doctrinal and controversial facets of doctrines of epis-

---

*Where a bishop is sent as pioneer evangelist and strategist to bring the Gospel, and thus in due course a church organisation, into a previously unevangelised area.

copal ordination and succession. This makes it difficult both to reduce the vast interest and vested interests in the subject, and yet also chart a way through the overheated controversies. The subject will not go away, remains integral to Anglican self-understanding and to relationships with other Churches today, and therefore demands some consideration.

Firstly, the Reformation was led from the top down. This made it almost inevitable that the orders of bishop, presbyter and deacon would be retained; for the progress of the Reformation in both Henry's and Edward's reigns depended in large part upon the clergy using the offices they already held to promote the newly reformed liturgy and doctrine. Had the archbishops and bishops of the Church of England at any point called into question the sufficiency or propriety of their own ordination, they would have cut off the branch they were sitting on. Thus, even when individuals were reluctant to fall into line, ordinations were conducted regularly and 'according to law' (the law of England from 1534 onwards was the law of the Church, and vice versa). This type of Reformation was bound to function with emphasis on 'continuity' of authority. The monarch now took sole responsibility for choosing new bishops, and for commanding deans and chapters of the cathedrals of vacant dioceses to 'elect' them,* and archbishops and/or other bishops to consecrate them – and in the Church of England itself (though, of course, not in the rest of the Anglican Communion) diocesan bishops are still to this day appointed under the terms of Henry VIII's act of parliament of 1534.[1] So the orders (and offices and appointments) in the Church of England continued, from the legal aspect and in terms of their places in the Church's structures, unchanged *faute de mieux*. By the time of Elizabeth's reign there was also the force of martyrdom – five bishops had been burned for their reformed faith, and they were being celebrated in Foxe's *Book of Martyrs*, the next book after the Bible to be read in English homes till *Pilgrim's Progress* came out. In the next

---

*The word 'elect' is put in inverted commas, because the dean and chapter had no choice whatsoever, and were required (under threat of appalling penalties) to 'elect' the royal nominee. No dean and chapter from 1534 to 1998 has declined to elect, although in recent years the penalties have been repealed.

century or so, the matter of episcopacy became so entangled with the defence and support of the monarchy that it was seen as a non-negotiable infrastructure of the throne. This meant that it was crucial for all royalists to leap to the defence – indeed, sometimes to assert the necessity – of episcopacy for the safety of the throne. This is interesting (and doctrinally it was bound up with the divine right of kings), but it has to be recognised as rather different from some of the doctrines that have since been wished upon the sixteenth century retrogressively. And in the text of Article XXIII, at the point where (for example) the Tracts of the 1830s, or the modern Anglican presuppositions in inter-Church talks, would have made some statement about the historic episcopate, there is instead the most general statement about ministering in the congregation, formulated in a way which would probably unite us with non-episcopalians on the spot.* Other Articles do refer to bishops, presbyters and deacons – but none refer to the need of them!

The way in which these orders were 'continued' was by means of successive revision of the ordination rites, which yet retained 'bishops, priests and deacons', and ordained the candidates by the laying on of episcopal hands. The revised Ordinal was published by authority in 1550. Because the Ordinal arose separately from the rest of the Book of Common Prayer, it has traditionally not been a legal part of it, though it has normally been bound between the same set of covers. The title page of the 1662 Book of Common Prayer (the book that is still part of the foundational documents of the Church of England), the canons on doctrine and the present declaration of assent all distinguish between 'The Book of Common Prayer' and 'The Ordering of Bishops, Priests and Deacons' – though the Church of England (Worship and Doctrine) Measure 1974 and its related canon on worship treat both

---

*The text of Article XXIII, 'Of Ministering in the Congregation', runs as follows: 'It is not lawful for any man to take upon him the office of publick preaching, or ministering the Sacraments in the Congregation, before he be lawfully called, and sent to execute the same. And those we ought to judge lawfully called and sent, which be chosen, and called to this work by men who have publick authority given unto them in the Congregation, to call and send Ministers into the Lord's vineyard.'

alike as part of the Book of Common Prayer. Thus the three orders were 'continued' by authority, but that does not totally close the question. Many features of church life ordered by authority in the sixteenth and seventeenth centuries may still be questioned and changed; and it is frankly unclear from the mere fact of something being ordered by act of parliament in those centuries for universal observance whether such requirements have or should have the same doctrinal force as credal statements about the Trinity, or whether they are merely disciplinary, contingent and open to change.*

From a biblical standpoint, granted the 'connexionalist' character of the Church, 'ministers' with oversight of a number of parishes or congregations, and acting in organic unity with other such ministers (ideally on a worldwide basis), would appear to offer both a structure for pastoral efficiency, and a provision for holding the Church in visible unity. As bishops in England in the sixteenth century had to assume the discipleship to Christ of every citizen within their dioceses, they obviously did not have what in our terms would be labelled an evangelistic ministry, or responsibility for a strategy for mission. But it is only a short step from that English 'established' situation to the concept of a bishop sent to spearhead a missionary endeavour in unevangelised areas. All bishops, in their role as 'overseers', have responsibility for ordaining or providing presbyter-pastors for congregations and for ensuring that evangelism is initiated and sustained in unevangelised parts of their dioceses.

I find all this entirely reasonable, wholly compatible with Scripture, and not wholly divorced from reality (I cannot put it higher at this stage) in England today. But that is a far cry from a doctrine of bishops which makes them 'the Essential Ministry' (a phrase from Gregory Dix), a 'note' of the true

---

*A comparable ambiguous requirement in this category might be the 'excepted ceremonies' – the wearing of the surplice, or the use of the sign of the cross in baptism – ceremonies which were not urged as of divine commandment, but which were nevertheless imposed by strict church discipline, to the chagrin of the Puritans. Forms of ordination appear to have been viewed by the Reformers in much the same way – required by authority, and therefore not to be opposed or evaded, but not actually immutable nor beyond theoretical question.

visible Church, and the exclusive guaranteed channel of God's grace to his people. Such a doctrine appears to have been invented out of a romantic view of tradition, by means of a sleight of hand with the Scriptures – and to have an implicit touch of the psychological need for a 'fundamentalism'.* It interprets 'apostolic' in the creed as meaning 'having bishops in the historic succession', rather than as meaning 'holding fast to apostolic truth' (see pp. 154–8).

Such a view has to look back to the early centuries of the Christian Church, and invites us to test the theory by its own claims.

In the first instance this is an historical claim. It is stating that the apostles left, by a form of laying on of hands with prayer, an apostle-like office to their own immediate successors, and that this was then handed on by an unbroken tactual succession conferred by the laying on of hands in every part of the Christian Church for all the centuries until the Reformation. But we have seen above that there is no historical evidence to give this other than the flimsiest support (pp. 141, 158–61 above). It *is* just about true to say that 'from the apostles' times there have been bishops, presbyters and deacons in the Church' – but, even if 'ancient authors' lead us to believe that Peter was, at least in around AD 65, the bishop of Rome, and that one or more of the other apostles exercised a bishop-like ministry, the gaps in the evidence are still enormous. We know nothing of when and how bishops arose in virtually every city of the Roman empire; we know nothing of any of the apostles passing on their office; we know nothing of the laying on of

---

*This last point is an admitted attempt to turn the theological tables. I hear devotees of this doctrine saying that they know by this means of the 'historic episcopate' that their sacraments are both guaranteed and fruitful, and that their ecclesial context is also guaranteed. It runs very near to the accusations made that those who are conservative on Scripture are compulsive fundamentalists – persons who need through personal insecurity to believe that the particular foundation on which they are resting their lives is beyond all question as firm and unshakeable as a rock, and will therefore commit intellectual suicide and repel all questions unexamined in order to sustain their otherwise untenable position. My task here, forced upon this exposition of the Church, is to examine coolly what credibility there can be in such a stance, and, if possible, to get the fundamentalists out of their chosen hyper-episcopalian ghetto.

hands or of 'ordination' till the beginning of the third century (and then the Hippolytan text is open to grave suspicion); the extant shreds of first-century and second-century evidence give no hint of a common pattern of 'ordained' ministry at all; where bishops, presbyters and deacons first appear as a 'threefold' ministry (i.e. in Ignatius of Antioch) there is no hint of 'ordination' or 'succession'; where 'succession' first appears (i.e. in Irenaeus of Lyon in the late second century) it is innocent of any concept of 'ordination' or of passing special 'grace' from one to another, and is solely about teaching – and is only a tiny corner of the whole Irenaean corpus at that; the actual laying on of hands cannot be demonstrated until the third century. A theory totally wrapped up with a 'historic' linking back to the apostles lacks virtually all the links we actually need from, say, AD 60 to 200 – five generations of bishops, if we gave each a (generous) 28 years in office.

Thus the highest contention we can make for the episcopal system of the Church of England is that it is of the *bene esse* (perhaps even the *optime esse*) of the Church, and certainly not of the *esse*, and therefore not non-negotiable. This position, which is closest of all to the reticence of the Articles on episcopacy, has always been agreed to be an allowable theoretical position to be held in the Church of England, but the Church of England corporately has, for a century or more, been nervous of acting on this theory.

What, then, is to be said for the suggestion that the 'historic episcopate' is of the *esse* of the Church? The 1550 Ordinal, the first revision of the Sarum uses, provided the 'continuity' terminology. The actual word occurs in the preface to the Ordinal:

> to the intent that these orders should be continued, and reverently used and esteemed, in this Church of England, it is requisite, that no man ... shall execute any of them, except he be called ... and admitted, according to the form hereafter following.

Vast edifices have been built upon the words 'that these orders should be continued'. Yet the words may be hardly doctrinal at all, but may be (a) asserting the propriety of the orders already held by ministers; and (b) exerting a discipline – both thrusts being designed to exclude sectarian upstarts rather than express a particular (let alone a conservative) doctrine of ordination. Cranmer himself was ready to argue that, if in any Christian country a succession of bishops ceased to appoint through failure or through an attack of the plague, the monarch had power in himself to appoint new bishops, without the participation of existing ones – and it is even arguable to the present day that the confirmation ceremony makes a man legally bishop of his diocese (at the monarch's command) even when other episcopal hands have not yet been laid on him!

For even while the orders were being 'continued', they were being so completely remodelled as to look like an almost new start. If there is a 'continuity' in titles and appointments and in episcopal ordination, yet there is a great 'discontinuity' in the contents of the rites: and it is the discontinuities in the Ordinal that I come now to examine. For this purpose I am looking at the ordination of priests, as that is the point of arrival of most ministers, and the parish priest is the minister most lay people encounter (see pp. 328–30).

These are the changes in the ordination of presbyters from Sarum to 1552 – i.e. through the two stages of change, firstly from Sarum to 1550, and then from 1550 to 1552.

1   There is a totally new question of a totally reformed sort: 'Be you persuaded that the holy Scriptures contain sufficiently all doctrine, required of necessity for eternal salvation through faith in Jesus Christ . . .?' The pre-Reformation use did not include questions to candidates for the presbyterate. So this stems from the Continental reformer Bucer (who had much influence with Cranmer), rather than from any pre-Reformation question.

2   The central task of the order was changed: it ceased to be 'to offer sacrifice for the living and the dead'; and it became 'to preach the word of God and to minister the holy sacraments' (the sacraments having been reduced to two only).

3   The subsidiary laying on of hands of the Sarum rite became the central act (the 'matter') of ordination, still retaining the words from John 20:23 – not, however, to justify, let alone to make central, the Roman practice of 'penance', but because Cranmer saw no reason to dispense with scriptural words, and must have long since concluded

that Jesus' commissioning of his disciples in John 20 was not, and could hardly be stretched to be interpreted as, a command to go and spread a network of confessional boxes across the world. It is indeed typical of Cranmer to preserve pre-Reformation biblical material and give it a better context (as he does in many places in the Eucharist). And it is fairly clear that he must have conceived of the John 20 passage as a highly personalised way of chartering the original disciples to proclaim a gospel of repentance (cf. Luke 24:47, a passage which reports the same evening) throughout the world.

4   In two stages Cranmer completely changed the *porrectio instrumentorum*. In the Sarum rite, the new priest received paten and chalice (with their respective elements) with the instruction to offer sacrifice for the living and the dead. In 1550 the bishop handed over the actual sacramental symbols of a cup of wine and bread, but added a Bible as well; and in 1552 the sacramental symbols disappeared, leaving the Bible alone as the outstanding tangible indicator of the character of the reformed ministry. Gone were not only the 'instruments' of the Mass, but also the vesting of candidates, the anointing of their hands, and any possibility of 'concelebration'.

Nor was this all. The preface to the Ordinal prescribed episcopal ordination for the Church of England, but it did not proscribe those, in Reformation Churches elsewhere, who were being ordained by other means (usually Presbyterian); and for 100 years after the Reformation the Church of England was ready to receive them into the threefold order as presbyters as if they had been episcopally ordained.[2] Nor was it different when James I and Archbishop Bancroft insisted on the Church of Scotland becoming episcopal – for, although the first bishops were existing presbyters (presbyterianly ordained) who came to London to be consecrated bishop in 1610, they were not at that point first episcopally ordained deacon and presbyter before being made bishop; and when they returned to Scotland they did not attempt to ordain again the existing presbyters, but recognised and accepted them as true presbyters in the Church of God.

This latter loophole ceased at the Restoration. Charles II was called (or recalled) to the throne in May 1660. The resto-

ration of the Prayer Book took two years and it was finally
imposed by Act of Uniformity from 24 August 1662. Until then
there were, as a run-on from the Commonwealth, perhaps
thousands of ministers functioning as parochial clergy without
benefit of episcopal ordination. The returning Royalists were
episcopalian to their last bit of ermine – not so much because
episcopacy guaranteed the form of the Church, or provided an
exclusive channel of grace, but because the monarchical throne
of England, as they saw it, was settled upon a substructure of
monepiscopacy. Charles I could have saved his life and his
throne if he had been prepared to ditch episcopacy, but he
judged the loophole not worth the price. Thus the heaviest
possible reimposition of episcopacy was basic to the Restoration Settlement, and by the terms of the 1662 Act of
Uniformity the non-episcopal ministers, ordained by whatever
method during the Commonwealth, were forced to leave their
parishes or to submit to episcopal ordination as though they
had not been ordained at all. The preface to the Ordinal was
strengthened in an exclusive direction: 'No man shall be
accounted or taken to be a lawful Bishop, Priest or Deacon in
the Church of England ... except he be called, tried, examined,
and admitted thereunto, according to the Form hereafter following, *or hath had formerly Episcopal Consecration or
Ordination*'. (My emphasis on the last eight words indicates
that they were added in 1662.) The door open to presbyterianly
ordained ministers was now shut, and the episcopal framework
was complete and without exceptions. The Puritan ministers
who would not accept (re)ordination were chased out of their
parishes, and the Church of England looked as though it were
now a closed episcopal system.* And so it was – but closed for
what today we might well think were politico-religious reasons
rather than purely theological ones. The Church of England,
by design or perchance, left itself still some room to negotiate
as to the theological necessity of the office of a bishop, even

---

*The Scottish solution was again different: four presbyters came to
London to be made bishops; two had been episcopally ordained before
1637, two presbyterianly since – and this time the latter two were now
episcopally ordained priest, prior to all four being ordained bishop.
However, the four themselves did not attempt to ordain again existing
presbyters when they returned to Scotland.

while its formularies required unvarying domestic use of episcopal ordination.*

Nor, I submit, is the practice of episcopacy to be ignored. There is a genuine case for reasonably permanent chief pastors for a connexionalist church polity. There will always be some variation in the administrative powers allocated constitutionally to bishops, but the principle of oversight (*episcope*) – the 'care of all the churches' (2 Cor. 11:28) – will be common to all patterns of episcopacy. This involves the president's role in the Church's ordination rites, a generally agreed role which is wholly congruous with the 'chief pastor' role, and in the Church of England this has also involved the retention of ultimate discretion for the bishop as to who should be ordained, and who not.** However, it is the wider role of the bishop in his relationship to the visible Church which ought to occupy us.

As this book is intended as a sketched outline of a whole ecclesiology, and part of its execution has therefore to be *not* to give overmuch space to issues of ordination, lest it fall into the very error it is striving to refute, various related issues are here handled in Appendix 1.

(See Appendix 1, p. 321 ff for Notes on theories of orders, the 'priesthood' of the ordained ministry, the diaconate, the ordination of women, 'flying bishops' and presidency of the Eucharist.)

---

*The Lambeth Quadrilateral has, as its fourth side, agreement about orders. In its best form it claims that only the 'historic episcopate' is likely to provide that agreement, but the claim is in the form of a prediction rather than a statement of intent. And agreement about uniting through and around an historic episcopate does not of itself mean that all other ordinations would necessarily thereby be deemed invalid.

**It is wholly arguable that the tradition of 'Lord Bishops' (and even the occasional 'Prince Bishop') has in England left us with an unfortunate inheritance. It is possible to lead a diocese, to teach the faith, to resource the ministers and to care for the parishes without being engulfed by an episcopal subculture ... possible, but genuinely difficult. Episcopal subculture? Gaiters have gone, and 'Your Grace' and 'My Lord' are on the way out (they were abjured by the *1968* Lambeth Conference, but England is never in the forefront of such abjuration). Signing one's name with a cross before it, using the name of the see as one's own surname, mitres, rings, purple ...? And castles, chauffeurs and lifestyles?

16   The Character of English Anglicanism

We now draw out various further features of developed Anglicanism which, together with the issues handled above, give us good criteria for measuring the Church of England's claim on Christian believers in this land.

1   Credal but on pilgrimage

The Church of England is in formal terms a scriptural Church, with considerable credal orthodoxy built into its foundation formulas. However, herein lies a hidden dilemma. I may bring this out best by using an illustration from trusts. If a trust is tied up too tightly in one century, not only may it fail to serve its purpose well in the next, but it may do even worse and actually function contrary to the testator's intentions. Thus a rich man who dies in the sixteenth century bequeaths his wealth to a trust to provide an income for the widows and orphans who live in the streets beside the river that flows through the town, and by the terms of the will appoints trustees to administer it. Over the centuries, the hovels in the riverside streets are pulled down, and a new estate is built well away from the river to which the poorer citizens are moved. Gracious homes for aristocrats appear alongside the river – and the trustees of the fund find themselves disbursing to rich widows who conform to the letter of the terms of the trust, but are probably not the beneficiaries intended by the original founder of the trust.

On the other hand, if the trustees are given space to use their own charitable discretion more widely, they in turn may choose to favour recipients whom the testator would never have chosen.

This, *mutatis mutandis*, is the dilemma of any corporate

body formd by an initial constitution, but thereafter run by
actual people. If the constitution is too fixed, it may well fail
to serve the founder's or testator's purposes after a time; but
if it is too weak or too flexible, it may give far too much
discretion to the trustees in each generation, and also thus
defeat the original purposes. There may be ways in which, by
legal process, it can be demonstrated that the original purposes
are outmoded, and the trust correspondingly and officially
altered – but there also may be ways in which, without any
legal alteration in the trust deeds, the implementation of the
trust involves a little discretion on the part of the contemporary trustees.

I use this analogy, as it is close to the realities of the Church
of England, and it is important (despite all Anglican temp-
tations to the contrary) to engage with realities and to live by
them. I illustrate two sorts of living by unrealities as exemplified by the terms of the analogy.

Firstly, there have been those who thought the Church
of England was totally constituted and defined by the
Reformation formularies. Only those who were loyal to the
Thirty-Nine Articles and the Book of Common Prayer could
count as 'real' Anglicans. However much the parish life of
others derived from the same Reformation origins, if they had
since deviated from a tight loyalty to the formularies they
were not true Anglicans, but part of a widespread plot to
overthrow the true (document-based) way of being Anglican.

Conversely, there have been others who believed existent
church life to be infinitely pliable, and to be susceptible to
any changes they cared to introduce. It is then simply the
contemporary character of parish worship and of parish life,
etc., which determines how the actual Church of England is
to be understood. I suspect that, in almost any institution,
some place must be left in the understanding of it for the
original intentions, charter or constitution to be carrying a
message at its heart, but that the existent human corporate
life and community ways cannot be overlooked and there must
not be too doctrinaire an attachment to a fictional institution –
that is, the one indicated by the sixteenth-century charter.

In the case of the Church of England, its existent life is
further complicated by centuries during which people were

supposed to belong to their parish church, simply because it was the parish church, and not because of anything particularly that might be being taught there. If the point is taken, those who believe in Jesus Christ are to belong to their neighbours in Christ, to share God's word with them, to break the Lord's bread with them and to address them in psalms and hymns and spiritual songs – and to do so in the first instance as existent believers together, and not because of the detailed and registered fidelity to the Gospel which characterises their shared meetings. That is the underlying principle of the territorially defined parish, and it sits with extreme difficulty with a doctrinally sharply defined Church. The benefit of the neighbourhood concept is that it ought to operate contrary to being too sharply bounded by doctrinal or sacramental walls.

This can, no doubt, look like criminal indifferentism about scriptural faith. It is, however, defensible and viable and actually preferable on biblical grounds to most alternatives on the following considerations:

1 A *de facto* comprehensiveness should have at its heart a true confession of the Gospel of Jesus Christ, a basic credal continuity in preservation of this, and an assertion of the supremacy of the Scriptures for faith and life. These the Church of England has.

2 A maturing Church functions in part from historic 'givens', but in part by debating unresolved issues, and, by speaking the truth in love (sometimes quite robustly – but still in love), works *towards* agreement that will build up the body of Christ. In other words, not all division (even on issues of how to formulate doctrine, as well as on issues of immediate policy) is to be regretted, suppressed, or hushed up as though division of itself were destructive or shameful. Much such division may be constructive towards the nature and witness of the Christian people in the coming generations.

3 Furthermore, there may be genuine (if secondary) areas where ways of living which appear almost mutually exclusive, but are followed as a matter of Christian conscience by different groups of people, are wholly tolerable. Thus Paul writes: 'This person believes he may eat all things; but that one who is "weak" eats only vegetables' (Rom. 14:2). The

reference here is presumably to the 'weak' person's fear lest meat on sale is already 'offered to idols' (cf. 1 Cor. 8:4–7), and therefore compromises whoever eats it. Paul himself is fairly clear where doctrinal truth lies, but the opposite practice, driven by a scrupulous conscience, is not to be forbidden. In Romans 14, despite his own initial treatment of the subject as from the standpoint of the strong ('Him that is weak you [presumably "the strong"] are to receive' – Rom. 14:1; cf.15:1), he quickly moves to even-handed reciprocity, thus: 'He who eats [meat] must not despise him who does not; and he who does not must not judge him who does' (Rom. 14:3). Indeed, for the sake of love in a 'mixed' church, he will cross to the side of the 'weak' rather than let his practice hurt the other's conscience, and thus cause division – or schism: 'Do not destroy by your feeding one for whom Christ died' (Rom. 14:15); and similarly, 'Therefore if my feeding causes my brother to stumble, I will never ever eat meat, lest I cause him to stumble' (1 Cor. 8:13). This instance of strong and weak consciences about meat offered to idols may seem very distant from us; but it gives us a formative glimpse of a church life (in Rome as well as in Corinth), where differences of mores were developing, and yet, even when Paul could discern that one of the two divergent ways was truer than the other to God's revelation of himself, he declined to guillotine the opposite way, but in some circumstances would even be prepared to join it.* This suggests

---

*What kind of issues could present us with alternative policies, separable as issuing from the 'strong' and the 'weak'? There are, no doubt some which sound trivial to the strong, but are experienced as highly threatening by the weak (the asymmetry of the evaluation is exactly what characterises some of us as 'strong' and some of us as 'weak' – which is why the duty of love begins with the strong). Issues of, for example, drinking alcohol, embracing warmly at the Peace (*sic!*), frequencing places of entertainment on Sundays, or enjoying *risqué* jokes, will by definition sound trivial to the 'strong', and thus lead them to 'despise' the 'weak'. But in any case there are many self-evidently more far-reaching issues to be debated in the life of a vigorously alive but comprehensive Church – reaching at their most serious not only to issues of beliefs about eternal judgement, but to more earthly policies such as attitudes towards the principle of believers 'bearing arms'; towards capital punishment (and other forms of punishment), towards civil disobedience (including resis-

that we should exercise great caution about foreclosing upon disagreements in the life of the Church – and to that same extent we may find ourselves a Church which is not only comprehensive by accident of history but under the aegis of eternity is properly and defensibly so. It may paradoxically also involve our finding ourselves in a Church whose policies we believe to be disobedient to God's revelation or to be in breach of some obvious priority for immediate action on a moral or political front. In a biblically comprehensive Church, such actions are a call for renewed witness to the truth as we discern it, and only most exceptionally should be viewed as the imperative to divide the Church into two, or personally to secede.

4 There is a further issue of discipline. The Reformers generally set up a concept of 'discipline' as one of the 'notes' of the Church. The Church of England omitted that note, at least from its definitions, virtually from the beginning of its separate existence. While it has occasionally excommunicated persons attempting to combine being communicant with living openly in adultery (and that has occurred even in the last 20 years), there has been little examination of individuals' ways of life, such as to uncover more hidden impediments to sacramental sharing.* Thus the inclusiveness of the Church of England has often resulted in a very diluted pattern of personal discipleship, and a low level of spiritual attainment in and by congregations.

On the other hand, it may properly be objected, those Churches which have been concerned to examine people's inner lives before admitting them to communion have run enormous dangers of pharisaism, of judgemental attitudes, and of high-walled sectarianism. There is little evidence of mainstream Churches requiring doctrinal tests before

---

tance to the payment of unfair taxes), towards national (or local) sweepstakes, lotteries, or bingo, towards being an established Church, and possibly even towards abortion and euthanasia, and a host of others.

*This may be contrasted with the traditional discipline of the confessional for Roman Catholics, with the class leader's examination of the members in classic Methodism, and with the visit by the elder and the provision of the ticket in classic Presbyterianism.

admitting lay persons to communion. So on both fronts, moral and doctrinal, there may well be a measure of contemporary good sense in the text, 'Let both grow together till harvest' (Matt. 13:30).

The issue of discipline does, however, also touch the question of the teaching office within the Church. While no reformed Church can ever function with the traditional Roman distinction between *ecclesia docens* (the teaching church – i.e the ordained) and *ecclesia discens* (the learning church – i.e. the laity), and while, because all have an open Bible and are encouraged to read it for themselves, no teaching office can be pedagogically exclusive or can impose beliefs or behaviour by *force majeure* or beyond appeal, yet there is a great weight of responsibility for conserving and conveying the word of God laid upon the ordained ministers. The bishops, along with selectors, advisers, training staffs and diocesan officers hold responsibility for the standards of life and orthodoxy of those whom they ordain – but it is extraordinarily difficult to discipline or correct those who, once ordained, hold secure appointments within the life of the Church, but deviate doctrinally. Moral disgrace usually means that ministers resign their posts (either acknowledging that they are in the wrong, or at least persuaded that the Church at large thinks that they are and will repose no further confidence in them) – but doctrinal heterodoxy cannot be addressed in the same way, not least because heterodox opinions usually stem from those who believe themselves to be right, and will therefore (quite understandably) fight to retain their posts. It should also be added that heresy trials, which are nowadays extremely rare in the Church of England, have generally proved counterproductive in their effects, either because legal ways of proceeding fail to get to the heart of spiritual issues, or because, in an avowedly (though perhaps inadvertently) comprehensive Church, to find someone guilty of heresy and thus deprived of his or her post is in fact to flout the toleration factor in the life of the Church and to run a serious risk of creating the wrong sort of martyrs.

There has been a further flurry, in living memory, in relation to the nomination and consecration of bishops who were heterodox. I need not stay on John Robinson, who came to the suffragan bishopric of Woolwich in 1961 with a reputation as a careful biblical scholar, but shook the Christian world to its roots with the undigested (and arguably indigestible) *Honest to God* in 1963. He did not then resign, but later returned to academia – and to careful (indeed hyper-conservative) handling of the Scriptures. The more recent David Jenkins case was the more complex because in 1984 he had already been nominated to be bishop of Durham (he was previously professor of theology at Leeds), but had not yet been consecrated when he uttered his famous denial of the bodily resurrection of Jesus. The issue then became one of whether or not the then archbishop of York, John Habgood, would proceed with the consecration on the day named, or would seek some public attestation of the orthodoxy of the candidate.* He did proceed to the consecration without further public investigation or assurance, and arguably damaged the teaching authority and general standing of the episcopate in the process.**

Just as past constitutions cannot wholly prevent a subtle change *in via* in institutions, so contemporary legal defences may fail to defend the desired purity. The institution is, to an extent far greater than seems generally understood, supported, continued, expanded and subtly changed by the

---

*There was precedent for this. When Hensley Henson was nominated for the see of Hereford in 1917, grave doubt about his belief in the creeds was publicly expressed. He thought it wrong and perhaps undignified to have to answer to public disquiet, but Archbishop Davidson, who was, we gather, ready if necessary to refuse to consecrate, leant on Henson to express his assent to the creeds in a publishable letter – and Henson, though protesting against the indirect form of heresy trial to which he understood himself to be answering, nevertheless did give the archbishop of Canterbury the assurance he wanted, and the consecration went ahead.

**There is nothing *personal* being said about David Jenkins in these remarks. He brought all sorts of proactive and even prophetic dimensions to the office of a bishop, and I honour those; and I personally owe him, and gladly acknowledge, a debt for a significant personal kindness. But neither in teaching the Easter faith myself, nor in attempting an apologia for the Church of England to other Christians, did I ever find the heterodoxy of the then bishop of Durham other than a severe embarrassment.

sheer character of the weight of the clergy and the run of the faithful. Thus the breadth and relative shallowness of the Latitudinarians in the eighteenth century was an ill context for new and dynamic evangelical gospel life and so, although the Evangelical Revival was true to the doctrinal standards of the Church of England, the *de facto* parish life, was largely unaffected by it in the first three generations of its outbreak, and in that time vast numbers left the Church of England. Similarly, although it may be appropriate to wrestle over small nuances of meaning in proposed liturgical texts in the General Synod, the gospel character of the future Church of England is far more secured by developing effective evangelism, by communicating the Gospel from one generation to the next in families, by sustaining a social witness to the Gospel, by finding scriptural ways of uniting separated denominations, by providing intellectual integrity and depth to Christian theology, and by discerning and nurturing future Christian leaders.

Comprehensive? Yes, because biblical and organic. Unprincipled therefore? No, so long as a normative biblical and gospel core (both verbal and personal) remains central to the different variants.

2 Synodical

A 'syn-od' is a 'coming together' – little different in its etymological meaning from 'meeting', 'assembly' or 'council'. In Christian history the word has had a consistent further implication that a synod exercises governing powers, whereas the synonyms have carried this meaning somewhat less consistently. A synod also usually embraces a width of congregations or even of dioceses in its representation and its governmental scope. In its essence it reflects three biblical truths:

1 The Church of the New Testament is 'connexionalist', an organic whole.

2 The churches of the New Testament are instructed by apostolic letters to make 'ecclesial' (rather than merely oligarchic) decisions about their life.

3 For the people of God to mature 'into the fullness of the measure of the stature of Christ', they are to interact with each other out of conviction, speaking the truth in love.

Here then is the charter for representative governing bodies, striving to reach agreement by bringing constructive Christian minds to bear, in conjunction with each other, upon issues, questions and potential reforms or redresses which require corporate and representative action.

The synod is therefore as basic to the concept of a 'connexionalist' understanding of the nature of the Church as is the chief pastor, the bishop. Neither is quite demonstrable from Scripture and each is a construct built from scriptural starting-points. Furthermore the two institutions belong together: the bishop ought to be a 'bishop-in-synod', and the synod ought not to be without episcopal leadership, chairmanship, or steering.*

It should be understood that this is not an imitation of secular forms of government, and the differences ought to be self-evident. Thus, by way of illustration, the Church of England General Synod is distinguishable from the House of Commons which meets only a few metres away in the following respects:

1   It has three separate Houses – Bishops, Clergy (both deacons and presbyters being eligible for election), and Laity – and, in any voting where it seems appropriate, members can ask for a 'Vote by Houses', and a defeat in any one House defeats the whole motion. For final decisions on important issues (such as doctrine and liturgy), a two-thirds majority, in each House, of those present and voting is required. These provisions cut out the hurt involved when 49.8 per cent of a body are overruled by the will (or whim) of 50.2 per cent.

2   There is (obviously) no 'government' polarised from an 'opposition', and seating is, by secular standards, haphazard and even friendly. There are, inevitably, groupings, but hardly parties, and certainly not 'whips'; and – one of the

---

*The concept of 'steering' is a very attractive one for Christian synods. The steersman does not provide the power of a wind-driven ship, but he has a key role in harnessing and exploiting the power for the benefit of all. It has been a speculation of mine in times past that the 'gift' of *'kubernesis'* (1 Cor. 12:28) might be the facility to 'steer' an assembly. This might correspond today to the leadership of the event we call 'worship' (which also should not be a one-man-show), but it might also identify the 'chair' of a synodical assembly – and it might well be that in Corinth these were one and the same meeting!

most liberating distinctions – the upshot is that, on rising to speak, there is a good chance of changing some minds. This is almost unknown in the Commons, and the whole concept of debating is thus robbed of its central purpose; as a result, people do not stop to listen to each other.

3   For certain kinds of decision (for example, the ordination of women as deacons and later as presbyters), Synod can only proceed if it has referred the issue to diocesan synods (we currently have 44), and has a majority of them in favour. Other issues may also be referred to diocesan synods if the General Synod sees fit.

4   The members of General Synod are *ex officio* members of diocesan synods (and of deanery ones, and of parochial church councils). This means they must always be ready to account for the actions of General Synod to their diocese.

5   The elected members of General Synod are elected by 'fair voting' – the single transferable vote. This provides a system which is truly proportionate to the voting of the electors, and this encourages candidates to stand (two candidates duplicating a particular stance or policy will not 'split' a transferable vote – it will 'transfer' on, and not simply be wasted). Its great (theological) virtue is that there is no mileage in trying to 'beat the system' in favour of a particular result – the result cannot be manipulated by tactical voting or other such corrupt practices as are forced upon us by the parliamentary first-past-the-post system; the means are honouring to God and cannot be subverted (contrary to the Pauline integrity of Romans 3:8) for a particular end. This currently distinguishes synodical elections from parliamentary ones. All committtees and representatives of Synod are also chosen by fair voting.[1]

6   Another significant difference – but this time one that is deeply regrettable (and is, mercifully, unique to the Church of England) – is that parliament is sovereign (subject only to some powers transferred to the European Community), and the General Synod is a dependent body, set up by parliament, subject to parliament, and, in many areas, only able to legislate for the good of the Church of England by seeking parliamentary ratification of its drafting. There is a great need for General Synod to be free to take decisions for the

Church of England with an answerability only to God for
those decisions.

These distinctions add up to a considerable difference in ways
of operating, and no one should castigate Synod for 'having
been devised on a parliamentary model'. In particular the
Synod should be preserved from taking major decisions by
narrow majority voting. While it is impossible in a body of
some hundreds to wait until there is unanimity, there needs
to be a very strong verdict in favour for major change to go
ahead.

There has been a fashion for sneerers at Synod to say, 'The
Church is not a democracy'. If the term 'democracy' has to
carry all the existing parliamentary baggage (as sketched out
above), then of course we must abjure the term. But if we
mean by 'democracy' that the whole *'demos'* (i.e. the people of
God) are to take responsibility for governing themselves before
God, then the term seems fully reasonable and compatible
with the New Testament. The sneerers should also be asked
what their alternative model is, as it sometimes proves to be
'theocracy' – and that simply means that someone, or some
group, has to interpret the mind of God for the Church; where-
upon the true alternative model is disclosed, sometimes (in
human political terms) as an autocracy, or less often as an
oligarchy. It is not clear that these are more biblical patterns
than democracy, but the real danger lies in treating theocracy
as a univocal and genuinely viable candidate, while in fact it
is a non-thing being used as a kind of Trojan horse to introduce
a semi-oppressive and unwarranted pattern of church
government.

Another problem in Church government has lain in the question as to whether any lay person can properly engage in
synodical activity in his or her parish, deanery and diocese,
in addition to General Synod. It is clear that the weakest
link in this four-part chain is the deanery, and its synodical
life must come under serious question. For not a few active
synods-people, lay and clerical, the issue is not only how to
take part meaningfully in this four-part chain, but how also
to belong to committees, boards or councils attached to the
four parts, and possibly also how to represent the General
Synod at international and ecumenical gatherings. There are

various reforming proposals in the offing (for example, the Bridge report, published as this book went to press, the effects of Turnbull – and my own proposals outlined in Appendix 4, p. 352ff.).

Among the other serious criticisms of the General Synod pattern of church government, one in particular has been heard since the vote in November 1992 to provide for women to be ordained to the presbyterate. The charge has taken this form: the ordained ministry of the Church is an inheritance received by the Church of England from the undivided Church of the first thousand years of the Christian era and retained as a trust from that undivided Church (and perhaps from the apostles themselves and certainly from God); it is therefore beyond our authority for us to act as though we can, by simple voting, unilaterally change this inheritance of orders; and, whereas a general council of the worldwide Church might perhaps wrestle with the issue and come to a new conclusion, or possibly the pope might have theoretical power to do so (with or without his own bishops round him), it is extremely doubtful as to whether our General Synod is competent to take such a decision. Thus the bolder critics query in turn whether (despite the liturgical process called 'ordination' which they have undergone) women *have* genuinely been ordained to the presbyterate; and that query in turn means that each diocese is emitting a strange and unbelievable message as to who is in its college of presbyters and who is not.

This criticism is worth answering, both on behalf of General Synod, and on behalf of women presbyters and those who ordain them, those who receive their ministrations, and those who simply wish to recognise and honour them *as* presbyters. The reply therefore goes as follows:

1 The Church of England so separated from the pope in Henry VIII's reign (and again in Elizabeth's) as to have total autonomy in respect of its own internal life. That 'autonomy' may be exercised by the monarch in parliament (it was in the very case at issue), and this may be a very inappropriate instrument for our regulating our own life (it is); but the total responsibility for our own life, exercised by the Synod and by the monarch in parliament, is unquestionable. No unilateral action we take in separation from Rome can

match the enormity of the original Tudor decisions to defy the pope, and then defy his excommunication, to write our own doctrines of Scripture, justification and the Eucharist, and to continue to assert them over against the anathemas of the Council of Trent, many of which were overtly, avowedly and in their actual wording targeted precisely against us. Similarly, if Rome really has overreaching overarching authority in relation to orders and the transmission of true orders (even if only in the West), then again our enormity in snapping our fingers at the nearly-infallible *Apostolicae Curae* in 1896–7 is breathtaking. It would appear almost heroically self-contradictory to say: the pope is the patriarch of the West and (in some metaphysical or perhaps subliminal way) we are under his authority, although:

a he himself has failed to notice it;

b the Church of England's formularies and her existent leaders and Synod deny it;

c he excommunicates us and calls on us truly to submit to him; and

d he denies that we have true 'historic' orders or true eucharists as we are.

We are a constitutionally *independent* part of the historic catholic Church, and, whatever other associations or obligations we may have assumed, we are at no point dependent upon the pope, at no point under his authority, and are always ready to survey his pronouncements critically and to respond to them robustly. We are as free to decide to ordain women as we were at the Reformation to abolish Mass-sacrifice, or the subdiaconate, or the pope's own authority over us. We may make decisions which distress a minority among us, but they are decisions which we are as free to make today as any of those epoch-making affirmations of independence were then. The precedents are so strongly in place, and our Anglicanism today so strongly derived from those very precedents, that it is impossible to urge that we have no authority now for major independent reforming action.

2 There is then an *ad hominem* argument, but one that is neither unfair nor trivial. If it were beyond the powers of General Synod (and of monarch in parliament) to permit the

ordination of women as presbyters, two logical points follow. Firstly, the earlier decision to ordain women as deacons was also beyond our authority, and, secondly, the Synod's incompetence to process and permit their ordination as presbyters was known long before the final decision was taken in November 1992. The *ad hominem* argument then arises in its two stages as follows:

Firstly, when was the outcry made that the Church of England, inheriting the historic holy orders of the catholic Church, had no right or authority unilaterally to admit women to the order of deacons? The debate in the years 1983–7 was conducted solely on the basis of whether women could or should be deacons, and never (as far as I recall) on the 'we are not competent to decide' basis.

Secondly, and far more damaging, in the years 1988–92, when the ordination of women as presbyters was before the various levels of Synod, we never saw this 'not competent' argument synodically deployed. If it had been believed, and believed as determinative, then, at each stage at each Synod, someone should have stood to say (in effect):

Mr Chairman, I see that the next [*or* the present] item we are handling on our agenda is entitled, 'The ordination of women as presbyters'. As our orders belong to the historic Churches of the West and East together and not to us, it is improper for any Synod to purport to legislate on the subject or for any member to assist General Synod in that process; I therefore propose that we pass to next business.

I am unaware of such procedural motions being moved. If they were, but were unsuccessful, then those in sympathy with them should have protested *and then withdrawn*. No one should sit in a Synod which is debating motions beyond its competence – to be present is to help continue that which ought not to continue, and no one of that persuasion ought to have remained in any Synod as it started to address this improper subject.

My strong recollection is that no such procedural motions and no such walk-outs occurred. (See Appendix 1, pp. 333–6, for a discussion of the issues of women's ordination to the presbyterate.)

The General Synod is the final guarantee of the preservation of the faith within the living fellowship of the Church of England. It is arguable as to how it could be more representative and or more accountable. But the necessity of having such a body is self-evident, and any who have been deceiving themselves in relation to our autonomy under God need to come to terms with that.

3 Territorial

The origins of the Christian Church related people to their places of abode. People in the New Testament are very often known by their place of origin, but also by their place of current residence and sometimes by both. Although the Church was one across the world, it was integral to its life that people met, and so they became both 'the church of [Priscilla's and Aquila's] home' (Rom. 16:5) and 'all who are in Rome ... called to be saints' (Rom. 1:7). The whole of Christian history has identified the people of God by their location – appropriately so, as theologically the only recognisable and allowable distancing of one group from another has been sheer spatial apartness (see p. 103 above for the theological argument).

In the first instance, in the pre-Constantinian era, the believers of one town met together and were known as the church of that town, and their bishop as the bishop of that town. He had his 'seat' there – the symbol of his teaching office.* The place of the seat (*cathedra*) became in time his 'cathedral' – and its place his 'see' city. In essence the concept of a bishop's 'jurisdiction' (to use a rather later word) was that he would live in a city, and have an oversight of congregations in the city and in the surrounding countryside. Much of this pattern is still to be found in Italy to this day; but north of the Alps the picture was much more varied, and it was deeply affected by the ways in which the original evangelists came

---

*Compare Jesus' words, 'The scribes and the Pharisees sit in Moses' seat [*cathedra*]' (Matt. 23:2). Note also how Jesus himself in the synagogue at Nazareth 'sat down' to teach (Luke 4:20). The seat was more indicative of teaching the truth than of ruling with power, though as episcopacy developed in the early centuries the two roles were often indistinguishable.

into each country, and an ecclesiastical organisation was first established.

In England, from the first coming of Augustine to Canterbury in 597, bishops tended to have very large dioceses. The pattern that emerged from Saxon times was of a presbyter in each village, often 'presented' by the lord of the manor, sometimes by a local monastic community, sometimes by other ecclesiastical persons, and established upon a plot of glebe land to enable him to support himself. England was almost entirely rural until the end of the Middle Ages, and, with the obvious exception of London, was arguably still so as late as the early eighteenth century. During this time the rural population was largely static and, unless they were summoned to the king's wars, people usually died within a few miles of where they were born. All were necessarily Christian, and until Elizabeth's reign all infants were baptised very quickly after birth. The parish incumbent knew all the families and was in position to watch over their lives keenly. The parish itself was not only his unit of pastoral care, but also had a civic boundary; and his chief lay officers, the churchwardens, were both appointed by the parishioners, and had considerable administrative powers in relation to them.* In other words, the incumbent had a clear role in relation to the whole village; all were reckoned to be his flock, and none therefore escaped his care (or 'cure'). The model was very clericalist and wholly pastoral.

This relationship of exclusive spiritual responsibility for all parishioners started to break down before the end of Elizabeth's reign. There is clear evidence of 'recusants' (i.e. Roman Catholics) going semi-underground to evade notice; and, on the other side, Puritans (and particularly independents) were always striving to set up an alternative (properly reformed and sometimes politically egalitarian) pattern of church life.

---

*While wardens are today wholly ecclesiastical persons, the past lives on in the right of every parishioner (whether or not baptised, believing, on the electoral roll, confirmed or communicant) to share in the appointment of the wardens, and in the particular link between archdeacons and wardens, which goes back to the days when archdeacons had magistrate-like powers and wardens were their local deputies for disciplinary and law-enforcement purposes.

During the seventeenth century this all erupted into Civil War and the Commonwealth period – a time when any hope that the Church of England's parish system would keep people loyal and at peace with each other was totally vitiated by events. After the Restoration there was a brief period of attempting to impose 'uniformity', but it became clear that many would not conform. The Glorious Revolution in 1688 ended in toleration for Nonconformists, a new set of semi-underground disloyalists in the Nonjurors, and a slackening of spiritual zeal in all flavours of Christianity alike. In the eighteenth century, the Church of England clergy and parishes lapsed into widespread slackness, the Evangelical Revival proved more divisive in many parishes than the older Puritan nonconformity had ever been, travel became easier, and the traditional identity of parishioners and church began to break down. The drift to the towns coincided with the beginnings of the Industrial Revolution, and new patterns of schooling and education began also. Town parishes were formed by division of old ones, or country parishes were swallowed up into burgeoning towns. The urban incumbent with the 'cure of souls' found himself, by the mid nineteenth century, with thousands of such souls to 'cure', and the religious census of 1851 discovered that one-third of the population did not attend Sunday worship at all.

The Church of England has continued the principles of its rural pastoral parish structure right through to the present day, multiplying the actual provision of clergy and church buildings to meet the vast urban numbers, and thus, paradoxically, often providing people with a choice of several Anglican congregations within easy reach of their homes. Those varied Anglican parishes may also have displayed an astonishing range of churchmanship, thus presenting people who wished to worship with a correspondingly wide choice of where they would like to throw in their lot. The railways spread in the second half of the nineteenth century, public transport by road in the first half of the twentieth, and the private car in the second half of the twentieth. With such vastly increased mobility accompanying growing secularisation, only a tiny proportion of urban English people now take any cognisance of which parish they inhabit, and the information tends only to cross the threshhold of the consciousness of the rest of the population when there arise issues of baptism or marriage, procedures for which the Church of England still locates administrative and pastoral responsibility in the parish of residence and with the incumbent. Congregations may bear little sociological, educational or even ethnic resemblance to the inhabitants of the parish in which they meet, and an incumbent may well run a totally split ministry – one half of which is towards the congregation, and the other half of which is towards a wholly separate entity, the parish.

Thus far does the case against the parish structure run, enhanced by the obvious point that the Church of England has a wonderful capacity to live in fantasy land and function by unrealities. But the parish system, with its background pre-supposition of a wholly Christian locality and a single super-pastor, has also attracted in the past considerable Free Church antipathy – not least because the Free Churches by definition have had to justify their Nonconformity over against the position of the Church of England parish pattern. The standard alternative ideology, as developed in Free Church circles, has been the 'gathered church' concept. This phrase is regularly around, and needs a little unpacking.

It seems fairly certain that the phrase originated in the seventeenth century, and was a statement of Independents' ideology at that time. People who thought that the parish was too inclusive a concept to be formative of a credible flock of believers considered rather how the true believers could be 'gathered' from those who were merely outwardly professing the faith. The members of the 'gathered church' might well physically all come from the one geographical parish in which the meeting place was situated – indeed, in the country that was very likely to be the case. The church was 'gathered' out of the sinful society in which it was physically placed, and was relatively self-selecting, in that high standards of behaviour were required for membership, and a very firm discipline would protect the significance of being the 'gathered church'.

It is necessary to spell out this meaning of the 'gathered church', as the phrase is used all too often nowadays (and sometimes even by Anglicans) to signify that a particular congregation assembles in the relatively unprincipled way by people coming from near and far on a Sunday, because they happen to like the worship, or the teaching, or the company there, and so gather from whatever distance. To eclectic or non-territorial Anglicans alike, the phrase 'a gathered church' makes it sound as though they can claim a reasonably good ecclesiological basis for their 'catch-as-catch-can' (and therefore competitive) style of church life (see p. 231 on competitiveness). I would suggest that the concept is being misapplied, and that competitiveness is being rationalised into a virtue.

So can we rescue the parish system? Is there anything still to be said for being territorially based? Even if present parish boundaries often do not make much sense in town contexts, does that invalidate the whole principle? The revised apologia will have to look something like this:

1 First of all, we are asserting three principles which relate closely to our mission to the whole country, as follows:

- We believe in one church in each place, and thus by our practice demonstrate that, in the strictest sense, we are in fullest possible co-operation with our neighbours, without there being any overlap or competition.

- We do not now pretend that all who are resident in the parish are, by dint of birth or residence, thereby necessarily to be treated as Christian or believing – but we do see in the parish boundaries both a charter for evangelism and an immediate demarcation of the whole population with a church-allocated first responsibility for giving social help. A parish church congregation knows exactly *where* the heart of its mission must lie, and in principle therefore every district, street, home or institution in the land lies within that scheme as encompassed in the missionary trusteeship held by that particular (and identifiable) parish church.

- The incumbent lives in the parish, and has an element of the 'incarnational' in relation to his calling in that place.

2 Thus we must be content with a congregational count – i.e. a review of the actual worshippers – in order to measure who the church in practice is.

3 Equally we do not and must not pretend that the whole 'community' of, say, 6000 persons are really members of the

Church who mostly forgot to show up last Sunday, but do (in some not quite admitted way) belong to the parish as Christian believers. To this some may wish to respond that the 6000 (or most of them) are in fact baptised. We might then decide not to write off their baptism as meaningless, but rather to describe them as the 'self-excommunicate'. This certainly describes their present state, though the use of such a description should not be thought to imply that all have gone through a conscious decision to abandon the implications of their baptism. It is in many cases more likely that they have never actually known the implications.

4   Even so, we would be delighted if those who came to worship came from the parish. We ought to view the 'neighbourhood church' role of a parish church as fundamental to its *raison d'être*. Obviously, from the time of first creating electoral rolls, the Church of England settled for people who lived in one parish and worshipped in another. Sometimes people do not even know where urban parish boundaries run (and often the boundaries could do with adjustment); but the great majority who come from outside know very well that they are exercising a deliberate choice. If they begin to outnumber the 'neigbourhood' element in a congregation, then a marginally unstable situation is emerging, which may in the long run undercut the remaining credibility of our parish-based system.

5   It is part of the mission of the Church of England that even worshippers resident outside the parish should recognise that, in belonging to that parish, they are themselves part of the mission to that parish. That may or may not limit other, 'associational', opportunities for evangelism in their own lives – but it should not mean that they are exempt from responsibilities where they worship, and certainly should not mean that cumulatively a set of such people from outside skew the mission of the people of God within the parish.

4 National

For a Church to claim to be 'national', various different
elements may be implied. Thus one or more of the following
features may be part of the claim:

   1   that the Church is 'by law established';

   2   that the Church is historically in continuity with the first
planting of Christianity in that land;

   3   that it is the Church of which the largest number of
citizens are members;

   4   that the Church has a structure reaching all the citizens.

The Church of England would qualify on most of these counts,
and, although the Roman Catholic Church has slightly larger
numbers of regular communicants, in the other respects it
would neither rival the entrenched position of the Church of
England nor claim to.*

5 A resourcing by voluntary societies

It is a characteristic of discussions of ecclesiology that the
given structures of the Church (whether papal, episcopal, presbyterian, connexionalist, synodical, associational, federal,
independent, or any combination of these or variants on them)
are treated as constitutive of the Church without remainder.
This, however, is to fly in the face of the facts as we experience
them on the ground. For the truth is that there is a great
range of supportive 'service industries' to the Church, which
have come into being in a haphazard way, which are by defi-

---

*One of the points at which the Church of England far outstrips all
other denominations in England is in its various earthly assets. It
has not only the £3 billion or more of the Church Commissioners, but
also considerable further financial assets in the funds of the Central
Board of Finance, the Pensions Board, and the forty-four diocesan
Boards of Finance, in the astonishing inheritance of its thousands of
medieval buildings, its equally vast stock of other buildings, and in
upwards of 10,000 parsonages. Whilst no one would maintain that
having such assets is the equivalent of being the 'national Church',
it has to be acknowledged that it is the existence of so much inherited
from the past which enables the Church of England not only to
sustain a nationwide parochial structure, but also to run both a
central national staff and also a local structure in each diocese in
numbers which are not just larger than those of other denominations,
but often twenty or thirty times larger. To that extent the assets and
the 'national' credibility are closely linked.

nition 'voluntary' and separate from the structures, and yet which, rightly meshed with the structures, are a great reinforcement of their life and activities.

I refer, of course, to the 'societies'. These are not, of course, unique to the Church of England, and may even be universally a concomitant of being church. A quick look at some typical examples will go a long way to establishing the case. The following categories of societies have become virtually integral to the life of the Church of England:

1   overseas missionary societies;

2   theological colleges;

3   religious communities;

4   weekly church newspapers;

5   The Mothers' Union;

6   The National Society;

7   home missionary societies (e.g. the Church Pastoral Aid Society – CPAS – and the Church Army);

8   various agencies for spiritual healing (e.g. the Acorn Trust);

9   single-issue groups, dedicated to securing a certain end (e.g., the Movement for the Reform of Infant baptism – MORIB), or bonding people with a common interest (e.g. the Ecclesiastical Law Society – ELS – or the Society of Catholic Priests – SCP – or Anglican Renewal Ministries – ARM);

10   trusts and charities established to promote and assist one or more features of church life (e.g. the Corporation for the Sons of the Clergy).

The list could go on. Not only is it not exhaustive of the categories of Anglican voluntary societies, it is also limited by taking no account of the great interdenominational societies. The following list will indicate something of their scope and rationale also:

1   The Bible Society;

2   the daily Bible-study networks;

3   Christian Aid;

4   The Leprosy Mission;

5   The Society for the Protection of the Unborn Child (SPUC);

6   many Christian publishing houses;

7   Christian conference centres;

8 Christian arts and music agencies;
9 youth organisations (including YMCA, YWCA);
10 student Christian organisations;
11 The Association for Promoting Retreats (APR).

Both lists would run into hundreds of actual organisations – vegetarian, pacifist, matchmaking (yes, there is a Christian dating agency), promoting mission in various contexts, and so on. Their relationship to the structures of the churches varies enormously: some are striving to do that which the structures do not do (as, for example, with theological training and with worldwide missionary organisations), and they have gained some recognition from the structures and some answerability to them. Others exist to protect certain emphases or weightings within the life of the churches; and they rather endeavour to make the structures accountable in reverse to them – a nice instance of this would be the Prayer Book Society or societies devoted to protecting architectural or archival treasures. Others would be reckoned as zany, one-eyed, partisan or obscurantist – but the society framework enables persons who share a passion to join together and to bring pressure to bear upon Church structures.

The voluntary society is so widespread among the Churches, so full of energy (perhaps even divine energy), so equipped with vast resources, that any account of the visible Church must somehow bring this phenomenon within the account. I attempt to do this by setting out a range of possible ecclesial interpretations.

At the very positive end of interpretation, the voluntary society is a prophet – a voice from God, like John the Baptist in the desert, recalling the people of God to spiritual priorities, and to living righteously, and thus justifiably seeking their material support and their ecclesial confidence. Such in origin are the overseas missionary societies.

Less outstandingly, but nevertheless positively, some societies function like the attendants on Paul, as servants attempting to make the apostolic priorities easy to observe. This comparison would make them like Timothy (Phil. 2:19–24) or Luke (Col. 4:14 and Acts *passim*).

However, there is also a comparison to be drawn with false prophets. Here I mention no names, but point out that publishing houses are free to publish (or web sites to purvey) anything they wish. The Press are in no way accountable to the structures, and the structures run their risk with them. Whereas in the first three centuries the bishop was the normative teacher (or 'doctor') of the Church – for the faithful sat at his feet – today anyone who can find a publisher becomes a teacher, whether he or she is a pillar of God's revealed truth or is denying the resurrection, selling out to existentialism, advocating promiscuity, or propagating false testimony. That is not to condemn all publishers – but it is to admit that they are generally driven by commercial considerations ('What will sell?'), and the sensational and the way-out may well be more commercially attractive than true prophecy. Either way the ship of salvation would seem today to have many loose cannons on the deck, and it appears a matter of random chance as to whether, when they fire, they are aimed at useful targets or are more likely to demolish the ship's own rigging.

Where such work is good and carries the approval of the structures, there is often a desire to 'take it over'. This is not just a matter of concentrating power (though that suspicion may always attend such moves); for there is also a theological principle behind it. If the visible Church of God, for instance, has a recognised worldwide missionary and mission-support calling, can this calling actually be fulfilled by a voluntary society or panel of such societies? Are not the structures opting out of their God-given task, if they leave it to volunteers to organise, fund and support? Is there any point in *being* the Church of God, if so much of the front-line energies, vision and execution are left to particular, even random, volunteers?

Here any answer must be highly speculative. An account of the Church ought to find a place on the ecclesiological map for the voluntary agency. To be a 'volunteer' is not necessarily to be outside the Church; and the Church – at whatever 'level – ought both to recognise the volunteers and to make them welcome.

There is much more work to be done on this front. I have spent more of my adult life among the 'societies' than I have within the 'structures'; but I am not aware of any profound theological account of them and of their general setting within an ecclesiological framework which I judge to be deserved by their sheer existence and ways of working. If it is agreed that they are not only 'in' the Church, but are also fuelling the Church, then their value is being recognised even while they are functioning without conforming to the standard models of the structures of the Church.

17 Whither, then, the Church of England?

How then should this curio among Churches, the joy and the burden of its own children, conduct itself for the future and set its priorities? I can but offer some broad principles.

Firstly, if it is to be true to the essential principle of its life independent of Rome, it must reaffirm strongly the authority of Scripture, and turn its people to a deeper and greater knowledge of God's word, not only to deepen lives of devotion and approach God and worship and prayer aright, but also to fuel internal debates aright, to govern external relationships aright, and to address the mission of the coming kingdom in God-given terms. It is both a scandal and a seemingly endemic disease that across the board – among clergy and laity alike – there is so little practical taste for the Scriptures. We may well thus be missing the voice of God in the sphere of further reforms, or the new tasks that we should take up.

Secondly, the Church of England must hold to that catholicity of the Church which is to be discerned in the New Testament, and we should not be content unless or until every possible step is being taken to promote convergence, union, or at the very least narrowing of ground between us and other denominations. The catholicity also will take us out into the whole of the *oikoumene*, the inhabited world, delivering us from petty parochialism, English superiority, or class-ridden disdain. In principle, if the concept is caught at a deep level, believers will be less keen to leave and go elsewhere when a feature of the local church does not suit them. As the Church of God becomes visibly one, not only will believers know that they cannot now opt out and go elsewhere, but they may even come to know that they should not want that liberty. But let believers also travel the world, live as the international people of God and become flexible, adaptable, teachable and open to God and his future. The Church of God is the people bathed in his love.

Thirdly, the Church of England will recall that the original charge of our Lord to bring the world into discipleship is far from fulfilled, and at every level of the structures it will be planning and pursuing its mission. While not exhaustively defined by evangelism, nevertheless that mission must include evangelism. 'We have a Gospel to proclaim' – but do we only *sing* it? It is a paradox that Anglicans are so often dumb, without testimony, without good news, without a word from God or about God. Yet our services are full to bursting with words from God, to God and about God: it is only, it would appear, when worship is over that the worshippers recall that some things are too deep for words, and return to dumbness. A book like this must also add, however, that the Church is part of the Gospel, that being turned to Christ means being incorporated into his Church, and that the style of church life from which the good news goes out to neighbours is itself part of that good news.

Fourthly, the Church of England will corporately await the end of the world. The awaiting will be active, questing and purposeful. But it will also be time-conscious, death-conscious, heaven-conscious. The Church is here for us each to prepare the others for heaven – whilst also here to model, live out and proclaim the values of the coming kingdom in a world that has not yet surrendered to our Lord.

But, believers in the Lord, we are to do it all *together*.

Part IV

Appendices and Notes

Appendix 1 Notes to Chapters

The Greek word *ecclesia* (*Note to Chapter 2*)
The word regularly (and uniquely) translated 'church' in the New Testament is '*ecclesia*'. As this occurs in the Greek version of the Old Testament (the Septuagint) and as there is good reason to think that the quotations of the Old Testament in the New are largely drawing upon the writers' acquaintance with the Septuagint, rather than their engaging in lightning translation from the Hebrew, the Old Testament use of '*ecclesia*' might well be thought to bear upon its use in the New.

However, the Old Testament use corresponds to the classical Greek use and does not bring us into New Testament usage without a leap of meaning. In classical Greek (e.g. in Athens in the fifth and fourth centuries BC) the word means simply 'an assembly'. While its etymology suggests that the assembly were people who had been 'called out'* (as we might expect a town-crier or knocker-up to 'call them out'), its use in classical Greek no longer had reference to the means of summoning, but only to the actual result – an assembly. In democratic Athens, the assembly of the citizens was the decision-making body of the city, and, if anything, the word had more reference to the functions of the gathering than to its point of origin.

It looks as though the Old Testament usage is similar, though marginally less technical. A characteristic usage is in Deuteronomy 31:30 – the word described the Israelites when they gathered together, and meant exactly 'an assembly'. It is even used in that sense in the New Testament when Stephen

---

*The Greek words to which this etymology is traced are '*ek*' ('out of') and '*kaleo*' ('call').

is describing Moses' own place 'in the assembly' (Acts 7:38) and when the writer to the Hebrews is quoting Psalm 22 in the Septuagint version (usually translated in Hebrews as 'in the congregation' or 'in the assembly', for 'in the church' would look absurd – though that *is* the text New Testament believers were encountering in the Greek). The Acts of the Apostles gives us further instances of the untechnical pre-Christian usage in Chapter 19, where in verses 32 and 41 the word is used of a pagan town assembly – an assembly which was so untechnical as to have been an unlawful riot! The city clerk countenances the possibility of a 'legal assembly' (19:39) – but the word 'assembly' itself is clearly as capable of as different meanings as if we said today that parliament is a legislative assembly and that a riot in Parliament Square is an unlawful assembly. The word 'assembly' of itself is more or less neutral, and without great overtones of significance.

We conclude from this that the use of the word in the rest of the New Testament cannot be traced to the long-lost etymology of '*ek-klesia*' or have an automatic meaning of 'the called-out people' derived simply from the choice of the one Greek word. Rather, it looks as though the existing neutral word was taken and *from other truths* was invested with new concepts of bonding with each other and of being loved by God and being sent on a corporate purpose. (If a fundamental New Testament truth were applied to the Old Testament (or classical) usage then 'God loved the church' would be rendered as something like 'God enjoyed getting them together'.) If we are to conclude that in any sense the New Testament Church *is* a 'called-out people', we must stake that point upon other New Testament foundations and not upon this shakiest and most simplistic form of reasoning from remote etymology.

Baptism in the Holy Spirit *(Note to Chapter 4)*

While, as a general point of exegesis, references to 'baptism' in the New Testament ought to be reckoned to refer to water-baptism, the proclamation of John the Baptist draws a contrast between his own water-baptism and the impending provision by Jesus of 'baptism in the Holy Spirit' (Matt. 3:11; Mark 1:8; Luke 3:16; John 1:33). There is an issue as to the significance and status in the Church of today of 'baptism in the Holy Spirit'.

It is commonly agreed that the swamping by the Spirit which happened to the disciples on the day of Pentecost was the initial fulfilment of the Baptist's prophecy. Jesus himself promised it in those terms: 'John indeed baptised with water, but you will be baptised in the Holy Spirit not many days from now' (Acts 1:5).

The phrase 'baptism in the Spirit' is not used in Acts 2, where the crucial verb says that the disciples were 'filled with the Holy Spirit' (Acts 2:4). They must, however, have understood that Pentecost experience as the fulfilment of Jesus' own promise. Certainly, when Peter is later explaining how he came to evangelise and then baptise the first Gentiles, he says, 'As I began to address them, the Holy Spirit fell upon them, as he had upon us at the beginning; and I remembered what the Lord had said: "John indeed baptised with water, but you will be baptised with the Holy Spirit"' (Acts 11:15–16).

It does not appear that the phrase appears anywhere else in the New Testament, and it would seem most appropriate to expound the general run of Acts and Pauline references to baptism as being to water-baptism (water being actually mentioned on occasion). So was there a separate experience of 'baptism in the Spirit' which was going on all the time in the New Testament Church through the Mediterranean? It seems remarkable if this was a widespread practice, yet somehow no one ever mentions it. One of the traditional get-outs has been to insist that the passing references to baptism generally may have a far wider relationship to Spirit-baptism than has generally been allowed. But this attempt then presents its proponents with a painful dilemma: either the references include the fact of water-baptism (even if the emphasis is on the Spirit) or they do not. If they do include reference to water-baptism, then the conclusion must be that the overwhelming thrust of the New Testament is that the inward and outward come together (which is a conclusion the proponents are usually trying to avoid); and, if they do *not* include water-baptism, then this apparently removes references to water-baptism where most readers of the Bible had always thought they occurred and also makes Spirit-baptism the initial and initiating experience of believers.

The modern interest in this derives from the experience of believers of being 'swamped' by the Spirit in a most powerful and life-changing crisis related to Jesus Christ and often resulting in speaking in tongues (in the Pentecostalist Churches there has been a tendency to say that the only valid test of this coming of the Spirit is his 'overflowing through tongues'). The experience of baptism in the Spirit is offered and urged upon those who have been believers for many years, so that it becomes a second stage in discipling, and even separates between an in-group and an out-group in particular congregations. Such a determinative experience, where it happens, cannot be denied or diminished; and the only question is whether it should be called 'baptism in the Holy Spirit'.

The difficulty is that the New Testament really only allows a single inward initiation by the Holy Spirit – the disciple is born again of water and the Spirit, and if anyone does not have the Spirit of Christ he or she is none of his. There is little place in the New Testament for a believer who has not yet received the Holy Spirit.* A more appropriate terminology for

---

*Clearly the original disciples of Jesus 'believed' before they received the Spirit on the Day of Pentecost, but from then on they ministered in the Spirit with a ministry of the Spirit. Luke does say that the Samaritans 'believed and were baptised' (Acts 8:12), but that 'the Holy Spirit had not yet fallen upon them' (Acts 8:16), and this passage has been the great proof-text for a second stage in initiation (drawn upon equally by the Pentecostalists and the 'confirmationists'). The easiest way to understand this consistently with the rest of Scripture is to take 'believed' as simply meaning 'expressed belief that Jesus was the Messiah', which was sufficient for Philip to baptise them: then it appeared that they were lacking something vital, perhaps inhibited by the very fact of being Samaritans – the Messiah had come, he genuinely *was* the Messiah, they could not but believe that as fact, but he had come *to the Jews*, and they could not assimilate rightly that they also as Samaritans were true beneficiaries of his coming, and this never went to their hearts until Peter and John, the leading apostles, came down from Jerusalem to 'go solid' with them. On this account, the Samaritans are an instance of people receiving the outward water-baptism prior to receiving the Spirit, but that separation of the outward and the inward, while anomalous (and it is clearly something anomalous being described in Acts 8), is in

a later swamping or crisis experience is of being 'filled' with the Holy Spirit, which is used on the day of Pentecost of the initial experience then (Acts 2:4) and is offered to Saul as part of his conversion (Acts 9:17), but is also used elsewhere of conditions of discipleship further on in the life of believers (e.g. Luke 1:67 – arguably an *Old* Testament experience: compare 2 Chron. 24:20, etc – Acts 4:31; 6:5; 7:55; Eph. 5:18). 'Filling' may be a slow process, a sudden crisis, a sustained plateau or even a repeated experience, and is much better used in these post-conversion circumstances.[1]

The problem created by this kind of allocation of terminology is that an experientially uninteresting or even unnoticed (because slow) event of conversion has to be dubbed the 'baptism in the Holy Spirit', and the highly colourful swamping experience of a later crisis should not be. But we are neverthe-less wise to keep our categories of both thought and speech in line with the language of initiation in the New Testament; and we may be helped in that in recalling that the experience of the Spirit is reported by external observers in Scripture and is virtually never reported by the person undergoing the experience. In other words, we are told that on the day of Pentecost, there were 'tongues of fire' distributed to the dis-ciples, that they spoke in other languages, that they were bold in their bearing, and so on. Yet, despite all that, we are *not* told how they *felt*. The same would be true of other mentions of receiving the Spirit or being filled with the Spirit. One wonders how a Spirit-filled disciple with raging toothache is supposed to *feel*.

Tongues and languages *(Note to Chapter 4)*
When modern believers come to 1 Corinthians 14 they are at risk of being greatly influenced in their understanding by their

---

principle entirely consistent with the rest of the New Testament. The last possible instance is where, in Acts 19:1–6, Paul asks the 'disciples' whether they received the Holy Spirit when they believed – but this is testing whether they have ever truly believed, and their response suggests that they were not only in a category of 'those only knowing John's baptism', but were a degenerate form of that category such that they had not in fact received the Gospel until Paul met with them.

own experience, a clear danger-sign in hermeneutics. Those who have spoken in 'tongues' (I fear I have to use the quotation marks for the moment) are not only usually persuaded that all the references in 1 Corinthians 12—14 refer to their 'tongues of angels', but are also fairly confident that some of the apparently favourable things said (like, 'I would that you should all speak with tongues' – 14:5) are giving positive encouragement to the practice, and tend to go on themselves to urge others to pray for 'the gift of tongues'; and they fear the opposition of 'cessationists'. (Cessationists are those who believe that God gave his Church special miraculous powers for a short initial honeymoon period to bridge the gap from the ministry of Jesus to the general availability of the full New Testament, but that those gifts have now ceased – hence there has been a 'cessation'.[2] In broad terms, it is generally taken nowadays to have been the position of the Protestant Reformers of the sixteenth century. That stance makes 'spiritual gifts' wholly historically conditioned and undercuts any expectation or validation of them today. To the tongues-speaker it is a frontal attack upon his or her Christian experience, as well as upon the apparent proper meaning of Scripture – and is often thought itself to have been inspired by a lack of experience of these supernatural gifts.)

As a matter of fact, most scholarly commentators on 1 Corinthians nowadays don't usually take a formally cessationist stance, which tends to be a mark of either Protestant scholasticism or a despairing defensiveness by someone under pressure from charismatics. But the scholars do often write as though they are discussing something a long way off and very far from mainstream Christian experience. This is perhaps illustrated by the translation in the NEB as 'ecstatic utterances'. There must have been an element of scholarly guesswork, totally untutored by experience, for translators to come up with that. As a general rule, we seem to have to make a choice between those to whom 1 Corinthians 14 is so far off and unreal as to sterilise all their treatment of it, and those to whom the chapter is the main dwelling-place of the Church, justifying a rather narrow programme of corporate life which has been built out of an interplay between this chapter and their particular experience. What is also clear, and is brought out by many scholars, is that Paul will go a long way to meeting practices with which he does not really agree, and the status 'tongues' receives from him is one of generous concession (along with strict delimitation) to a pattern which, say the scholars, he actually thinks undesirable rather than to be promoted. Such a concessionary stance would exactly match the view he takes of not eating idol-meats.

However, whereas, for the purpose of the main discussion in Chapter 4, it is sufficient to note that 'tongues' are an unknown and incomprehensible sound-pattern for most, if not all, of the persons present, there may be a case for a closer, more critical, investigation of what it was. I offer three radically differing possible results of such investigation, with perhaps a hint of the answer which I believe should be preferred.

1 The 'received tradition'

There is around a widespread, virtually unchallenged, understanding of 'tongues' which goes like this:

1 The sounds are those of a language given by God and usually unknown to either the speaker or hearers.

2 Nevertheless there should be someone in any assembly where 'tongues' are used who can 'interpret' – and the interpreter will probably not have recognised anything familiar in the 'tongue', but will have a burning pressure within him that, following the 'tongue', a particular message should be given, and this will be received as the interpretation.

3 As 'tongues' involve both praise of God on the one hand, and release or other inner fulfilments on the other, it is a highly esteemed gift; and tongues-speakers, however constrained in the assembly, are not only free to exercise the gift privately, but have every encouragement to do so.

4 In shorthand, 'tongues' is one of the most prominent 'gifts' which marks out the charismatic persons or congregations, and for many years acted as a litmus test as to whether individuals or congregations were properly classified as charismatic, and whether or not they were exercising the gifts of the Spirit. In classic Pentecostalism 'tongues' was taught and practised not simply as one gift among many in the Church, nor even as a prominent one, but as *the* secure evidence of baptism in the Spirit. Latter-day charis-

matics have often been in danger of sliding into this
Pentecostalist position.

It will be clear that this 'received tradition' – however moving
or convincing it seems in practice – is insufficiently close to
the text or balance of Scripture to be left unchallenged. Even
if the 'gift of tongues' is the speaking of a God-given unique
language, it is only one function among many in the body, it
is raised in 1 Corinthians 14 only to be very carefully constrained, and its concomitant interpretation is beyond our
power to test. It is mentioned nowhere else in the New Testament. Even in this chapter, it should only be used when there
has been a check, *in advance of its use*, that there is someone
present who will interpret – and that is not how tongues-
speaking operates. And, above all, it is dependent upon a
unique sense given to the Greek word *glossai*, institutionalised
in the twentieth century as something specially religious
through the chance of old English translating it in the AV as
'*unknown* tongues'.

2   Could it be 'ordinary' languages?

I confess that, over the years, I have found the answer –
that 'tongues' was other ordinary languages – an increasingly
attractive approach, though it is ignored by most commentators (whether charismatic, distant or cessationist).[3] One of
the more sympathetic comments I have read is that of Leon
Morris: '[Other existent languages] is an alternative solution,
but nobody reading 1 Corinthians would think that this is
what Paul had in mind.'[4] I use his comment as a peg because
it is actually subjective – and it reminds me of those sketches
in which two faces can be discerned within one careful
drawing; but some people can only see one and others only the
other, and anyone in either of those two groups might say,
'Looking at this picture no one would think there is any other
face in it but the one I have seen.' But we know better. So here
goes on 'tongues', and my own attempt to 'see the other face'
on the terminology in 1 Corinthians.

Firstly, I revert to my translation points – we are going to
consider other 'languages' and 'translation' of them and from
them. The 'natural' or normal meaning of *glossai* is 'languages'.
We would only think it meant something else if other evidence

in the passage told us so. And what we then find is a classic begging of the question, or arguing in a circle: 'We know that "tongues" is a mysterious heavenly kind of language, so clearly it needed interpreting; and because it needed an interpreter we can be sure it was a heavenly kind of language.' But just suppose that it was earthly known languages, the natural normal meaning of *glossai*; then the circle disintegrates and we find we are in the world of 'translation'. Once we have established, or at least hypothesised, that, then the 'trailer' in 12:28–30 tells us we are in the field of existent languages: ' . . . administrations, other kinds of languages. Are all apostles? . . . Do all speak in other languages? Are all translators?'

Then in Chapter 13, the 'languages of angels' are a highly remote condition, not a reference to what is in actuality going on. It is fully in line with 'giving my body to be burned' – that is, if people can conceive of hitting amazing heights of spiritual attainment *far beyond what we actually do*, but still have not love . . . So the rendering of verse 1 is (loosely): 'OK, so suppose I have a range of earthly languages – or, come to that, even angelic ones – and yet do not have love . . .'

Then, in Chapter 14, the rendering will look something like this (I have not attempted to be 'inclusive'):

Whoever speaks in another language is not communicating with men but with God; the people cannot pick it up, and from their point of view he is uttering mysteries in the spirit. But whoever prophesies [speaks their language and addresses them]. Whoever uses another language is no doubt doing something beneficial to himself, but whoever prophesies is benefiting the Church. Now I am happy enough for you all to use other languages, but you would do better to prophesy. Prophesying is honestly better than speaking other languages – unless of course the speaker translates in order that the church may get the benefit. So, brothers, if I come to you using foreign languages, what use to you will I be, unless I can [presumably by translation] bring some revelation or knowledge or prophecy or teaching? In the case of lifeless things [the same applies, and] who will prepare himself for battle? Similarly, unless you produce intelligible words, how can what you are saying be understood? You will be speaking into thin air.

Now there are many kinds of sounds around in the world, and each one has a meaning: but if I do not know the force of what is being said, then I shall be alienated from whoever is speaking and the speaker will be alienated from me. So it is with you: since you are keen on 'spirits', try to excel in things that build up the church.

Therefore whoever is using a foreign language should pray that he can translate it aright. For if I pray in a foreign language my spirit is refreshed, but my mind is not communicating. What then? I will pray with my spirit, but I will pray with my mind also. I will sing in the spirit, but I will sing with my mind also. For if you give praise 'in the spirit', how shall the man in the place of no understanding say 'Amen' to your thankgiving, for he doesn't know what you mean? You are no doubt giving thanks well enough, but the other person is not being benefited.

Now for what it is worth I thank God that I speak other languages more than you all. But in church I prefer to speak five words in which my mind communicates so that I may instruct others, rather than ten thousand words in a foreign language.

Brothers, don't be young children as far as your minds are concerned (be children instead in respect of evil), but engage your minds so as to be mature. For it is written in the law:

'Through men of foreign languages and alien lips, I will speak to this people,
but even then they will not listen to me, says the Lord.'

Foreign languages, then, are for a sign not to the believers but to the unbelievers, and prophecy is not for the unbelievers but for the believers. If therefore the church comes together and all are speaking different languages and uncomprehending or unbelieving people come in, won't they say, 'You are mad'? But if all are prophesying and some uncomprehending or unbelieving person comes in, . . . he will fall on his face and worship God, and say, 'Surely God is among you'.

[verse 27] If anyone is to speak in a foreign language, let

two or at most three do so, one at a time, and then
let someone translate. But if there is no one to translate,
then let the would-be speaker keep quiet and simply speak
to himself and to God.

[verse 39] So, my brothers, seek to prophesy – and don't
forbid speaking in other languages; but let everything be
done decently and in order.

This rendering has certain great gains over the 'unknown
tongues' translation. It reflects Paul's own versatility in languages, as well as the temptation in the city which was the
crossroads of the commercial world for people just to join
the interaction of the assembly in their own language. It keeps
'languages' meaning the same as it does in Acts – i.e. real languages of this world, known and recognised by those present.
It allows for the speaker himself to translate, which is clearly
there in the text and is fully in line with polyglot experience
today, and it provides the sensible alternative, that is, for the
speaker to check out in advance whether there is a translator
present for the language he wishes to use. It looks slightly
difficult in terms of the 'spirit' and the 'mind' – and these have
been usually rendered as though the 'spirit' would speak the
unintelligible, whereas the 'mind' would speak the intelligible;
but I think it is consistent to understand the 'spirit' as impel-
ling whatever is uppermost in the mind to say (which in some
cases will be in a foreign language), and the 'mind' as considered communication with others – i.e. by translation. The
words, 'you are giving thanks well enough', mean, I submit,
that you actually *know* what you are saying, but you are using
a language others do not know.

The quotation from Isaiah is puzzling to all schools of
thought. But it has this much to be said for it on the 'foreign
languages' rendering:

- the foreigners of Isaiah were speaking their own current
  languages, even though the meaning was unknown to
  their hearers;
- believers can indeed, where appropriate, use foreign languages to communicate with unbelievers;
- but if they all use foreign languages 'in church' they will
  create confusion;
- people addressing each other and the assembly in the

standard vernacular are doing what is appropriate for
believers (and if an unbeliever comes in it will be good
for him too).

It will be noted that this rendering of the relevant parts of 1
Corinthians 12—14 has some immediate bearing upon charismatics. On the one hand it does not have any recourse to
cessationism; but on the other it ceases to find an unambiguous
lodging in the New Testament for the distinctive contemporary
practice of 'tongues-speaking'. It does not, of course, *invalidate*
such practice; but it does place it – like, say, the 'Toronto
blessing' – into the category of manifestations that are not
clearly grounded in the New Testament. Then, just because it
is not clearly grounded in the New Testament, it is not a
matter of surprise or concern if it has not occurred at all
times and in all places. Nevertheless, where it is practised,
the principles outlined in 1 Corinthians clearly still apply –
that such strange sounds must be translated if they are to be
of benefit in the congregation – but it would be by extension of
the principle rather than by direct application. I think that
those who believe that the passage is positively validating
'tongues-speaking' must face the following exegetical factors:

- Why is 'tongues' in 1 Corinthians so different from
  'tongues' in Acts?
- Why does this so-important 'gift' not appear anywhere
  else in the New Testament?
- How can 'interpretation' be verified as accurate – or
  falsified?
- How can the tongues-speaker either interpret himself or
  herself – or alternatively find out, *before* speaking in
  tongues, that there is an interpreter present? (Are
  'tongues' ever practised this way?)

I add three further comments.

1 On any view of 'tongues' or languages, it would seem
inappropriate to urge others to '*seek* the gift of tongues' –
such an urging seems to fly in the face of 1 Corinthians 12,
where 'tongues' are listed as part of the evidence of the great
variety of functions within the body. This would appear to
mean that to have only one particular function as the normal
goal for all enthusiastic disciples is exactly providing a

cartoon illustration to fulfil the warning, 'If the whole body were an ear, where would the sense of smell be?'

2   If the above rendering appears to downgrade some much-valued experience, it is not a one-sided issue. While my whole purpose in Chapters 3 and 4 has been to discover what the apostolic Church was like and how it lived, it is perhaps useful to see what this understanding of 'tongues-speaking' in 1 Corinthians might mean in practice in a current situation. I have recently met a bilingual woman in Brussels (surely as nearly a crossroads of the world as Corinth?), who speaks happily in both French and English, but only prays aloud in prayer meetings in English – which done, she then herself translates into French. Clearly her *pneuma* urges her to pray aloud in English, but her *nous* then enables her to translate and connect with the French-speaking members of the meeting. It was actually worrying her that she was doing this, and she experienced a sense of release on discovering how biblical she was being! Similarly, at the time of writing I have recently attended a Bible Convention in Uganda where preachers (often actually bilingual or trilingual in their own persons) preached in their own first languages and were then translated by others – and it seemed very close to the Corinthian position in my judgement.

3   If any issue of down-grading does arise, then it should be put on record that much practice and theory of 'tongues-speaking' does itself downgrade those who do not have it. Yet it would be surprising, I would have thought, if anyone reading 1 Corinthians 14 with an open mind could ever have concluded that this one 'gift' is the great key to spiritual release or Christian growth and maturity, and that those who did not practise it were somehow second-grade believers.

3   Are 'tongues' inchoate thoughts that need to be put into words?

There is a slight variant on 'unknown tongues' – a variant put forward by Anthony Thiselton in 1979 and quoted since. He argues for a meaning of the 'interpretation' stem as being to 'put into words', and backs this key to the passage by a word-study in Philo and Josephus. On this view, new converts (and presumably Paul himself in private) have praise and other responses welling up within them non-verbally, and, if those are allowed to have premature vocal expression, they emerge at that stage as some form of ululation. However, they are not meaningless or incomprehensible to the utterer, and, if he will calm down and reflect, he will be able to 'put into words' that which has spilled out from him in inchoate form. There is much precedent in these two Jewish authors for using *hermeneuo* and its compounds for this purpose, and, if we work with the hypothesis, a reasonably coherent picture of the Corinthian assembly can be gleaned from it. However, it needs to be cross-examined as follows:

1   Is it methodologically secure to discover an attractive possible meaning for 'interpret' and use that to fasten a highly speculative meaning upon 'tongues'?

2   Anthony Thiselton acknowledges that many of the uses of *hermeneuo* and its compounds in Philo and Josephus are perfectly normal instances of 'translate' or 'interpret'; but his case rests upon there being many other cases where the meaning *must* be 'put into words'. He then appears to produce a sharp disjunction – saying, in effect, that in any particular context it must mean 'translate/interpret' *or* it must mean 'put into words'. The word, he reckons, has two (or perhaps more) separable meanings and it jumps from one to another in different uses. But this disjunction may in fact be over-sharp (and there are a host of other minor variants of meaning in the literature). If we try the hypothesis that it is in fact a very broad word and acquires the exactness of its meaning from its context, then we may be on a better track. Suppose, for the sake of argument, that the closest English word we can find for it – a word with its own breadth of nuance and application – proved to be 'render'. This would then take on its meaning in Philo and Josephus from the needs of each context, but it would not of itself tell us what its meaning would be in another context, or what weighting should be given in any general understanding of the word to any particular nuance of meaning it may have had in this or that context. I submit that the range of uses of *hermeneuo* and its compounds in the New Testament, the early Fathers and in Jewish authors is such

that its meaning in 1 Corinthians 14 has to be determined by the meaning of 'tongues' – and not vice versa. I think the onus of proof is then on Anthony Thiselton to show that *glossai* means what he says it means.

3   While this meaning of *glossai* is carefully distinguished by Thiselton, I confess that I do not think it would amount to anything very much different in practice. The distinguishing feature is something internal to the 'tongues-speaker'. In the charismatic case, the 'tongues-speaker' is using a sweet language of heaven which channels his non-rational side into expression; but in the Thiselton case he is using 'out-pourings' of a thrilled life, outpourings which are in essence 'his own' rather than heavenly, a jumbled sound which is by definition *not* a language. Behind this sequence of non-verbal sound, he knows what he is saying, and retains a clear understanding of it – and when he has finished he is then able to give the verbal form of it. But, firstly, do we in fact work that way psychologically – to be prompted to utter an unreflective jumble of sound, but to know what it means in such a way that we can 'put it into words'? Secondly, is it acceptable to understand the Greek word 'tongue' or 'language' in such a way that the one thing it *cannot* be is a 'language' (known or unknown)? Thirdly, while the Thiselton meaning makes good sense for the occasions when the person who has uttered the 'tongue' is to do the 'putting into words', it would seem that on other occasions the expectation would be that *someone else* would 'put it into words' – and that would not work at all well as the sense of the passage.

Prophecy *(Note to Chapter 4)*

'Prophecy' and its connected verbal forms are a more common phenomenon in the text of the New Testament than 'tongues', but the nature of this function within the life of the Church is also open to dispute. The difference is that the choice of understanding here has to be made by a careful selection from a spectrum of overlapping possibilities, while with 'tongues' the alternatives look to be severely polarised. The phenomenon has been subjected to considerable academic and scholarly enquiry.

1   The New Testament reveals the last of the Old Testament prophets, John the Baptist. He is a classic example in that

he foretells the imminent special time of God's dealing with his people in judgement and mercy through the coming of the Messiah; and he exhorts the people to prepare themselves by repentance and conversion to God's ways immediately.

2   There are reasonings within the gospels as to whether or not Jesus is a prophet, culminating in the call for him, when blinded before his crucifixion to 'prophesy' – i.e to discern who has struck him.

3   There is the judgement of John the Evangelist that, when Caiaphas said that it was better 'that one man should die for the people, and not that the whole nation should be destroyed' (John 11:50), he was 'prophesying' (11:51), even if not knowing the full weight of what he was saying.

4   There are at intervals prophets occurring in the narrative of Acts – for example Agabus (one of a group in Acts 11:27–8; on his own in 21:10–11) and the daughters of Philip (21:8–9). There are also at Antioch 'prophets and teachers' (13:1) who, listed by name (but not differentiated as to which were 'prophets' and which 'teachers'), send out Barnabas and Saul on the first missionary journey. Judas and Silas, sent with Paul and Barnabas from Jerusalem to Antioch, were prophets (15:32). The Ephesian converts who spoke in 'languages' also 'prophesied' (19:6) – though that might be that the languages were actually conveying prophecies, rather than being a totally separate channel of expression. While the general look of Acts would not be greatly affected if there were no mention of prophets, yet they are sufficiently frequent as to require some explanation.

5   In the Pauline letters, the existence of prophets and the practice of prophesying occur in several places:

- In Romans 12:6, 'prophesying' is among the differing functions of the body;
- In 1 Corinthians 11:3–4, 'prophecy' is bracketed with praying as twin public ways of speaking in church;
- In 1 Corinthians 12 and 13, 'prophecy' is similarly cited (12:10; 12:28; 12:29; 13:2; 13:8–9);
- In 1 Corinthians 14, 'prophecy' is opposed to 'languages' (*passim*), but is to be preferred in the assembly;
- In Ephesians 2:20 and 3:5, 'prophets' are bracketed with 'apostles' as the channels of God's revelation;

- In Ephesians 4:11 the 'prophets' are one of the donations of the ascended Christ to his Church;
- In 1 Thessalonians 5:20 there is to be no despising of 'prophesying';
- In 1 Timothy 1:18 Timothy is to act in accord with previous prophecies about him;
- In 1 Timothy 4:14 there was prophecy given when hands were laid on Timothy.

6   The book of Revelation is itself characterised as being 'prophecy' (Rev. 1:3; 22:18–19).

The overall picture is very inclusive. While the contrast with '(other) languages' in 1 Corinthians 14 means that we can be certain that prophecy was an utterance in clear, transparent, vernacular speech – and would then 'build up' the church – we cannot so easily determine either the content or the style. Clearly there was *something* distinctive of the particular function. The nearest to an overall understanding is that of Wayne Grudem, who suggests that prophecy was the utterance of one who thought he (or she) had a message from God, but was taking responsibility for phrasing and expressing it in his or her own way.[5] That still leaves special cases. And it may not of itself enable us to determine whether or not this or that form of contribution to a shared interchange about the word of God in the assembly is to be labelled 'prophecy'.

What priesthood has the ministry? *(Note to Chapter 4)*

There are in the New Testament various historical references to persons who are *hiereis*, 'priests', or *archiereis*, 'high priests' – we can identify Zachariah, the father of John the Baptist (Luke 1:5, etc); Annas (John 18:13ff); Caiaphas (John 11:49, etc.); and there are several references in Acts, including 'a large number of priests became obedient to the faith' (Acts 6:7). These are all persons holding an Old Testament priesthood, being not only Jews, but also descended from the tribe of Levi (of whom the members had originally been divided among the territory of all the other tribes in order to provide priestly ministry in each locality – see Joshua 21). They appear to have no equivalent – in name, descent or function – in the emerging New Testament Church. A reading of the letter to the Hebrews reveals why.

Hebrews (as I shall call it hereafter, and take for granted in biblical references) is seized of three vital truths about Jesus: his incarnation ('like his brothers' – 2:17); his atoning sacrifice ('to put away sin by the sacrifice of himself' – 9:28); and his ascension into heaven ('passed through the heavens' – 4:14). The writer apparently knows that Jesus referred Psalm 110:1 to himself – 'The Lord said to my Lord "Sit at my right hand until I make your enemies your footstool"' (Matt. 22:44; Mark 12:36; Luke 20:42–3). He has therefore a greater than usual incentive to treat the psalm as messianic, and, as a matter of fact, it looks as though all our credal references to Jesus sitting 'at the right hand' of the Father stem from Hebrews' use of Psalm 110:1. But Hebrews also moves to verse 4 of Psalm 110 and, with the author presumably taking his cue from verse 1, maximises on that verse as messianic also – 'You are a priest for ever after the order of Melchizedek' (5:6; 5:10; 6:20; 7:17; 7:21). The argument then develops from a twin set of Old Testament sources: firstly from the priesthood of Levi and Aaron, as far as the functions of a priest are concerned; and secondly from the priesthood of Melchizedek as far as the method of appointing a priest is concerned.

Firstly then, the Levitical references are largely to the annual day of Atonement rituals in Leviticus 16. The high priest then, i.e. Aaron, had first to offer sacrifice for himself, in order, being a sinful man, to be qualified to act on behalf of the people, and this sacrifice was a bull. He was then in position to offer sacrifice on behalf of the people, and he did so, and it was a goat. He then entered into the 'Most Holy Place' (9:8) to appear there on behalf of the people.* This day of Atonement ritual had a 'shadow of good things to come, but not the substance of them' (10:1). The system was of itself not effectual, for it had the following weaknesses:

* the high priest was himself a sinful man (7:27–8);

---

*Hebrews does not mention the further relevant features of Exodus 28, including, for instance, the binding of the names of the tribes on to the garments, or the provision of golden bells whereby the people could tell that the high priest was still alive (because the bells tinkled) even when he had entered the Place where he might expect to be slain on entry – and thus the people knew that the sacrifices were accepted.

- 'it is impossible for the blood of bulls and goats to take away sins' (10:4);
- the high priests themselves could not continue in office because they were prevented by death (7:23);
- the event was repeated annually because it never achieved what it portrayed (10:1–2);
- earthly imitation is not comparable to heavenly reality (9:24–5).

Nevertheless the system provided a fairly detailed model whereby the readers could be led to understand the priesthood of Jesus.

Secondly, there is the contrast of appointment. Jesus is a priest 'after the order of Melchizedek' – which is wholly separable from that of Aaron, and involved an enormous change.* Melchizedek is a mysterious person who appears in Genesis 14. He is 'without father or mother or genealogy or beginning or end' (7:3). This does not mean that the historical king of Salem (whoever he may have been) had not been born in the normal way! But it means that his priesthood is not signalled, labelled and validated in Genesis 14 by statements that he is 'son of X of the tribe of Y'. His qualification to be a priest, if subjected to that sort of Levitical dynastic test, remains mysterious – even God-given – and is clearly not dependent upon birth or tribal factors; and that is in complete contrast to the Aaronic qualifications (7:16). The case is clinched by the fact that Abraham – and, we might almost say, Levi in his father's loins (7:10) – paid tithes to Melchizedek (7:4) and was blessed by him (7:6). And these two transactions establish Melchizedek as far greater than Levi, and any priest 'after the order of Melchizedek' as far greater than Levi or Aaron.

Jesus then is made priest by God's oath (6:16–18), and, because he belongs to this greater priesthood, he supersedes the temporary and shadow-acting priesthood of Aaron (7:11–19). His priesthood is 'for ever', so he fulfils the role to

---

*Hebrews is relatively indifferent as to any difference between 'priest' and 'high priest'. The messianic figure in Psalm 110:4 is only told he will be a 'priest' and Melchizedek himself (great though he was) is only called a 'priest'. But the Aaronic model and its day of Atonement functions are those of a 'high priest', and so Jesus is at intervals said to be 'a high priest for ever after the order of Melchizedek' (6:20).

which the Aaronic priesthood and its functions pointed, but does so in a once-for-all, and thus eternally effective, way. The fulfilments may now be spelled out:

- He is securely appointed by God as high priest (5:4–6);
- He is fully qualified by being 'like his brothers' (2:10–18);
- He is sinless, so he does not need to offer preliminary sacrifice for himself (7:27);
- He therefore can offer a perfect sacrifice for the people – the sacrifice of himself (7:27);
- He did this once-for-all on the cross ((9:28);
- He then entered the Most Holy Place (4:14; 9:24);
- He is alive for ever, fulfilling his priesthood by his presence in heaven (7:24–5);
- We all have confidence to come to the throne of grace *because he is there on our behalf* (4:14–16; 10:19);
- He will in his time return (9:28).

I have laboured this a little, because the total teaching is of some importance. Hebrews is stating that 'every high priest who is selected from among men is appointed to represent them in respect of the things of God, to be able to offer gifts and sacrifices for sins' (5:1). That is the function of priesthood, and, for the purposes of the letter, is its defining function. The thrust of the letter is to give the people of God total confidence in Jesus as their one high priest who lives forever, and has wound up all other priesthoods in providing and fulfilling the reality to which the Old Testament rituals pointed.*

Various corollaries follow:

1 Obviously there is within the Church of Christ no distinctive priesthood 'to offer gifts and sacrifices for sins', for all such sacrifices have been superseded by the priesthood and sacrifice of Christ once for all for ever.

2 There is no hint of any other kind of priesthood, or other

---

*While the priesthood of Jesus is not discussed or named in other books of the New Testament, it has become conventional to name the prayer Jesus made in the Garden of Gethsemane (John 17) as 'the high priestly prayer'. This is derived directly from the recognition that Jesus is, in this prayer (the only lengthy prayer he prayed which has come down to us), 'appearing in the presence of God on our behalf' (Heb. 9:24). But it anticipates the priestly work of his sacrifice on the cross and his entry into heaven, and to that extent the title is slightly stretched.

connotation of the word 'priest', in the New Testament – and no point at which the ministers of the Church might be called 'priests'.

3   There is no way, as far as Hebrews is concerned, in which Jesus might delegate the functions of his high priesthood, for those functions are bound up in the once-for-allness of his sacrifice of himself on the cross, and the once-for-allness of his entry into heaven, and the eternal character of his living for us 'at the right hand of the Father' in the heavenlies.

4   There are, however, elsewhere in the New Testament references to the Church itself, as a whole, as a priesthood (see pp. 101–2). The two major ones are in 1 Peter 2:5 and 2:9, and they themselves draw upon the passage in Exodus 19:5–6 where God prepares the fleeing Israelites for the giving of the law by affirming his love for them. This usage, while it has a fascinating continuity from the Old Testament Israel to the New Testament Church, must be viewed as metaphorical, or at least as a second order 'priesthood'.

The Church is a priesthood in that it has access to the throne of grace, coming in the wake or train of Jesus, the true high priest – and in that it 'offers' metaphorical or responsive sacrifices, but not atoning or propitiatory ones. In 1 Peter 2:5 these are said to be 'spiritual sacrifices', and further instances are found in Romans 12:1 (where offering our bodies as a living sacrifice is obviously responsive to 'the mercies of God' and is itself 'service' or 'worship'), and, most interestingly, in Hebrews itself (13:15–16), where 'through Jesus' we are to offer a 'sacrifice of praise' continually to God – a sacrifice which is the 'fruit of lips which confess his name' – and our doing good and sustaining fellowship are also sacrifices with which God is well pleased. So the Church as a whole has (derivatively) priestly functions towards God. These also cannot be delegated to a special class of ministers – they are the function of the whole Church, are very clearly commanded as such in Romans 12, Hebrews 13 and 1 Peter 2, and cannot be given away.

In Revelation 5:10 and 20:6, the glorified people of God are said to be 'kings and priests to God', which says little about function, but would seem to be a way of saying all in one breath that the people have an authority over the rest of the new creation as kings and serve God as priests – but both terms are clearly metaphorical and cannot be translated into any implication (beyond the 'priesthood of the whole Church') for the Church on earth down history.

Our review of Church history shows how the 'priestly' terminology has crept into the life of the Church. But here the point is that not only is there no support for such a title for Christian ministers in the New Testament, but there is actually a coherent and fully argued theological doctrine of the priesthood of Jesus, the Son of God, which totally precludes the possibility of some special priesthood vested in Christian ministers. This is visibly worked out in the whole range of denominational Churches which have sprung from the Reformation or have arisen as biblical fellowships since – it has not occurred to any of them to create or ordain a 'priesthood', and in general their leaders are known as 'ministers', or sometimes 'presbyters', 'elders', 'deacons', 'pastors' or 'bishops'. That result is the upshot of studying the Scriptures. Nor has the point escaped Roman Catholics – the liturgist Robert Taft states very clearly, 'I was made a priest at my baptism, a presbyter at my ordination'.[6]

Sacraments *(Note to Chapter 14)*

Article XXV of 1571 includes a section not in the 1553 Article on the Sacraments. It runs as follows:

> Those five commonly called Sacraments, that is to say Confirmation, Penance, Orders, Matrimony, and extreme Unction, are not to be counted for Sacraments of the Gospel, being such as have grown partly of the corrupt following of the Apostles, partly are states of life allowed in the Scriptures; but yet have not like nature of Sacraments with Baptism and the Lord's Supper, for that they have not any visible sign or ceremony ordained of God.

The adverb 'commonly' when used by the Reformers regularly implies 'wrongly', and it would appear that it is the negative aspects of these five which are to the forefront of the argument. Matrimony and Orders might well be 'states of life allowed in the Scriptures', but confirmation, penance, and extreme unction would appear to be derived from 'the corrupt following of the Apostles' and the Article clearly distances them from any biblical justification. In brief compass the 'five' were handled by the Reformers as follows:

1 Confirmation

Though the Reformation liturgies reverted to the sign of the imposition of a hand ('after the example of thy holy Apostles') it was only in the use of that outward sign that they saw any scriptural precedent – for the rest the rite which they received arose from 'the corrupt following of the apostles'. It was not a sacrament, not ordained by Christ, not the channel of some particularised grace, not traceable to Acts 8 or Acts 19, and not the 'completion of baptism'.[7] It was instead the occasion of catechising youngsters who had come to years of discretion, with the laying on of a hand and a prayer for strength in discipleship. The prayer was not a sacramental formula, and could thus be used by anyone for anyone else in any context. According to the rubric, none were to be admitted to communion unless they were confirmed, but this was drafted in this way to ensure that they were catechised (i.e. truly instructed) as a basis for receiving communion.

In 1662 the catechism was separated from the rite, and candidates were instead asked directly whether they viewed themselves as bound by the baptismal obligations their godparents had expressed for them at their baptism. It thus became very explicitly a ratification in person of the baptismal vows. Also in 1662, as for the first time there was provision for baptising those of 'riper years', there was also a requirement written in that those thus baptised should then go on to be confirmed. No theological reasons were given for this, and the text of the confirmation rite itself, as I have shown in Chapter 14, actually now rested even more clearly upon the basis of proxy vows made at infant baptism, and made little sense if candidates had only a few days before in their own persons made their own profession of faith at their baptism. So the reason for the requirement must lie elsewhere and was almost certainly political and probably last-minute.

In the late nineteenth century, as confirmation became readily available in all parishes for the first time, the second generation of Anglo-Catholics started to teach the absolute necessity of the rite in order to 'complete' baptism and to confer the gift of the Holy Spirit. This teaching became known, through its two most notable proponents, as the 'Mason-Dix Line'.[8] It deeply affected Anglicanism throughout the world, and held the field as the norm until around 1970. Since then, the particular scholarship involved has been exposed as flawed, and a growing tide of exposition has demonstrated water-baptism to be 'complete sacramental initiation'. This has led to more openness to receiving non-episcopalians to communion, and, more latterly, to admitting baptised children to communion without confirmation. But the provision of confirmation for those baptised in 'riper years' or adulthood runs on, often in the combined rite of baptism and confirmation, without there being theological or other justification for it.

2 Penance

In the Ten Articles of 1536, penance was included with baptism and Eucharist to produce three sacraments. By 1549 the necessity of it had been dropped, and in the warning exhortation to holy communion those who were 'satisfied with a general confession' were warned not to be 'offended' with those who used 'the auricular and secret confession to the Priest', and similarly those who would 'open their sins to the Priest' were not to be offended with those who did not. In the Visitation of the Sick there appeared the 'indicative formula' ('. . . and by his [Jesus'] authority committed to me I absolve thee from all thy sins') to be used over those confessing their sins at the point of death – but before it there was also a rubric which said '. . . *and the same form of absolution shall be used in all private confessions*'. In 1552 the warning exhortation dropped all reference to 'auricular confession . . . to a priest' and spoke instead of anyone who could not calm his own conscience going to 'me, or some other discreet and learned minister of God's word' and 'by the ministry of God's word' receiving then 'the benefit of absolution'. Equally the rubric before the formula in the Visitation of the Sick was dropped, so that no reference to 'private confessions' now remained, and the wording in the warning exhortation to communion reads more like two people sitting beside each other, with one conveying 'ghostly counsel, advice and comfort' to the other from the Scriptures.

The indicative absolution remained in the Visitation of the Sick still in 1662, though now it was only to be used if the sick person *'humbly and heartily desire it'*. But it appears to be a provision for someone at point of death, and the preceding confession (labelled 'special') is not necessarily even private, as others may be around the bed. It is very difficult to argue from this for a 'sacrament of penance', though at intervals from the seventeenth century onwards – and very determinedly from the 1830s onwards – there have been Anglicans urging the necessity or desirability of auricular confession to a priest. The judgement of the Articles remains that it springs from 'the corrupt following of the apostles'.

It is a curiosity that, even while Cranmer was abolishing the 'sacrament of penance', he promoted the liturgical formula drawn from John 20:23 into a central place in the ordination of presbyters. It can only be concluded that he read, 'whose sins thou dost forgive, they are forgiven: and whose sins thou dost retain, they are retained', as not referring to the confessional. There is certainly little evidence from Acts or the epistles (or, come to that, from the first three centuries) to suggest that the Church understood Jesus' words to mean that the confessional was to be central to their mission. So Cranmer must have had some wider understanding of the Johannine text, and if, for example, he thought Jesus was charging his disciples generally to preach the Gospel, then he no doubt thought that very apt as an injunction to ordinands at the point of the laying on of hands.

In 1980 the Liturgical Commission produced draft forms for 'The Reconciliation of a Penitent', and I (with one other) dissented from the provision of the 'indicative formula' for regular rather than emergency use, as giving a misleading concept of the status and role of presbyters in conveying God's forgiveness. I also urged that private ministry does not need officially authorised forms, but each minister may make whatever textual provision he or she thinks appropriate (not authorising the formula would not actually stop anyone from using it). Certainly it was not self-evident that a rite for the reconciliation of a penitent was a liturgical alternative to the Visitation of the Sick in the Book of Common Prayer, which alone would have been a basis for seeking full synodical approval of it.

In the event, the House of Laity declined to give the draft rite the necessary two-thirds majority in February 1983, so no such rite was authorised. The legal advice then swung about 180 degrees, and in the services of *Lent, Holy Week, Easter* (SPCK, 1986), 'commended' by the House of Bishops as not needing synodical approval because lying beyond the scope of services 'alternative' to those in the Book of Common Prayer, there appeared 'A Form of Absolution, which may be used for the quieting of the individual conscience', and its text at the sensitive point ran 'by the ministry of reconciliation ... I declare that you are absolved from all your sins'.

3   Orders

Ordinations continued through the Reformation (see Chapter 15). The issue was not whether or not there should be 'these orders' in Christ's Church. There was a remodelling of the liturgical rites, and a rewriting of the tasks of the various orders, but ordination itself was not in question. All that Article XXV appears to be saying is that we cannot demonstrate that the laying on of hands with prayer for ordination is traceable to a command of Jesus himself, and therefore the rite is not technically a sacrament, but it would seem that ordination was a 'state of life allowed in Scripture', and it is not in question as needed in the Church.

4   Matrimony

Matrimony is, obviously, 'a state of life allowed in Scripture'. It became labelled as a sacrament partly through the influence of the Vulgate, where Ephesians 5:32, 'This mystery [marriage] is great', was rendered '*Hoc est magnum sacramentum*', which in turn became in English, 'This [marriage] is a great sacrament'. It has been traditionally expounded in Roman Catholicism as a sacrament which husband and wife minister to each other in the consummation of the marriage bond. Clearly, there is a tremendous truth within this exposition, and in the economy of God the physical act of marital union is an outward and experiential sign of exclusive love and permanent commitment. It is, however, a creation ordinance and was not originated by Jesus in the gospels, and we should be wary of creating a Christian (sacramental) marriage, supposedly ontologically different from unbelieving matrimony. The marriage of Christians should indeed be 'solemnised' with Christian ritual, and all pastoral efforts should be used to sustain and support couples in their marriage; but these points hardly bear upon the issue of ontology.

5 *Extreme unction*

This usage, called '*extrema*' as it was by definition the 'last' anointing anyone would receive, came as part of the preparation for death.* It too qualified as arising from 'the corrupt following of the apostles', since there is no hint of such preparation for death in the New Testament. There is one mention of the disciples anointing the sick and healing them (Mark 6:13), and one instruction from James for the elders to come and anoint the sick (James 5:13–16). The ministry of anointing the sick obviously stands close to the ministry of Jesus, but we lack his specific command – and the purpose of such anointing was physical healing, not 'last rites'. In 1549 the Reformers reinstated anointing for healing in the Visitation of the Sick, though without suggesting it was a sacrament. It was removed again in 1552, and has been revived as a spiritual ministry only over the last century or so, being authorised within official services for the first time in 1983 in *Ministry to the Sick*.

Theories of orders *(Note to Chapter 15)*

There are three subsequent trends to be examined in relation to a theory of orders:

1 the rise of Catholicism in the Church of England;
2 controversies related to *Apostolicae Curae*;
3 modern revisions of the Ordinal.

---

*The total preparation, known to non-Roman Catholics today in the phrase sometimes seen in notices of deaths: 'So-and-so died on such a date, fortified by the rites of Mother Church', included confession and absolution, the receiving of the bread of communion (called the '*viaticum*', i.e. 'for the journey'), and this particular anointing, with commendation and prayers surrounding the actual departure.

1   The rise of Catholicism in the Church of England

This issue is well known. Keble insisted on apostolic succession in his Assize Sermon in July 1833. Newman wrote in September 1833 in Tract no. 1: '[when all else fails] There are some who rest their divine mission ... upon their temporal distinctions. This last case has, perhaps, been too much our own; I fear we have neglected the real ground on which our authority is built – OUR APOSTOLICAL DESCENT'. And John Mason Neale wrote a hymn which is still to be found in *Hymns Ancient and Modern Revised*:

> His twelve apostles first he made
> his ministers of grace:
> And they their hands on others laid
> to fill in turn their place.
>
> So age by age and year by year
> this grace was handed on;
> and still the holy Church is here,
> although her Lord has gone.

It would be my contention that the theological doctrine of apostolic succession, drawing upon the rubrical uniformity of the sixteenth and seventeenth centuries, then began to engulf Anglicanism in a way previously unknown (though perhaps adumbrated in the narrow sectarianism of the Nonjurors). It produced its own concepts of ministerial authority (with its concomitant clericalism), its own insistence on episcopal confirmation for true Christian initiation (with its concomitant Anglican exclusiveness), and its own magnification of the bishop's office in all accounts of ecclesiology (and thus of terms for intercommunion and reunion). That which was viewed as a near-rebellion in the 1830s had become a respectable and accepted valid way of being Anglican by the 1870s, and had, in effect, changed *de facto* Anglicanism enormously. The strand went on to become the dominant form of Anglicanism in the first 60 or 70 years of this century, until its tenets were taken for granted as 'normal' (or perhaps normative) Anglicanism. We need to note these effects – relatively new to the nineteenth century – but need not now stay on them.

The basic insistence on episcopal succession and ordination as necessary to the being (the *esse*) of the Church is neither integral to the Gospel nor grounded in the Reformation settlement, but is a partisan and over-narrow view which has deeply affected and damaged our relationships with Reformed Churches. It will be clear that 'succession' had no meaning in the first two centuries save in the sense of 'successive handing on of an unchanged Gospel'. It is equally clear that, once the content of Christianity *had* been altered as substantially as it was altered in the West between the fifth century and the fifteenth, then the second-century rationale of 'succession' became virtually unsustainable – and the needed reform of the received religion in the sixteenth century meant again that 'succession' was a matter of legalities rather than unchanging truth, and, although the Reformers were keen to ordain episcopally and to have the bishops themselves consecrated by those who were already bishops, the 'succession', when written down, in doctrinal terms looks distinctly odd.* Nor is it at all clear that an unchanged and unchanging adherence to the same Gospel has marked the Anglican episcopate since the Reformation. The only alternative theory – the one espoused by the Oxford Movement and still lingering today – is that episcopal consecration conveys grace or authority, which is passed down history in the persons of the bishops thus consecrated, irrespective of what they have taught or believed. This clearly would not pass muster with Irenaeus, and yet has no other point of reference in the first and second centuries apart from him. In crude terms, it is the pipeline theory. But, if we cannot fasten a pipeline theory of grace upon the first two centuries, then it must be doubtful indeed whether such a pipeline could ever have come into existence later.

What then are we to make of the episcopal office and sequence (if we are not to call it 'succession') of bishops? Once we have got past the breathtaking claims of Kirk's book, *The Apostolic Ministry* (1946),[9] and have started a slow descent to more modest claims for the episcopate, then there are two

---

*I have, after all, served in the diocese of Rochester, where, when the present diocesan bishop was enthroned, we gave thanks for the previous bishops, mentioning in quick 'succession' Fisher and Ridley . . .

stopping-points worth noting. Both function by admitting the lack of evidence for the Kirk position, but by looking around for more modest defences of the importance of the episcopate. The first of these was the 1954 Westcott House symposium relating to the Church of South India, *The Historic Episcopate in the Fullness of the Church* (edited by K. Carey),[10] and the second is the recent document from the Council for Christian Unity of the Church of England, *Apostolicity and Succession*.[11] The first of these is a bold rewriting of the argument of the Tractarians and their followers down to Kirk and Dix, that historic episcopacy (as it is regularly called) is of the *esse* of the Church; and the Westcott symposiasts come up instead with a new theological dictum, that the historic episcopate is of the *plene esse* of the Church. The second takes very seriously the locating of true succession and continuity in the continuance of the whole Church on earth from the apostles' times, but then presses the argument that, within the Church's continuity, the historic succession of episcopal ministry is a 'sign' of the Church's continuity. The two books have a major point in common – that is, both are resiling from the unsustainable and harsh *esse* argument, while still wanting to give high preferential treatment to the historic episcopate in their doctrine of the Church; and thus both end up with an apologia that the episcopate *makes the Church look right*. I suspect that this essentially cosmetic argument is not half as theological as it is dressed up to appear. On the other hand, each of the two books has a totally different 'political' impact – the Westcott House book reads as loosening an over-rigorous position in the days of the Anglo-Catholic hegemony; while the CCU document reads as looking for some shreds of argument with which to hang on to the importance of the historic episcopate in days of a rising Evangelicalism, and relative indifference about various forms of ministry.

Over against the erroneous and the cosmetic, it is time to restate the *bene esse* argument. This returns to the thesis that a connexionalist Church is appropriately led by supraparochial chief pastors, and that responsibility for resourcing, stimulating and monitoring the congregation, rightly called '*episcope*' or oversight, is well exercised by such pastors, who may thus be *episcopoi* or 'bishops'. But they should be genuinely resourcing the local congregations, and they are doing less than that when they are only valued for their scarcity, and only have rare contact with the general run of parishes. Rightly structured and rightly deployed, episcopal ministry might well claim to be of the *optime esse* of the Church. But the institution may well vary from place to place, and from generation to generation, in the powers and accountability of individual episcopal ministers; it may well also vary as to whether episcopacy is practised in an episcopal team or through a severely monepiscopal constitution, and as to the formation of provinces or other supra-diocesan frameworks. There may even be variety in the ways of appointing to episcopal office.[12]

Before we go further into discerning and tracing the jungle pathways of history, episcopal succession and theories of orders, there is a need for a larger protest about the whole enterprise. It takes this form: does the nature of the Church depend as exclusively upon connections through history as this exploration would suggest. If we look at, 'this grace was handed on; and still the holy Church is here, although her Lord has gone' (quoted on p. 322), we get the cartoon in its most colourful form. According to this view, the Lord is directing and resourcing his Church, because he started it off in a certain shape in the first century, and grace has been channelled down to us along all the centuries through those means – and that is how we know we receive grace through sacraments, etc. But in the New Testament it would appear that God resources his Church by dynamic grace-full encounter with his people through the ascended and glorified Christ and the gift of the Holy Spirit, and by word and sacrament and other kinds of ministering – but the encounter is live, immediate, and dynamic because it is a contemporaneous direct heaven-to-earth communication, not a first-century-to-twenty-first-century linear conveyancing down time. Whatever weight is given to historical continuity, and whatever disqualifications it is appropriate to issue in relation to schisms and breakaways and the formation of 'new Churches' without respect for history, yet the immediacy of Christ's reign within his people is to be tested by results, not by pedigree: the ultimate validation of a Church is its living Christianity not its history. Of course we should be seeking to unite the parts of the visible Church, but we should remember that in the economy of God it is not an episcopal succession, however well ordered, which is the major achievement or characteristic of the Church of England, or the best proof of our obedience, or the finest evidence of God's special care for us. It is terrifying that it has so often come top of our agenda when conversations are joined with others.

2   *Controversies related to* Apostolicae Curae

Secondly (and with that caveat) we come to the Roman Catholic condemnation of Anglican orders in the encyclical, *Apostolicae Cuarae* (1896). This was a condemnation of the liturgical texts. It included a statement that the orders conferred were not clearly identified in 1552, but that is (a) special pleading, and (b) likely to pull out the rug from early rites also. The major objection was 'defect of intention'; and the defect was that the Edwardine Ordinal was not intended to make priests whose role was to offer the sacrifice of the Mass. This argument was threefold:

1   Orders are conferred in order to provide priests to offer the sacrifice of the Mass;

2   Cranmer's eucharistic rites had abolished all hints of the sacrifice of the Mass;

3   Cranmer's Ordinal therefore could not be said to ordain priests for that task (and the more so as it gave no hint in its own text that it did so ordain them).

While *Apostolicae Curae* undoubtedly arose from English Roman Catholics manoeuvring to get the pope to put Anglo-Catholicism out of court, it needed refuting rather than merely dismissing. A robust Anglican answer (such as Jewel would have given in Elizabeth's reign) would have been that we had never claimed that the validity of our orders rested upon any acceptance of (1), and thus it was unnecessary and even misleading to argue about (2) and (3) – points which, once (1) had been challenged, a good Anglican might well concede! It might however be argued back that what was needed was not robustness, but sensitivity – and that if any *rapprochement* were ever to happen (which was not what the pope or the cardinal archbishop of Westminster in 1896 actually wanted), then

Roman Catholics would have to be convinced, on *their* terms, that Anglicans had retained a valid succession. This was how the archbishops of Canterbury and York went about replying: their 1897 document, while profoundly and satisfyingly scathing of the pope and his scholarship on most points of both history and logic, veered a bit near him on this point of the Eucharist. It virtually allowed (1), denied (2) and thus dismissed (3). But I think that both the polemical needs of the 1890s and the Reformation formularies themselves, and a constructive laying of foundations for the future, actually called for the 'robust' reply on this point which would have challenged the basis of the papal condemnation, and I do not think we ought to concede the starting-point of the two archbishops.

Modern revisions of the Ordinal
Modern revision of the ordination rites has happened round the world since the early 1970s. In my collection of the rites,[13] I have traced their origins to the Church of South India rites of 1950, the Lambeth Conference document of 1958, and the Anglican–Methodist Ordinals of 1967 and 1968. Almost all of these have seen a shift from an indicative or imperative formula at the laying on of hands to a prayer of thanksgiving (indeed a 'eucharistic' prayer), within which or following which comes the laying on of hands. It is a move sufficiently sharp to raise the question as to whether we had a sufficient rite before! – and I recall Arthur Couratin telling me, in the early days of my time on the Liturgical Commission, 'I never assist at an ordination in Durham Cathedral without saying to myself, "Invalid orders – defect of form"'. But *that* would be to open a retrospective can of worms . . .

There is one other issue arising from our Ordinals which needs some brief attention. The Anglican world has at intervals thrown up a concept of 'unifying' or 'reconciling' episcopal and non-episcopal orders by an ordination-like mutual ritual. This arose because the Anglo-Catholic hegemony at the time of the formation of the Church of South India in 1947 opposed that form of integration so forcefully that they compelled others into the 'unifical' pattern of rites. Paul Bradshaw, in *The Anglican Ordinal*,[14] gives a chapter to such ritual concepts, and thus groups them under the 'ordination' title of his whole book. The dilemma is that, if such rites can be understood as subliminal ordination, then they are morally out of court – whereas if they cannot be understood in any way as a kind of ordination, then they are out of court for the purposes of getting the school of thought which originally precipitated them now to accept them.

For the rest, I must cite myself from the Introduction to my collection of Anglican ordination rites: 'What ordination _is_ and _does_ remains elusive'.

The 'priesthood' of the ordained ministry _(Note to Chapter 15)_

The English word 'priest' remained with the 'second order' of the threefold orders of ministry at the Reformation. It is the word used in the rites of ordination, in the rubrics of the services in the Book of Common Prayer, and in the references in the Thirty-Nine Articles to 'bishops, priests and deacons'. It caused some confusion in Elizabeth I's reign, as in the New Testament '_presbuteroi_' was translated as 'elders', and only '_hiereis_' was translated as 'priests' – but all were clear that the Church of England 'priests' were not '_hiereis_' but '_presbuteroi_'! When the Articles are read in their (equally authoritative) Latin form, then the truth stands out – the three orders are '_episcopi, presbyteri, diaconi_'. Anglicans are, I think, the only English-speaking Church of the Reformation to leave the misleading English title 'priest' in place, and it has brought confusion that they did so. The misleading effects include the following:

1 a reinforcing of reintroduced pre-Reformation notions of eucharistic sacrifice;

2 a notion that there is a connection between 'priesthood' and sacraments;

3 a tendency to want to link the 'priesthood' (i.e. presbyterate) of the ordained ministers with the 'priesthood' (i.e. '_hierosune_') of Christ or the concept of the whole Church as a 'priesthood' (i.e. '_hierateuma_'), and this is clearly illegitimate, and those who suffer from the tendency ought to be made to argue the case in Latin or Greek.

The true translation has never been left without a witness, and the Scottish Episcopal Church, to take a strange example, has always said 'the presbyter' in the rubrics of its liturgical rites. Over the last 50 years the united Churches of South India, North India, Pakistan, and Bangladesh have come into being, each of them eschewing (in their definitive English-language formulations) the term 'priest' for the second order of ministers, each of them using 'presbyter' – and each of them involving Anglicans. There are more signs today of the Church of England itself getting its linguistic house in order. The ASB rite for ordaining the second order of ministers is entitled 'The Ordination of Priests (also called Presbyters)', which both clarifies the standing of the word 'priests' and gently encourages us to make the transition to the biblical term.

There was a threat of a set-back to this trend in General Synod in the 1980s. In 1983 the Synod passed a motion asking for the Standing Committee to provide a study of 'ordained priesthood' within the Church of England in order to bring the Church of England 'towards agreement' from the 'different, and deeply held, convictions' on the subject. The Faith and Order Advisory Group (FOAG) then drew up a report, *The Priesthood of the Ordained Ministry*.[15] The conclusion of its investigation of the New Testament, in a section headed 'The priesthood of the distinctive ministry' (*sic*!), was, 'No priesthood is attributed to the distinctive ministry' (p. 28) – though the report appears not keen to state this too cleanly, but instead nudges away with hints as to why it was inappropriate for first-century Christians to call their ministers 'priests', as though they were itching to do so all along, but managed to restrain themselves because they knew they would be misunderstood! This is itself loaded nonsense, with a heavy burden of proof on those who would so nuance their presentation of the New Testament evidence. We respond:

1   It is true that 'no priesthood is attributed to the distinctive ministry'.

2   No functions which could be called distinctively 'priestly' are attributed either.

3   The positive teaching of the letter to the Hebrews makes it clear that there are not and cannot be 'distinctive priests' within the people of God, for all such priesthood has been fulfilled inalienably and non-transferably in the priesthood of Christ (see pp. 311–16 above).

4   The natural reading of the New Testament suggests that
it did not occur to the early Church to call their leaders,
officers or ministers 'priests'.

The report's passing hints do not and cannot greatly affect the
cleanness of the New Testament picture. As might have been
expected, the report instead gives first some authoritative
standing to 'tradition', and then argues from the growing use
in Church history of 'priestly' language for the ordained ministry that this was not a mistake but represented the inner
reality of the 'distinctive ministry'. So the last chapter begins:
'[The ministers] are priestly only by grace and only by participation in his unique priesthood' (p. 97 – is not 'participation'
here a thoroughly weasel word?), and ends:

> Although the terms "priest" and "priesthood" are not used
> in the New Testament with reference to the work of Christ's
> special ministry, nevertheless ... they indicate *essential
> aspects* of the ministry of presbyters and bishops (p. 102,
> emphasis mine).

This does not quite say that the terms are themselves 'essential', but it reads as though the authors hoped that those who
believe that about 'priesthood' would think they *had* read it
there.

At any rate, the report was short-lived. Having done all
that human ingenuity could do to make 'the priesthood of
the ordained ministry' a credible concept, the report came to
General Synod in November 1986 to help the Church of
England to solve its problems of ecumenical relationships and
to find internal accord between 'different, and deeply held,
convictions'. The debate afforded no such happy result. An
eminent member moved as an amendment that 'this Synod
views Chapter XIII of [the report] as inconsistent with Chapters I–IV and asks the House of Bishops to give consideration
to this issue'. The amendment was lost by 224 votes to 207,
but the report was now dead in the water. The most that could
be plausibly said for the 'priesthood of the ordained ministry'
had now been said, and had totally failed to convince and
thus had defeated its own purposes.

The diaconate *(Note to Chapter 15)*

Deacons are the 'third order' of the threefold order of ministries. It has to be recorded that they are an order in quest of a place on the ecclesiological map. Since long before the Reformation the diaconate has been generally used as a short probationary time prior to ordination as a presbyter. That is the clear teaching of the 1662 Ordinal. This has in turn led by reaction to various attempts to locate a calling and even a job description for 'permanent deacons'. It is my own conviction that these attempts are unsuccessful, for they are impaled on the horns of a dilemma – either there are distinctive diaconal functions or there are not. If there are such functions, then they can only be made 'distinctive' by denying them to lay people – and all ministries of 'service' to the world are fundamental to the whole calling of the whole people of God, and commissioning for them therefore comes sacramentally in baptism and not through specialist ordination. There are currently some minimal 'in-church' liturgical functions for a deacon, the traditional one being 'reading the gospel' at the Eucharist. If, however, we canonise that job description, and ordain *permanent* deacons for the task, then:

1 we shall deprive lay people of the chance to read the gospel in the rite;

2 we shall rather trivialise ordination if such a small service is to be conferred by ordination for life;

3 while any of the existing expectations is still in place, and non-stipendiary and local non-stipendiary presbyters are being created all round our 'permanent' deacons, then they will come under pressure to be ordained as presbyters and thus be *truly* useful rather than have holy orders with minimal functions.

If, on the other hand, the deacons do not have any distinctive functions, then the whole concept of a diaconate becomes cosmetic. There are those in the Church of God who revel in making, say, a eucharistic liturgy *look* right (and I am well aware of that as a bishop, whose presence is sometimes valued for its cosmetic – though hardly ornamental – contribution to a celebration), and in those circles to have a genuine deacon available apparently adds to the cosmetic completeness of a rite. I confess I am not of this persuasion, and I conceive that the authenticity of a worship event is to be measured, even outwardly, by other criteria. At any one time in about 95 per cent of the parishes of the Church of England there is unlikely to be a deacon – and in somewhere over 80 per cent there quite probably never will be. Yet the worship and mission of those parishes proceeds apparently unhampered.

Gregory Dix, in his famous chapter on orders in Kirk's *The Apostolic Ministry*, does not set up an immutability of threefold orders, but rather works with a division between 'the essential ministry' (i.e. the episcopate) and 'the dependent ministry', a phrase which suggests that it is capable of finding expression in practice in differing ways. There may or may not be a case for abolishing the diaconate as a 'holy order', but I suggest that, despite the apparent attractiveness of the idea, there is little positive mileage in saying, 'The diaconate is a "given"; it is one of the threefold orders revealed from heaven; and, as we have it in its evanescent form, let us now pin it down and give it some lasting substance.' If Dix is right, even on his presuppositions about the episcopate (which are difficult to share), there is no need to impale ourselves on the horns of the diaconal dilemma – and the case can at least be considered as to whether the probationary diaconate is worth preserving. Curiously enough, the advocates of a restored 'permanent' diaconate are now to be heard urging that those who are to become presbyters should be ordained by 'direct' ordination to the presbyterate – on the grounds that, as long as there are probationary presbyters passing through the order of the diaconate (usually for a year in England, but often less in other parts of the world), so long will these 'transitional deacons' muddy the waters and obscure the true nature of the diaconate. If there were direct ordination to the presbyterate, then it would be almost a matter of empirical inspection as to whether or not candidates for a permanent diaconate were emerging. If they were (and could be defended against pressures to become presbyters, which are often strong!), then we would have such an order. If there were no candidates, the order would not be abolished, but would simply be in abeyance.

The ordination of women *(Note to Chapter 15)*
There can be little doubt that in the New Testament the
leaders of the Church were male, and certainly the twelve
specially chosen by Jesus were male, the appointed successor
to Judas was to be male, the seven in Acts 6 were male, Saul
converted on the road to Damascus was male, and the elders
('presbyters') appointed in the churches arising, for example,
from the first missionary journey, appear to have been male
(Acts 14:23). At various well-known points the women in the
churches are exhorted to be quiet and submissive (1 Cor. 11:
3–16; 14:33–8; 1 Tim. 2:9–15). Community life inside the
churches appears to have been as patriarchal as community
life outside. And the general practice of Christian history since
the first century has shown little change in the situation
until the twentieth century.

It is no doubt possible to put in qualifiers to this New Testament account. There is the role of the Virgin Mary (Luke 1—
2; John 19:25; Acts 1:14), the initial resurrection appearance
to Mary Magdalene (John 20:11–18), the role as head of a
household in Philippi of Lydia (Acts 16:14–15), Phoebe the
woman *diakonos* of the church in Cenchrea (Rom. 16:1),
the allowance by Paul that women can 'pray or prophesy' (1
Cor. 11:4–5), and other verses which suggest parity between
the sexes. An obvious foundation principle is established in the
assertion that '[in Christ] there is neither male nor female'
(Gal. 3:28) – though this refers to justification in Christ and
not at all to holding distinct office in the Church.

However, these are but qualifiers, and the question retains
this shape: if for good reason we wish to appoint women to
leadership in the Church (such as is integral to being presbyter
or bishop), is the de facto patriarchal context and content of
the New Testament writings such as to forbid in principle and
de jure that appointment of women? There are three considerations which have led me to say 'no' to this question.

1 The issue of office-holders is not a foundational gospel
issue in any case. The leadership given by office-holders is
not autonomous, but is itself to be subject to the revealed
word of God. So the issue is partly of the form: can women
be mature believers, rightly handling the word of truth?

2 Is there any way in which the New Testament is histori-

cally conditioned? Of course, we must not disallow the
radical nature of the Gospel itself, or the readiness of both
Jesus and his followers to confront evil and to prophesy new
ways. But, to take what is to us a moral issue, did not the
New Testament writers 'go along with' the principle of
slavery as exercised in the Roman empire, even while
planting the radical seeds of mutual love, of the breaking
down of racial barriers, and of respect for human dignity
which ultimately were to sweep human slavery away in
Christian-led countries? There is obviously *some* historical
conditioning in relation to women and their roles in the
community – as, for example, in covering the head and
the regard for the angels! Is there some such conditioning
of the Church also in the general according to women of
second place in home and community, such that in general
it would not have occurred to first-century Christian leaders
to call or appoint women to leadership roles? Could the 1
Timothy passage, for instance, be read that way?

If we put this the other way round, we have to say that it
is no doubt true that the emergence of women into a promin-
ence challenging that of men in Western (and other) societies
in the twentieth century is often attributable to secular
egalitarian principles. But the converse is that societal pressures in virtually all kinds of community on earth were
previously holding women down by what we might also dub
'secular inegalitarian principles'. Most people in most
societies for most of the history of the world have lived with
the prejudices they have received from the generation before
them (consider the position of women in Islamic countries
to this day). The prophet who challenges is rare – the one
who challenges and succeeds is even rarer – and thus attitudes from the past live on. The oppression of women
(whether petty or horrific) is part of the secular history of
the world, and the Christian Church was just as much under
secular misguidance when its women were oppressed – or
at least not valued for their gifts – as it may be accused of
being when it brings women into leadership.

3   There is a self-cancelling character of advocacy against
the ordination of women. I do not now mean 'Catholic' argumentation, which so often appears to have resolved itself

into an issue of 'authority' in this form: it may not be impossible for women to be ordained, but Anglicans, who are merely
a 'separated' part of the Western Church, have no authority
to take such a decision on their own, and must await a
Roman Catholic (presumably papal) decision before they will
know whether they should be ordaining women or not. The
specifically biblical arguments raised relate to whether
women may teach, and to the 'headship' of men over women.
Each of these, once invoked, raises problems rather than
solves them.

The teaching issue, which seems to be the main thrust of
the Pauline prohibitions, is impossible to apply and sustain,
except perhaps in the narrowest of Brethren assemblies.
The difficulty is partly in knowing where 'teaching with
authority' stops and 'communicating with accuracy' starts.
And if a woman was allowed to prophesy in Corinth (and it
seems she was), then any amount of 'teaching' might well
have entered her prophecies. Anglicans allowed women to
be lay parish workers, deaconesses, lay readers and Church
Army officers (and catechists and evangelists in some parts
of the world), and all these offices canonised the principle of
women as teachers of the congregation long before they ever
crossed the line into 'holy orders' and became first deacons
and later presbyters. There may be a case for a protest, but,
if so, the protest was due decades before the ordination issue
came up, and is quite inappropriate and hollow-sounding
now.

The headship issue is equally difficult to apply. 'Headship'
may denote 'dominance', but does not necessarily do so, and
there are suggested translations which would locate the root
sense of 'head' in a concept like 'source' (as in 'head-waters',
'fountain-head', etc.), or even like 'that which complements
or completes' (as in 'the stone which has become the head of
the corner', or the verb for 'completing all things in Christ'
(Eph. 1:10), where the Greek has a compound verb formed
from *kephale* a head). Either of these senses would fit many
of the uses of 'head' or 'headship', and the 'dominance'
concept has itself places where it does not seem to fit well.

But let it be that 'headship' has its strongest possible
connotation, that (as in 1 Cor. 11:2–3) Christ is to be sub-

missive to the Father, the man is to be submissive to Christ, and the woman is to be submissive to the man, or that (as in Eph. 5:22–4) the woman is to be submissive to the man, as the Church is to Christ. In each case the 'woman' (*gune*) might mean more narrowly the 'wife', thus not touching on the submissiveness of single women and widows. But even so, while this passage may say much about marriage, it does not actually accord a 'headship' role to a male pastor or leader in relation to a congregation; and, even then, if we wished to go beyond Scripture and were determined to apply the text to leadership in the congregation, we would still not know what role, if any, a woman pastor might fulfil. Is a woman pastor leading a daughter church in a 'headship' role? Is a woman pastor temporarily responsible during a vacancy in the chief pastor's position in a 'headship' role? If a team of presbyters functions together, is the convenor of the team a 'head' and the others not? Or do they have to watch their respective roles in relation to the lay people of the congregations to discover whether they are being 'heads' or not? Is a hospital chaplain in a 'headship' role? Is the 'head' of a woman's community in this 'headship' role – or is she not to be 'head' of the community anyway? Or is any presbyter who is canonically obedient to his or her bishop a 'head' of any sort? And is a suffragan or assistant bishop a 'head' of any sort? In short, even if it is thought that 'headship' could apply to leadership within the Christian community, and it is simultaneously articulated that women must not exercise that headship, could we even then know what it is we are wanting to forbid to them, and would that prohibition of itself exclude them from being ordained as presbyters – or even as bishops? I fear the headship argument dies the death of a thousand imprecisions.

'Flying bishops' *(Note to Chapter 15)*

One extraordinary feature of life in the Church of England since women were made presbyters in 1994 has been the creation and consecration of 'flying bishops'. They have received the publicity, but they are really only a particular instance of a general principle, which is that, under the terms of the Episcopal Ministry Act of Synod in 1993, in each diocese provision is made for 'extended episcopal care' for parishes which oppose the ordination of women to the presbyterate. The 'Provincial Episcopal Visitors' only visit some dioceses, and in others arrangements may be made for this 'care' within the diocese or (as is the case in my own diocese, Southwark) with the help of a bishop from a neighbouring diocese.

Such parishes which have asked for extended episcopal care remain fully part of the diocese within which they are physically placed, and there is no diocesan or provincial administration or jurisdiction to which they belong except that of their existing diocese. They tend to reject the sacramental and episcopal ministry of those bishops who will ordain women largely, it seems, on the grounds that those who ordain women, when they either cannot or should not have done so, have so muddled the nature of the presbyteral college in the process that clear and open sacramental relationships with them are impossible. The upshot is a 'Catholicism', which is itself but a splinter of the Catholic strand in the Church of England – of a strand, that is, which is itself but part of the Church of England, and of a Church of England, that is, which is itself split from the truly 'Catholic' Church of the West, the Church of Rome. If 'Catholic' means anything, it means something worldwide and fully comprehensive, and not, surely, as sectional as the constituencies of the flying bishops appear to be.

The provision of extended episcopal care is the outworking and fulfilling of a promise made before the vote in November 1992, a promise which may even have been determinative in the vote being sufficient for the ordination of women to go ahead. It would be quite improper to abrogate it now. Furthermore, while in formal terms the Church of England is a Church in which women are ordained, the provision of extended episcopal care allows the opposing view – i.e. that the Synod was mistaken and its decision ought to be reversed, to remain alive without any charge of disloyalty or disobedience. Thus those who ask for such care are formally able to work for the reversal of the decision, and are, *as far as such formal terms go*, given that hope of what, for them, would be light at the end of the tunnel. They do not *have* to believe that the night is closing in on them, or that they merely have the dubious benefit of a

delay in execution. To remain as parishes of the Church of
England they have needed some hope. Informally, as a matter of
sheer prediction, we may or may not think they can survive –
but formally they can.*

It remains to use this opportunity to reflect briefly upon a
pretentious word 'reception'. As I understand it, 'reception'
was a Roman Catholic term to describe the process by which
either a popular belief or a decree of council or pope passed
into full acceptance, as it made its impact upon the whole
Church, and as minds grappled with it, came to terms with it,
and accepted it. In such Roman terms, the faithful had no
option, and therefore such formulations were and are totally
'received'. The difficulty has been that Anglicans (and others
in the ecumenical movement) have tended, when putting out
a statement or formulation that is not yet fully agreed, and is
at least open to rejection, to say that the process of 'reception'
has just begun. Thus it has been with the ordination of women
to the presbyterate; but it should be noted that, because of the
overtones that full acceptance is bound to follow in time, to
propose a change like this – that is, one which has only partial
support – and to say that the process now is one of 'reception'
is actually pre-emptive and unfair to opponents. Alternatively,
if 'reception' actually means 'testing to see whether or not the
whole Church is ready to receive [the particular change]', then
a most peculiar and even weasel meaning is put upon 'reception'. If we mean 'testing' or 'vetting' or 'putting on probation'
(with a view to a period of time being used for this), then we
would do better to use such words, and not the misleading
'reception'. And, with that terminological warning, we must
insist that the present mode of ordaining women within the
Church of England's structure is not one in which all must
agree from the outset (or even, technically, at the end of the
day) that women can be ordained; rather it is that a large
majority is being enabled to test out that which it has seemed
good to them before God to implement, and the final outcome
of that testing is yet to be registered. It is actually a situation

---

*My impression is that they themselves do not think they could
survive the ordination of women as bishops. But that is another story.

where persons holding to the two theological positions ought
to be in continued theological debate.

Presidency of the Eucharist *(Note to Chapter 15)*
We do not know who presided at the Eucharists of the New
Testament Church. When Paul writes to the Corinthians and
calls for a redressing of their unloving ways, he simply tells
the whole church to correct its behaviour (1 Cor. 11:17–31).
Similarly, when, a few years later, he comes to Troas as he
returns to Jerusalem from his third missionary journey, Luke
(infuriatingly) records merely, 'When we gathered on the first
day of the week to break bread' (Acts 20:7). There was a
precedent in the clear presidency exercised by Jesus at the
Last Supper; there was an oral textual account of his institution of the Eucharist being recited; but we cannot tell what
manner of man (or woman) actually presided or read this
account. We can only approach the subject through the New
Testament by asking ourselves what kind of churchly event
this supper may have been (and should have been), and then
asking whether our answer to the first question would give
any clues as to what kind of person would most appropriately
preside at the event.

Ignatius of Antioch wrote at the beginning of the second
century AD that 'that Eucharist can be considered safe [trust-
worthy/valid/reliable – Greek *bebaia*] which is under the
bishop or someone to whom the bishop shall have delegated
it'. From then until now the presidency of the Eucharist has
been confined in the main 'historic' Churches to bishops and
presbyters. It would appear that the prime role of these ministers has been as leaders and ministers to the congregation,
and presiding at the Eucharist has been an expression of that
pastoral and leadership role. Certainly it is as chief public
officers of the Church that their exclusive role in presiding at
the chief public corporate celebration of the Church would
have to be defended – it is their relationship to the Church
which must be the key, not some ontological and perhaps
divinising change in their persons conferred by ordination.

The Church of England's Reformation, whatever its benefits
on other fronts, was, in respect of the ministry of word and
sacraments, totally clericalist. As noted earlier, this clericalism

was further narrowed and strengthened in 1662 in order to provide an exclusively episcopalian system; and it is not therefore surprising that the Act of Uniformity of 1662 imposed a heavy fine on anyone, not being a properly (i.e. episcopally) ordained presbyter, who presumed to consecrate the sacrament of the body and blood of Christ. The fine was £100 (worth perhaps 400 times as much today). While this was directed primarily against ejected ministers, it incidentally completely ruled out lay presidency.

So the Church of England's rules ran and (through the 1969 canons) still run. The nineteenth century saw the rise of the Anglo-Catholic movement, with an increasing emphasis upon both priesthood and sacrament, and an ample supply of priests also. There was no groundswell seeking for permission for lay people to preside. It has only been in the late twentieth century that the issue has really arisen – and it has arisen both from a sacramental need on the one hand and a desire for an anti-clericalist gesture on the other. Both are incomprehensible to average clericalists; but the 'sacramental need' part of the causation is worth careful consideration.

Many parts of the world Church, and not least the provinces of the Anglican Communion, have developed in the last 50 years a pattern of eucharistic life – that is, a main weekly congregational celebration of communion as *the* centre of corporate worship of the week – which is resonant of the Church under persecution and traceable to early in the second century, and only slightly less certainly back to the Church of the apostles themselves. This in turn has provided large numbers of communicants with the expectation that such a eucharistic celebration will always occur; and that those who quite properly developed a pattern, or even rule of life, which reckoned on receiving communion each week, would not be disappointed. The provision of a presbyter-president each week becomes difficult when there are no assistant or retired clergy to help during holidays, illness or a vacancy in the incumbency. There are also places in the world (though probably few such in England) where presbyters rarely come, and the issue is not so much whether people can receive communion weekly, as whether they can receive it at all, even over periods of some months.

The old Prayer Book answer, which is still heard occasionally nowadays, was to make do with 'spiritual communion', as set out in the 1662 Book of Common Prayers.

But there are two more usual modern answers to this shortage of eucharistic presidents, both of which are intended to meet the actual expressed need – that is, both terminate in a general communion (and both were mentioned as such in the 1988 Lambeth Conference Statement on Worship). They are:

1 Use 'extended communion', by providing consecrated elements at a distance (in time or space) from where the full celebration of communion has taken place.

2 Ordain 'local' presbyters, often by specially constructed selection and training methods.

However, there lurks in the offing another possibility – lay presidency of the Eucharist. This has traditionally been viewed as so unthinkable a subject as to be literally unspeakable. It was the theme of a serious publication for the first time in *Lay Presidency at the Eucharist?*, edited by Trevor Lloyd.[16] It came up once, briefly, in the General Synod of the Church of England in February 1983, when a private member motion was moved to ask the House of Bishops to set up a group to consider the issue. On that occasion, after only two speeches in the debate, the Synod was invited to move to next business – and duly did so without voting on the motion. Since then it has been a live issue among Anglicans in the Southern Cone of South America (where, in 1986, the Provincial Synod voted by eight votes to seven not to allow the diocese of Chile to adopt an experimental practice of lay presidency);[17] it has led to a General Synod report in the Anglican Church of Australia (and very nearly to implementation in Sydney) and to a recommendation for implementation by a different kind of working party in the diocese of Cape Town. The 1988 Lambeth Conference managed to avoid thinking about it or commenting on it; but the subject has not gone away. More recently it has become a genuine subject for genuine debate, and the upshot is a 72-page report by the House of Bishops, entitled *Eucharistic Presidency*.[18]

Eucharistic Presidency is very thorough, and it concludes that lay presidency should not be encouraged or allowed. It does, however, treat this as a contingent (or probabiliorist!) outcome of a contested argument. In so doing it sets up a defence for the present exclusive presbyteral or episcopal presidency, and it is this defence which will have now to be pierced if future debate is to change the Church of England's discipline. The main thrust of the report is to draw out the congruity of having those who preside over the Church's life preside also over its eucharistic liturgy, and this is done with great care. The report became the subject of a kind of seminar of the General Synod at York in July 1997.

If lay presidency is not available, at least for the moment, then Anglicans have to consider the alternatives mentioned above for ensuring that communion is available for the people. We may thus note:

1 'Extended communion', while very apt for the taking of communion to the sick and thus in effect keeping them in well-fostered fellowship with their own local church, appears far less apt as a way of providing a quasi-celebration of a 'main service' at a distance (whether in time or space) from the main celebration at which the elements were consecrated. The theological controversies involved in institutionalised 'reservation' of consecrated elements have so far only been addressed in long-range polemics and shrill voices, and need a weightier and more urbane approach.

2 'Local ordained ministry' also looks very difficult (although schemes for such ordinations are burgeoning all round the Anglican world). If they are too closely or exclusively linked to the need of a eucharistic presidency, they begin to look like 'massing priests' – and if they are only needed for a relatively brief period (e.g. during a vacancy in a parish), then to ordain *for life* (as ordination involves) would appear a considerable overkill of a solution. That is not to say that, if there is an overall need for ordained leadership in any local situation, there is never a case for 'local ordination' to meet it; but the problems of sustaining an identifiable watershed – between those who are presbyters, in principle able to minister anywhere, and those who are 'local ordained presbyters', in principle unable to minister anywhere save the named 'locality' – are legion, and are only fully discoverable after some years of operating a scheme.

I suspect that the problems inherent in these two alternative

solutions mean that the issue of lay presidency will not quickly
go away.

Appendix 2 The Worldwide Anglican Communion

Anglicanism is a worldwide phenomenon, and a full treatment of Anglican ecclesiology would properly give full attention to its worldwide character. It arose through a series of historical chances and ventures, in which the spread of the British empire in the eighteenth and nineteenth centuries was one large feature, the Evangelical Revival and its zeal for world evangelism was another, and the Tractarian Movement was a third. Between the seventeenth and twentieth centuries it fumbled its way into observing on a worldwide basis the principle of the self-government of 'every particular and national Church', so that, at the time of writing, there are 32 independent and autonomous provinces of the Anglican Communion, with four United Churches, including ex-Anglicans and having the 'historic episcopate', as member Churches also. There are further relationships of communion with the Lutheran Churches of the Nordic and Baltic countries, with the Old Catholics, and with the Mar Thoma Church in South India.

The Churches of the Communion define themselves as 'Churches in communion with the see of Canterbury', and the archbishop of Canterbury holds a focal role, which is expressed in his *ex officio* presidency of the various 'instruments' which provide a bonding across the communion.

While the scriptural argument for the Church of God being a single organic unity across the surface of the earth might point towards a single supreme governing agency (whether or not like the papacy of Rome), the principle of national autonomy which originally separated the Church of England from Rome has worked similarly within the fabric of worldwide Anglicanism, and it is thus that, one by one, the separate provinces have been created. There may be something inconsistent in not pressing the logic of connexionalism to its international limit, but the internationalism of the Communion is preserved by the less tangible bonds of love, and common ethos and purpose.

The rationale for planting Anglican Christianity in a country like Kenya has simply been that English overseas missionary societies originally evangelised in a British colony, and created a pattern of church life much resembling that in England. In addition, there then developed all sorts of human and financial links between the Churches of Kenya and England, and the creation of a separate autonomous Anglican province arose at roughly the time of Kenyan decolonisation and independence. In other countries – as, for example, in the Southern Cone of South America – Anglicanism has been planted in countries already predominantly Roman Catholic. In neither case can the English apologia, of simply continuing the pre-Reformation Church but in a reformed pattern of life, be sustained – and, to that extent, Anglicanism appears all the more as one option among many, distinguished by its cultural style and its episcopal ministry, with the risk of simply attracting those who go for its specific culture.

The effect of such provincial autonomy is that each province can decide its doctrinal standards, its liturgy, and its discipline. Provinces may decide differently from each other about making women presbyters or even bishops, and about relationships with non-episcopal Churches. It is least possible that, in that power to act differently, the destruction of the Communion is somehow inherent; but it is also notable that provinces hold on to each other and are mutually supportive. The power to take initiatives in one place has led since 1970 to various pioneering moves which have in turn led on to adoption by others – as, for example, the creation of synodical patterns of church government in the USA in 1789, South India's entry into a United Church in 1947, New Zealand's allowing of the communion of unconfirmed children in 1970, Hong Kong's first ordination of women as presbyters in 1971, or Southern Africa's pioneering of interchangeability of ministers with non-episcopal Churches in 1996. There are now enormous variants to be found in liturgical forms, styles of music, election of bishops, appointment of pastors, relationships with other faiths, and political stances.

In two major respects the rest of the Communion differs from England, and differs sufficiently for it to be arguable that it is the Church of England which is out of step. In England a folk-religion still attaches to the Church of England, such that it is still natural in most of the country to call the local vicar to conduct an Anglican funeral when someone dies, except in those cases where it was known that the dead person had other definite religious affiliations – or was a professed unbeliever. The upshot is that the Church of England still reckons that somewhere between 25 and 30 million baptised persons are in some sense 'CE', and is sometimes tempted to put them into the count of the total numbers of Anglicans in the world.*

Separable from the folk-religion, and yet closely linked with it, is the legal establishment, the subject of Appendix 3 below. Anglicans from elsewhere can hardly credit it when told, among other fantasy-yet-fact features of this extraordinary arrangement, that the monarch appoints our bishops on the nomination of the prime minister. This hardly bears upon other Anglican provinces directly, so they usually just shake their heads in polite incomprehension, and leave the English to their impenetrable ways. But it does bear upon them in the appointment of the archbishop of Canterbury, as the see of Canterbury is that by which the communion is defined, the archbishop himself is focal to the various 'instruments' of unity and co-operation in the Communion, described in the next paragraph. At the 1988 Lambeth Conference, some Australian bishops led an unsuccessful attempt to require the opening of the office of archbishop of Canterbury to persons of any nationality, thinking that an African or Asian archbishop would model and inculcate a thorough internationalism to the Communion. Their instinct was right, though their proposed

---

*Thus, for example, the statistical information distributed before the 1978 Lambeth Conference showed the Church of England with 27,800,000 baptised members and 1,600,000 Easter communicants (*The Lambeth Conference 1978 Preparatory Information*, CIO, 1978, p. 16).

means was probably a mistake.* Their instinct would have been better deployed if they had called upon the Church of England to seek a church process for appointing the archbishop of Canterbury, so that the occupant of the prime see in the Communion should be above any suspicion of being the blue-eyed boy of a past prime minister (of whatever political hue or personal prejudice) or someone particularly beloved of the palace (whoever is in residence there in 2008).

The actual 'instruments' of unity in the Communion are in principle four:

1   The person of the archbishop of Canterbury, backed by a personal staff employed for Anglican Communion purposes;
2   The Lambeth Conference, to which the bishops of the Communion are summoned every ten years through the personal invitation of the archbishop of Canterbury.
3   The Primates' Meeting, chaired and summoned by the archbishop of Canterbury, and meeting roughly every two years and apparently of increasing significance.
4   The Anglican Consultative Council, which is composed of a bishop, a presbyter and a layperson from each province, with the archbishop of Canterbury as its *ex officio* president. It has an office at 157 Waterloo Road in London, sustains a permanent secretariat and services a series of inter-Anglican networks.

The existence of the worldwide Communion is a warning to the English, including this author, not to think solely of an English setting. That would be as fatal as judaising, and has some resemblances to it. But to my regret, both time and space

---

*Because, as long as the see of Canterbury is led by an English bishop, so long will it be clear that the relationship of other provinces with Canterbury is solely fraternal, and the definition of the communion as Churches in communion with the see of Canterbury can stand unaltered. If a national of another country could be appointed to Canterbury, then it would be clear that some supra-national powers were being claimed by the office-holder – other parts of the world were not simply aligned with Canterbury fraternally, but were in some sense *under his authority*. That is not the case at the moment, but to internationalise the post is to start towards a papacy. It would be better to have the focal defining point of reference leave Canterbury and move on (say every decade) than to cross the watershed into an internationalised Canterbury.

forbid my doing more here than note that an enquiry into the Church of England's credentials as subject to the word of God is not the last word for Anglicans, but merely the first; and a worldwide Anglicanism has to hold itself *sub specie aeternitatis*, as ready before God for that principled organic union which would lead to a truly catholic Church.

Appendix 3 The Establishment of the Church of England – A Shameful Captivity

I have avoided in Part III of this book making any comment on the legal establishment of the Church of England. It is clear from Parts I and II that the Church of Jesus Christ, while it may have apologetic or prophetic words to address to the secular rulers, while it may in some circumstances be ready to be martyred by the rulers and in others to be favoured by them, and while in all circumstances it has the duty and the habit of praying for them, can hardly be credible if it is *owned* by them. However, the history of Western Europe, from the Decree of Constantine (313) onwards, tells a different story. As Christianity became the official religion of Western nations, and as papal power grew in the Dark Ages, so monarchs and parliaments in the Middle Ages, if not actually in hock to the popes (who at times had their own troubles weakening their hold), were at all times engaged in wheeling and dealing with the Roman Catholic Church, sometimes manipulating the organs of church government to their advantage, sometimes being manipulated to the Church's – and yet, as all were Catholic Christians, rarely quite making that sharp polarisation, for all that two distinguishable power bases existed in relation to each sovereign or sovereign state.

It is against that background that Henry VIII's expropriation of the papal assets and powers, temporal and spiritual, in respect of England should be seen, and the consequent state ownership of the Church of England should be understood. Since that nationalisation of the English branch of the transnational company in the sixteenth century, there has been an intermittent process of lengthening the chain by which the Church of England has been bound to the slowly secularising state. Thus the position today is one where, like a goat on a very long chain, the Church of England can pursue its business most of the time with a great sense of freedom to move and to take decisions unfettered by outside forces. However, at intervals the goat reaches the end of the chain, and discovers that the sense of being free was deceptive – there are limits set by the state and, when those limits are reached, the goat can go no further.

Thus at the moment, the Church of England hits the limits of the chain in the following ways:

1 Its constitution and laws are subject to parliament by a procedure known as a Measure. Thus the decision of General Synod in November 1992 to ordain women as presbyters could not be implemented until parliament had, by votes in Lords and Commons, also agreed the legislation (and it took twelve months).

2 Its diocesan bishops (and deans of cathedrals) are appointed by the monarch, on the advice of her chief adviser, the prime minister of the day (I need not discuss how he or she is appointed). In respect of bishops, there is a prior Church procedure, via Vacancy-in-See committees and the Crown Appointments Commission, which in theory delivers two names to the prime minister who chooses one to nominate. The power of the prime minister has been defended by political leaders, since the convention was first agreed in 1976, because diocesan bishops go in due course to the Lords, so it has to be a political appointment.

3 The historic assets of the Church of England are held by the Church Commissioners, which, in the last analysis, is a parliamentary trust.

4 There are various issues bearing upon the person of the monarch, who is 'supreme governor' of the Church of England, and thus upon the form of coronations, and upon the behaviour (and any sanctions upon the behaviour) of the monarch.

5 There are also a variety of smaller issues which bear upon parish life in the Church of England – some favourable, some less so.

I restrain myself here from further denunciation of the ungodly and improper structural captivity of the Church of England to the state. I have argued the case against it elsewhere.[1] The proper persons to oppose such a captivity are the captives; but, partly because of the illusion of freedom, the captives appear in large measure to enjoy their captivity and oppose attempts to strike off the chains. It would probably take a crisis to change the mind of the Church of England's leadership.

Appendix 4 Making Episcopacy Credible

I have always believed the English practice of episcopacy to be incredible. To the average lay person a bishop gains his value not from his ability to resource or help either the person or the parish, but rather (as with royalty) from his sheer scarcity value; and this in turn means that you are honoured if he comes near you, delighted if he shows any knowledge of your local scene, and frankly astonished if he does anything which might actually be useful. He for his part faces vast amounts of driving if he is truly to be known and to give anything of spiritual benefit, with frequent returns home late at night.

I confess I made an exception to this verdict of incredibility when I went to be bishop of Aston (suffragan of Birmingham) in 1985; and I decided then that episcopacy could in that city be made *just* credible, though as like as not I had a hand in the scales in my own favour. The point was that this see was centred entirely upon a single major city – a city with ample dual carriageways and motorways, so that, living in Handsworth, I had all 200 parishes within 25 minutes of my home by car (and the diocesan bishop, in the south of the city, was in nearly as strong a position). There were other parts to the diocese – Solihull, and parts of Sandwell and north Warwickshire – but it was essentially a city-diocese of compact size, structured to relate to the civic city, but also a missionary diocese in a secular, multicultural and multi-religious (and multi-suffering) urban context. When I was forced to resign from there, I reflected that there was no other diocese in the Church of England to compare with it – but at the time of writing I find myself bishop of Woolwich, with around 95 parishes in an area of three London boroughs, little more than 12 miles from east to West and six from north to south (and not unlike Birmingham in its sociological conditions and its missionary context). Here too I find I may stretch a point in my own favour and profess to myself that episcopacy is just credible. I am also aware that at times a very big man as bishop (and I enjoyed, if that is the right word, one such in Hugh Montefiore) can be felt as omnipresent, even in a see which would otherwise make episcopacy totally incredible. But I have also had the experience, between my two periods as a suffragan, of being the incumbent of a town parish in the Rochester diocese; and I retain a strong suspicion that both parochialism on the one hand, and the relatively non-interventionist exercise of episcopacy on the other, leave the average parish going its way (cheerfully or otherwise) without much thought or interaction, let alone resourcing, from the episcopate – and that is so much the norm that it is rarely questioned. Consequently, any use a bishop does prove to be is treated as a kind of uncovenanted bonus over and above what might normally be expected. That is fine in its way (I do not query its workability and I applaud its 'successes') – but it is nothing like either the episcopacy of the first four centuries, nor the usual Anglican rationales for the institution. Of course one can maximise the benefits of a commodity with a scarcity value; of course one can use such a provision (as one can use royalty) for heightening ceremonial and special events; even with such events as confirmation (as currently practised) it is possible to use effectively the relative rarity with which the candidates will encounter a bishop;* but none of those possibly useful outcomes can justify the warped state of diocesan episcopacy in the Church of England today.

Now it is fully arguable that, because episcopacy obtrudes on the life of the average Christian believer and normal Christian congregation so little, and because, when it does, it has the character of a festive bonus, no one should lose too much sleep

---

*One has to say 'a bishop' rather than 'their bishop', as the actual ministering of confirmation is currently delegated to all manner of suffragan, assistant, neighbouring, retired and even visiting bishops – giving further evidence of the relative unavailability of the 'real' bishop, and the relative meaningless of rationales for confirmation which make it somehow a 'coming into relationship with *the* bishop'.

over its central incredibility. It is an awareness of that which makes me put this material into an appendix. Nevertheless, if we were to take our own rationales seriously, and were to endeavour seriously to commend episcopacy to those who do not have it, then we ought to interest ourselves in how it might be re-formed to become a truly pastoral and resourcing office within the Church of God. That is the purpose of this appendix.

I fear there will be an element of unlikelihood in what follows. This is not a practical policy for the incoming Archbishops' Council to implement the day after they take office. It is made difficult by the near-necessity of bringing it in all in one single change; and, for *that* to be practical, years of preparation would be needed in order to achieve near-consensus – and the very prospect of spending years doing it would so open the authorities of the Church of England to the charge of rearranging deckchairs on a certain doomed liner that it would be easy to abort the whole process. I know these things well. But perhaps a dream (with, I trust, some internal coherence, even if little external credence) may be allowed in an appendix. And, despite these disclaimers, I shall write the coming paragraphs as though we were in fact about to implement the plan.

What shape, then, could a reconstituted Church of England take, if getting episcopacy right were deemed a high priority in itself, and, perhaps derivately, a good instrument of mission? I set out four *desiderata* in such a shake-up:

1   Each diocese should have one bishop and should ideally have 80–90 incumbencies;

2   Each parish should have direct representation on the diocesan synod;

3   As far as is possible without loss of efficiency, existing diocesan non-parochial persons, posts and payments should be streamlined and reduced, rather than multiplied as dioceses divide;

4   General Synod should be as accessible and as manageable as it is at present, and preferably more so.*

---

*I write this without prejudice to the actual Archbishops' Council concept, as that is *sub judice* as I write, and is in large measure an issue internal to the running of General Synod and its department.

These criteria would point to the following organisational principles:

1 England would be divided into not more than 90 dioceses, arranged as far as possible along the grain of sociological units and areas.

2 The present diocese of Europe would be distanced from this procedure, and, whatever other arrangement were made, would not be described as a diocese of the Church of *England*, and would not function as part of the synodical structure of the Church of England.*

3 Each of the 90 dioceses would have a single diocesan bishop and two archdeacons. It would have a synod composed of the bishop, all the licensed clergy and one, two or three lay representatives per parish, depending upon their size. The election of a bishop would involve participation by the diocesan synod and by some representatives of the province, perhaps with weighting towards neighbouring or 'clustering' dioceses.

4 The General Synod would have three clergy and three laity from each diocese, the laity being elected either by all on the electoral rolls or by all on the diocesan synod. It would have a House of Bishops of 90 (or nearly 90) members, the most obviously altered feature from the present Synod. There would probably have to be provision for slightly more co-options to the Houses of Clergy and Laity than at present, though that would be in part dependent upon the outcome of the processes leading to the formation of the Archbishops' Council.

5 Dioceses would be encouraged to form clusters and to run joint boards (e.g. of finance, education, social responsibility, etc.) located in and answerable to each cluster of dioceses. These clusters *could* be deemed 'provinces', but that would be a self-defeating and unwelcome move if it meant that we either created more archbishops (scarcity value has some value at that point!) or started to create another layer of synodical government – or both. What they

---

*Shortly before going to press, I have heard with considerable approbation of an outline scheme to create an Anglican province on the Continent of Europe.

could have would be a senior or chairing bishop who spoke on occasion for the cluster within the region.

6   Deaneries might well be retained, but they would have to justify themselves in terms that were not synodical. If non-parochial archdeacons had an oversight of 40–45 incumbencies each, they could almost certainly fulfil all that existing rural deans with full-time parochial commitments can achieve.

7   Cathedrals would be otiose, as dioceses would be 'travelling light', and it would be a matter of chance as to whether any particular diocese inherited an existing cathedral or not when the great division came. The broad answer is that the 15 or so cathedrals which are parish churches would be retained as parish churches; that the 45 or so bishops who found themselves without a cathedral of any known sort would each have the opportunity to place his 'seat' in any parish church he chose, and certain resources would then be allocated to that parish. The 27 or so existing extra-parochial cathedrals would have the choice between becoming diocesan and parochial (and then being subject to all usual forms of pastoral reorganisation, etc.) or of becoming 'peculiars', remaining as independent ecclesiastical units, comparable in many ways to Westminster Abbey, but perhaps subject to a national synodical council.*

If such dioceses could truly 'travel light', then they would be in a good position to adjust boundaries to provide a sensible 'ecumenical map'. Bishops would live rather closer to the actual parishes, and diocesan synods also would have more idea of the church life of the diocesan area whose life and ways they were considering. Both would address the mission of the Church from a more credible standpoint. And a city like London would have a regional council of bishops and a secretariat which had the whole of London in its purview.

---

*The nearest comparison I can summon is to the Forces chaplaincies!

Notes and references

Introduction

1 There is an account of the founding of Latimer House in the splendid recent portrait, A. McGrath, *To Know and Serve God: A Biography of James I. Packer* (Hodder & Stoughton, 1997), pp. 101–16. I think there will be more to tell when the reputed memoirs of John Wenham reach publication, and I had a small finger in the pie myself. While the later history of Latimer House (since 1973) has been sadly defensive and retrogressive, the initial hopes were much higher, and the sheer coming in of the initial finance and the founding of the institution had enormous symbolic value.

2 *Conversations between the Church of England and the Methodist Church: A Report* (Church Information Office and Epworth Press, 1963).

3 J. I. Packer (ed.), *The Church of England and the Methodist Church* (Marcham Manor, 1963) – the Aunt Sally is in Jim Packer's Introduction on p. 5.

4 The Keele statement is contained in Philip Crowe (ed.), *Keele '67* (CPAS, 1967), and the two sections which most concern the points made here are numbers 5 and 6, 'The Church and its worship' and 'The Church and its unity'. The former of these is reprinted in Grove Worship Series 90, Colin Buchanan, *Evangelicals and Liturgy* (Grove Books, 1984), and the latter in the symposium, Colin Buchanan (ed.), *Unity on the Ground* (SPCK, 1972). While I was personally responsible for the pre-congress drafting of these texts, I was in no way responsible for the adoption of them by the congress: I was not at Keele, as our second daughter was born that week.

5 Jim Packer was invited on to the second round of negotiations, the Anglican-Methodist Unity Commission, which sat from 1966 to 1968 – although he made it clear on joining that he would have to distance himself from any 'service of reconciliation'. The resultant report in two parts (1968) was a far better-crafted scheme doctrinally than the 1963 report of the Conversations had been, though this time there were, by definition, no dissenting

Methodists, and Jim Packer dissented specifically over the proposals to 'reconcile' the ministries. In the process a large amount of literature was generated by Evangelicals: J. I. Packer (ed.), *The Church of England and the Methodist Church* (Marcham Manor, 1963); J. I. Packer (ed.), *All in Each Place: Towards Reunion in England*, (Marcham Manor, 1965); J. I. Packer (ed.), *Fellowship in the Gospel*, (Marcham Manor, 1968).

6 Jim Packer and Michael Green were heavily involved in the Commission's report, *Subscription and Assent to the Thirty-Nine Articles* (SPCK, 1968), which led to the present Declaration of Assent; and in *Prayer and the Departed* (SPCK, 1971), which has provided a signpost for all later debate about a controverted subject.

7 Julian Charley, who became vice-principal of LCD in 1969, was one of the founder-members of ARCIC, and from an early stage was, jointly with Jean Tillard, entrusted with much sensitive drafting – and this led (to the genuine amazement of most Anglicans) to the agreed statement on the Eucharist – the Windsor Statement of September 1971 (to which Julian Charley then contributed the first published commentary and commendation, published as Grove booklet on Ministry and Worship 1 on 31 December 1971, *The Anglican-Roman Catholic Agreement on the Eucharist*).

8 This is recorded in all sorts of places, but quite a bit is brought together in my own *Evangelicals and Liturgy* (Grove Worship Series 90, Grove Books, 1984).

9 In the opening essay in the first issue of the new evangelical Anglican journal *Anvil* in spring 1984 – 'Anglican Evangelicalism: the state of the "party" ' – I noted four 'phases' of post-war Anglican Evangelicalism:

   a the public school and Inter-Varsity Fellowship phase;
   b the neo-Puritans;
   c the ecclesiologists;
   d the charismatic movement.

10 See *Encountering Charismatic Worship* (Grove booklet on Ministry and Worship 51, Grove Books, 1977) and the official Church of England report (which I drafted), *The Charismatic Movement in the Church of England* (CIO, 1981).

11 This was published as a pamphlet by the Fountain Trust and the Church of England Evangelical Council, and also in *Renewal* (around March 1977) and in *Churchman* (vol. 91, no. 2, April 1977).

12 See Dave Tomlinson, *The Post-Evangelical* (Triangle/SPCK, 1995). The logic of this is being worked out as this book goes to press, provoking a further symposium, *The Post-Evangelical Debate* (Triangle/SPCK, 1997).

13 I should perhaps add a recent addition from a non-Anglican

source: Everett Ferguson, *The Church of Christ: A Biblical Ecclesiology for Today* (Eerdmans, 1996). This covers the same New Testament ground as Kevin Giles' book, and engages in equal depth of argument, though it betrays anti-pedobaptist and Independency presuppositions – and consequent conclusions! There has also just been published a remarkable book by Paul Zahl, an American Episcopalian evangelical, *The Protestant Face of Anglicanism* (Eerdmans, 1998).

14 S. Sykes, *Unashamed Anglicanism* (Darton, Longman & Todd, 1995), pp. 101–9; J. Robert Wright (ed.), *Quadrilateral at One Hundred* (Forward Movement Publications, 1996), p. 156f.

1   Scriptural Authority

1 The exact wording here is of 1662, but 1550 and 1552 have only minute differences (e.g. '*the* faith').

2 Thus C. S. Lewis most illuminatingly shows at the beginning of *Mere Christianity* (1952, Collins) that Roman Catholics and Protestants will not only give different answers to questions about the Virgin Mary, but will also give vastly different status to the questions.

3   The New Testament and Christology

1 John A. T. Robinson, *The Body: A Study in Pauline Theology* (SCM, 1952), pp. 51–2.

2 See Colin Buchanan, E. L. Mascall, J. I. Packer and the Bishop of Willesden (Graham Leonard), *Growing into Union: Proposals for Forming a United Church in England* (SPCK, 1970), p. 47 – and cf. p. 50. We did not there make the link with John 20:21, but it offers the intriguing possibility that the Father had sent the Son for an incarnate mission which, as far as ministry in the body on earth was concerned, would reach its consummation in the resurrection – revealed there before the disciples' faces as, risen from the dead that day, he commissioned them for an apostolic mission reflecting his. It is therefore wholly compatible with his invoking of the incarnation for us to view ourselves as the 'extension of the resurrection'. See also the quotation from John Robinson on p. 46.

4   The New Testament and Derived Ecclesiology

1 This is slightly elusive in its New Testament significance – but see the article by Geoffrey Cuming, 'Service endings in the epistles', in *New Testament Studies* 22 (1976), pp. 110–13; and also my own booklet, *The Kiss of Peace* (Grove Worship Series 80, Grove Books, 1982) and Edward Phillips, *The Ritual Kiss of Peace* (Alcuin GROW Joint Liturgical Study 36, Grove Books, 1996).

2 '[Kasemann attempts] to argue that in Acts "the word" has been

subordinated to the Church. Not so! – a central theme of Acts is the free and victorious progress of the word of God. It is not so much a case of the Church carrying the word from Jerusalem to Rome as the word carrying the Church to Rome' (J. D. G. Dunn, *Unity and Diversity in the New Testament*, SCM, 1977, p. 357).

3 I wrote a booklet 20 years ago called *One Baptism Once* (Grove booklet on Ministry and Worship 61, Grove Books, 1978) intended pastorally to make the requisite points of this paragraph, and at somewhat greater length.

4 In my *A Case for Infant Baptism* and (with David Pawson) *Infant Baptism under Cross-Examination* (Grove Booklets on Ministry and Worship 20 and 24, Grove Books, 1973 and 1974); and also, in slightly more summarised form but with 20 years more reflection and debate, in an opening chapter to my *Infant Baptism and the Gospel: The Church of England's Dilemma* (Darton, Longman & Todd, 1993).

5 *The Gospel and the Catholic Church* (Methuen, 1936), p. 59 (in 1956 edition).

6 The relevant books are A. J. Mason, *The Relation of Confirmation to Baptism* (Longmans, 1890, 1891) and Gregory Dix, *The Theology of Confirmation in Relation to Baptism* (Dacre/Black, 1946).

7 In terms of the scriptural data, the best demolition job on the 'confirmationists' (as he calls them) is J. D. G. Dunn, *The Baptism in the Holy Spirit* (SCM, 1970 – a significant year when, in part through this book, the climate of theology began to change). My own contributions have been *Anglican Confirmation* (Grove Liturgical Study 48, Grove Books, 1986) and an essay 'Confirmation' in David Holeton (ed.), *Growing in Newness of Life* (Anglican Book Centre, Toronto, 1993). In respect of the patristic evidence see Part II below, and also the Introduction in E. C. Whitaker (ed.), *Documents of the Baptismal Liturgy* (2nd edition, Alcuin/SPCK, 1970).

8 Thus J. D. G. Dunn: 'In Romans 12 and 1 Corinthians 12 Paul is describing *the local church* . . . It is particularly clear from the way he develops the metaphor of the body in 1 Corinthians 12 that the body referred to was the Corinthian body of believers' (*Unity and Diversity in the New Testament*, SCM, 1977, p. 110).

9 I have myself speculated elsewhere that there might be just a hint of a 'steersman' of the assembly of its programme in the 'administration' function in 1 Corinthians 12:28 (see my *Leading Worship*, Grove Worship Series 76, Grove Books, 1981). The point is that the Greek here is *kubernesis*, the ability to steer a ship. And chairing an assembly has much in common with steering – though J. D. G. Dunn suggests that it may be what we would call 'spiritual direction' – another form of 'steering'!

10 W. Grudem, *The Gift of Prophecy* (Kingsway, 1988), pp. 50f. Grudem deals very convincingly with other possible exegeses.

6 The Authority of the Early Church

1 Kenneth Woolcombe, 'The Ministry and Order of the Church in the Works of the Fathers', in K. Carey (ed.), *The Historic Episcopate in the Fullness of the Church* (Dacre, 1954), p. 41.

7 Apostles and Apostolicity

1 Letter of Clement of Rome to the Corinthians chapters 42–3.
2 Letter of Clement of Rome to the Corinthians chapter 40 (my translation from Greek).
3 Magnesians 6:1; 7:1; Smyrnaeans 8:1 (and compare Ephesians 6:1 and Magnesians 3:1).
4 Magnesians 13:1; Romans 4:3.
5 Philippians 9.1.
6 This point is strongly made by T. Francis Glasson in 'Second-century episcopacy: its non-diocesan character', in *The Expository Times* (vol. LXXIX no. 2, November 1967), pp. 52–4. See also note 3 above.
7 Justin, *Dialogue* XLII.
8 *Adv. Haereses* I.xxvii.2.
9 A. M. Ramsey, *The Gospel and the Catholic Church* (Longmans, 1956, 2nd edition) p. 57.
10 Gregory Dix, 'Ministry in the early Church', in K. E. Kirk (ed.), *The Apostolic Ministry* (Hodder & Stoughton, 1946), p. 186.
11 G. L. Prestige, *Fathers and Heretics* (SPCK, 1940), p. 13.
12 The text provides forms for the ordination of a bishop, of a presbyter and of a deacon. These might bear witness to Roman use before 200, but there is great uncertainty on several fronts. Paul Bradshaw, for instance, follows E. C. Ratcliff in his passing suggestion that bishops were consecrated by presbyters, and that a later practice of drawing in bishops from surrounding sees has been dubbed into the text during its transmission (P. Bradshaw 'Ordination' in G. J. Cuming (ed.), *Essays on Hippolytus* (Grove Liturgical Study 15, Grove Books, 1978), pp. 3–4 – drawing upon E. C. Ratcliff, 'Apostolic Tradition: questions concerning the appointment of a bishop', in A. H. Couratin and D. Tripp (eds), *E. C. Ratcliff: Liturgical Studies* (SPCK, 1976) p. 160).
13 J. D. G. Dunn, *Unity and Diversity in the New Testament* (SCM, 2nd edition 1990), p. xxxi.

8 The Universality of the Church

1 *Epistle to Diognetus*, paras 5–6.
2 Hilary, *in Aux. 6, c.* AD 364.

9 The Early Development of Sacraments

1 *Apol.* 1. XV.
2 Irenaeus, *Adv. Haereses* 2. XXII. 4.

3   *Commentary on Romans* (re 6:5–7).
4   *De Baptismo*, XVIII.
5   *De Baptismo*, VI.
6   *De Baptismo*, VII.
7   Smyrnaeans 8.
8   Tertullian, *Apology* XXXIX.
9   Philadelphians 3.
10 Smyrnaeans 6.
11 *Apology* 1:LXVI.
12 Didache 14.
13 *Dialogue*, XXVIII, XLI and CXVII.
14 *Adv. Haereses* 4:XVII–XVIII.
15 E. W. Benson, *Cyprian: His Life – His Times – His Work* (Macmillan, 1897), p. 33 – my italics.

11   The Reformation

1   From 'The First Part' of 'A Fruitful Exhortation to the Reading and Knowledge of Holy Scripture', the first homily in the *First Book of Homilies* (1547), usually attributed to Cranmer.
2   I have set this out in my Grove Liturgical Study 7, *What Did Cranmer Think He was Doing?* (Grove Books, 1976, 1982) – it is a view endorsed by Cranmer's latest biographer, Diarmid McCullough.

12   Scripture and Tradition

1   *Conversations between the Church of England and the Methodist Church: A Report to the Archbishops of Canterbury and York and the Methodist Conference* (SPCK/Epworth, 1963), p. 58.
2   Decrees of the Council of Trent, 'Concerning the Canonical Scriptures' (8 April 1546).
3   G. L. Carey, *The Meeting of the Waters* (IVP, USA/Hodder and Stoughton, 1985), pp. 60ff.
4   See, for instance, this extract (my italics):

This commission [from Christ to his apostles to minister the Gospel] was faithfully fulfilled by the apostles who, *by their oral preaching*, by example, and by ordinances, *handed on* what they had received from the lips of Christ, from living with him, and from what he did, or what they had learned through the prompting of the Holy Spirit. The Commission was fulfilled, *too, by those apostles and apostolic men* who under the inspiration of the same Holy Spirit *committed the same message* of salvation *to writing* . . . This sacred *tradition*, therefore, *and* sacred *Scripture* of both Old and New Testament are like a mirror in which the pilgrim church on earth looks at God.

(*Dei Verbum*, para 7 in Walter Abbott (ed.), *The Documents of Vatican II* (Chapman, 1965), p. 115)

5 Anglican–Roman Catholic International Commission, *The Final Report* (CTS/SPCK, 1982), pp. 69–70, quoted in G. L. Carey, op. cit., p. 66.

6 Anglican–Roman Catholic International Commission, *Clarifications on Eucharist and Ministry* (CHP/CTS, 1994), p. 9.

7 Pope John Paul II, *Ut Unum Sint*, paras 39, 66 and 79. The quotation within para 66 is from the Vatican II Decree on Ecumenism.

8 See, for good instances of this, both Cranmer's five volumes, *On The Lord's Supper* (as the Parker Society edition labels them), and the debate in the House of Lords over the 1548 Act of Uniformity imposing the 1549 Book of Common Prayer (published in Colin Buchanan (ed.), *Background Documents to Liturgical Revision 1547–1549* (Grove Liturgical Study 35, Grove Books, 1983), pp. 15–33).

9 A good instance of this is Jewel's challenge to his Romanist opponents in his Sermon at Paul's Cross or in his *Apologia Ecclesiae Anglicanae*.

10 Canon Law Commission, *The Canon Law of the Church of England* (SPCK, 1947).

11 P. C. Rodger and L. Vischer (eds), *The Fourth World Conference on Faith and Order: The Report from Montreal 1963* (SCM for WCC, 1964), pp. 51–2.

12 *Conversations between the Church of England and the Methodist Church: A Report to the Archbishops of Canterbury and York and the Methodist Conference* (SPCK/Epworth, 1963), p. 17.

13 ibid. p. 18.

14 'Despite the care with which it was formulated, it has to be asked whether the Montreal Statement on "Scripture, Tradition and Traditions" has not, after all, had the unfortunate side-effect of de-canonizing the canon' (J. D. G. Dunn, *Unity and Diversity in the New Testament*, SCM, 1977, pp. xxxi–xxxii).

15 *Anglican-Methodist Unity: 2 The Scheme* (SPCK/Epworth, 1968), p. 18.

16 ibid. p. 19.

17 Colin Buchanan, E. L. Mascall, J. I. Packer and the Bishop of Willesden (Graham Leonard), *Growing into Union: Proposals for Forming a United Church in England* (SPCK, 1970), p. 38.

18 *Lambeth Conference 1948: Encyclical Letter from the Bishops together with the Resolutions and Reports* (SPCK, 1948), Part II, pp. 84–5.

19 See his *Credible Christianity* (Mowbray, 1993), pp. 5–13; or, in more popular form, his *Reaffirming the Church of England* (Triangle/SPCK, 1995), pp. 14–17. In this latter book, he manages to father the threefold authority of Scripture, tradition and reason on to both Jewel and Hooker (p. 11), though Robert Wright concedes that 'this triad . . . cannot be proven to originate

with Richard Hooker' (op. cit., p. 236). I think it would take some doing with Jewel.

13 The New Testament Church and the Church of England
1 He had, of course, made his name in this field with his great book, *Unity and Diversity in the New Testament* (SCM, 1977).

14 A Sacramental Church
1 I have written in some detail, to show that Cranmer so far moved the Eucharist from being centred in 'consecration' as to dispense with an objective or liturgical consecration altogether, in my *What did Cranmer think He was Doing?* (Grove Liturgical Study 7, Grove Books, 1976, 1982).
2 See, for instance, G. W. Bromiley, *Baptism and the Anglican Reformers* (Lutterworth, 1953). For a treatment of how infants might be said to receive 'rightly' (*'recte'* – Article XXVII of 1571), see my essay 'Adult initiation and the Anglican churches' in Donald A. Withey (ed.), *Adult Initiation* (Alcuin/GROW Joint Liturgical Study 10, Grove Books, 1989), p. 27.
3 See J. C. D. Nias, *Gorham and the Bishop of Exeter* (SPCK, 1951), p. 98. While fuller accounts can be found, including Gorham's own careful documentation of the whole theological case, Nias gives a fine overview of the whole matter, with a sufficiently detailed documentation for the full story to be followed.
4 'Indiscriminate baptism' is roundly denounced in the Lima document, *Baptism Eucharist and Ministry* (WCC, 1982) and in the Statement on Worship in the Lambeth Conference report of 1988. I have written up the history of growing concern about such indiscriminate practice in the Church of England in my *Infant Baptism and the Gospel: The Church of England's Dilemma* (Darton, Longman & Todd, 1993). I am also president of The Movement for the Reform of Infant Baptism (MORIB), the pressure group within the Church of England to give expression to this growing concern.
5 There is a fuller treatment in my *One Baptism Once* (Grove Worship Series 61, Grove Books, 4th edition 1987).
6 The 'significant ceremonies' may even include a submersion, provided that the event as a whole be protected from any interpretation which would suggest that it is itself baptism. See my *Renewal of Baptismal Vows* (Grove Worship Series 124, Grove Books, 1993).
7 See my *What did Cranmer Think He was Doing?* (Grove Liturgical Study 7, Grove Books, 1976, 1982).
8 See my *Anglican Confirmation* (Grove Liturgical Study 48, Grove Books, 1986), p. 31.

15   The Ordained Ministry

1   See my book on disestablishment, *Cut the Connection: Disestablishment and the Church of England* (Darton, Longman & Todd, 1994), pp. 81–5.
2   Norman Sykes' book, *Old Priest New Presbyter*, works carefully over the evidence for this.

16   The Character of English Anglicanism

1   For further discussion of my shorthand description 'fair voting', see my study, *The Christian Conscience and Justice in Representation* (Grove Ethics Series 53, Grove Books, 1983).

Appendix 1   Notes to Chapters

1   The joint evangelical–charismatic statement of 1977, *Gospel and Spirit*, (on which see p. 14) stated:

> There are problems attaching to the use of this term [baptism in the Holy Spirit] to describe an experience separated, often by a long period of time, from the person's initial conversion to Christ . . . However, we see that it may be hard to change a usage which has become very widespread, although we all agree in recognising its dangers.

> (*Gospel and Spirit*, Fountain Trust and Church of England Evangelical Council, 1977, p. 4 – the charismatic signatories of this included John Collins, Michael Harper and David Watson)

2   See, for instance the brief mention (with a footnoted list of cessationist authors) in J. D. G. Dunn, *Baptism in the Holy Spirit* (SCM, 1970), p. 225.
3   Anthony Thiselton draws attention to earlier essays by J. G. Davies and R. H. Gundry in favour of 'ordinary' languages in his own article 'The "interpretation" of tongues', *Journal of Theological Studies* (1979). Davies (in 'Pentecost and Glossolalia' in *JTS* n. s. vol 3 (1952), pp. 228–30) is concerned to demonstrate that Acts 2 and 1 Corinthians 14 must be in harmony and use 'tongues' in the same way as each other; Gundry (in ' "Ecstatic Utterances" (NEB)?' in *JTS* n.s. vol. 17 (1966), pp. 299–307) is confronting the odd presuppositions of the NEB translations, and emphasising that *glossai* must be 'known languages'.
4   Leon Morris, *1 Corinthians* (Tyndale Bible Commentary, IVP, 1965), p. 172.
5   See W. Grudem, *The Gift of Prophecy* (Kingsway, 1988) *passim*. Grudem helpfully distinguishes 'that which has come forcefully to mind' (i.e. prophecy) from the 'teaching' of the apostles – a known corpus of material about Jesus which had to be repeated and handed on and enforced.
6   Similarly Jean Tillard, a member of the Anglican Roman Catholic International Commission (ARCIC), wrote Grove booklet on Min-

istry and Worship 13, *What Priesthood has the Ministry*? (Grove Books 1973 – now out of print), a preliminary paper for ARCIC's consideration of ordination, and itself putting forward a very biblical presentation, in which he emphasises that in the New Testament the Church has no 'priests' to fulfil ritual sacrificial acts on its behalf.

7 For a fuller handling of it see my *Anglican Confirmation* (Grove Liturgical Study no. 48, Grove Books, Bramcote, 1986).

8 A. J. Mason wrote *The Relation of Confirmation to Baptism* (Longmans, 1890, 1891), and Gregory Dix wrote *Confirmation or Laying on of Hands* (SPCK, 1936) and *The Theology of Confirmation in Relation to Baptism* (Dacre/Black, 1946).

9 K. E. Kirk (ed.), *The Apostolic Ministry: Essays on the History and Doctrine of Episcopacy* (Hodder & Stoughton, 1946).

10 K. Carey (ed.), *The Historic Episcopate in the Fullness of the Church*, (Dacre, 1954).

11 Council for Christian Unity of the Church of England, *Apostolicity and Succession* (Church House Publishing, 1995).

12 I have suggested in *Cut the Connection: Disestablishment and the Church of England* (Darton, Longman & Todd, 1994), my book on disestablishment, a radical alternative scheme for appointing diocesan bishops in the Church of England, where an outrageously Erastian power is still held and sometimes exercised by prime ministers (see Appendix 2, p. 344ff). But other proposals might well have mileage.

13 Colin Buchanan (ed.), *Modern Anglican Ordination Rites* (Alcuin/GROW Joint Liturgical Study 3, 1987).

14 Paul Bradshaw, *The Anglican Ordinal*, (Alcuin/SPCK, 1972).

15 Faith and Order Advisory Group, *The Priesthood of the Ordained Ministry* (GS 694, Board of Mission & Unity, 1986).

16 Trevor Lloyd (ed.), *Lay Presidency at the Eucharist*? (Grove Books, 1977).

17 See the account in Alan Hargrave, *But Who Shall Preside*? (Grove Worship Series 113, Grove Books, 1990).

18 House of Bishops, *Eucharistic Presidency* (Church House Publishing, 1997). The stages which led to this were:

> (a) the tabling of a private member's motion in General Synod in November 1993 asking the House of Bishops to state the theological reason why the presidency of the Eucharist is reserved to bishops and presbyters;
> (b) the immediate rallying to that private member's motion of enough signatures to take it straight to the top of the list for such motions;
> (c) its consequent scheduling for July 1994;
> (d) the House of Bishops devising a reasoned amendment (which avoided giving a positive affirmation to lay presidency),

which was accepted by the Synod, which then passed the amended motion in this form:

That this Synod, while accepting that lay presidency at the Eucharist is incompatible with Anglican tradition, would welcome a statement from the House of Bishops about the theology of the Eucharist and about the respective roles of clergy and laity within it.

(e) more than two years of careful drafting before its sifting and final adoption by the House of Bishops.

Appendix 3 The Establishment of the Church of England – a Shameful Captivity

1 I wrote a chapter on 'Mission and disestablishment' in a pre-Lambeth pan-Anglican symposium for the 1988 Lambeth Conference – see Philip Turner and Frank Segano (eds), *Crossroads are for Meeting: Essays on the Mission and Common Life of the Church in a Global Society* (SPCK, USA, 1986). My fully focused and deployed argumentation comes in *Cut the Connection: Disestablishment and the Church of England* (Darton, Longman & Todd, 1994), in which I provide a fairly full (and evaluated) bibliography of writings on the subject.

INDEX

Scripture references

Only specified references including verse numbers are listed here.

Genesis
49:29 — 38n
50:14 — 38n

Exodus
13:19 — 38n
19:5–6 — 101, 315

Deuteronomy
31:30 — 295

Joshua
24:31 — 38n

Judges
2:18–19 — 39

2 Kings
17:24–41 — 41

2 Chronicles
24:20 — 299
26:16–23 — 215n

Psalm
110:1 — 312
110:4 — 312, 313

Isaiah
49:7 — 66

Jeremiah
7:4–11 — 40n
7:12 — 40n

Hosea
1:9–10 — 101

Malachi
1:10–11 — 177

Matthew
1:21 — 43
3:11 — 296
11:11 — 63n
12:29 — 63n
13:30 — 271
16:18 — 44, 92
18:17 — 44, 92
18:18 — 44, 103
18:19–20 — 44
22:44 — 312
23:2 — 280n
23:15 — 76n
26:30 — 107
28:16–20 — 52, 68
28:19 — 82n

Mark
1:8 — 296
6:13 — 321
10:13–16 — 240

10:35–49 — 138
10:38–9 — 71n
12:34 — 63
12:36 — 312
14:9 — 104n
14:26 — 107
16:9–20 — 126n

Luke
1:1–4 — 104n
1:5 — 311
1:67 — 299
2:1 — 166n
3:16 — 296
4:20 — 280n
11:1 — 106n
12:50 — 71n
17:21 — 63n
20:42–3 — 312
21:10 — 63
24:26–8 — 53
24:35 — 111
24:47 — 263

John
1:33 — 296
2:19–22 — 47
3:5 — 71, 85
3:24 — 84
5:28–9 — 113n
6:35 — 112
6:39–40 — 113
6:48 — 112
6:51 — 112, 113
6:53 — 112
6:54 — 113
6:58 — 113
11:49 — 311
11:50–51 — 310
17:20–3 — 97
18:13 — 311
19:25 — 333
20:11–18 — 333
20:21 — 52, 359
20:23 — 319
20:30–1 — 104
20:31 — 140
21:24 — 140

Acts
1:1–2 — 51
1:2 — 131
1:5 — 297
1:6–8 — 52
1:8 — 51, 90
1:13 — 131
1:14–15 — 49

1:14 — 333
1:15 — 50
1:21–2 — 55
1:24 — 51
2:1 — 49, 103
2:4 — 127, 297, 299
2:6 — 126
2:7 — 131
2:8 — 126
2:11 — 76n, 127
2:14 — 131
2:22 — 53
2:27 — 53
2:29 — 53
2:31 — 53
2:32 — 53
2:33 — 51
2:37 — 53
2:38 — 69, 70, 76n, 82n, 85
2:39 — 76n
2:41–7 — 164
2:41 — 49, 69
2:42–6 — 50
2:42–7 — 56, 57
2:42 — 49, 58, 60, 104, 105n, 107
2:46 — 106
2:47 — 51
3:16 — 51
3:20–1 — 51
3:26 — 51
4:11–12 — 51
4:23 — 50, 103
4:31 — 299
4:32–5 — 50
4:36–7 — 132n
5:11 — 50
5:12 — 50, 103
5:16 — 50
5:33 — 50
6:1–6 — 60
6:1 — 50
6:2 — 50, 103
6:3 — 50
6:5 — 76n, 299
6:7 — 50
7:38 — 296
7:55 — 299
8:1 — 50, 90n, 92, 131
8:3 — 50
8:4–25 — 90n
8:12–13 — 70
8:12 — 298n

8:14–17	89
8:14	131
8:16	298n
8:17	127
8:26–40	89
8:26	90n
8:36–8	70
9:1	50
9:2	50, 90n, 92
9:10–25	90n
9:10	50
9:15–16	66
9:17	299
9:18	70
9:19	50
9:27	132n
9:31	90n, 92
9:32	50, 90n
9:35	90n
9:36–43	90n
10:44–8	77, 85
10:46	127
10:47–8	70
11:1	131
11:15–16	297
11:15	127
11:26	50n, 103
11:27–8	310
11:27	133
11:29–30	164
11:30	133
13:1	92n, 133, 310
13:43	76n
13:47	66
14:4	132n
14:22	64
14:23	66, 93, 133, 333
15:2	133
15:6	133
15:22	133
15:32	310
16:4	133
16:5	93
16:14–15	70, 333
16:15	77, 78
16:33	70, 77
17:6	90
18:8	70, 77, 82n
18:21	66
18:27	91
19:1–6	89, 299n
19:5	70
19:6	127, 310
19:21	66
19:26	90
19:39	296
20:7	103, 106, 175, 339

20:17	93, 133
20:25	64
20:27	93
20:28	93, 133
21:8–9	310
21:10–11	310
21:10	133
21:17	133
22:4	92
22:16	70, 85
24:14	92
26:11	90n
26:28	50n
28:22	90
28:23	64
28:31	64

Romans

1:4	45
1:5–7	132
1:7	280
1:10	66
3:8	275
4:11	75
5:12–21	48
5:19	48n
6:3–4	74, 75, 78, 83
8:1	49
8:23	64n
10:9	88, 104n
11:17	58
12:1	314
12:4–6	123
12:5–6	95
12:5	46, 122
12:6	120, 122, 310
12:7–21	123
12:7	124
12:8	124
12:13	58
13:11–12	113
13:11–14	67
14:1	269
14:3	115, 269
14:7	59
14:15	269
14:17	64
15:1	269
15:14–22	131
15:21–9	92
15:24	66
15:25–8	66
15:26–7	58
16:1	133, 333
16:3	93
16:5	93, 280
16:7	132n, 133
16:16	93
16:21	136

1 Corinthians

1:9	58
1:10–12	125
1:13–15	130
1:13	78, 85
1:16	77
1:18–25	130
3:5–9	125
3:16	47
4:20	64
5:4	103
6:1–11	115
6:9	64
6:11	71
6:12	115
6:14	47
6:15	47
6:16	47
6:19	47
6:20	47
7:1–9	117
7:10–11	117
7:12–16	117
7:17–20	117
7:17	93
7:21–4	117
7:25–38	117
7:39–40	117
8:1–13	125
8:4–7	269
8:4	116
8:6	104n
8:10	116
8:13	269
9:1	55, 131
9:23	58
10:1–4	78, 84, 85
10:1–6	73
10:1	39
10:14–11:1	125
10:16	57, 58, 107, 108
10:17	94, 108
10:18	58
10:20	58, 59
10:23	116
10:24–5	116
10:26	116
10:29	115
11:2–3	335
11:2–16	117
11:2	118
11:3–10	118
11:3–16	333
11:3–4	310
11:11–15	118
11:16	93
11:17–31	106, 339
11:17	103
11:20	103

11:29	108, 109
11:33	103
12:1	119, 124
12:3	73, 88
12:4	119, 120, 123
12:5	123
12:6	123
12:8–11	120, 121
12:9	119
12:10	310
12:12–26	119, 130
12:12	122
12:13	78, 85, 94
12:14–20	123
12:14–26	120
12:21–6	123
12:27	46, 94
12:28–30	133, 135, 303
12:28	94, 119, 120, 123, 136, 274n, 310, 359
12:29–30	121
12:29	310
12:30	119
12:31	119, 120, 121, 126
13:2	119
13:8–9	310
14:1–40	303–5
14:1	119, 124
14:2	128
14:12	119, 124n
14:16	128
14:18–19	128
14:19	103
14:24–5	129
14:26–40	124
14:26	103, 129, 130
14:27–8	129
14:28	103
14:30	129
14:31	129
14:32	129
14:33–4	103
14:33–8	333
14:35	103, 129
14:37	119
14:40	129
15:1	61, 130
15:3–4	60, 104
15:5–8	132
15:6	67n
15:8	55, 131
15:12–19	130
15:18	67n
15:20	67n
15:21–2	48
15:24	64
15:29	85

15:35	67n
15:45–9	48
15:49	49
15:50	64
15:51	67
16:1	93, 106
16:3	91
16:10	136
16:19	93
16:22	113

2 Corinthians
1:17	58
2:13	136
3:3	91
5:14	45
6:14	58
6:16	47
7:6–16	136
8:4	58
8:9	93
8:16–24	136
8:18	93
9:13	58
11:8	93
11:28	93, 138, 255n, 265
12:18	136

Galatians
1:2	93
1:15–17	131
1:19	132n
2:1–3	136
2:8–10	131
2:9	58
2:11–16	131, 230
3:16	45
3:26–7	71
3:26	78
3:27	78, 85
3:28	77, 333
4:6	59

Ephesians
1:1	91n
1:10	95, 96, 335
1:14	64n
1:22–3	95
2:7	96
2:13	47
2:14	47
2:16	47, 95, 96
2:17	100
2:18	100
2:19–22	100
2:20–2	47
2:20	54, 133, 135, 310
3:2–6	54
3:5	133, 310

3:6	100
3:8	135
4:4–5	104n
4:4	74, 78, 95, 96, 108
4:11–16	47
4:11	133, 135, 136, 137n, 311
4:12	137n
4:13–16	95
4:13	46, 96
4:14–15	105
4:15	46, 185
4:16	46
4:21–2	104
4:22–4	104
4:25	95, 96
5:5	64
5:11	59
5:14	105
5:19	130
5:22–3	96
5:22–4	335
5:23	95
5:26	71
5:30	95
5:32	320

Philippians
1:1	133, 136
1:5, 7	59
2:1	59
2:6–11	104n
2:19–24	288
2:25–31	164
2:25	132n
3:10	59
3:20	91
4:14–15	59
4:14–16	165
6:21	91n

Colossians
1:7	90
1:9	92
1:12–13	64
1:15–19	104n
1:17–19	96
1:18	95, 96
1:24	95, 96
2:1–5	132
2:9	51
2:10	95
2:11–12	76
2:19	95, 96
3:9–11	96
3:12–17	46
3:15	95, 96, 105
3:16	105, 130
4:7–8	91n

4:7	134
4:11	64
4:13	90
4:14	288
4:15	93
4:16	91n
4:17	136n

1 Thessalonians

1:7–8	90
1:9–10	67
2:7	138
4:13–18	65, 67
4:15	66
5:1–2	67
5:12	67
5:12	134
5:20	134, 311

2 Thessalonians

1:10	67
3:6–13	67

1 Timothy

1:7	136
1:18	311
2:7	134
2:9–15	333
3:1–7	134
3:8–13	134
4:14	134, 311
5:1–2	136n
5:1	
5:17–20	134
5:17	136n
5:22	59, 134
6:18	59

2 Timothy

1:6	134
1:11	134
1:13–14	139
2:2	139
3:14	139
4:1	64
4:5	134
4:18	64

Titus

1:5	134, 255n
1:6–9	134
1:7	134
3:5	71, 85

Philemon

2	93
6	59
17	59

Hebrews

1:2	100
1:13	312
2:1–3	100
2:10–18	314
2:17	312
3:6	100, 101
4:14–16	314
4:14	312
5:1	314
5:4–6	314
5:6	312
5:10	312
6:16–18	313
6:20	312, 313n
7:3	313
7:4	313
7:6	313
7:10	313
7:11–19	313
7:17	312
7:21	312
7:23	313
7:24–5	101, 314
7:27–8	312
7:27	314
9:8	312
9:24–5	313
9:24	101, 314n
9:27–8	101
9:28	312, 314
10:1–2	313
10:1	312
10:4	313
10:10	101
10:14	101
10:19	314
10:21	101
10:23	59
10:25	100, 103
11:10	101
11:16	101
12:22–4	101
12:22	100
12:28	64, 101
13:7	134
13:14	101
13:15–16	315
13:17	134
13:30	101

James

5:13–16	321
5:14	134

1 Peter

1:1	101
1:22–3	71
2:4–9	48
2:4	101
2:5	101, 102, 315
2:9	101, 102, 315
2:10	101
2:11	101
2:12	101
3:15–16	50n
3:15	140
3:21	71
4:10	120
4:13	59
5:1	135
5:2	135, 136
5:3	138
5:5	135

2 Peter

1:4	57, 59
1:11	64
1:12–15	140
1:20	33n
1:21	33n
3:2	135
3:15–16	34n

1 John

1:1–2	140
1:3–7	57

2 John

1	135
11	59

3 John

1	135

Jude

12	113
17	135

Revelation

1:3	311
1:4	93
1:9	59
1:10	106
1:20	93
4:4	135
5:7	126n
5:8	135
5:10	102, 315
7:9	126n
10:11	126n
11:9	126n
13:7	126n
14:6	126n
18:4	59
20:6	102, 315
22:16	93
22:18–19	311
22:20	113

Index of biblical names

Aaron 179, 312–13
Abraham 38–9, 75, 97
Adam 48–9
Agabus 133, 310
Alexander the Great 42
Amos 41
Ananias 66
Annas 311
Antiochus 42
Apollos 114, 125, 133
Archippus 136n

Barnabas 132n, 164, 310

Caiaphas 310, 311
Cornelius 84
Cyrus, King 41

David, King 40, 53

Elijah, 41
Elisha 41
Epaphras 90
Epaphroditus 132n, 165
Esau 38
Ethiopian Eunuch 84

Herod the Great 42
Hosea 41

Isaac 38
Israel *see* Jacob

Jacob 38, 38n, 75
James 91n, 131, 132n
Jeroboam 40
John 91n, 131, 136, 140, 155, 298n
John Baptist 63n, 76, 77, 84, 85, 288, 296–7, 309
Joseph 38n

Joshua 39
Judas 56, 131
Judas (Acts) 310
Jude 91n

Korah 178

Luke 78, 92, 288, 298n
Lydia 78m, 333

Mark 160
Mary Magdalene 333
Mary, Virgin 333
Matthias 51, 131
Melchizedek 312–14
Micah 41
Moses 38–9, 53

Paul (Saul) viii, 34n, 61, 65–6, 75, 90n, 91, 92, 97, 114, 125, 131, 134, 136, 138, 139, 153–4, 164, 232, 288, 310, 333
Peter (Simon) Authorship of 2 Peter viii, 33n–34n
  confession 44
  leader of early Church 49, 53, 65, 91n, 97, 114, 131, 135, 136, 140, 154, 230, 260, 297, 298n
Philip 70n, 89n, 90n, 133, 298n, 310
Phoebe 136n, 333

Rehoboam 40

Silas 66, 136
Solomon, King 40
Stephen 65, 295–6

Timothy 66, 134, 136, 139, 288
Titus 134, 136, 164
Tychicus 91n, 134

Zachariah 311

Index of names

Abbott, Walter 362
Ambrose 203
Anicetus, Bishop of Rome 166, 181
Anne Boleyn 214
Augustine of Canterbury 281
Augustine of Hippo 75, 168, 203, 246

Bancroft, Archbishop of Canterbury 263
Barth, Karl 19
Baxter, Richard 220
Beckett, Thomas à 189
Benson, E. W. 362
Booth, General William 223
Bradshaw, Paul 327, 361, 366
Bradshaw, Tim 19
Bridger, Gordon vii
Bromiley, G. W. 364
Bucer 216

Buchanan, Colin
  author/editor of various publications 357–60, 363–7
  context of writing vii–viii
  Cut the Connection 350, 366, 367
  founder of Grove Books 12
  Growing into Union 359
  limitations 22
  Liturgical Commission 327
  personal credo ix
  personal history 4, 9, 352
  vicar of St Mark's, Gillingham vii, 14
  Visible Unity and the Ministry of Oversight viii

Carey, George 202, 362
Carey, Kenneth 324, 361, 366
Catherine of Aragon 29
Charles I, King 217

Charles II, King 263
Charley, Julian 358
Chrysostom, John 90, 203
Clement of Rome 89, 152, 155, 177
Couratin, Arthur 161n, 327
Collins, John 365
Cranmer, Thomas 29, 195, 215–16, 240–1,
    249, 251, 262, 319, 326, 362, 364
Crowe, Philip 10n, 357
Cuming, Geoffrey J. 175, 359, 361
Cyprian of Carthage 161, 166–7, 178, 179,
    182, 232 *see also* E. W. Benson

Darby, J. N. 223
Davidson, Randall 272n
Davies, J. G. 365
Deacon, Bishop Thomas 35n
Didache 152, 169, 170, 173, 175
Dimock, Nathanael 3
Dix, Gregory 89, 159, 175, 259, 318, 332
    The Apostolic Ministry 361
    *Confirmation of the Laying on of
        Hands* 366
    *The Theology of Confirmation in
        Relation to Baptism* 360, 366
Dunn, James D. G. 162, 234
    The Baptism in the Holy Spirit 360
    comment on 'Montreal' 363
    *Unity and Diversity in the New
        Testament* 360, 361, 364
Du Plessis, David 14

Edward VI, King 30, 190, 190, 192, 197,
    215–16, 239, 254
Eleutherius of Rome 155
Elizabeth I, Queen 199, 217–18, 254,
    277, 326
Epistle of Barnabas 169
Epistle to Diognetus 165
Eusebius of Caesarea 160

Ferguson, Everett 359
Fisher, John, Bishop of Rochester 189,
    323n
Fletcher of Madeley 204
Foxe's *Acts and Monuments* 218, 257
Franklin, William 32n

Giles, Kevin 18, 19, 359
Glasson, T. Francis 361
Goode, William, Dean of Ripon 244
Gorham, George 243–5, 364
Graham, Billy 4, 4n
Green, Michael 10n
Grindal, Archbishop of Canterbury 217
Grudem, Wayne 311
    The Gift of Prophecy 360, 365–6
Gundry, R. H. 365

Habgood, John 272
Hadrian, Emperor 169n
Hardwick, Charles 238n

Hargrave, Alan 366
Harper, Michael 365
Henry VIII, King 20, 29, 190, 214–16, 254,
    257, 277
Henson, Hensley 272n
Hermas 89
Hippolytus of Rome 87, 148, 160, 169, 170,
    172, 175, 241–2n, 250, 261
Holeton, David 360
Hooker, Richard 363–4

Ignatius of Antioch 90, 153, 154, 167, 169,
    173, 175, 178–9, 180, 261, 339
Irenaeus 151n, 152, 154–9, 166, 171, 180,
    261, 323

James I, King 218–19, 263
James II, King 220
Jenkins, David 32n, 272
Jeremias, Joachim 77
Jerome 160
Jewel, John, Bishop of Salisbury 326, 364
    Apologia Ecclesiae Anglicanae 363
    sermon at Paul's Cross 363–4
John of Damascus 160
John Paul II, Pope 363
Josephus 308
Justin Martyr 89, 148, 170–1, 173, 175,
    176
    Dialogue with Trypho 154, 178

Keble, John 322
Kirk, Kenneth E. 323, 332, 366

Lampe, Geoffrey W. H. 174–5
Leonard, Graham, Bishop of Willesden
    359, 363
Lewis, C. S. 359
Lapide, Pinchas 68n
Linus of Rome 155
Lloyd, Trevor 341, 366
Lombard, Peter 238

McCullough, Diarmid 362
MacGrath, Alister 357
Manning, Henry 245n
Mant, Bishop 244
Marcion 156–7, 162, 174
Mary, Queen 216
Mascall, Eric 359, 363
Mason, A. J. 89, 318
    *The Relation of Confirmation to
        Baptism* 360, 366
Montefiore, Hugh 211, 353
    *Credible Christianity, Reaffirming the
        Church of England* 364
Morris, Leon 302, 365

Neale, John Mason 322
Newbigin, Lesslie 13, 14n
Newman, John Henry 19, 205, 245n, 322
Nias, J. C. D. 364

Oliver, Gordon vii
Origen 171

Packer, James I. 5, 6n, 10n, 210
  All in Each Place 358
  *The Church of England and the
    Methodist Church* 357
  Fellowship in the Gospel 358
  Growing into Union 359, 363
  Guidelines 10n, 24
  see also Alister MacGrath
Peterson, David vii
Philip of Spain 216, 218
Phillips, Edward 360
Philpotts, Henry, Bishop of Exeter 244–5
Pius IX, Pope 226
Pius XII, Pope 226
Philo 308
Pliny the Younger 169n
Polycarp of Smyrna 153, 154, 155, 166,
  170, 181
Prestige, G. L. 361

Ramsey, Michael 88–9, 158
  The Gospel and the Catholic Church
    360, 361
Ratcliff, E. C. 361
Reid, Gavin 10n
Ridley, Nicholas 323n
Robinson, John 11, 46, 272, 359
Rodger, P. C. 363
Runcie, Robert 13n

Segano, Frank 367
Seymour, Edward 216

Seymour, Jane 216
Stephen, Bishop of Rome 167, 183
Stuart Kings 199, 254
Sykes, Stephen 20–1
  Unashamed Anglicanism 359

Tertullian 159n, 169, 171–4, 178, 241–2n
Thiselton, Anthony 308–10
  'The "Interpretation" of tongues' 365
Tillard, Jean 358, 365–6
  What Priesthood has the Ministry? 366
Tomlinson, Dave 358
Turner, Philip 367

Valentinus 156
Victor, bishop of Rome 181
Vincent of Lerins 30
Vischer, L. 363

Ward, W. G. 245n
Watson, David 365
Wenham, John 357
Wesley, John 204, 222, 223
Whitaker, E. C. 175
  *The Documents of the Baptismal
    Liturgy* 360
Whitefield, George 222
Wilberforce, Robert 245n
Wimber, John 14
Withey, Donald 364
Woolcombe, Kenneth 147
  *The Historic Episcopate in the Fullness
    of the Church* 361
Wright, J. Robert 363–4

Zahl, Paul 359

Index of subjects

absolution 318–21
Acts of Parliament 249, 257, 259, 350
Act of Uniformity 1662 220, 264, 340
Agape 107, 112–13, 149, 175–6, 251
Alternative Service Book 246, 329
anamnesis 179
angel 135
anglican 2
Anglican Communion 2, 14, 250, 256,
  344–8 *see also* Church of England
Anglican Consultative Council 347
Anglican Evangelicals *see* Evangelicals
Anglican-Methodist relationships 5, 13,
  199–200, 208–10, 327, 357–8, 362
Anglican-Roman Catholic relationships
  see ARCIC
Anglo-Catholicism 3, 9, 17, 19, 25, 161n,
  205, 242, 244–5, 250, 321–6 *see also*
  Tractarian Movement
anointing the Sick 321
antinomianism 115
Apocrypha 192
Apostolic Succession 47, 54, 56, 61, 131–3,
  134–5, 138–41, 143, 151–63

Apostolicae Curae 324, 366
archbishopric of Canterbury 346–7
ARCIC (Anglican-Roman Catholic
  International Commission) 19, 202,
  251, 358, 366
  Clarifications 363
  The Final Report 363
Arminianism 7n
Articles of Religion *see* Thirty-Nine
  Articles
auricular confession 205, 318 *see also*
  penance
Authorized Version 163, 219, 302

baptism 4n, 38–9, 50, 68–88, 130, 167,
  169–75, 213, 239–47
  formula of 87–8
  infant 75–83, 170–2, 236, 240–7
  of John 70n, 127, 173
  mode of 83–7
  see also household baptism,
    confirmation
baptism in the Spirit 14,1 5, 90, 296–9
Baptists 86, 221–2, 242

Bible *see* Scripture
Birmingham 229n, 352
Bishop of Rome *see* Papacy
bishops 93, 133–5, 152–3, 167
'Black-led' Churches 224–5
Bodily Assumption of Mary 226
body 45–8
Book of Common Prayer 7, 163, 198, 205,
    216, 220, 239, 246, 250, 258–9, 267,
    288, 317, 328, 341
Brethren Movement 15n, 199, 223
British Israelites 41n
broadcasting 5

Caister 13n
Canon Law 206–7, 216, 217, 240, 246, 252
Canon of Scripture 149, 152, 157, 161–3,
    192, 201
Canterbury 189, 344 *see also*
    archbishopric of Canterbury
catechism 205, 239, 317
Catechumenate 170
cathedrals 356
Catholicism *see* Anglo-Catholicism,
    Roman Catholics
ceremonies 191, 193, 251, 259n
Cessationists 300, 306, 365
Chalcedonian Creed 36, 192, 196
charismata see gifts
Charismatic Movement 13–16, 118n,
    300–2
    *The Charismatic Movement in the
        Church of England* 358
children in church 78–82, 197, 252, 318
Christology 43–55
Church
    Evangelical treatment 3–16
    theme of book ix, 165–8
    see also Church of England, ecclesiology
Church Assembly 5, 206–7
Church Commissioners 350
Church of England ix
    as institution 1, 20 and *passim*
Church of England (Worship and
    Doctrine) Measure, 1974 258
churchwardens 281
circumcision 38, 75–7, 117
Clarendon Code 220
Commonwealth, The 217, 219, 264
comprehensiveness 220, 268–70, 273
confirmation 88–90, 159n, 172–5, 316–18
Congregationalists 220
connexionalism 221–2, 254–6, 259, 273–6
consecration 191, 248–9, 364
constitutionalism 7–10, 16–17, 268
conversion 4n, 43, 74, 230
copyright viii
Council, Regency 216
Council of Arles 166
Council of Carthage 167

Council of Jerusalem 132n *see also*
    Jerusalem
Council of Nicea 166
Council of Trent 162, 200, 201n, 254,
    277, 362
covenant 38
Creeds 30, 35, 182, 192, 205, 212
Credal affirmations 104, 196, 267
crucifixion 45, 48, 191

Daily Offices 191
Declaration of Assent 207, 212
Decree of Constantine 166, 180, 349
denominationalism 3, 144, 220–37
Diaconate 60, 133–5, 265, 331
dispersed authority 210–12
divine right of kings *see* royal supremacy
Doctrinal Commission 12
    Reports 38
Donatists 168, 182–3

early church 20
Easter 166, 170, 181, 248, 272n
Eastern Orthodoxy 36, 87n, 150, 163,
    214n, 225, 229, 248n
Ecclesia 42, 44, 295–6
ecclesiologists 12–13
ecclesiology 3–4 and *passim*
Eclectics 10n
elders 93, 133–5, 152–3, 155
electoral roll 1, 285
enthusiasm 204
episcopacy 2, 6, 20, 167, 235, 254–65,
    322–6, 352–6
episcopi vagantes 168
eschatology 61, 64–8, 96, 113, 194, 223
Eucharist 11, 85–6, 106–13, 130, 137, 138,
    143–4, 175–9, 191, 213, 247–53
eucharistic presidency 176–7, 251, 265,
    339–43
    Eucharistic Presidency 341–2, 366–7
eucharistic sacrifice 177–9, 205, 248, 262,
    278, 326–7
Europe, diocese of 355
Evangelicals 2–24, 74, 204, 250, 273
    Free Church 11
evangelism 16
Evangelists 133–5
excommunication 109, 176, 179, 181, 183,
    254, 270, 278
exorcism 14
extended communion 340, 342
extreme unction 317, 321

Fall, the 38
fellowship 57–60, 230
Flying Bishops 265, 336–9
Forty-Two Articles 192–4, 238
fundamentalism 260

gathered church 283–4

General Councils 30, 162, 166, 180, 182, 184, 193, 277
General Synod 12, 274–9, 320, 342, 350, 355
Gentiles *see* Jewish and Gentile Christians
Gideon Bible 197
gifts 15, 118n, 119–30, 149
Gillingham, St Mark's Church vii, 14
Glorious Revolution 220, 282
Gnosticism 156–7, 165, 176, 180–1
Godparents *see* Sponsors
Gorham Judgement 224–5
Gospel and Spirit 14, 358, 365
Grove Books 12, 23

Hail Mary 248n
Handsworth 229n
headship 335–6
healing 14
hermeneutics 4, 19, 20, 32
historical conditioning 17, 333–4
Holy Spirit 14, 51–2, 62, 64, 121, 124, 127, 199, 298–9
homilies 7, 192, 195, 216
homosexual relations 17
household baptism 77–8

idol-meats 115–16
Immaculate Conception 226
immersion *see* baptism, mode of
Incarnation viii, 51–2, 192, 194, 284
Independent Evangelical Churches 224
infant baptism *see* baptism, infant
intercession of the saints 200
internationalism 100–2, 164–8, 291–2
interpretation 14, 126–8, 300–9
Inter-Varsity Fellowship 5
Irvingites 15n

Jerusalem 40–1, 139
Jewish and Gentile Christians 76, 94–102, 141
Judicial Committee of Privy Council 244–5

Keele, National Evangelical Anglican Congress, 1967 10–12, 13, 357
kingdom of God 62–8, 253, 292
kingship 40
kiss 57, 170, 173–4, 176, 252, 359–60

Lambeth Conference
 general 347
 1948 210–11
 1958 327
 1968 265n
 1988 341, 346
 1998 213, 364
Lambeth Quadrilateral 265
Last Supper 92
Latimer House, Oxford 5, 357

Latitudinarians 204, 273
lay presidency *see* eucharistic presidency
laying on of hand(s) *see* confirmation, ordination
Liberalism 5, 24–5, 212
Lima document 364
Liturgical Commission 9, 319–20
Liturgical Movement 250–2
Liturgy 148–9, 151n, 189, 190–2, 196, 198, 235, 249
local church life 103–41
Local Ecumenical Partnerships 236
London 356
Lord's Prayer 64, 81, 105–6n, 227, 248n
Lord's Supper *see* Eucharist
Lutheran Churches 156, 344

magisterium 163, 203
marriage 65, 117, 316, 320–1
Mary, Virgin 191, 202, 226–7, 359
mass *see* Eucharist, eucharistic sacrifice
meeting 56, 100, 103, 129
membership
 of any Church 4n
 of Church of England 1
 of New Testament Church 46
Methodism 5–6, 15n, 222, 228, 237, 270n
 see also Anglican-Methodist relationships
Middle Ages 200
Millenary Petition 218
ministers 131–41, 254–65
mission 52, 67–9, 194, 246, 253, 284, 359
missionary bishops 256
Montreal Faith and Order Conference 208, 209n, 363
MORIB (The Movement for the Reform of Infant Baptism) 364

Neo-Puritan 6
New Churches 15, 199, 224
New Testament vii–viii, 69, 125, 300, 320 and *passim*
Non-jurors 35n, 204, 322
Nottingham, National Evangelical Anglican Congress, 1977 14

Oak Hill vii
officers 133–8, 143–4
Old Testament 38–42, 53–4, 60–1, 105, 192
oral traditions 200, 202–3 *see also* traditions
Doctrines of Orders 21–2, 316, 320, 321–8
Ordinal 7, 191–2, 261, 331
ordination 160, 178, 191–2, 256
ordination of women *see* women's ordination

papacy 30, 189, 217–18, 254, 277
parish system 1, 9, 246, 268, 281–3
patristics 4, 20, 147–85, 206

patronage 5, 9
penance 262, 316, 318–20
Pentecostalism 13, 118, 224, 298n, 301
porrectio instrumentorum 263
post-evangelicalism 17–18
Preface to Ordinal 264
Presbyterians 218–21, 270n
presbyters *see* elders
priesthood 6, 40, 137–8, 144, 153, 177–9, 265, 311–16, 328–30
Priesthood of the Ordained Ministry, The 329
Primates' Meeting 347
Prophecy 14, 41, 47, 54, 120–9, 130, 133–5, 288–9, 303–11
proeselytes 77
purgatory 193, 200, 205, 248
Puritans 7, 199, 204, 218–21, 259n, 264, 281–2

Quakers 15n, 220n
Quartodecimanism 166, 181

reception 338–9
redemption 39, 110–11
Reformation 8n, 29–31, 184, 189–94, 213–18
reservation of eucharistic elements 251
restoration from exile 41–2
resurrection 32, 45, 52, 53–4, 68n, 111–12, 131, 143, 212, 359
Rome
  ancient 42, 56, 66, 131–2, 148–9
  authority of Church of 183–5
  see also Papacy
Roman Catholics 13, 32, 196, 200, 225–8, 270n, 281
royal supremacy 189–90, 194, 254–5, 258

sacramentalism 6, 21, 85–6, 169–79, 193, 238–53, 316–21
Salvation Army 15n, 223
Samaria 40, 41n, 51, 70, 89n, 127, 298n
Savoy Conference 163, 219
schism 40

Scripture 6, 15–16, 30–7, 143
Septuagint 44, 295–6
singleness 117, 193
slaying in the Spirit 15
Socinianism 204
Spirit *see* Holy Spirit
sponsors 171–2, 241–2, 246, 317
state control 189, 215–16, 235, 275–6, 286, 346, 349–51
submersion 364 *see also* baptism, mode of
Sunday 11, 106, 148–9, 175, 176, 253
synods 235, 273–80

temple 40, 41–2, 45, 46–8, 100
territorial concept of Church 230, 235
Thirty-Nine Articles 7, 30, 35, 192–4, 196, 198, 204, 238n, 239–40, 243, 247, 249, 255, 258, 267, 316, 328
tongues 14, 124–9, 130, 299–309
Toronto 14, 306
Tractarian Movement 20, 204–5, 258, 322
tradition, Scripture and 6, 21, 147, 150, 158, 184–5, 190–4, 195–212, 235
transubstantiation 177, 193, 205, 248
Trinity, doctrine of 33, 36, 87–8, 98, 120n, 166, 192, 195–7, 205, 212, 252, 259
Tyndale Hall 5

United Reformed Church 221, 237

validity 84n, 167–8
Vatican II 227, 250
  Decree on Ecumenism 363
vernacular 191
Virgin Mary *see* Mary
visibility of Church 100, 109, 167, 193, 239–40
voluntarism 142, 230
Voluntary Societies 287–90

Westminster Confession of Faith 31
women's initiation 76–7
women's ministry 118, 129
women's ordination 16–17, 275, 277, 333–6
words of knowledge 14